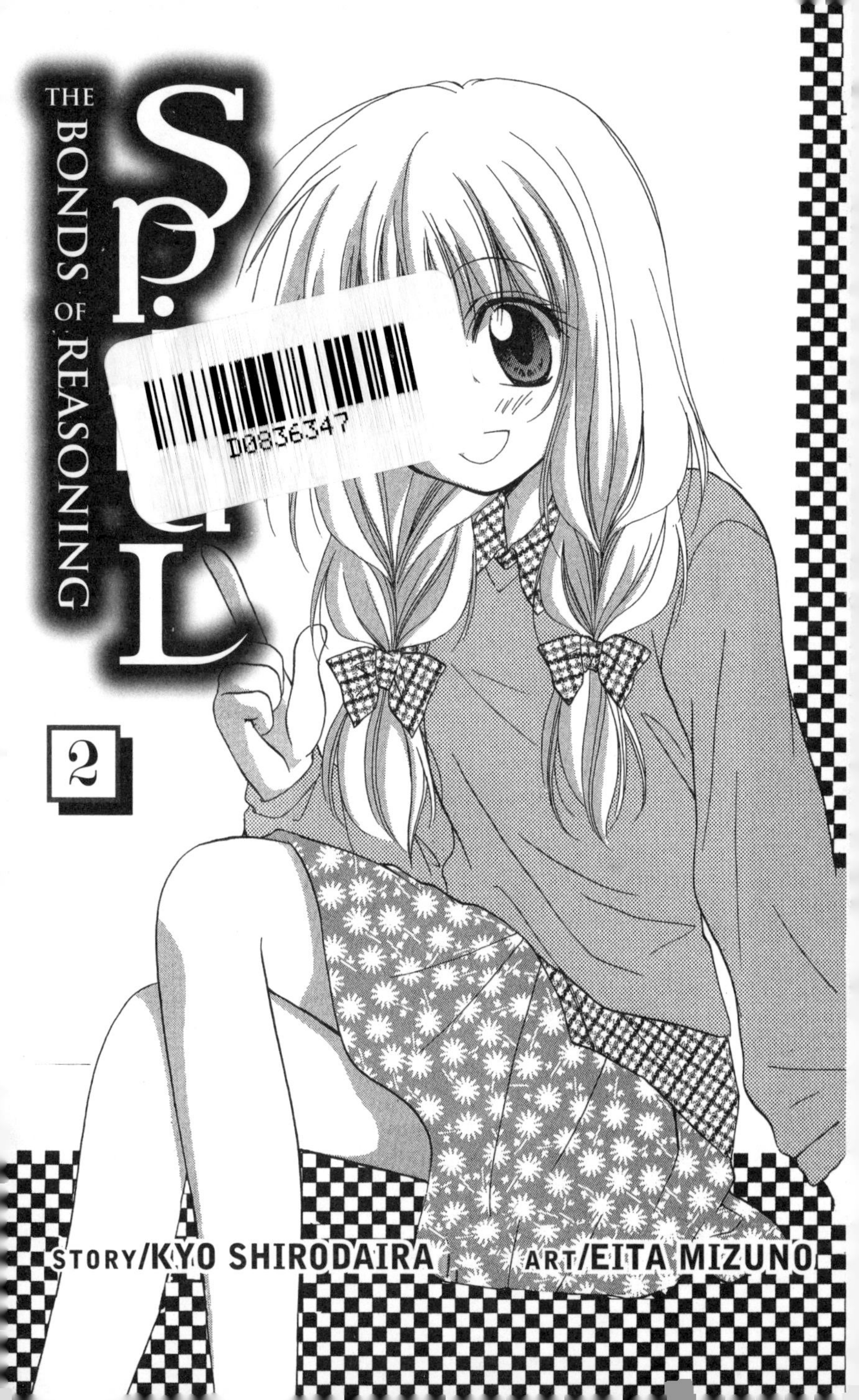
THE BONDS OF REASONING
2
STORY/KYO SHIRODAIRA
ART/EITA MIZUNO

THERE ONCE WAS A MAN CALLED
"THE GREAT DETECTIVE" AT
POLICE HEADQUARTERS.

IN OTHER WORDS, HE IS NO MORE.

HE LEFT BEHIND THE MYSTERIOUS WORDS
"I'M GOING AFTER THE BLADE CHILDREN"
AND THEN VANISHED.

HIS WHEREABOUTS ARE
STILL UNKNOWN.

SO THIS IS THE TALE
OF HIS LITTLE BROTHER,
AYUMU NARUMI.

His

Destiny is

On the

SPIRAL

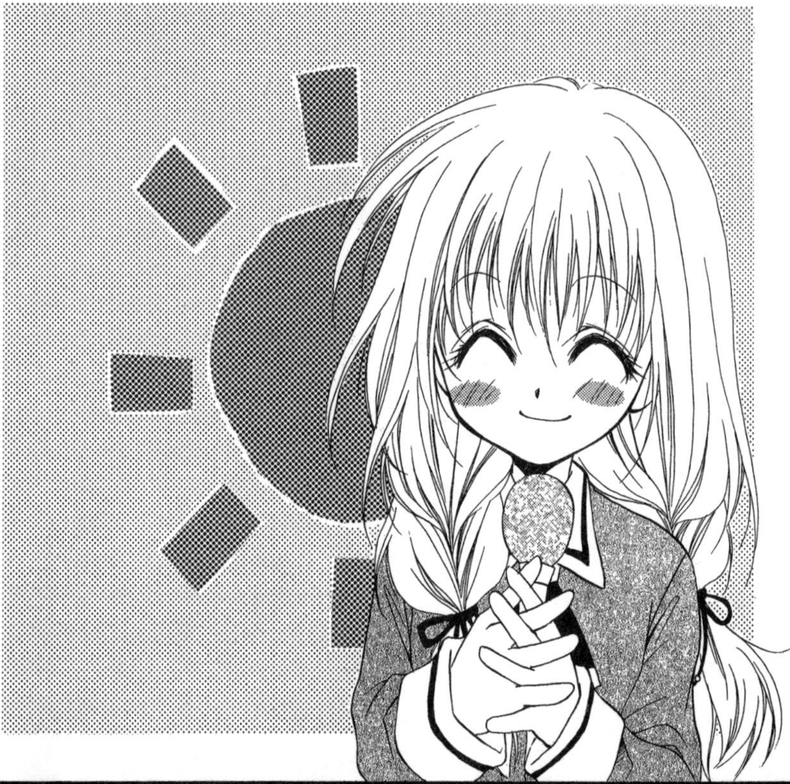

CONTENTS

CHAPTER SIX

ROOM BEHIND THE WARD LOCK (PART III)

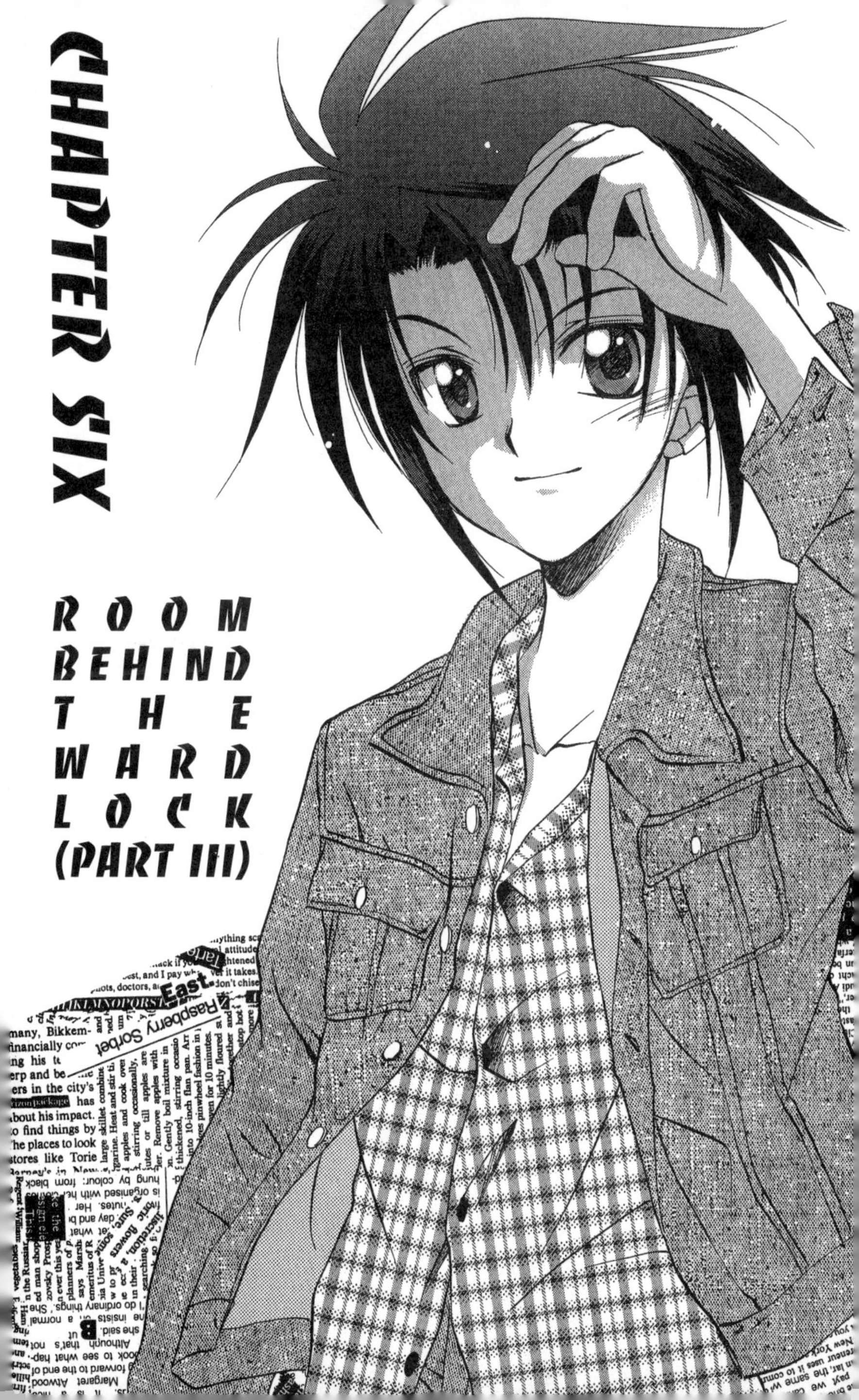

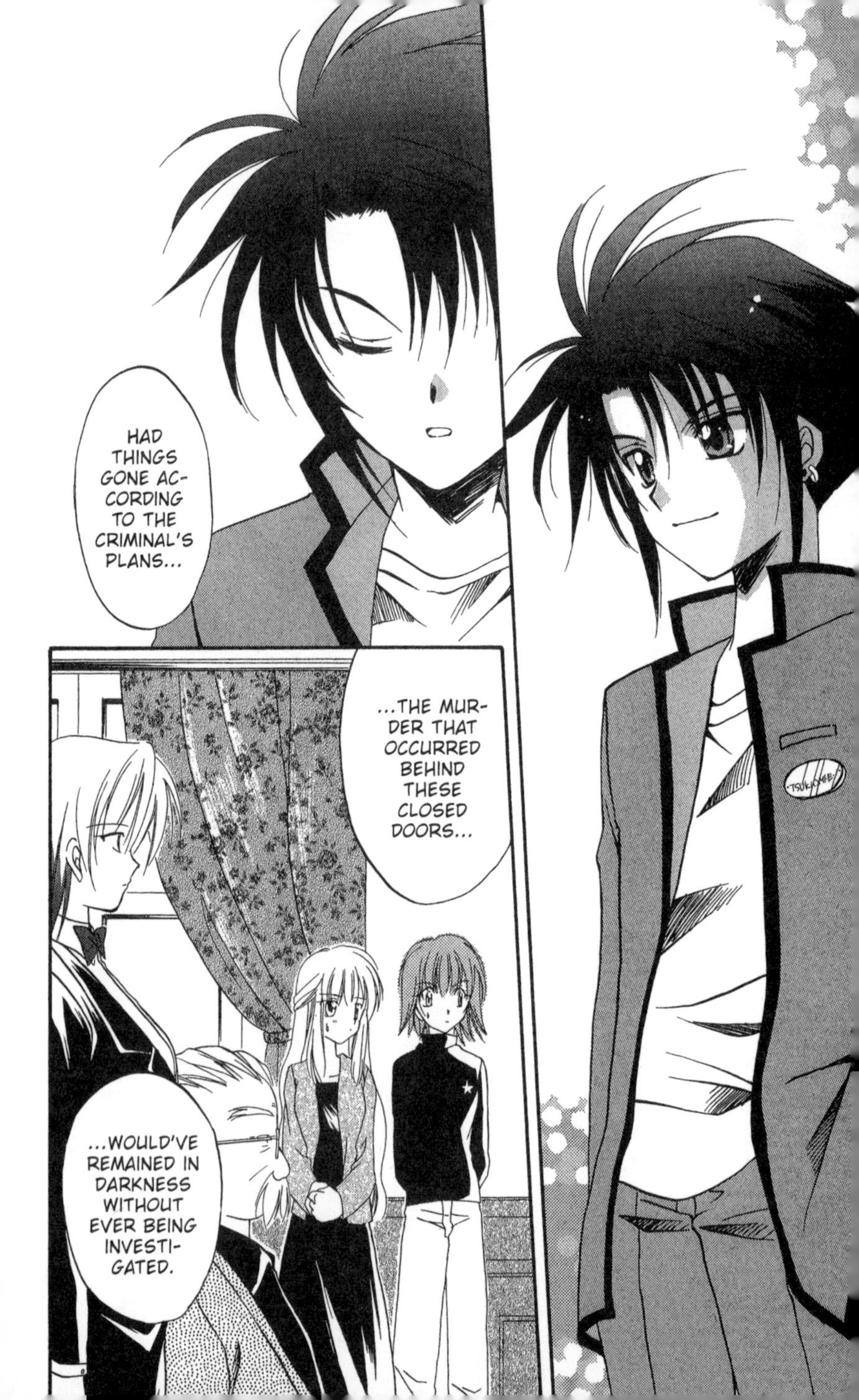
HAD THINGS GONE ACCORDING TO THE CRIMINAL'S PLANS...
...THE MURDER THAT OCCURRED BEHIND THESE CLOSED DOORS...
...WOULD'VE REMAINED IN DARKNESS WITHOUT EVER BEING INVESTIGATED.

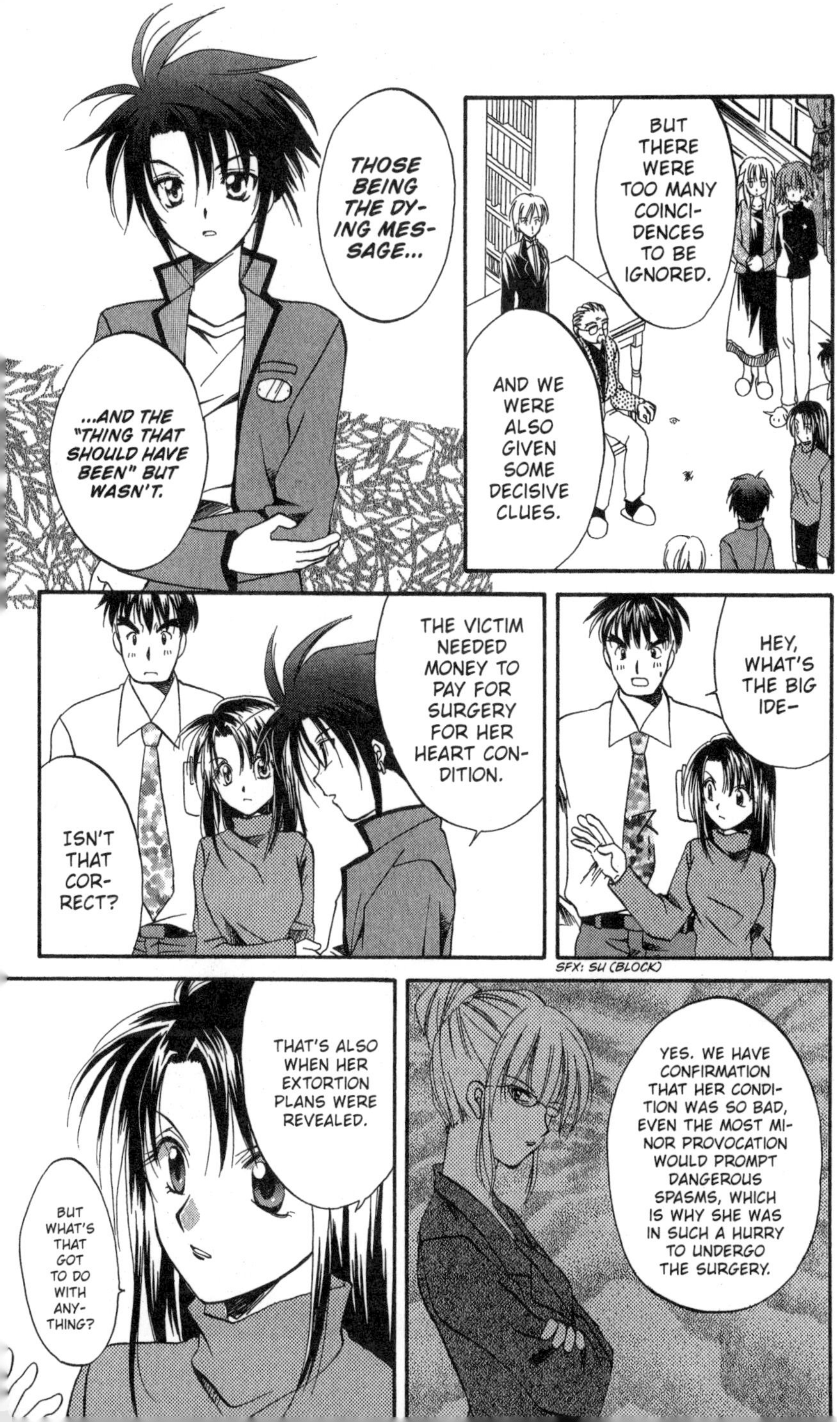
BUT THERE WERE TOO MANY COINCIDENCES TO BE IGNORED.
AND WE WERE ALSO GIVEN SOME DECISIVE CLUES.
THOSE BEING THE DYING MESSAGE...
...AND THE "THING THAT SHOULD HAVE BEEN" BUT WASN'T.
HEY, WHAT'S THE BIG IDE-
SFX: SU (BLOCK)
THE VICTIM NEEDED MONEY TO PAY FOR SURGERY FOR HER HEART CONDITION.
ISN'T THAT CORRECT?
YES. WE HAVE CONFIRMATION THAT HER CONDITION WAS SO BAD, EVEN THE MOST MINOR PROVOCATION WOULD PROMPT DANGEROUS SPASMS, WHICH IS WHY SHE WAS IN SUCH A HURRY TO UNDERGO THE SURGERY.
THAT'S ALSO WHEN HER EXTORTION PLANS WERE REVEALED.
BUT WHAT'S THAT GOT TO DO WITH ANYTHING?

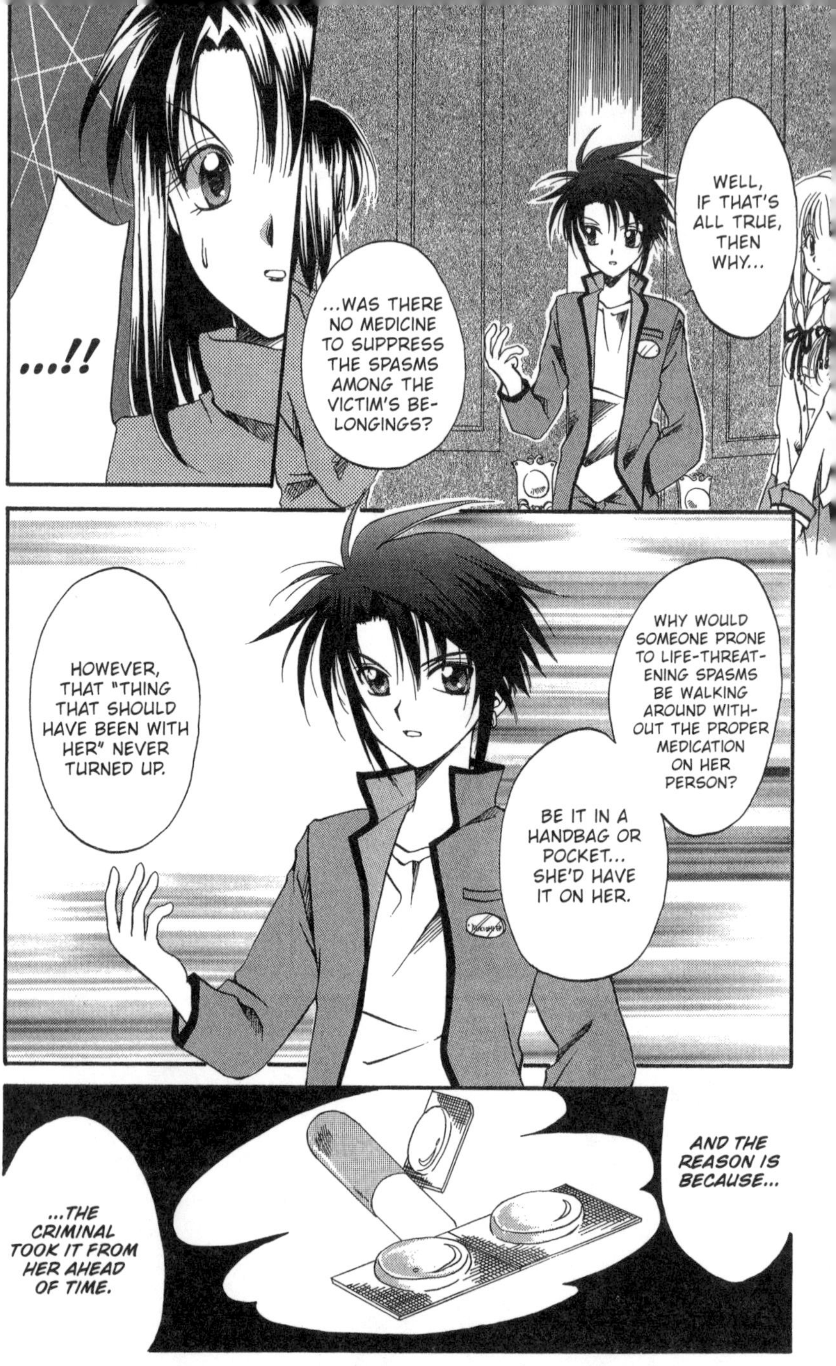

WELL, IF THAT'S ALL TRUE, THEN WHY...
...WAS THERE NO MEDICINE TO SUPPRESS THE SPASMS AMONG THE VICTIM'S BE-LONGINGS?
...!!
WHY WOULD SOMEONE PRONE TO LIFE-THREAT-ENING SPASMS BE WALKING AROUND WITH-OUT THE PROPER MEDICATION ON HER PERSON?
BE IT IN A HANDBAG OR POCKET... SHE'D HAVE IT ON HER.
HOWEVER, THAT "THING THAT SHOULD HAVE BEEN WITH HER" NEVER TURNED UP.
AND THE REASON IS BECAUSE...
...THE CRIMINAL TOOK IT FROM HER AHEAD OF TIME.

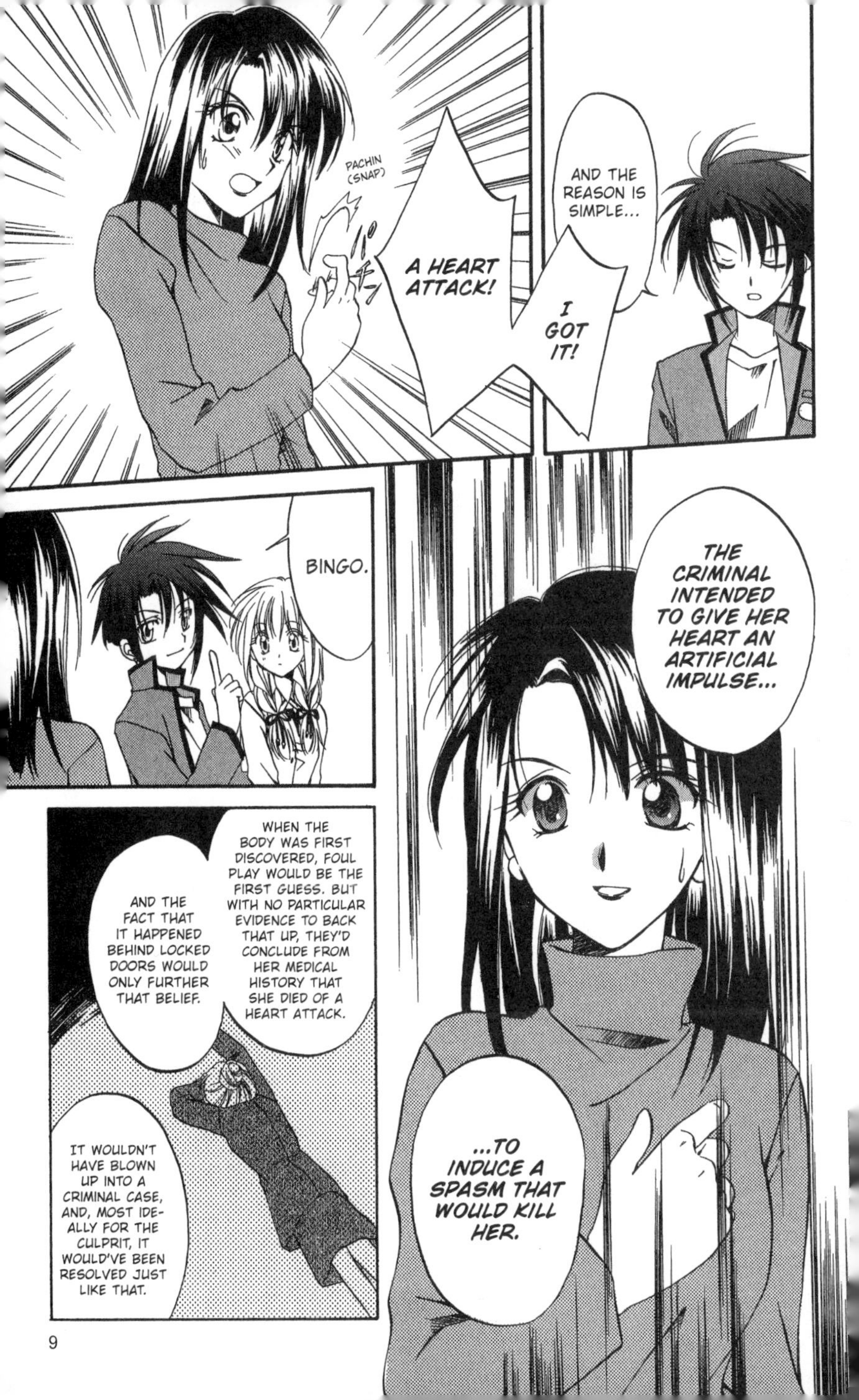

AND THE REASON IS SIMPLE...
I GOT IT!
A HEART ATTACK!
PACHIN (SNAP)
THE CRIMINAL INTENDED TO GIVE HER HEART AN ARTIFICIAL IMPULSE...
...TO INDUCE A SPASM THAT WOULD KILL HER.
BINGO.
WHEN THE BODY WAS FIRST DISCOVERED, FOUL PLAY WOULD BE THE FIRST GUESS. BUT WITH NO PARTICULAR EVIDENCE TO BACK THAT UP, THEY'D CONCLUDE FROM HER MEDICAL HISTORY THAT SHE DIED OF A HEART ATTACK.
AND THE FACT THAT IT HAPPENED BEHIND LOCKED DOORS WOULD ONLY FURTHER THAT BELIEF.
IT WOULDN'T HAVE BLOWN UP INTO A CRIMINAL CASE, AND, MOST IDE-ALLY FOR THE CULPRIT, IT WOULD'VE BEEN RESOLVED JUST LIKE THAT.

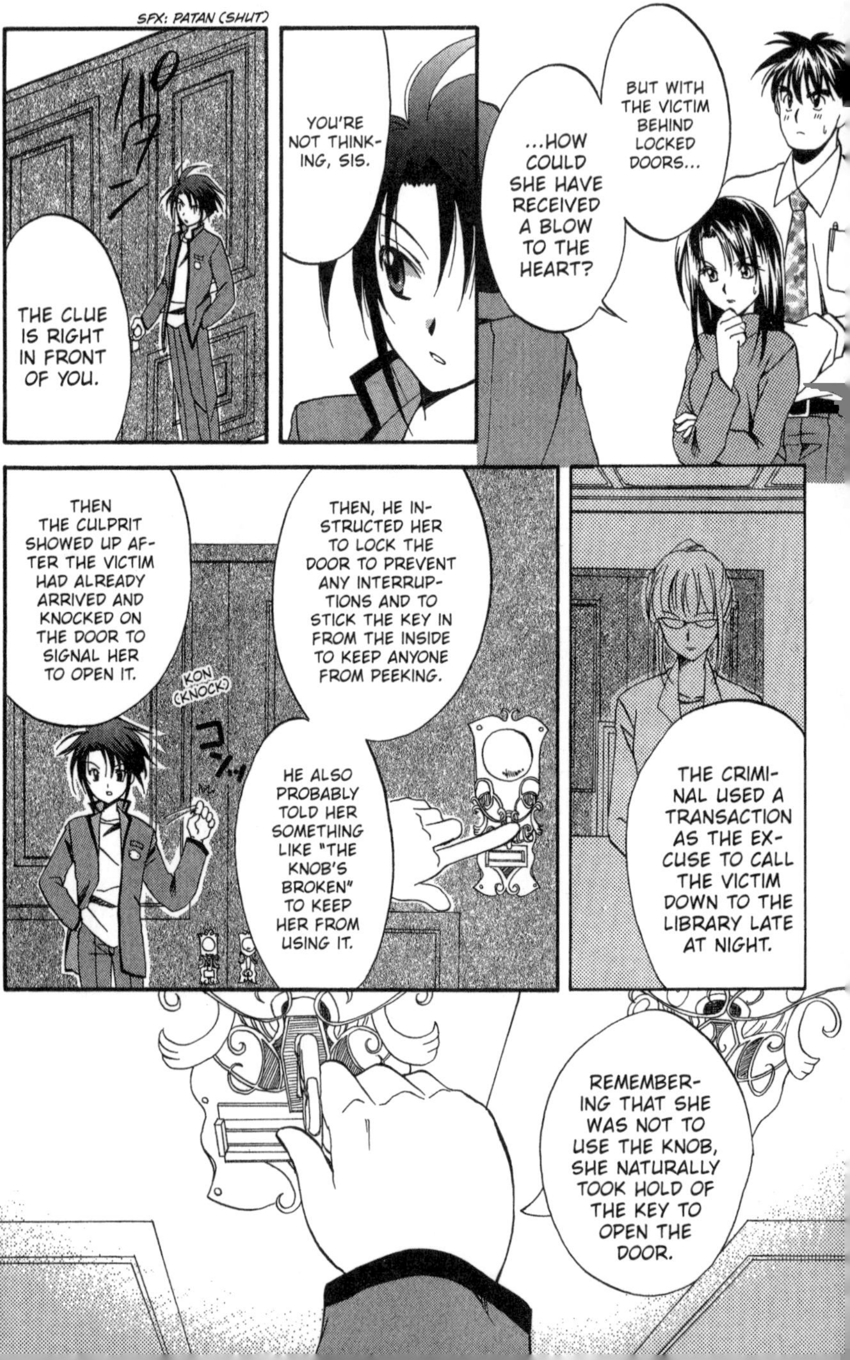
BUT WITH THE VICTIM BEHIND LOCKED DOORS...
...HOW COULD SHE HAVE RECEIVED A BLOW TO THE HEART?
YOU'RE NOT THINKING, SIS.
SFX: PATAN (SHUT)
THE CLUE IS RIGHT IN FRONT OF YOU.
THE CRIMINAL USED A TRANSACTION AS THE EXCUSE TO CALL THE VICTIM DOWN TO THE LIBRARY LATE AT NIGHT.
THEN THE CULPRIT SHOWED UP AFTER THE VICTIM HAD ALREADY ARRIVED AND KNOCKED ON THE DOOR TO SIGNAL HER TO OPEN IT.
THEN, HE INSTRUCTED HER TO LOCK THE DOOR TO PREVENT ANY INTERRUPTIONS AND TO STICK THE KEY IN FROM THE INSIDE TO KEEP ANYONE FROM PEEKING.
KON (KNOCK)
HE ALSO PROBABLY TOLD HER SOMETHING LIKE "THE KNOB'S BROKEN" TO KEEP HER FROM USING IT.
REMEMBERING THAT SHE WAS NOT TO USE THE KNOB, SHE NATURALLY TOOK HOLD OF THE KEY TO OPEN THE DOOR.

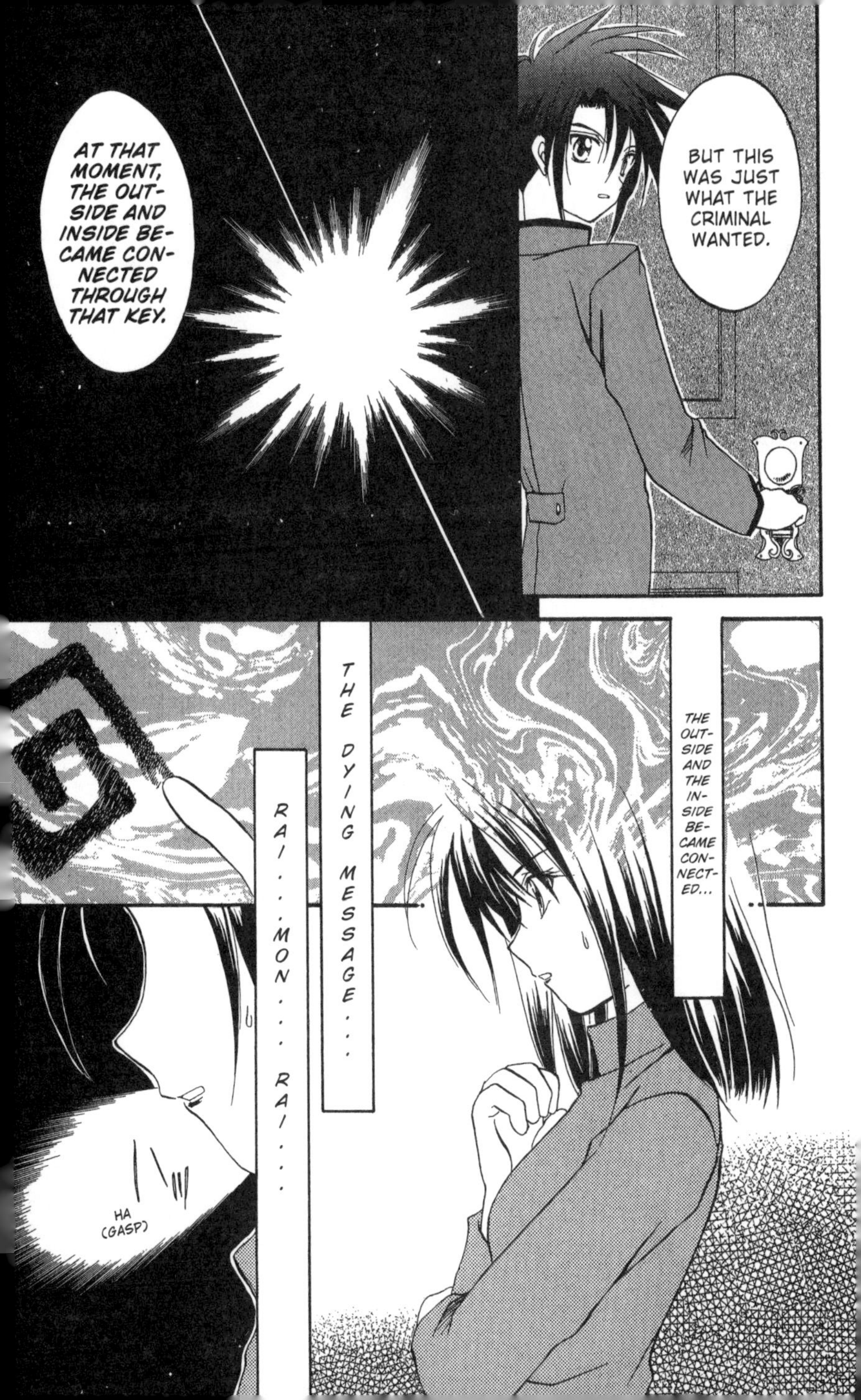
BUT THIS WAS JUST WHAT THE CRIMINAL WANTED.
AT THAT MOMENT, THE OUT-SIDE AND INSIDE BE-CAME CON-NECTED THROUGH THAT KEY.
THE OUT-SIDE AND THE IN-SIDE BE-CAME CON-NECT-ED...
THE DYING MESSAGE...
RAI...MON... RAI...
HA (GASP)

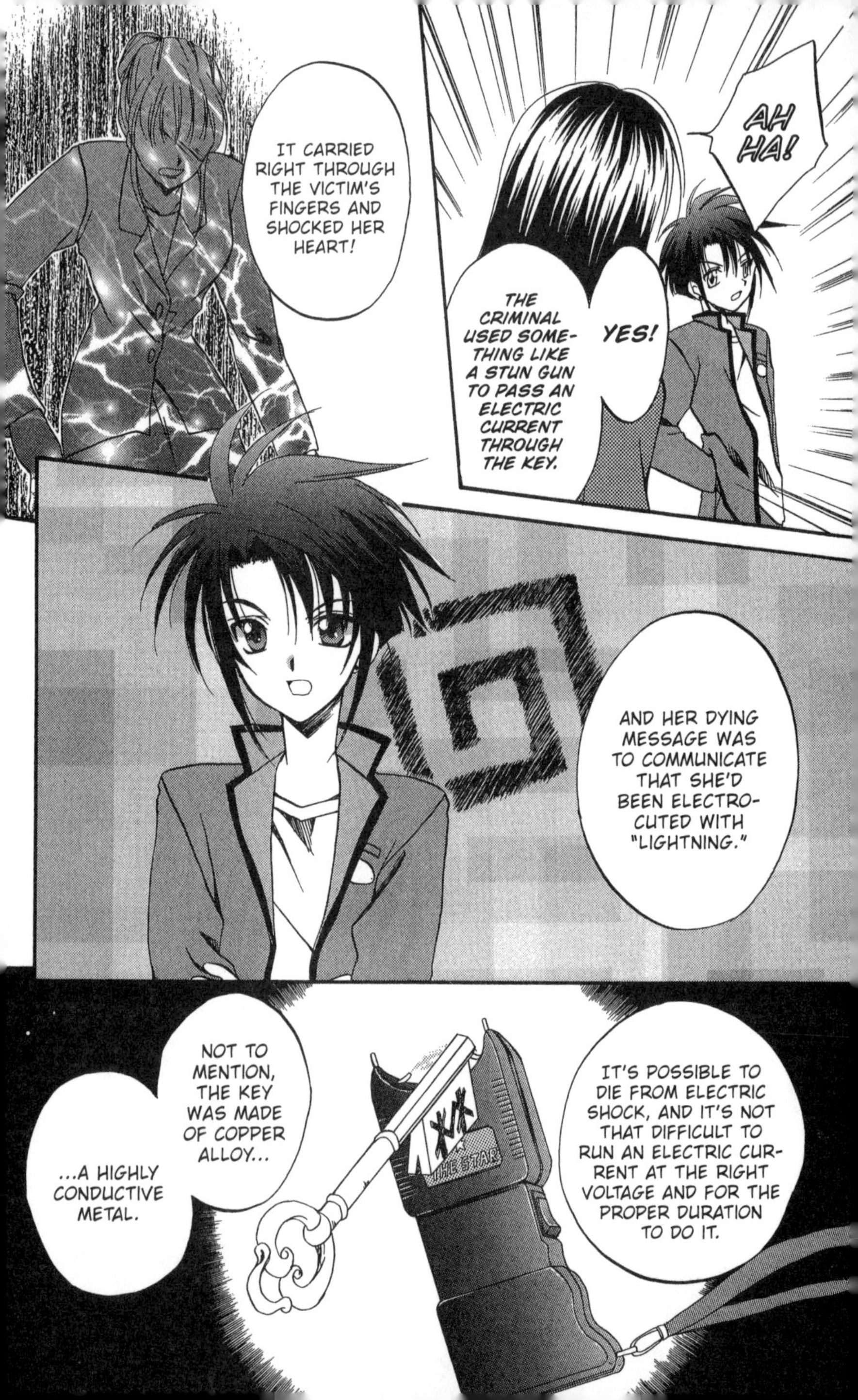
AH HA!
YES!
THE CRIMINAL USED SOMETHING LIKE A STUN GUN TO PASS AN ELECTRIC CURRENT THROUGH THE KEY.
IT CARRIED RIGHT THROUGH THE VICTIM'S FINGERS AND SHOCKED HER HEART!
AND HER DYING MESSAGE WAS TO COMMUNICATE THAT SHE'D BEEN ELECTROCUTED WITH "LIGHTNING."
IT'S POSSIBLE TO DIE FROM ELECTRIC SHOCK, AND IT'S NOT THAT DIFFICULT TO RUN AN ELECTRIC CURRENT AT THE RIGHT VOLTAGE AND FOR THE PROPER DURATION TO DO IT.
NOT TO MENTION, THE KEY WAS MADE OF COPPER ALLOY...
...A HIGHLY CONDUCTIVE METAL.
THE STAR

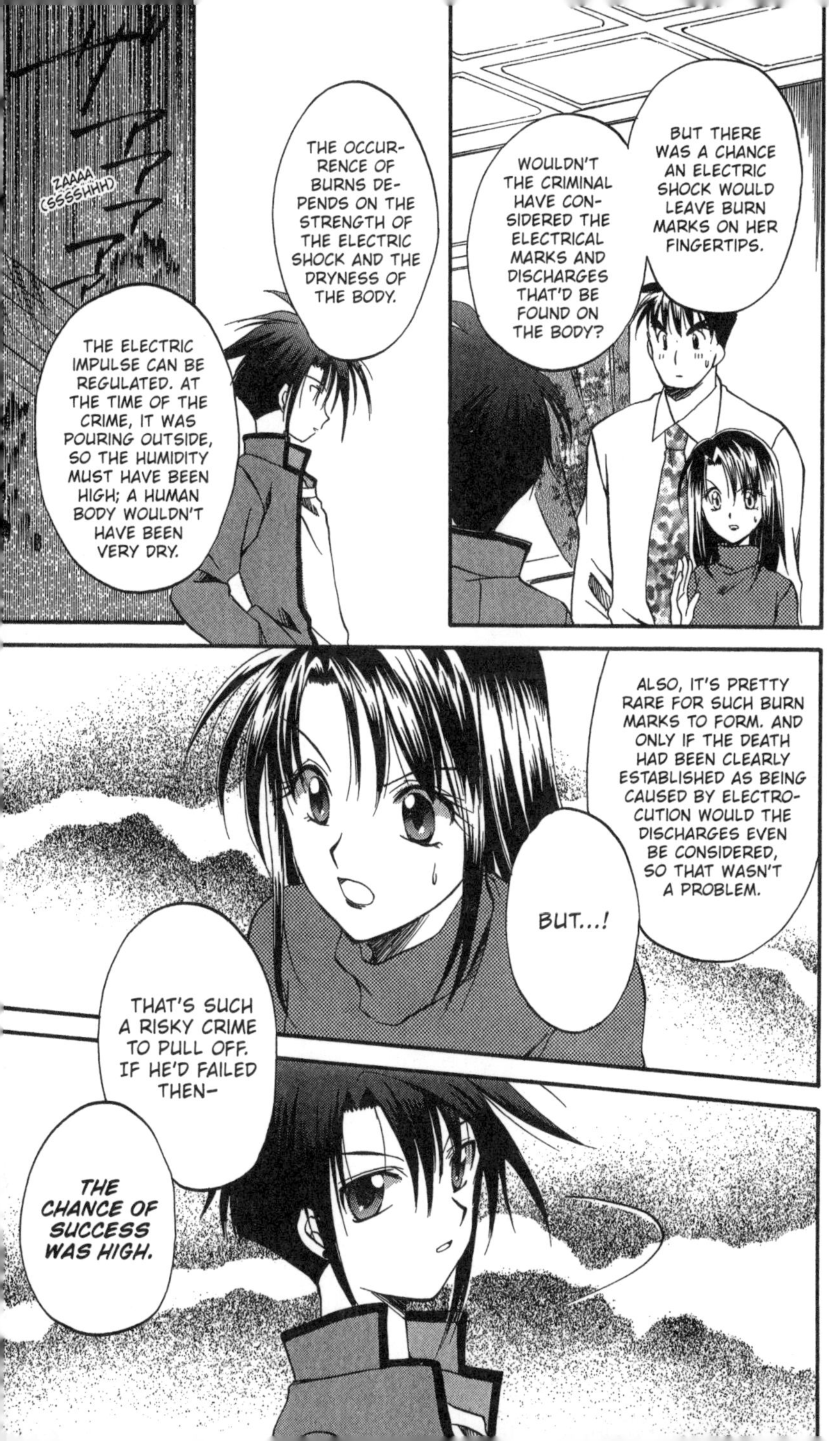
BUT THERE WAS A CHANCE AN ELECTRIC SHOCK WOULD LEAVE BURN MARKS ON HER FINGERTIPS.
WOULDN'T THE CRIMINAL HAVE CONSIDERED THE ELECTRICAL MARKS AND DISCHARGES THAT'D BE FOUND ON THE BODY?
THE OCCURRENCE OF BURNS DEPENDS ON THE STRENGTH OF THE ELECTRIC SHOCK AND THE DRYNESS OF THE BODY.
ZAAAA (SSSSHHH)
THE ELECTRIC IMPULSE CAN BE REGULATED. AT THE TIME OF THE CRIME, IT WAS POURING OUTSIDE, SO THE HUMIDITY MUST HAVE BEEN HIGH; A HUMAN BODY WOULDN'T HAVE BEEN VERY DRY.
ALSO, IT'S PRETTY RARE FOR SUCH BURN MARKS TO FORM. AND ONLY IF THE DEATH HAD BEEN CLEARLY ESTABLISHED AS BEING CAUSED BY ELECTROCUTION WOULD THE DISCHARGES EVEN BE CONSIDERED, SO THAT WASN'T A PROBLEM.
BUT...!
THAT'S SUCH A RISKY CRIME TO PULL OFF. IF HE'D FAILED THEN–
THE CHANCE OF SUCCESS WAS HIGH.

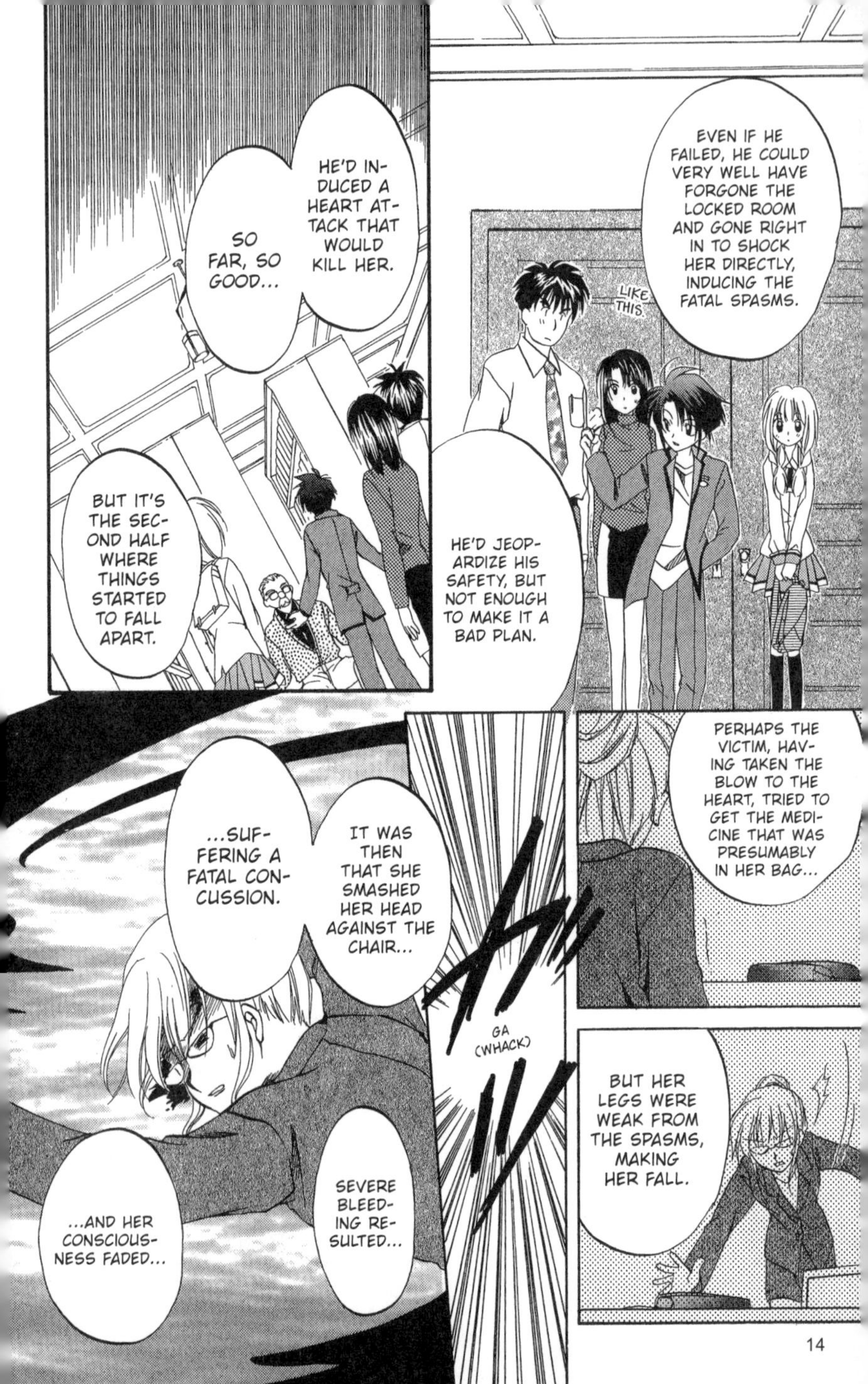
EVEN IF HE FAILED, HE COULD VERY WELL HAVE FORGONE THE LOCKED ROOM AND GONE RIGHT IN TO SHOCK HER DIRECTLY, INDUCING THE FATAL SPASMS.
LIKE THIS.
HE'D JEOPARDIZE HIS SAFETY, BUT NOT ENOUGH TO MAKE IT A BAD PLAN.
HE'D INDUCED A HEART ATTACK THAT WOULD KILL HER.
SO FAR, SO GOOD...
BUT IT'S THE SECOND HALF WHERE THINGS STARTED TO FALL APART.
PERHAPS THE VICTIM, HAVING TAKEN THE BLOW TO THE HEART, TRIED TO GET THE MEDICINE THAT WAS PRESUMABLY IN HER BAG...
BUT HER LEGS WERE WEAK FROM THE SPASMS, MAKING HER FALL.
GA (WHACK)
IT WAS THEN THAT SHE SMASHED HER HEAD AGAINST THE CHAIR...
...SUFFERING A FATAL CONCUSSION.
SEVERE BLEEDING RESULTED...
...AND HER CONSCIOUSNESS FADED...

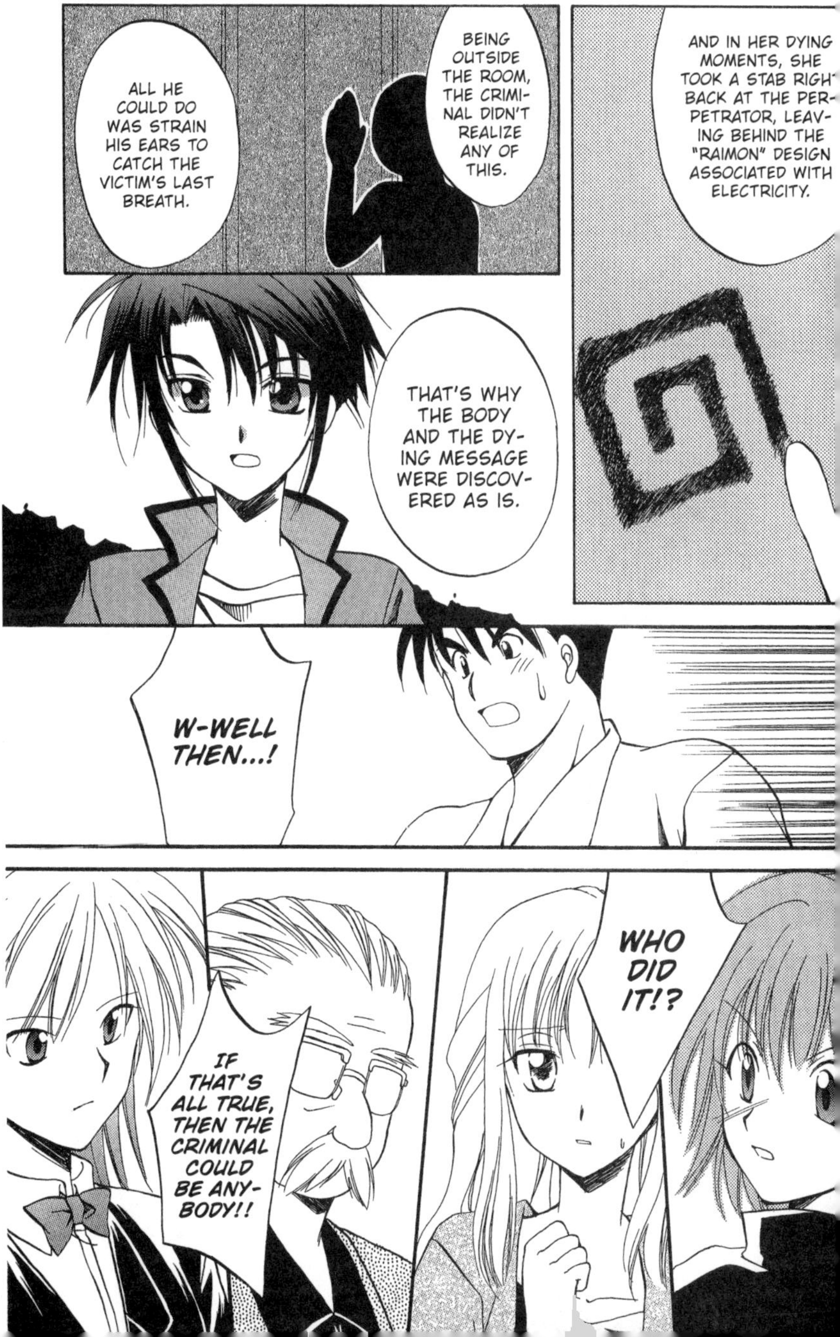
AND IN HER DYING MOMENTS, SHE TOOK A STAB RIGHT BACK AT THE PERPETRATOR, LEAVING BEHIND THE "RAIMON" DESIGN ASSOCIATED WITH ELECTRICITY.
BEING OUTSIDE THE ROOM, THE CRIMINAL DIDN'T REALIZE ANY OF THIS.
ALL HE COULD DO WAS STRAIN HIS EARS TO CATCH THE VICTIM'S LAST BREATH.
THAT'S WHY THE BODY AND THE DYING MESSAGE WERE DISCOVERED AS IS.
W-WELL THEN...!
WHO DID IT!?
IF THAT'S ALL TRUE, THEN THE CRIMINAL COULD BE ANYBODY!!

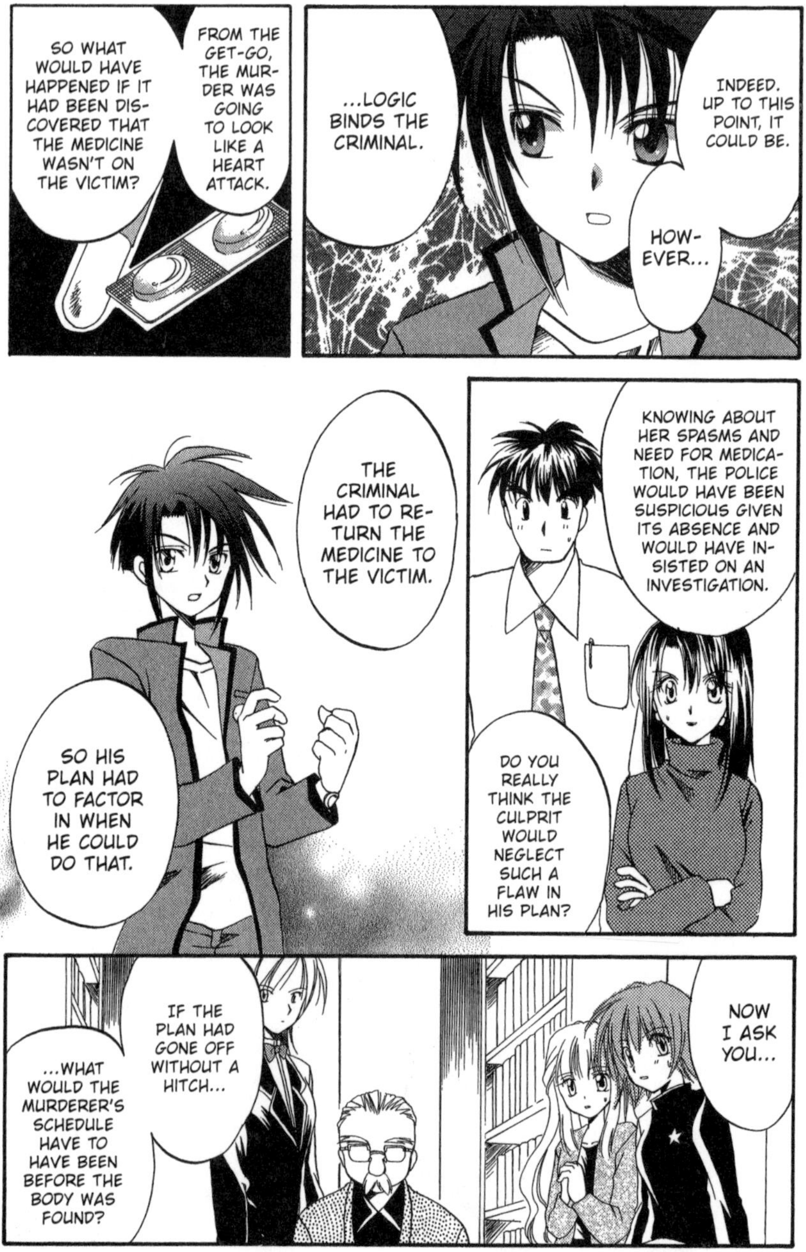
INDEED. UP TO THIS POINT, IT COULD BE.
HOW-EVER...
...LOGIC BINDS THE CRIMINAL.
FROM THE GET-GO, THE MUR-DER WAS GOING TO LOOK LIKE A HEART ATTACK.
SO WHAT WOULD HAVE HAPPENED IF IT HAD BEEN DIS-COVERED THAT THE MEDICINE WASN'T ON THE VICTIM?
KNOWING ABOUT HER SPASMS AND NEED FOR MEDICA-TION, THE POLICE WOULD HAVE BEEN SUSPICIOUS GIVEN ITS ABSENCE AND WOULD HAVE IN-SISTED ON AN INVESTIGATION.
DO YOU REALLY THINK THE CULPRIT WOULD NEGLECT SUCH A FLAW IN HIS PLAN?
THE CRIMINAL HAD TO RE-TURN THE MEDICINE TO THE VICTIM.
SO HIS PLAN HAD TO FACTOR IN WHEN HE COULD DO THAT.
NOW I ASK YOU...
IF THE PLAN HAD GONE OFF WITHOUT A HITCH...
...WHAT WOULD THE MURDERER'S SCHEDULE HAVE TO HAVE BEEN BEFORE THE BODY WAS FOUND?

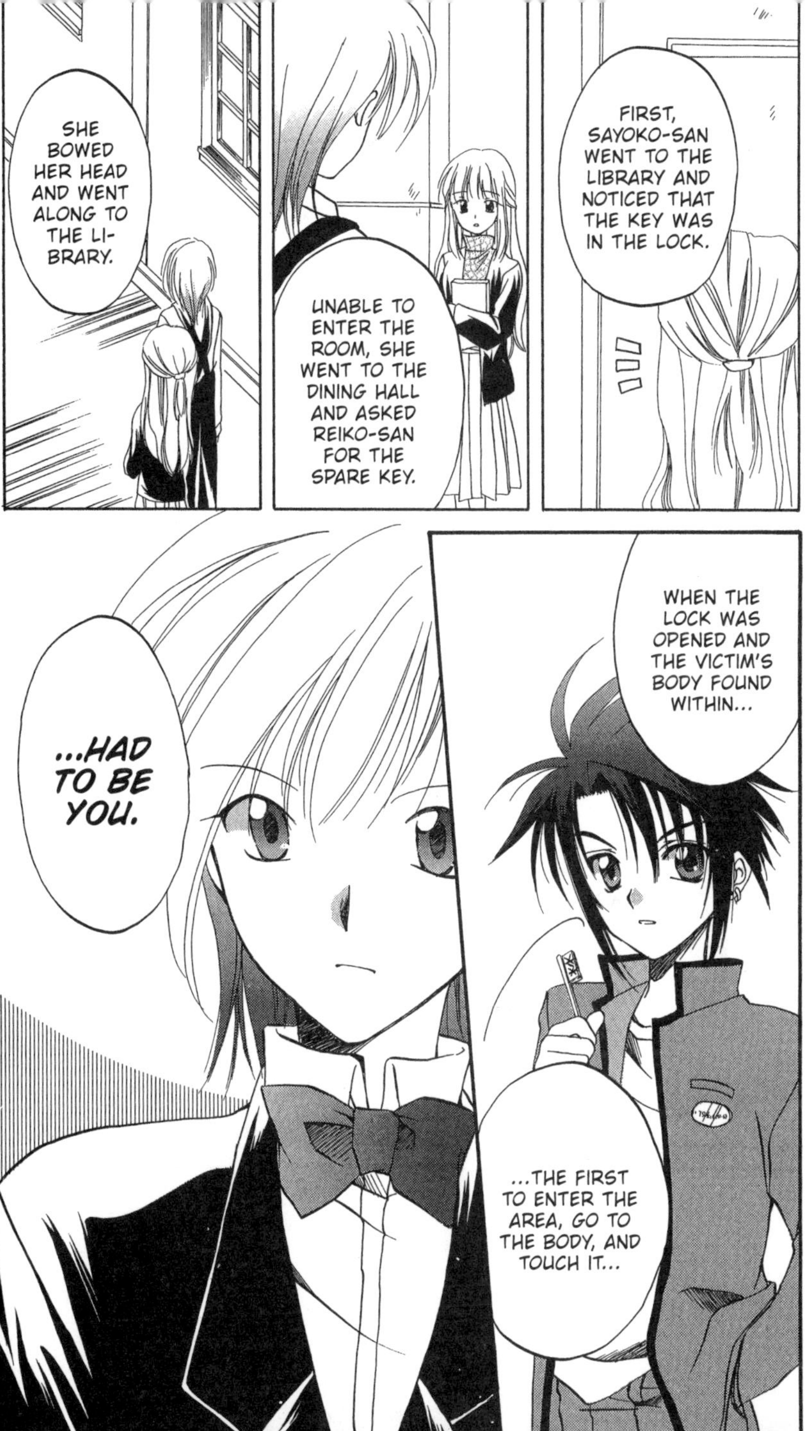
FIRST, SAYOKO-SAN WENT TO THE LIBRARY AND NOTICED THAT THE KEY WAS IN THE LOCK.
UNABLE TO ENTER THE ROOM, SHE WENT TO THE DINING HALL AND ASKED REIKO-SAN FOR THE SPARE KEY.
SHE BOWED HER HEAD AND WENT ALONG TO THE LI-BRARY.
WHEN THE LOCK WAS OPENED AND THE VICTIM'S BODY FOUND WITHIN...
...THE FIRST TO ENTER THE AREA, GO TO THE BODY, AND TOUCH IT...
...HAD TO BE YOU.

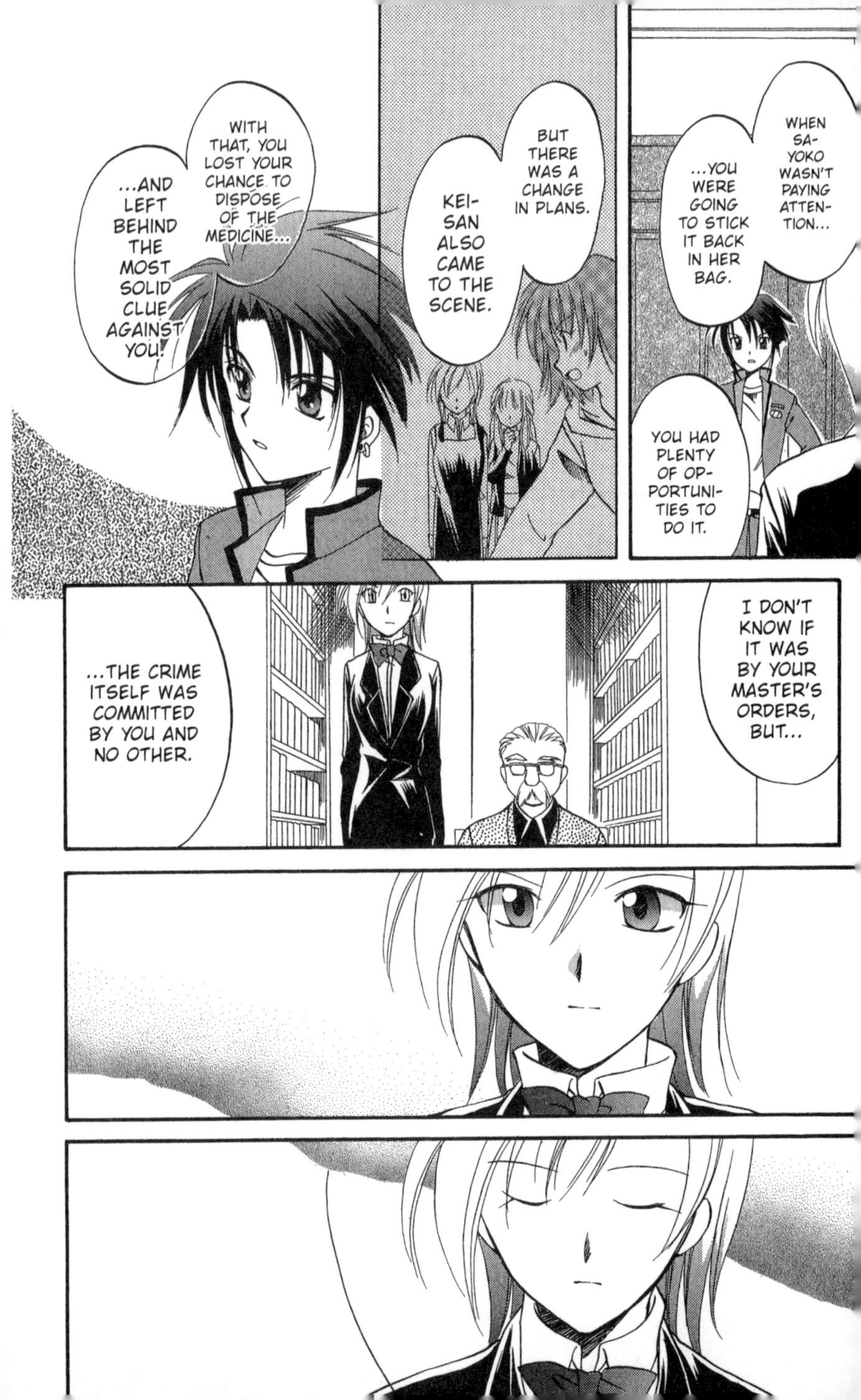
WHEN SA-YOKO WASN'T PAYING ATTEN-TION...
...YOU WERE GOING TO STICK IT BACK IN HER BAG.
YOU HAD PLENTY OF OP-PORTUNI-TIES TO DO IT.
BUT THERE WAS A CHANGE IN PLANS.
KEI-SAN ALSO CAME TO THE SCENE.
WITH THAT, YOU LOST YOUR CHANCE TO DISPOSE OF THE MEDICINE...
...AND LEFT BEHIND THE MOST SOLID CLUE AGAINST YOU!
I DON'T KNOW IF IT WAS BY YOUR MASTER'S ORDERS, BUT...
...THE CRIME ITSELF WAS COMMITTED BY YOU AND NO OTHER.

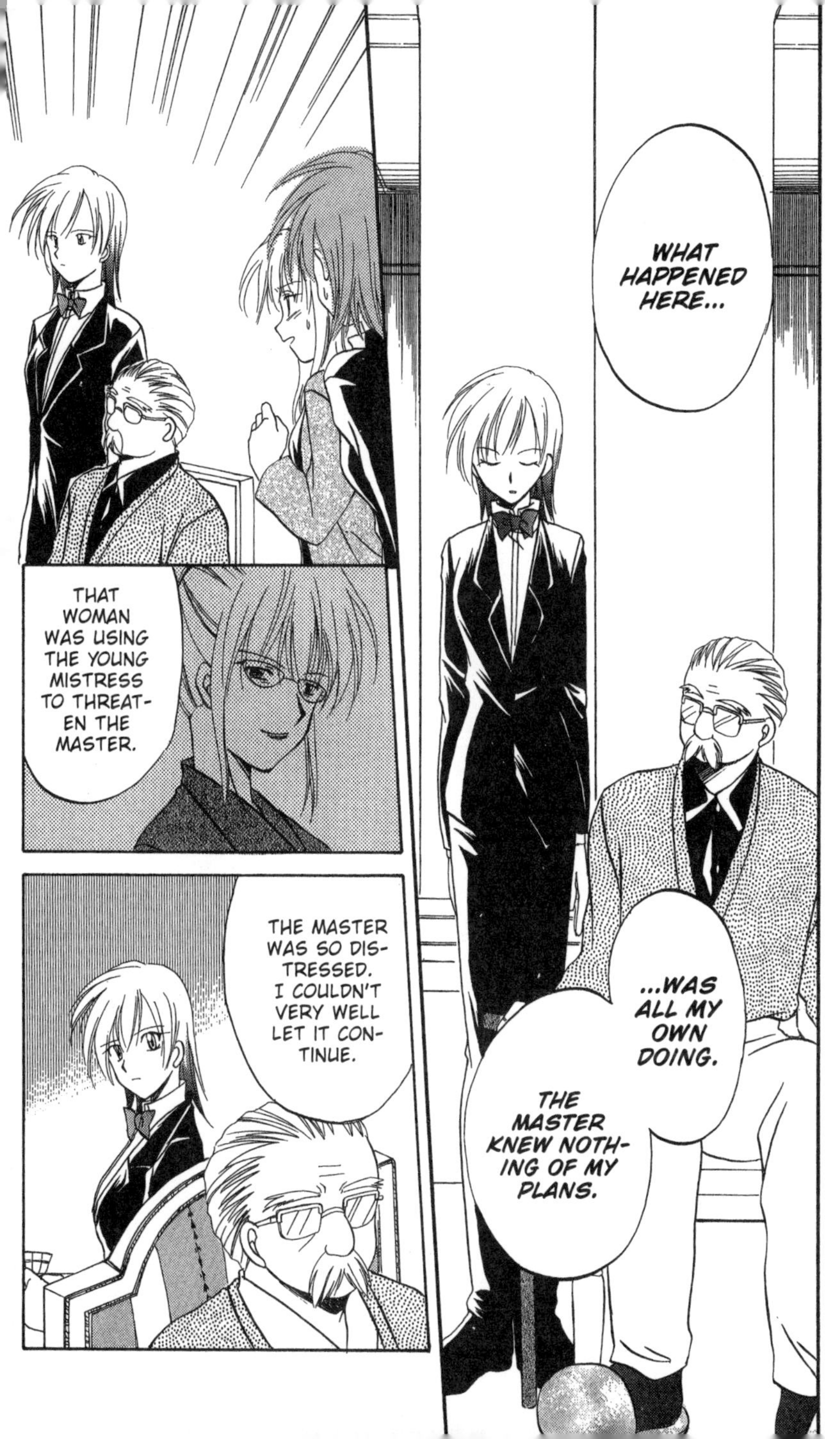
WHAT HAPPENED HERE...
...WAS ALL MY OWN DOING.
THE MASTER KNEW NOTHING OF MY PLANS.
THAT WOMAN WAS USING THE YOUNG MISTRESS TO THREATEN THE MASTER.
THE MASTER WAS SO DISTRESSED. I COULDN'T VERY WELL LET IT CONTINUE.

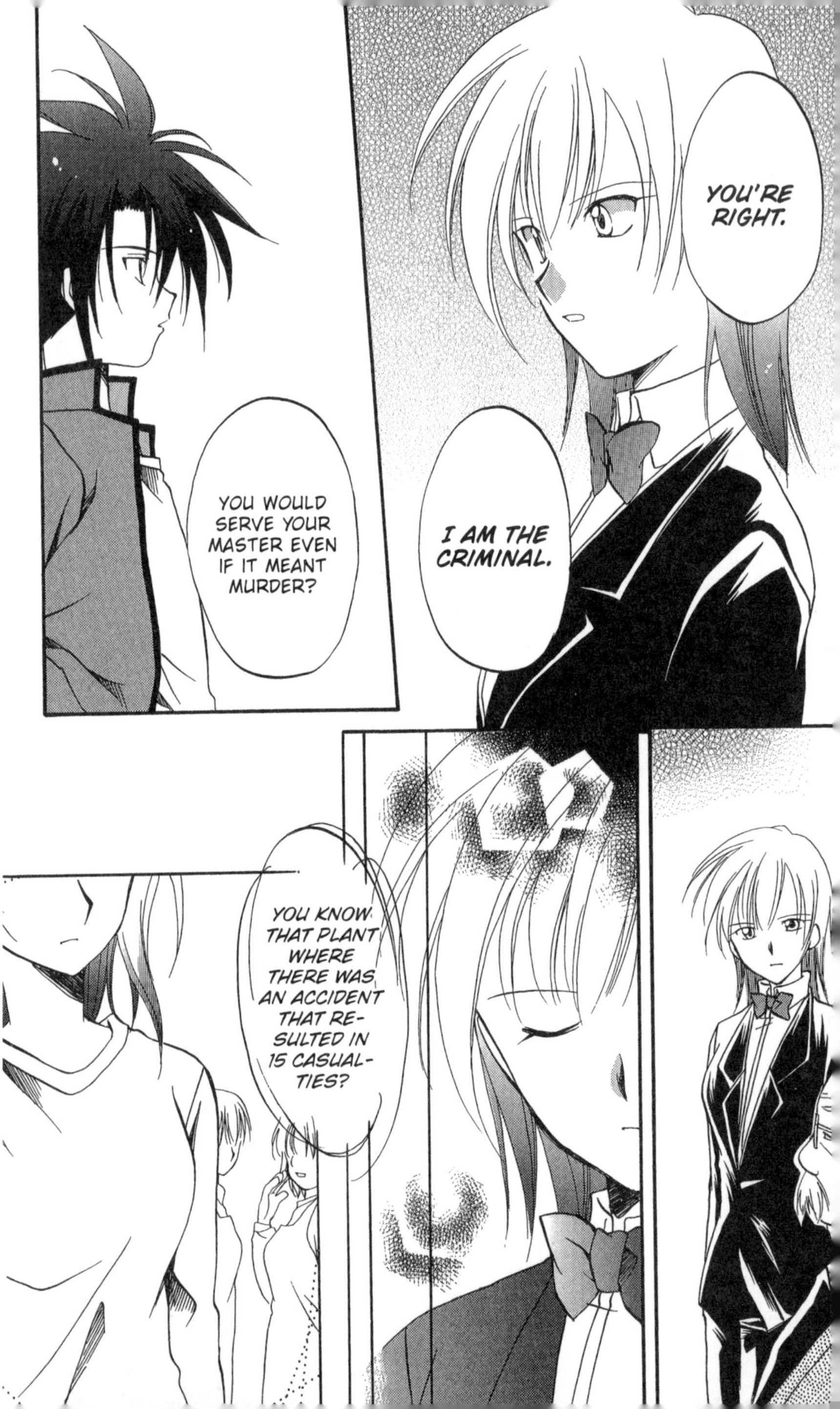
YOU'RE RIGHT.
I AM THE CRIMINAL.
YOU WOULD SERVE YOUR MASTER EVEN IF IT MEANT MURDER?
YOU KNOW THAT PLANT WHERE THERE WAS AN ACCIDENT THAT RE-SULTED IN 15 CASUAL-TIES?

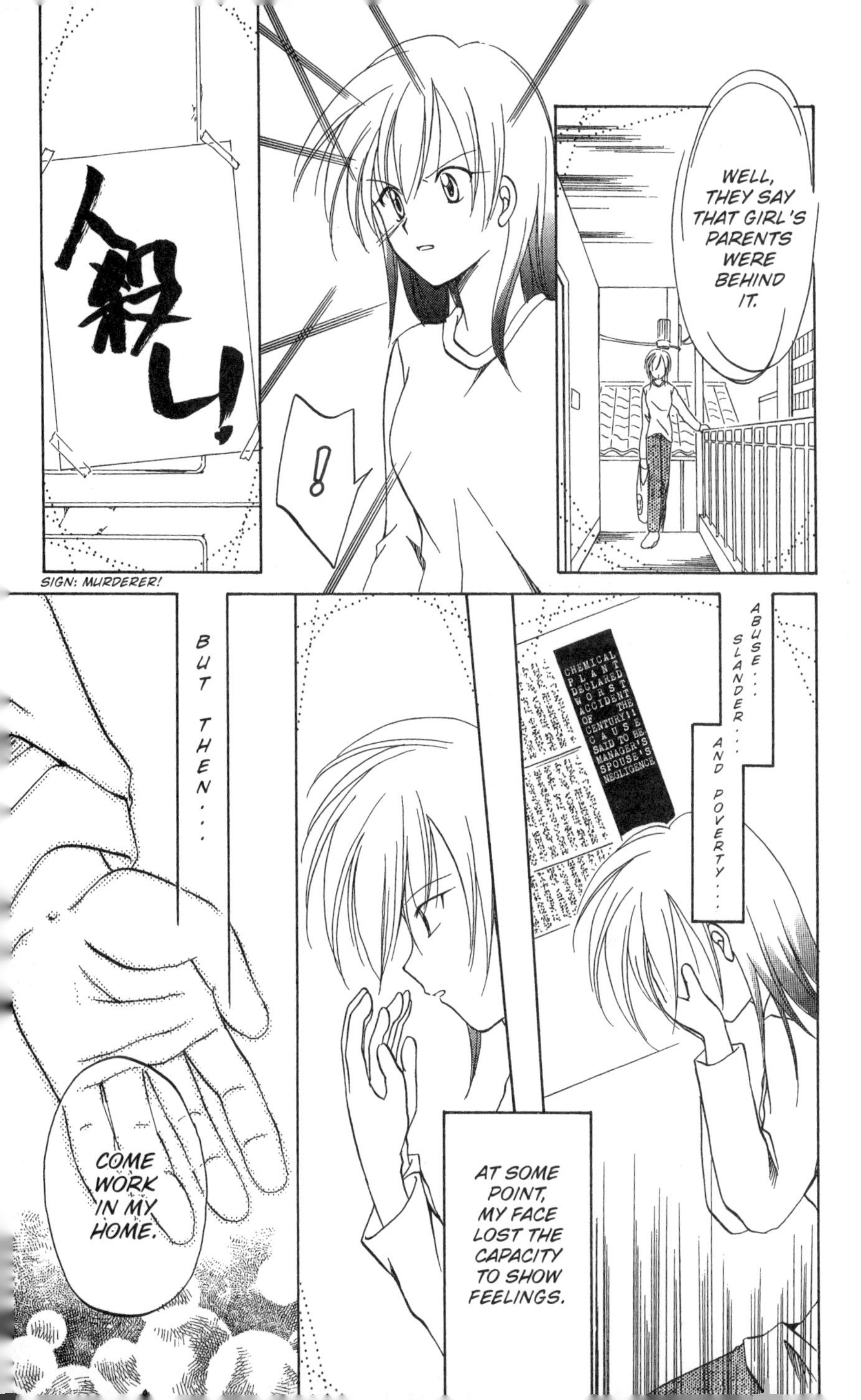
WELL, THEY SAY THAT GIRL'S PARENTS WERE BEHIND IT.
!
殺し!
SIGN: MURDERER!
ABUSE... SLANDER... AND POVERTY...
CHEMICAL PLANT DECLARED WORST ACCIDENT OF THE CENTURY!! CAUSE SAID TO BE MANAGER'S SPOUSE'S NEGLIGENCE
AT SOME POINT, MY FACE LOST THE CAPACITY TO SHOW FEELINGS.
BUT THEN...
COME WORK IN MY HOME.

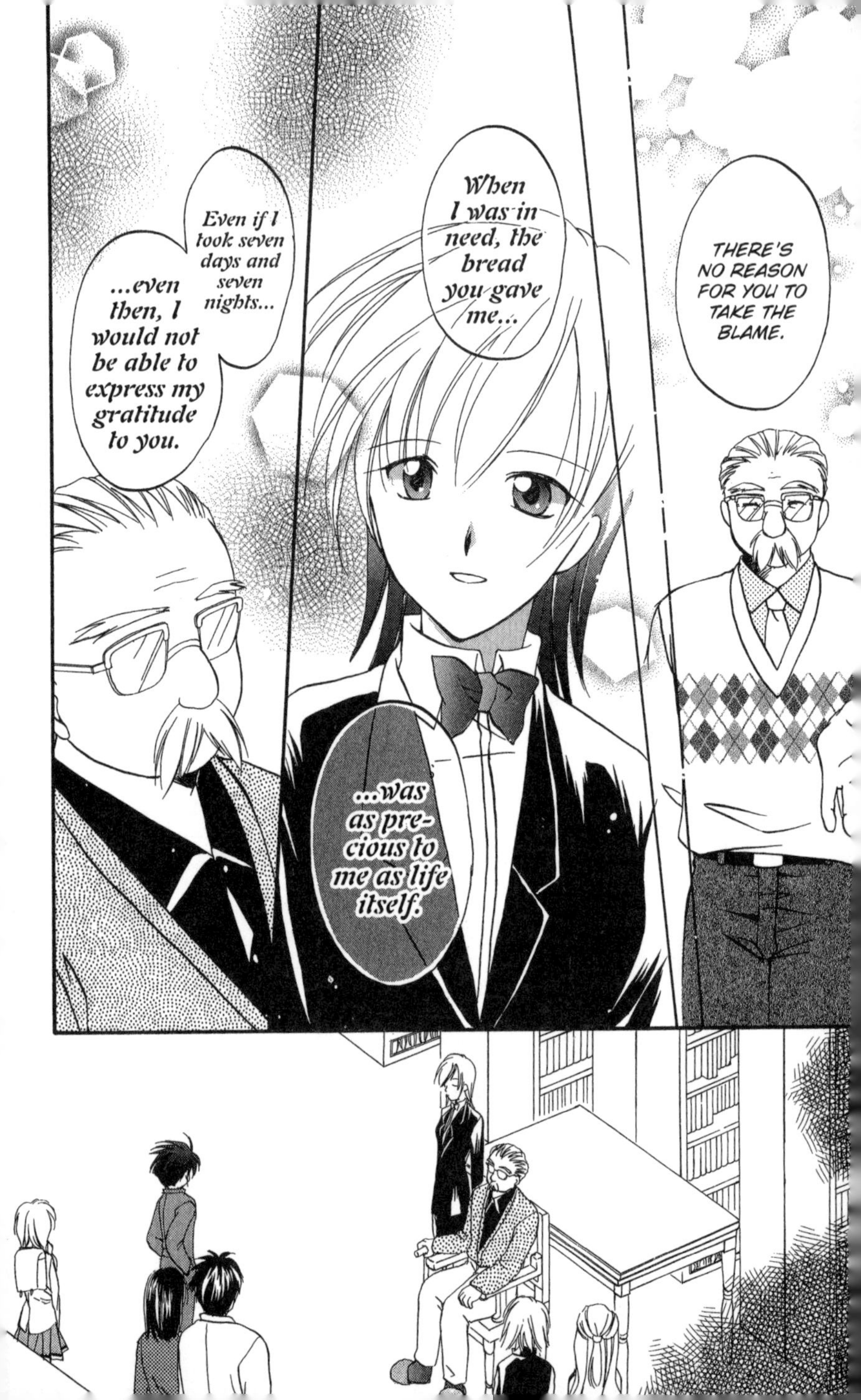
THERE'S NO REASON FOR YOU TO TAKE THE BLAME.
When I was in need, the bread you gave me...
...was as precious to me as life itself.
Even if I took seven days and seven nights...
...even then, I would not be able to express my gratitude to you.

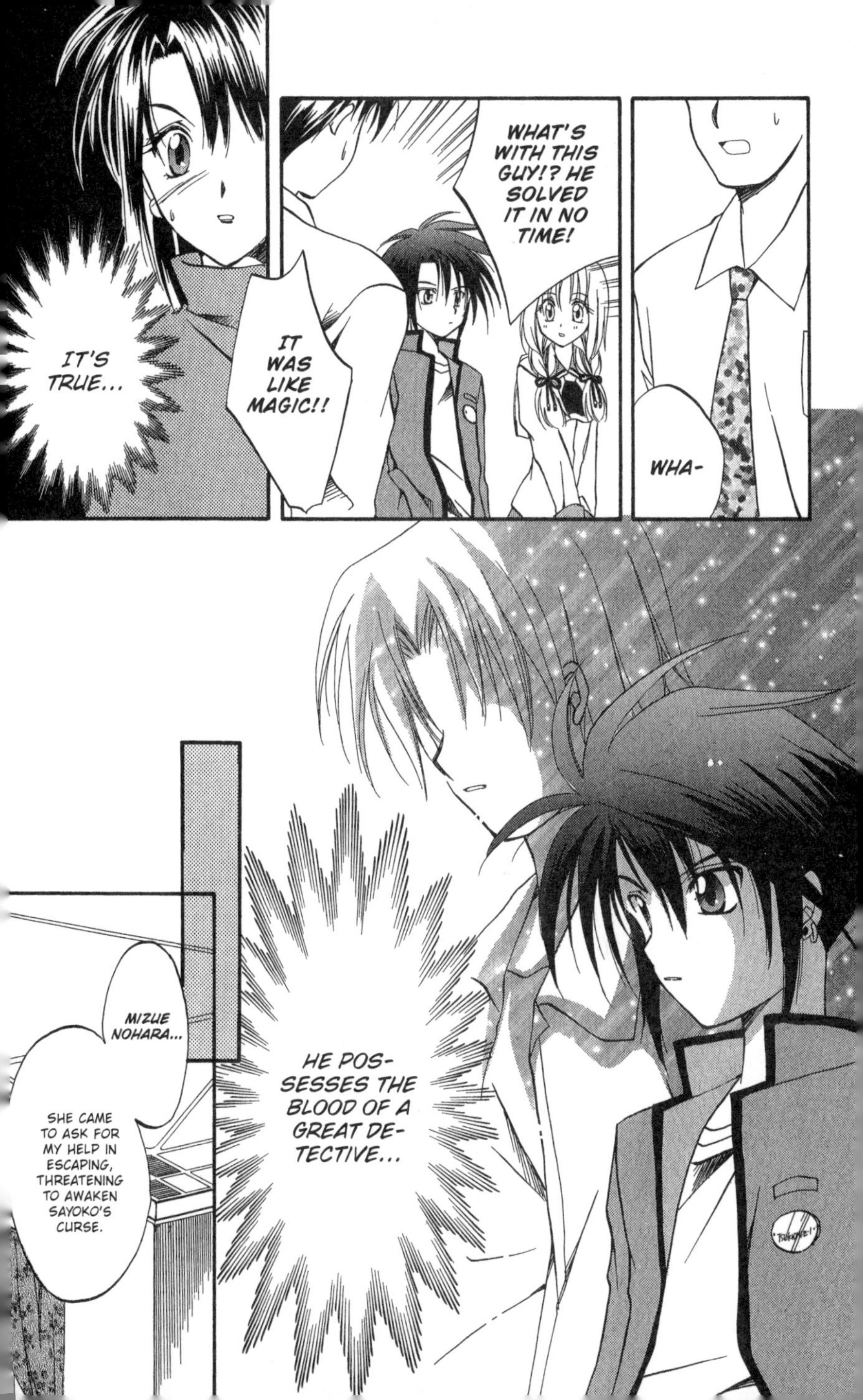
WHA-
WHAT'S WITH THIS GUY!? HE SOLVED IT IN NO TIME!
IT WAS LIKE MAGIC!!
IT'S TRUE...
HE POSSESSES THE BLOOD OF A GREAT DETECTIVE...
MIZUE NOHARA...
SHE CAME TO ASK FOR MY HELP IN ESCAPING, THREATENING TO AWAKEN SAYOKO'S CURSE.

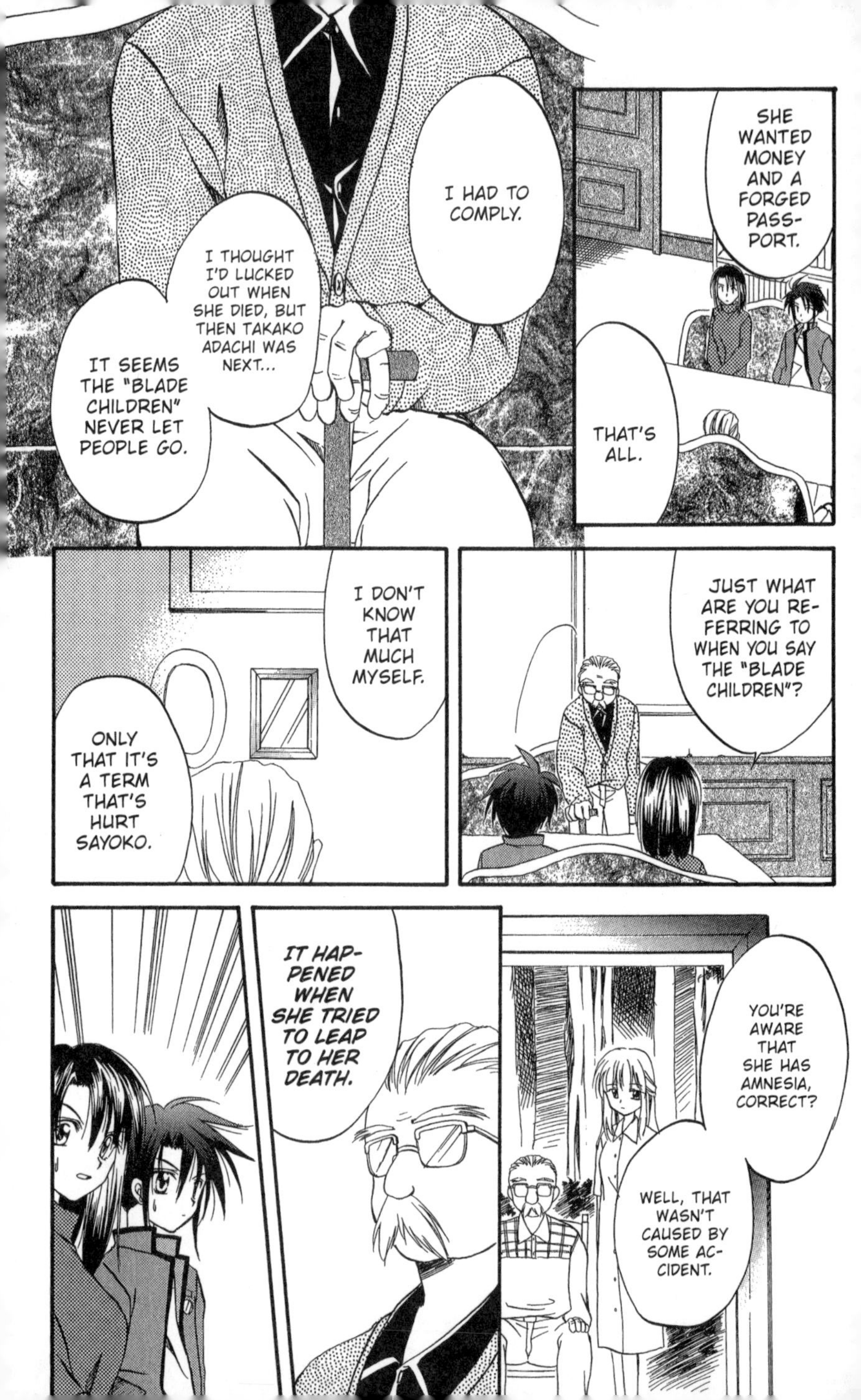
SHE WANTED MONEY AND A FORGED PASSPORT.
THAT'S ALL.
I HAD TO COMPLY.
I THOUGHT I'D LUCKED OUT WHEN SHE DIED, BUT THEN TAKAKO ADACHI WAS NEXT...
IT SEEMS THE "BLADE CHILDREN" NEVER LET PEOPLE GO.
JUST WHAT ARE YOU REFERRING TO WHEN YOU SAY THE "BLADE CHILDREN"?
I DON'T KNOW THAT MUCH MYSELF.
ONLY THAT IT'S A TERM THAT'S HURT SAYOKO.
YOU'RE AWARE THAT SHE HAS AMNESIA, CORRECT?
WELL, THAT WASN'T CAUSED BY SOME ACCIDENT.
IT HAPPENED WHEN SHE TRIED TO LEAP TO HER DEATH.

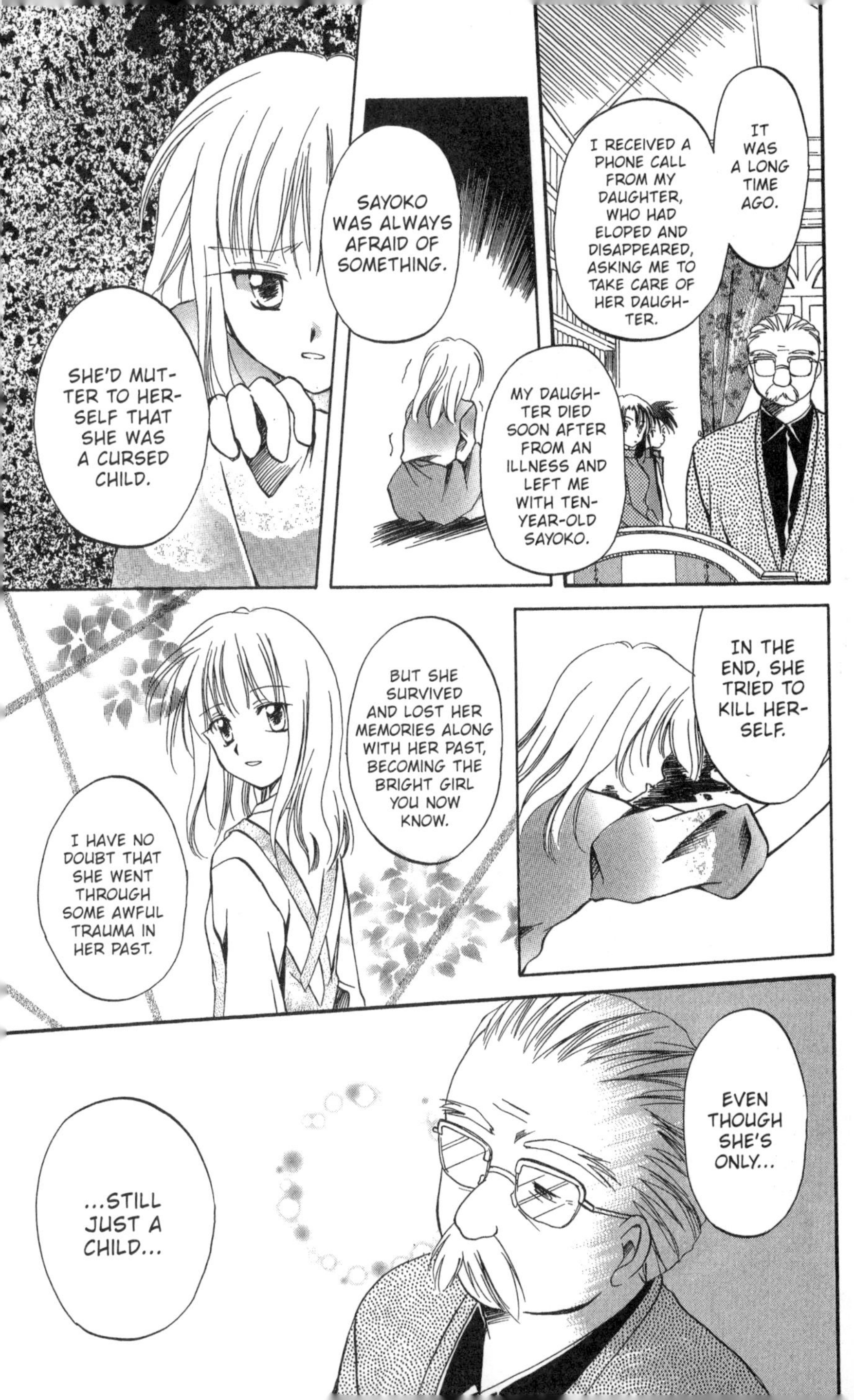
IT WAS A LONG TIME AGO.
I RECEIVED A PHONE CALL FROM MY DAUGHTER, WHO HAD ELOPED AND DISAPPEARED, ASKING ME TO TAKE CARE OF HER DAUGHTER.
MY DAUGHTER DIED SOON AFTER FROM AN ILLNESS AND LEFT ME WITH TEN-YEAR-OLD SAYOKO.
SAYOKO WAS ALWAYS AFRAID OF SOMETHING.
SHE'D MUTTER TO HERSELF THAT SHE WAS A CURSED CHILD.
IN THE END, SHE TRIED TO KILL HERSELF.
BUT SHE SURVIVED AND LOST HER MEMORIES ALONG WITH HER PAST, BECOMING THE BRIGHT GIRL YOU NOW KNOW.
I HAVE NO DOUBT THAT SHE WENT THROUGH SOME AWFUL TRAUMA IN HER PAST.
EVEN THOUGH SHE'S ONLY...
...STILL JUST A CHILD...

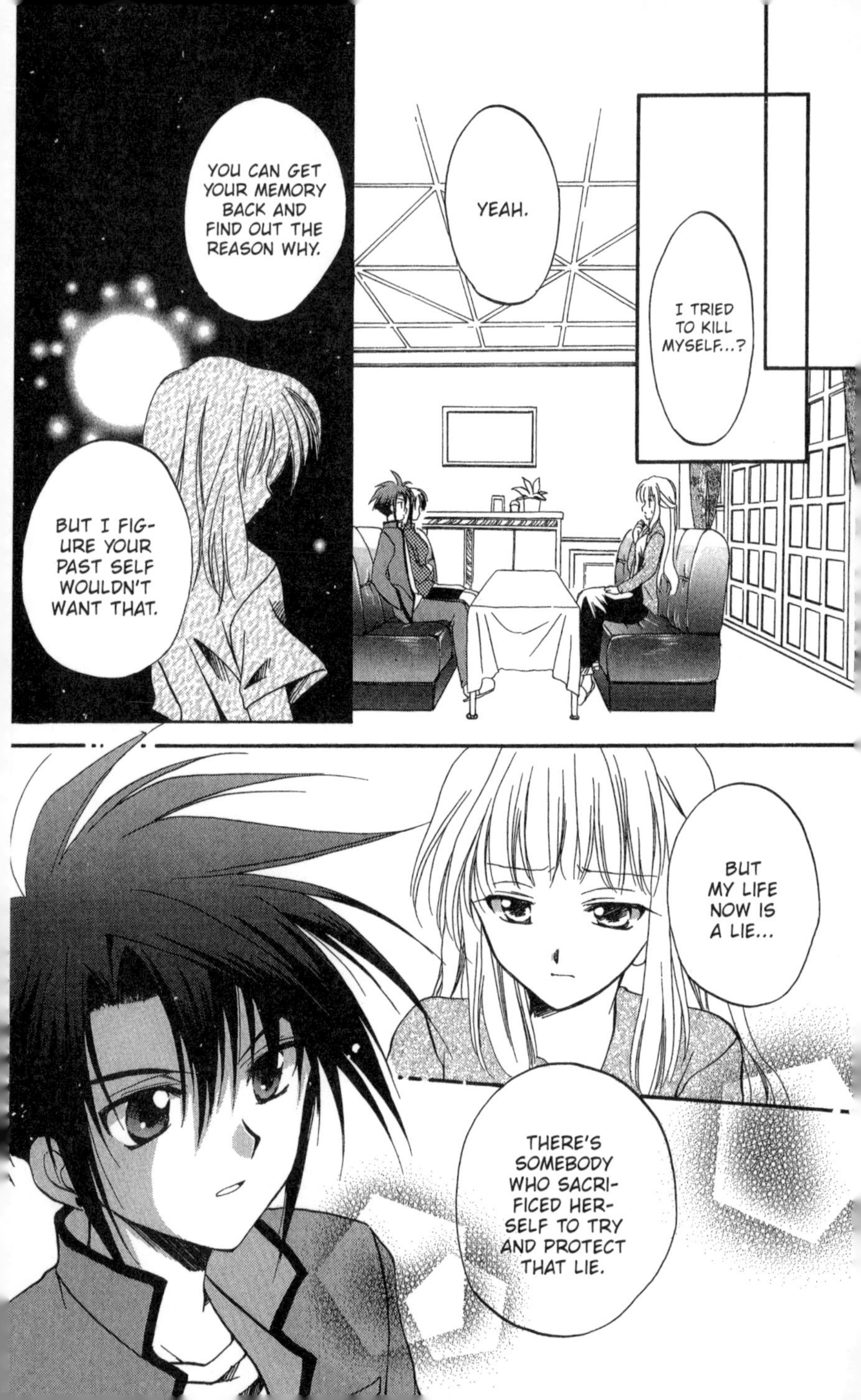
I TRIED TO KILL MYSELF...?
YEAH.
YOU CAN GET YOUR MEMORY BACK AND FIND OUT THE REASON WHY.
BUT I FIG-URE YOUR PAST SELF WOULDN'T WANT THAT.
BUT MY LIFE NOW IS A LIE...
THERE'S SOMEBODY WHO SACRI-FICED HER-SELF TO TRY AND PROTECT THAT LIE.

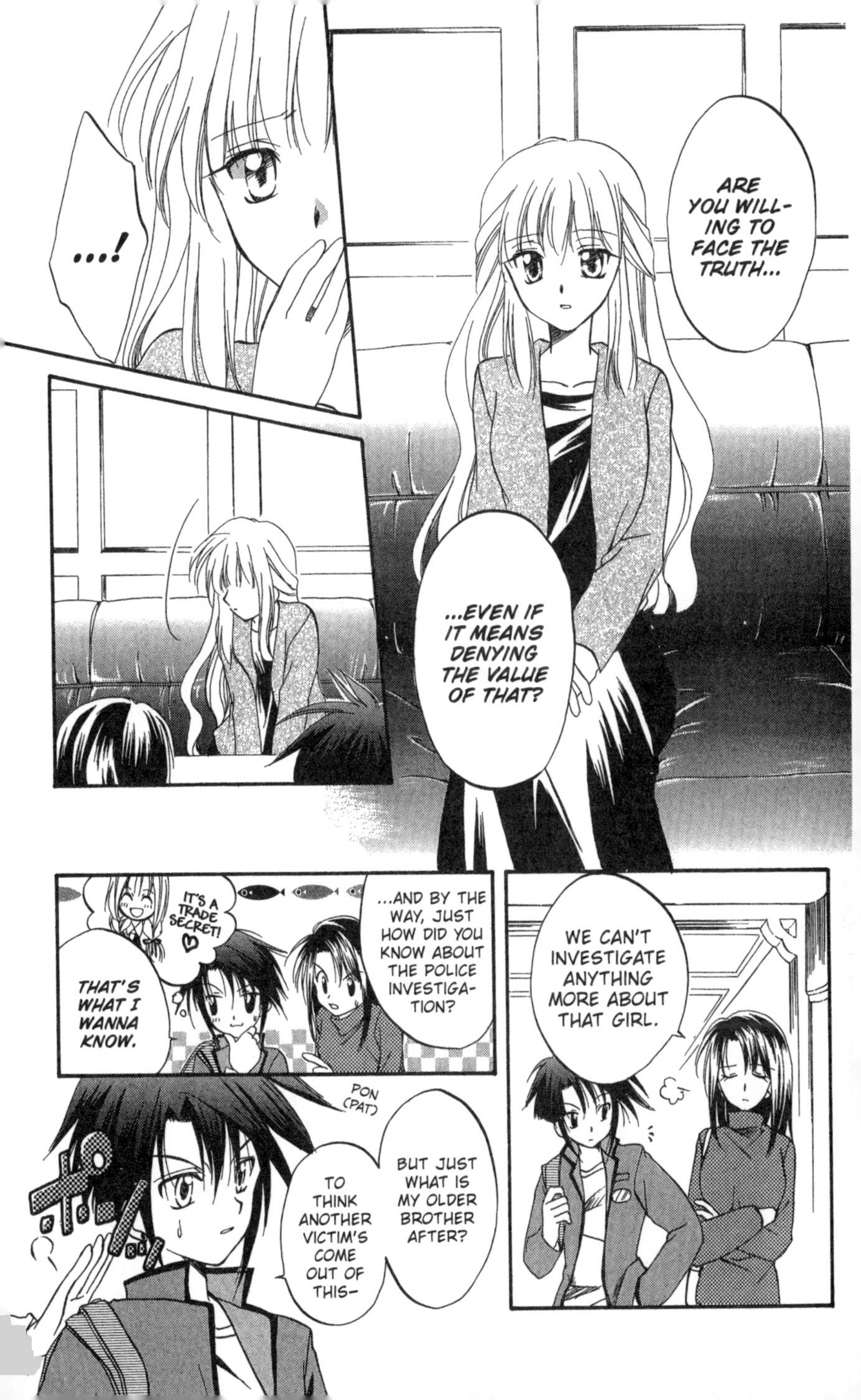
ARE YOU WILL-ING TO FACE THE TRUTH...
...EVEN IF IT MEANS DENYING THE VALUE OF THAT?
...!
WE CAN'T INVESTIGATE ANYTHING MORE ABOUT THAT GIRL.
...AND BY THE WAY, JUST HOW DID YOU KNOW ABOUT THE POLICE INVESTIGA-TION?
IT'S A TRADE SECRET!
THAT'S WHAT I WANNA KNOW.
PON (PAT)
BUT JUST WHAT IS MY OLDER BROTHER AFTER?
TO THINK ANOTHER VICTIM'S COME OUT OF THIS-

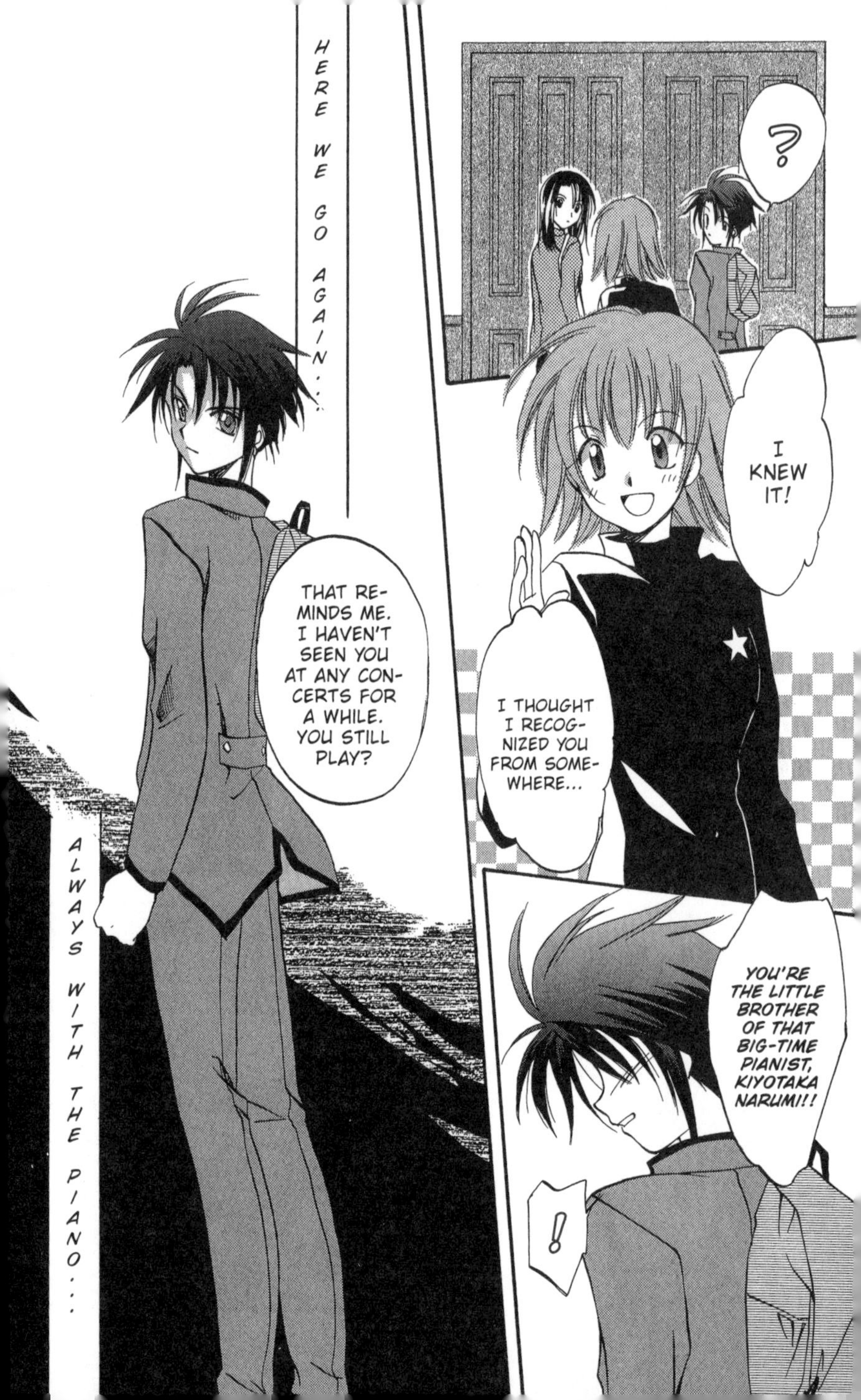
?
I KNEW IT!
I THOUGHT I RECOGNIZED YOU FROM SOMEWHERE...
YOU'RE THE LITTLE BROTHER OF THAT BIG-TIME PIANIST, KIYOTAKA NARUMI!!
!
HERE WE GO AGAIN...
THAT REMINDS ME. I HAVEN'T SEEN YOU AT ANY CONCERTS FOR A WHILE. YOU STILL PLAY?
ALWAYS WITH THE PIANO...

CHAPTER SEVEN
EXPLOSIVE ADVENTURE

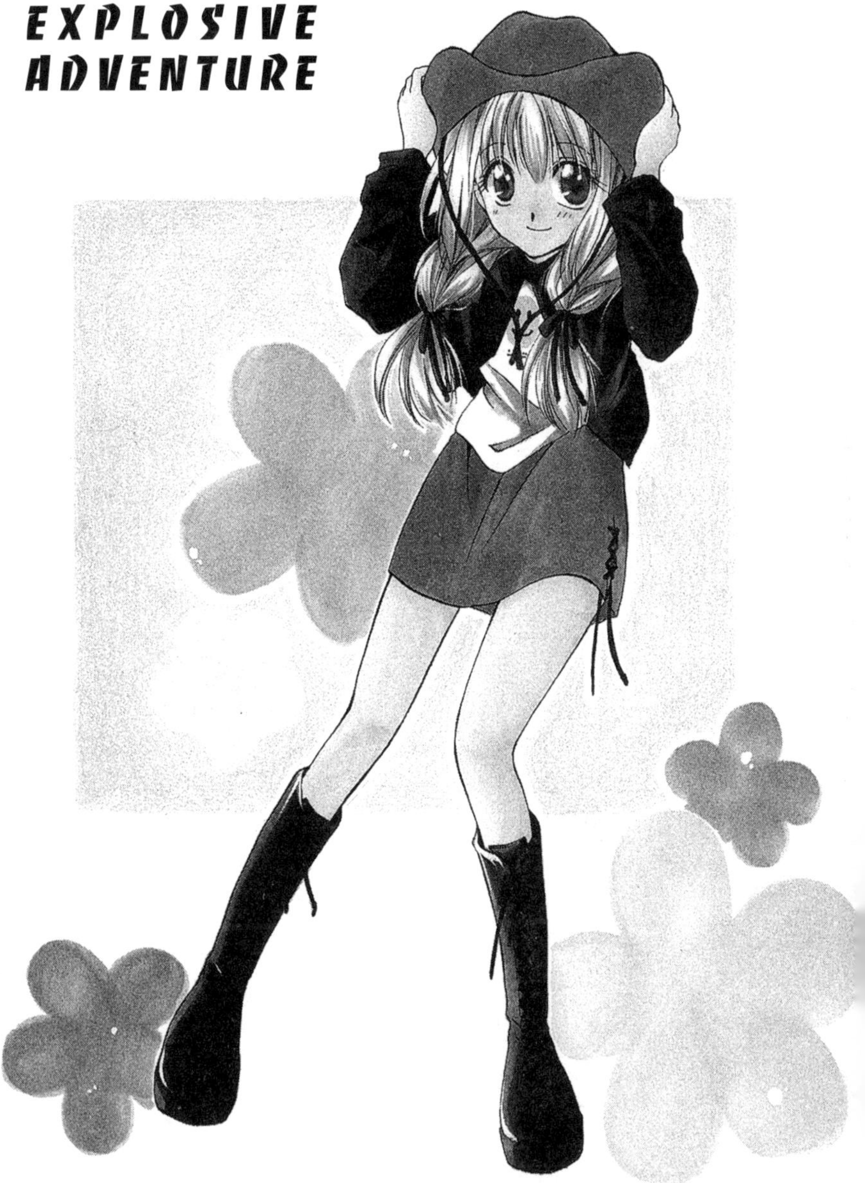

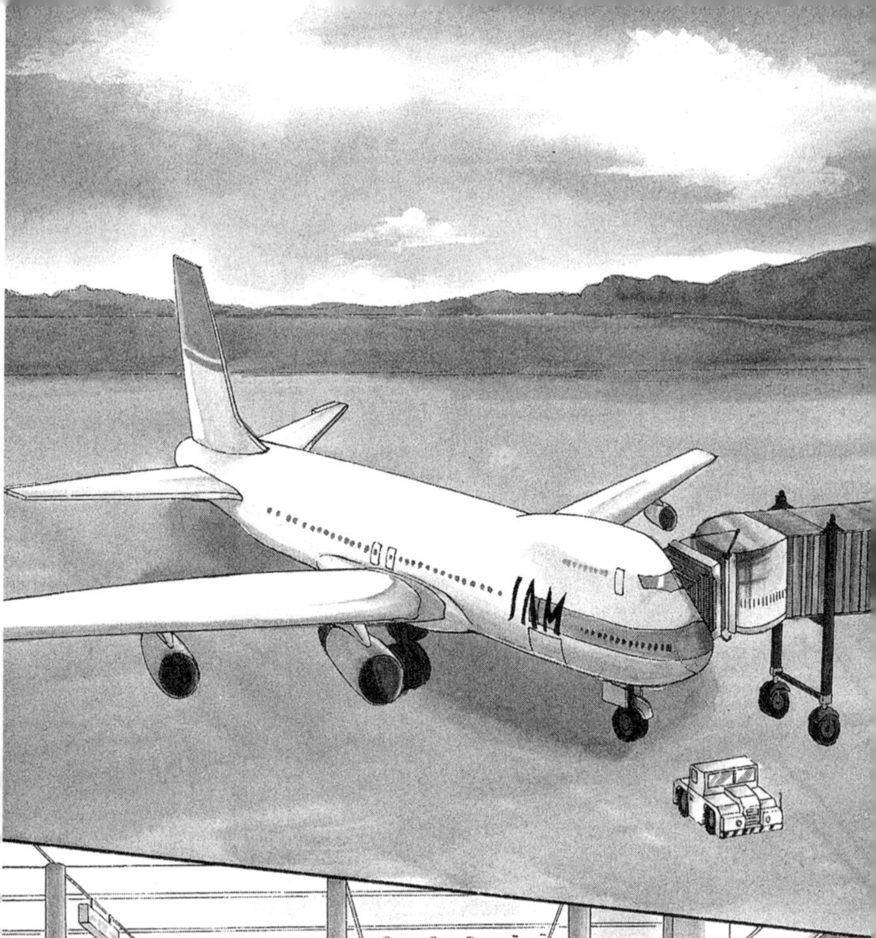
JAM

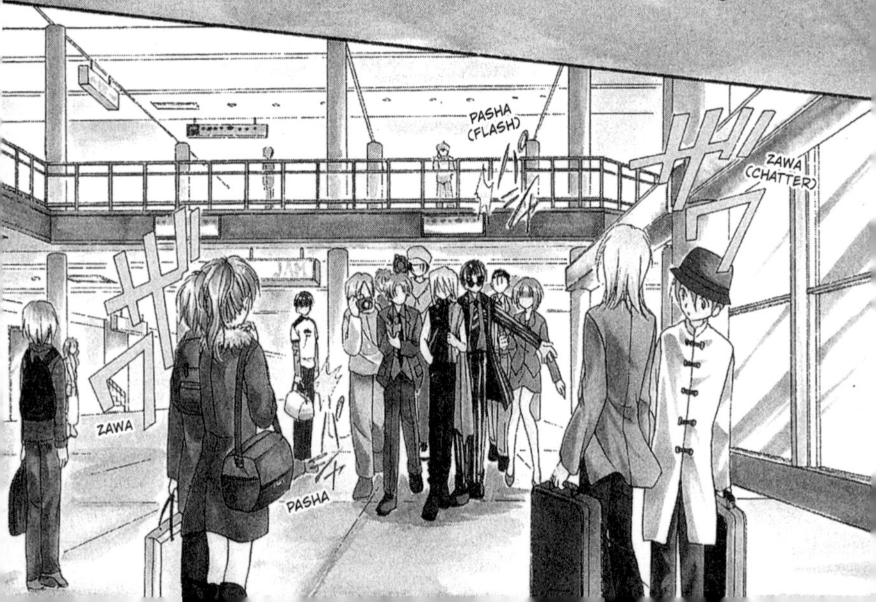
ZAWA (CHATTER)
PASHA (FLASH)
JAM
ZAWA
PASHA

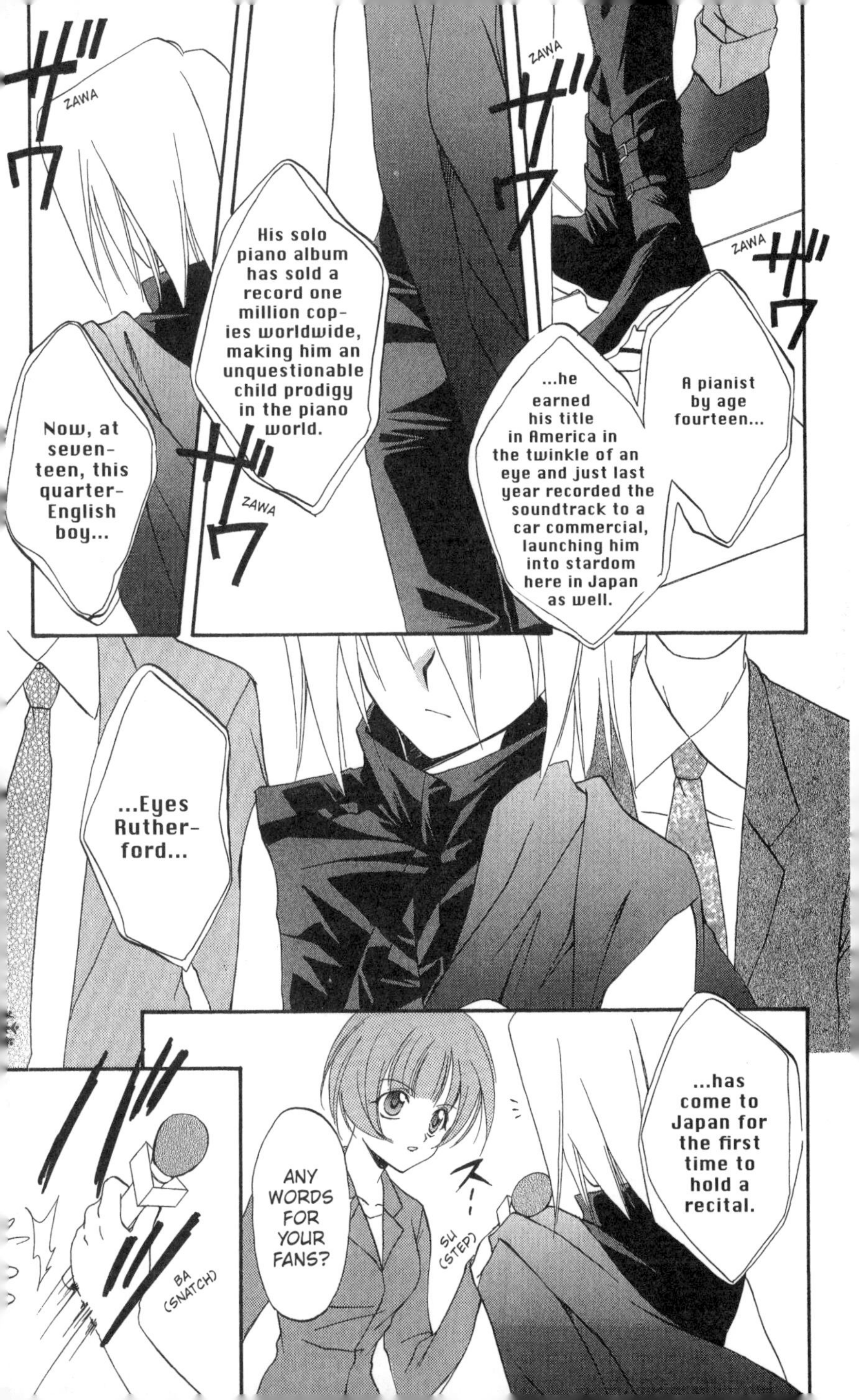
ZAWA
ZAWA
A pianist by age fourteen...
...he earned his title in America in the twinkle of an eye and just last year recorded the soundtrack to a car commercial, launching him into stardom here in Japan as well.
His solo piano album has sold a record one million copies worldwide, making him an unquestionable child prodigy in the piano world.
ZAWA
ZAWA
Now, at seventeen, this quarter-English boy...
...Eyes Rutherford...
...has come to Japan for the first time to hold a recital.
SU (STEP)
ANY WORDS FOR YOUR FANS?
BA (SNATCH)

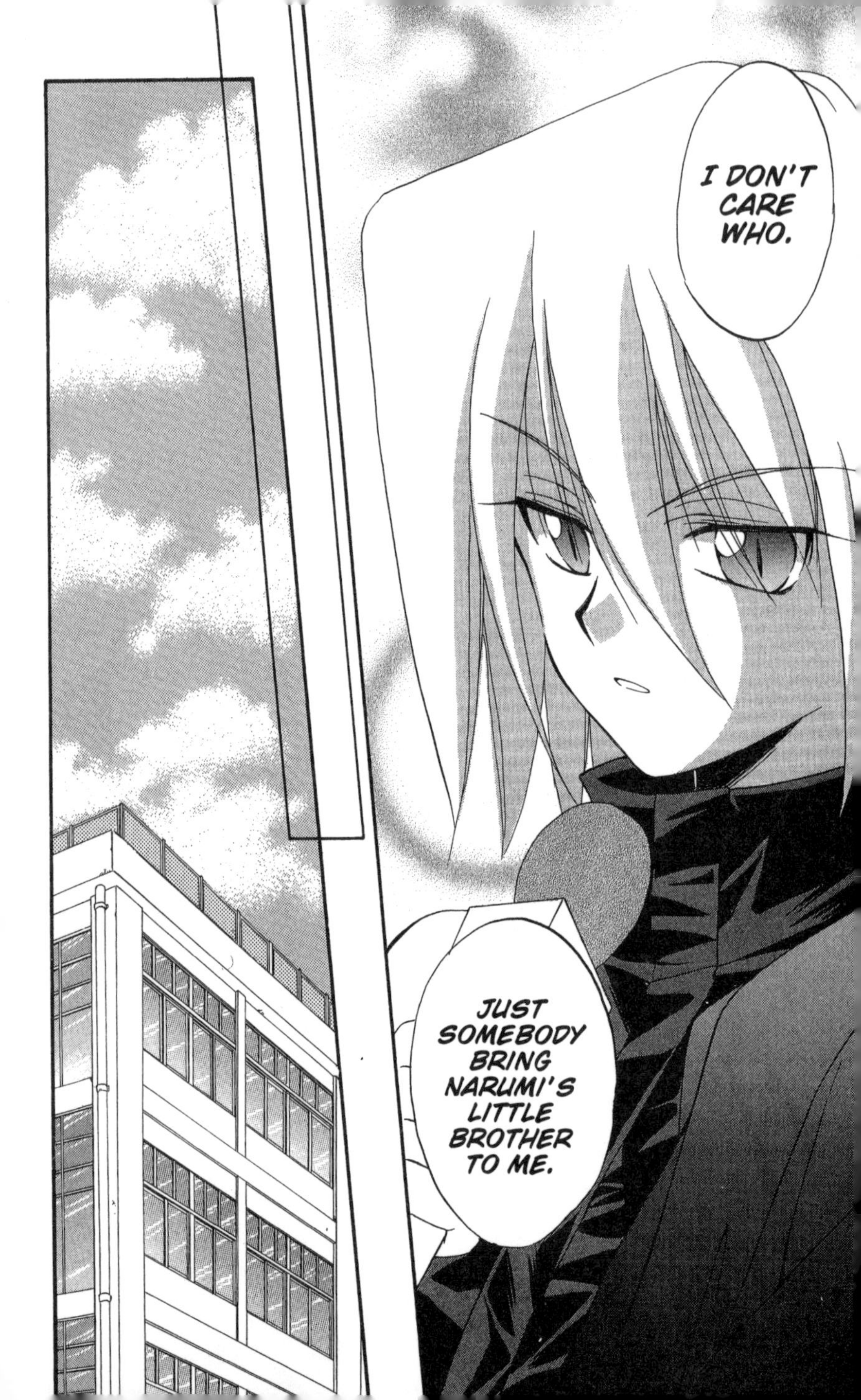
I DON'T CARE WHO.
JUST SOMEBODY BRING NARUMI'S LITTLE BROTHER TO ME.

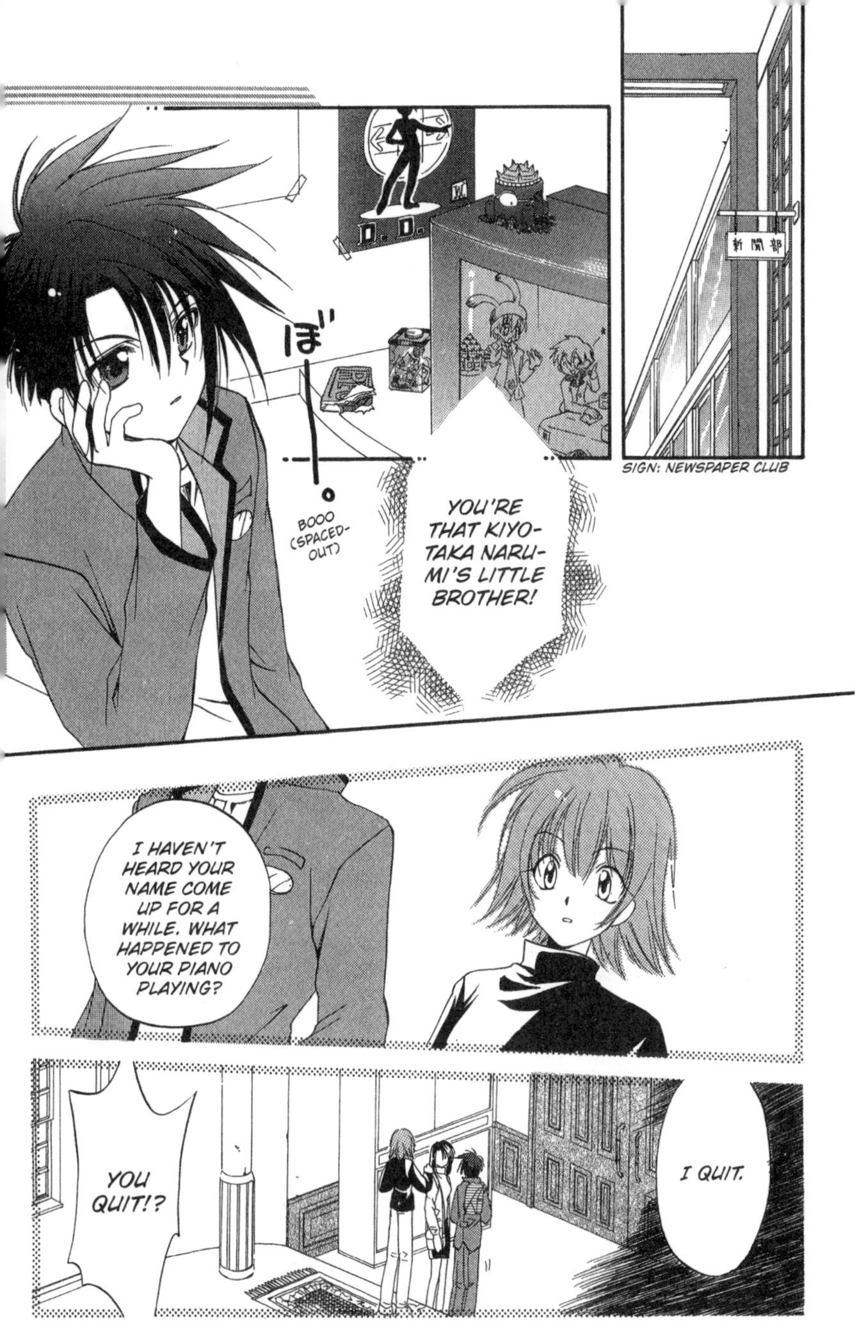
新聞部
SIGN: NEWSPAPER CLUB
YOU'RE THAT KIYOTAKA NARUMI'S LITTLE BROTHER!
ぼー
BOOO (SPACED-OUT)
I HAVEN'T HEARD YOUR NAME COME UP FOR A WHILE. WHAT HAPPENED TO YOUR PIANO PLAYING?
I QUIT.
YOU QUIT!?

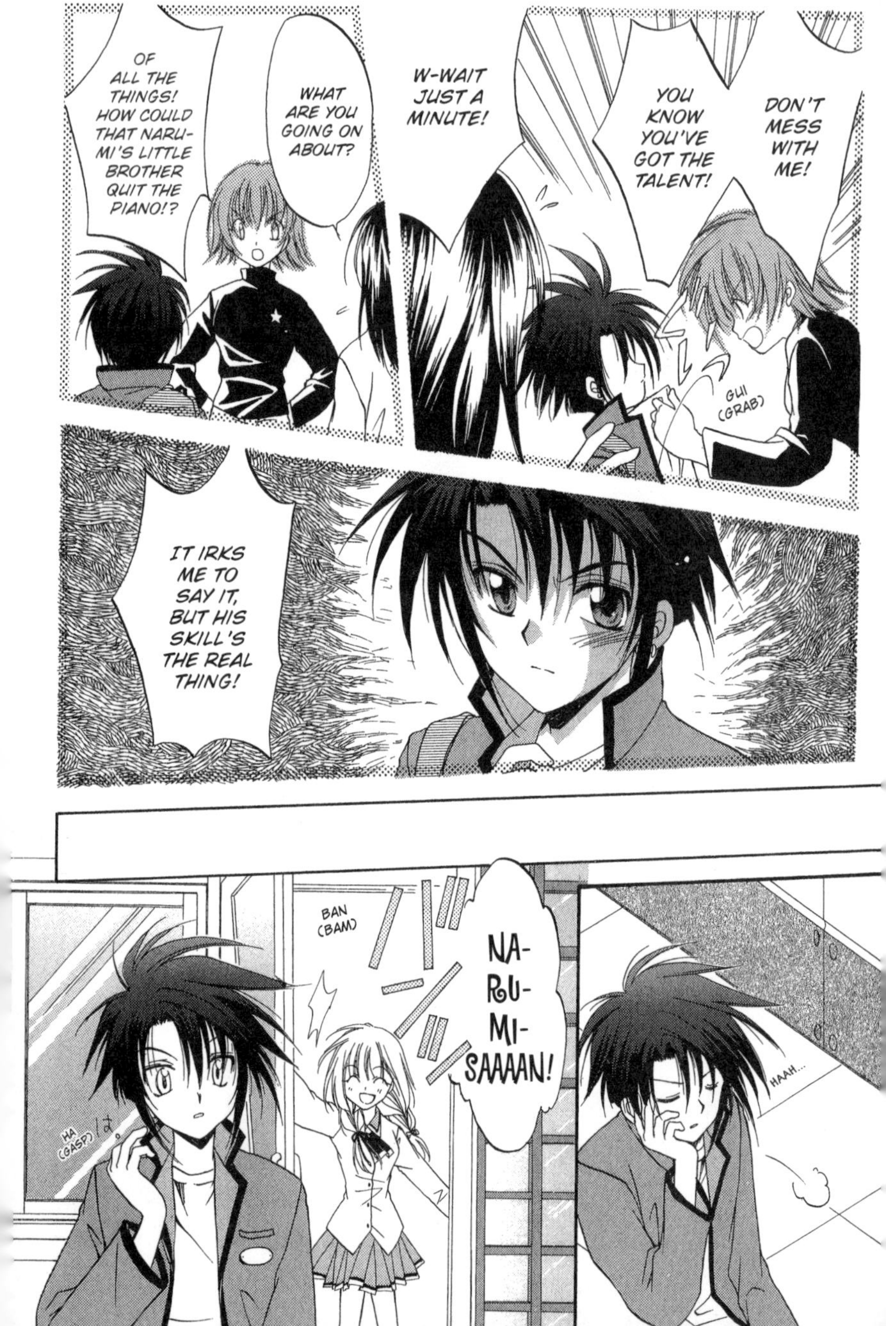

DON'T MESS WITH ME!
YOU KNOW YOU'VE GOT THE TALENT!
GUI (GRAB)
W-WAIT JUST A MINUTE!
WHAT ARE YOU GOING ON ABOUT?
OF ALL THE THINGS! HOW COULD THAT NARUMI'S LITTLE BROTHER QUIT THE PIANO!?
IT IRKS ME TO SAY IT, BUT HIS SKILL'S THE REAL THING!
HAAH...
NA-RU-MI-SAAAAN!
BAN (BAM)
HA (GASP) は

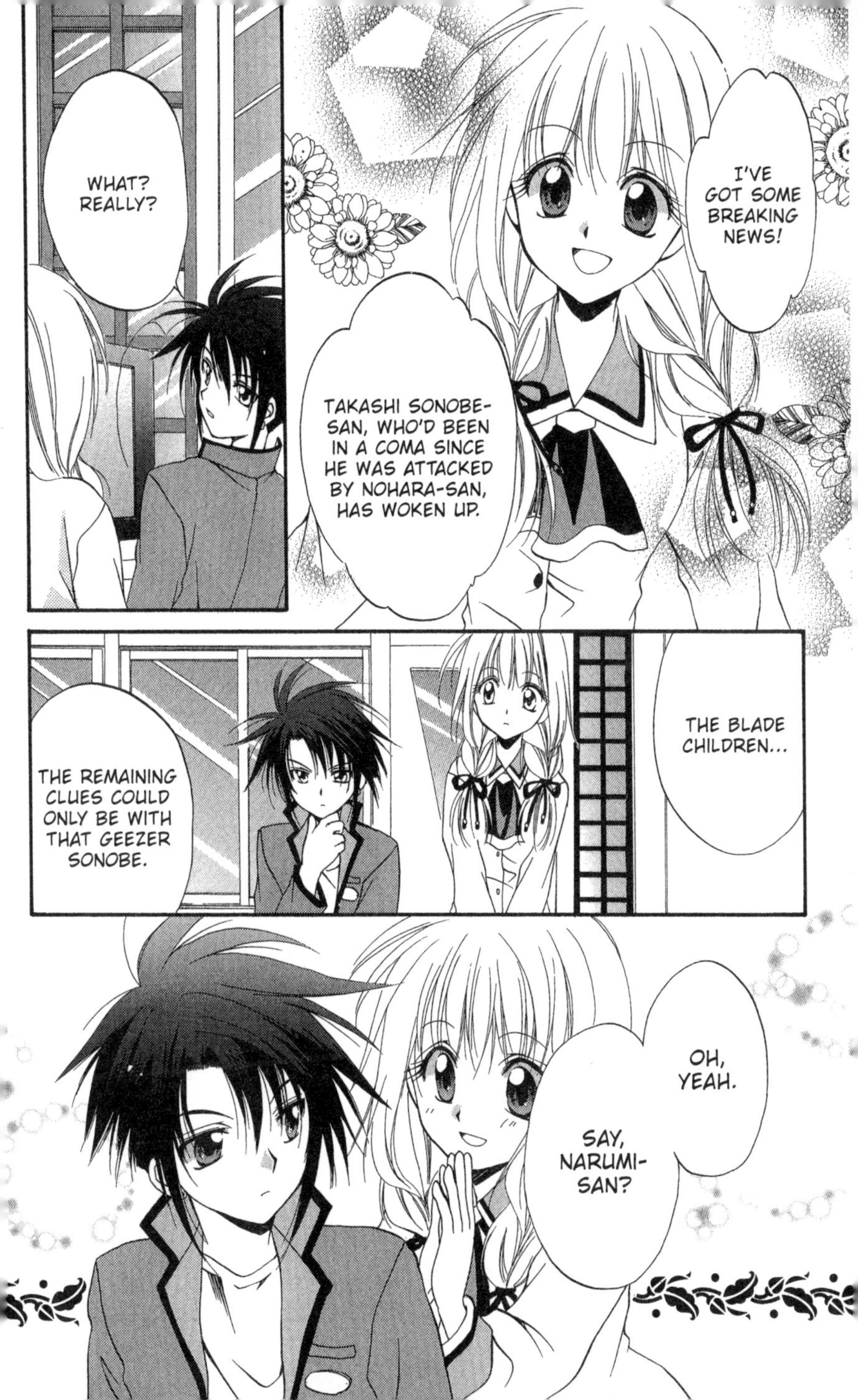
I'VE GOT SOME BREAKING NEWS!
TAKASHI SONOBE-SAN, WHO'D BEEN IN A COMA SINCE HE WAS ATTACKED BY NOHARA-SAN, HAS WOKEN UP.
WHAT? REALLY?
THE BLADE CHILDREN...
THE REMAINING CLUES COULD ONLY BE WITH THAT GEEZER SONOBE.
OH, YEAH.
SAY, NARUMI-SAN?

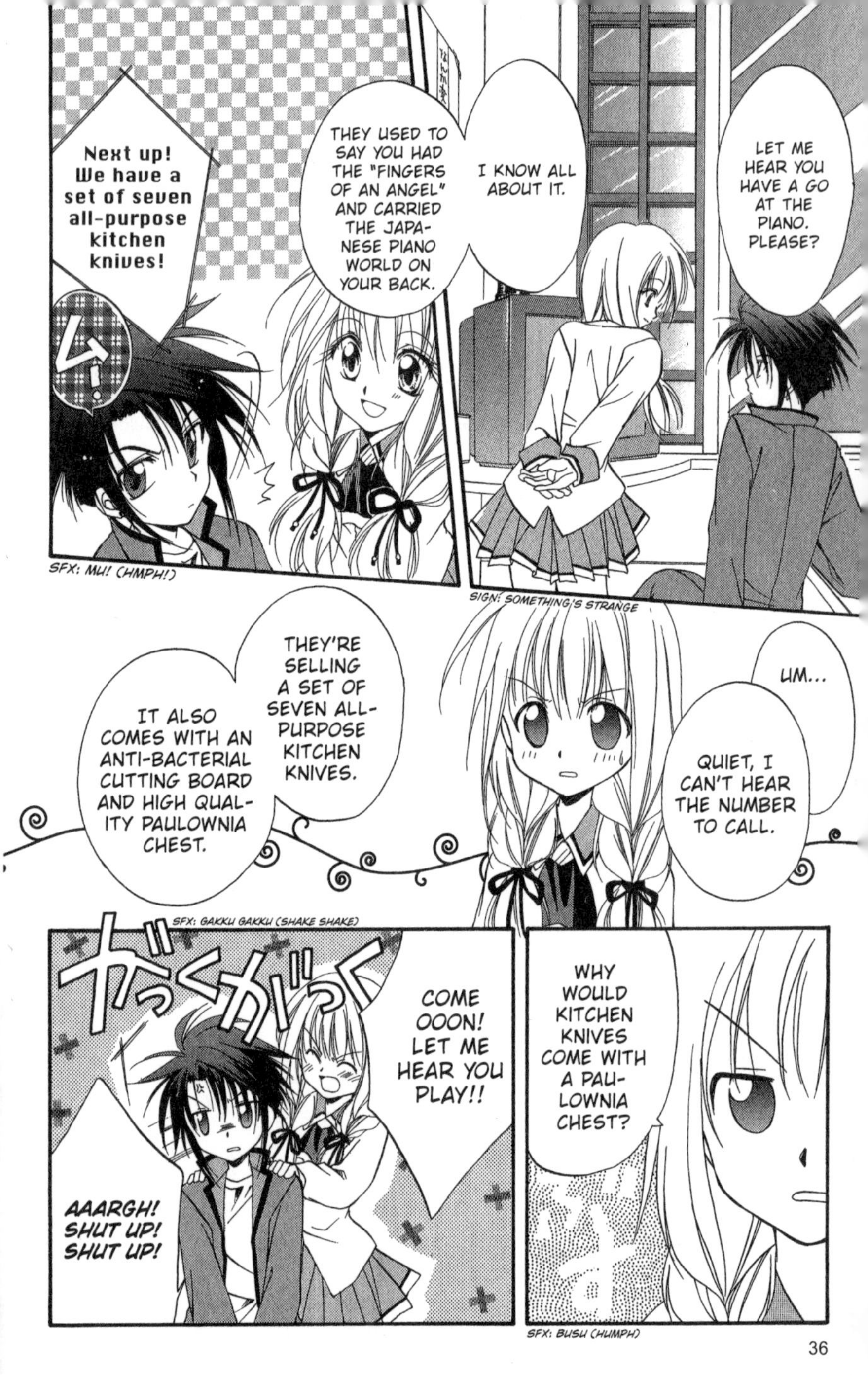
LET ME HEAR YOU HAVE A GO AT THE PIANO. PLEASE?
I KNOW ALL ABOUT IT.
SIGN: SOMETHING'S STRANGE
THEY USED TO SAY YOU HAD THE "FINGERS OF AN ANGEL" AND CARRIED THE JAPANESE PIANO WORLD ON YOUR BACK.
Next up! We have a set of seven all-purpose kitchen knives!
ム!
SFX: MU! (HMPH!)
UM...
QUIET, I CAN'T HEAR THE NUMBER TO CALL.
THEY'RE SELLING A SET OF SEVEN ALL-PURPOSE KITCHEN KNIVES.
IT ALSO COMES WITH AN ANTI-BACTERIAL CUTTING BOARD AND HIGH QUALITY PAULOWNIA CHEST.
SFX: GAKKU GAKKU (SHAKE SHAKE)
WHY WOULD KITCHEN KNIVES COME WITH A PAULOWNIA CHEST?
SFX: BUSU (HUMPH)
がっくがっく
COME OOON! LET ME HEAR YOU PLAY!!
AAARGH! SHUT UP! SHUT UP!

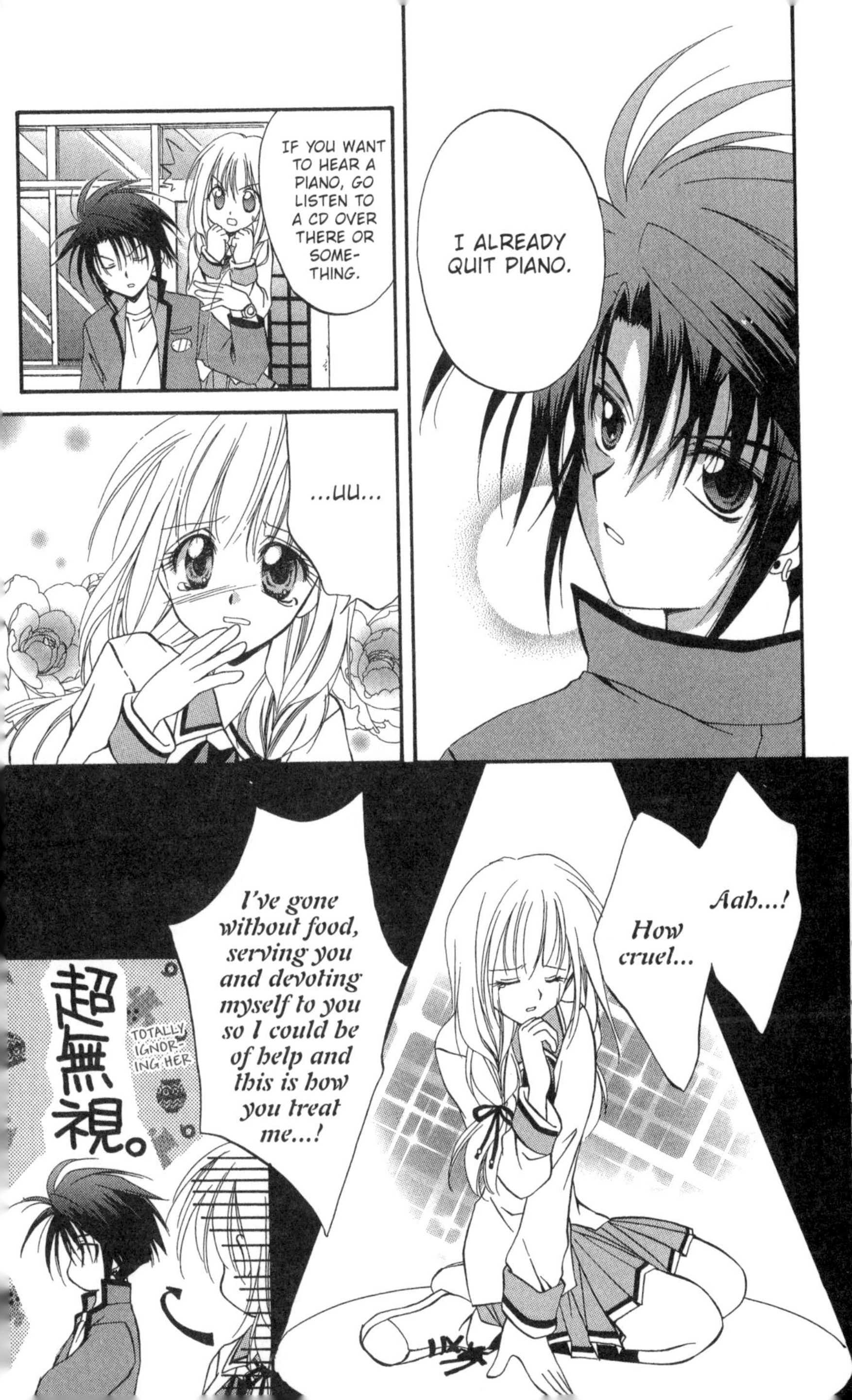
I ALREADY QUIT PIANO.
IF YOU WANT TO HEAR A PIANO, GO LISTEN TO A CD OVER THERE OR SOME-THING.
...uu...
Aah...!
How cruel...
I've gone without food, serving you and devoting myself to you so I could be of help and this is how you treat me...!
超無視。
TOTALLY IGNOR-ING HER

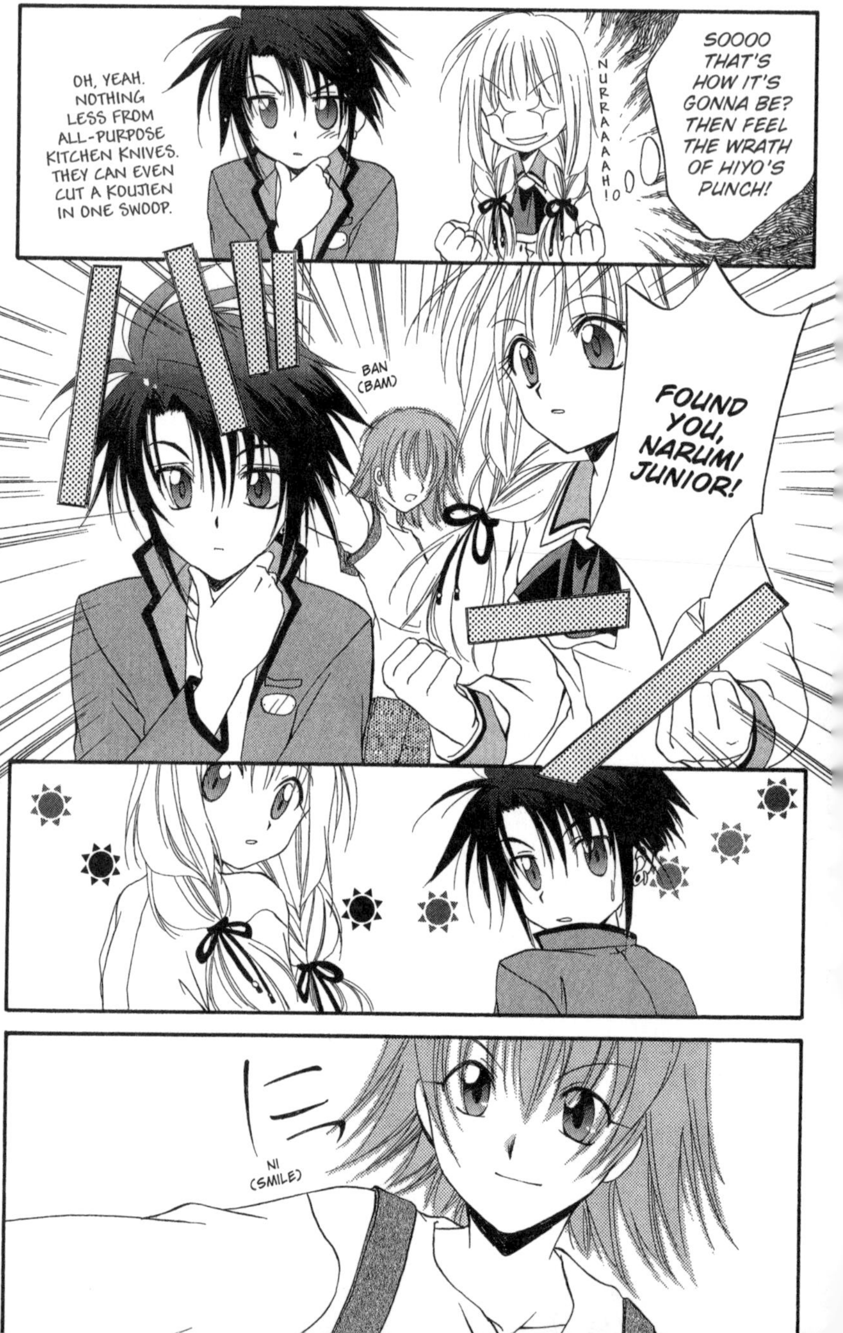
SOOOO THAT'S HOW IT'S GONNA BE? THEN FEEL THE WRATH OF HIYO'S PUNCH!
NURRAAAAH!
OH, YEAH. NOTHING LESS FROM ALL-PURPOSE KITCHEN KNIVES. THEY CAN EVEN CUT A KOUJIEN IN ONE SWOOP.
FOUND YOU, NARUMI JUNIOR!
BAN (BAM)
NI (SMILE)

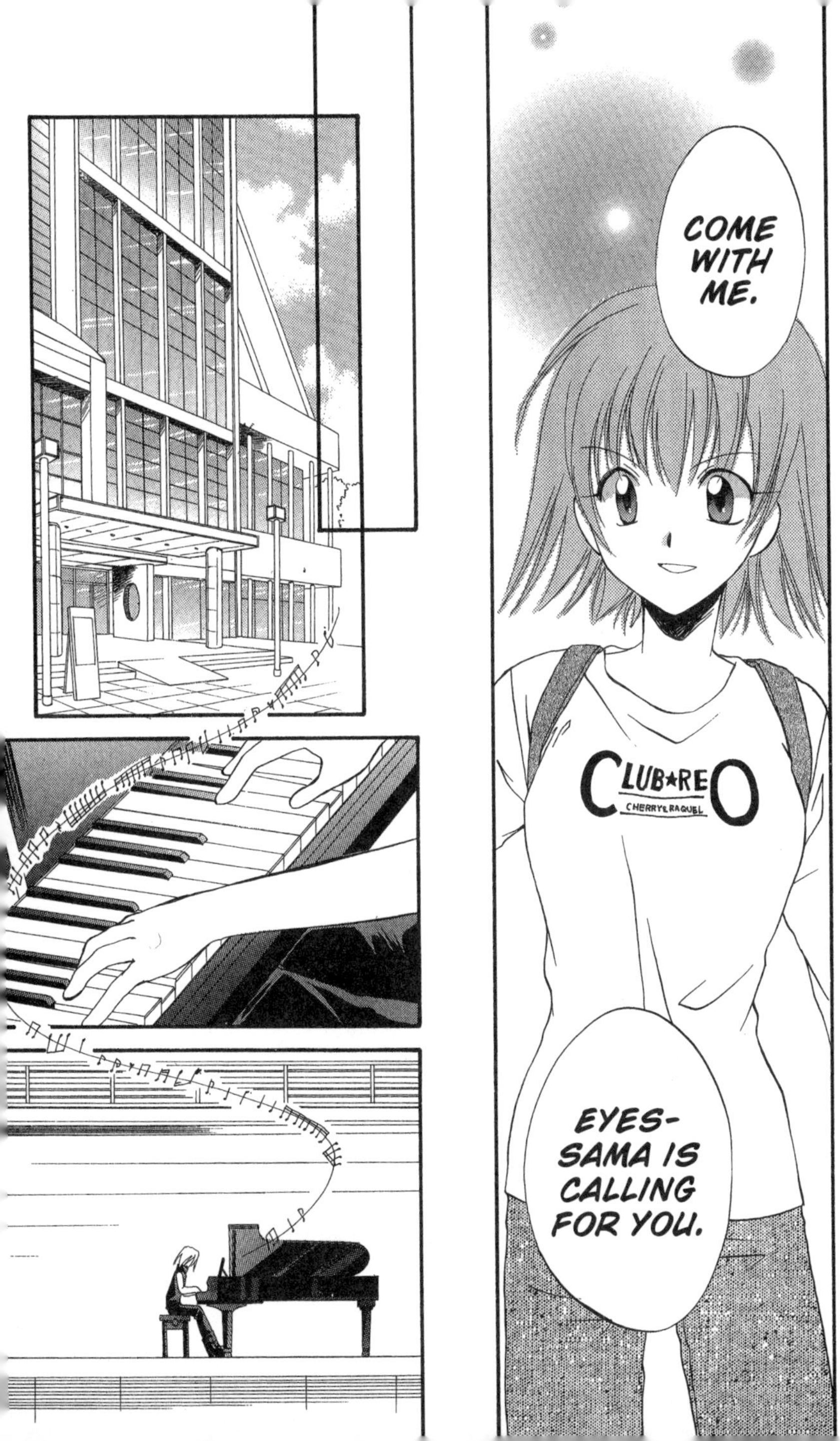
COME WITH ME.
CLUB★REO
CHERRY&RAQUEL
EYES-SAMA IS CALLING FOR YOU.

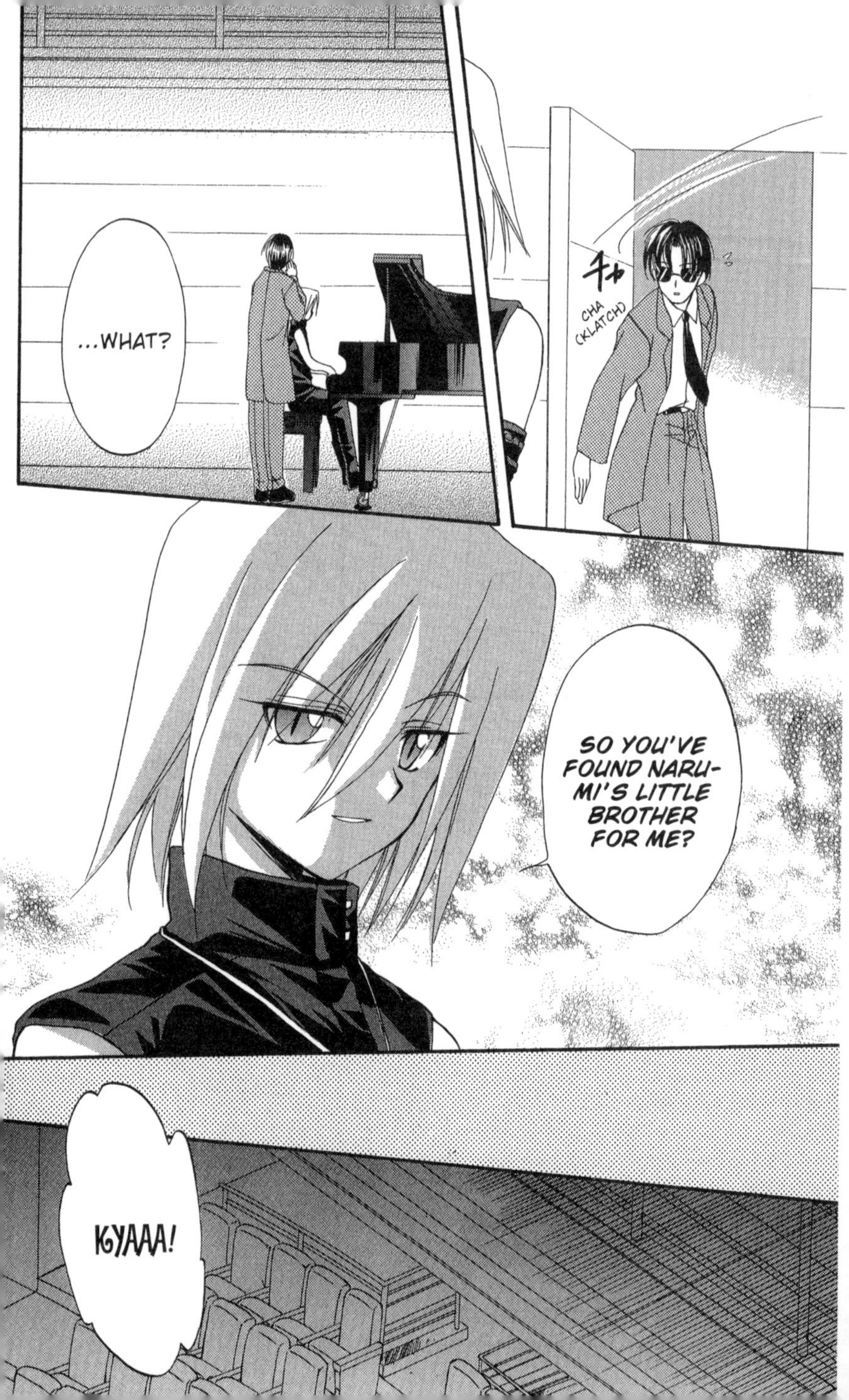
チャ
CHA (KLATCH)
...WHAT?
SO YOU'VE FOUND NARU-MI'S LITTLE BROTHER FOR ME?
KYAAA!

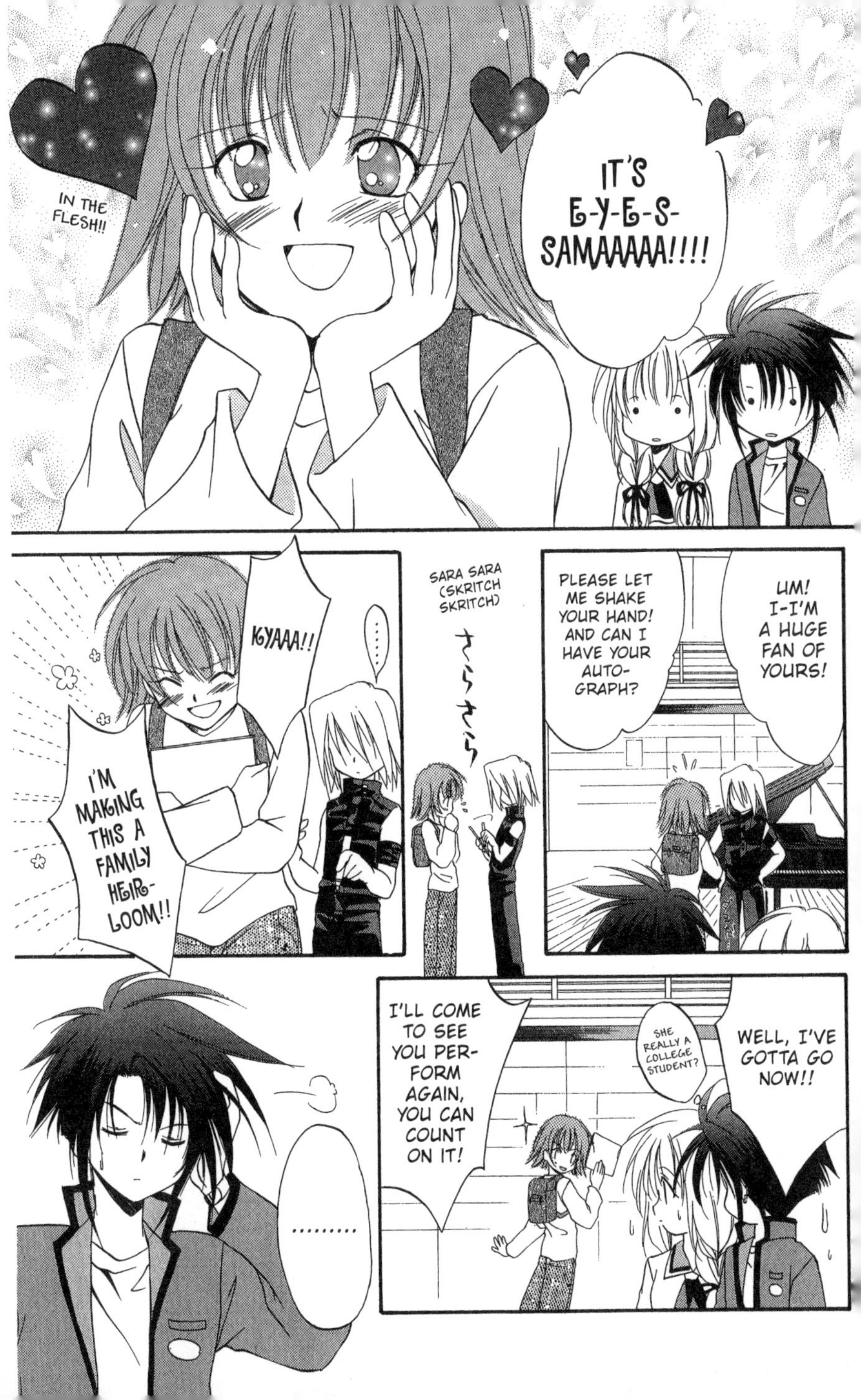
IT'S E-Y-E-S-SAMAAAAA!!!!
IN THE FLESH!!
UM! I-I'M A HUGE FAN OF YOURS!
PLEASE LET ME SHAKE YOUR HAND! AND CAN I HAVE YOUR AUTO-GRAPH?
SARA SARA (SKRITCH SKRITCH)
さらさら
KYAAA!!
......
I'M MAKING THIS A FAMILY HEIR-LOOM!!
WELL, I'VE GOTTA GO NOW!!
SHE REALLY A COLLEGE STUDENT?
I'LL COME TO SEE YOU PER-FORM AGAIN, YOU CAN COUNT ON IT!
....

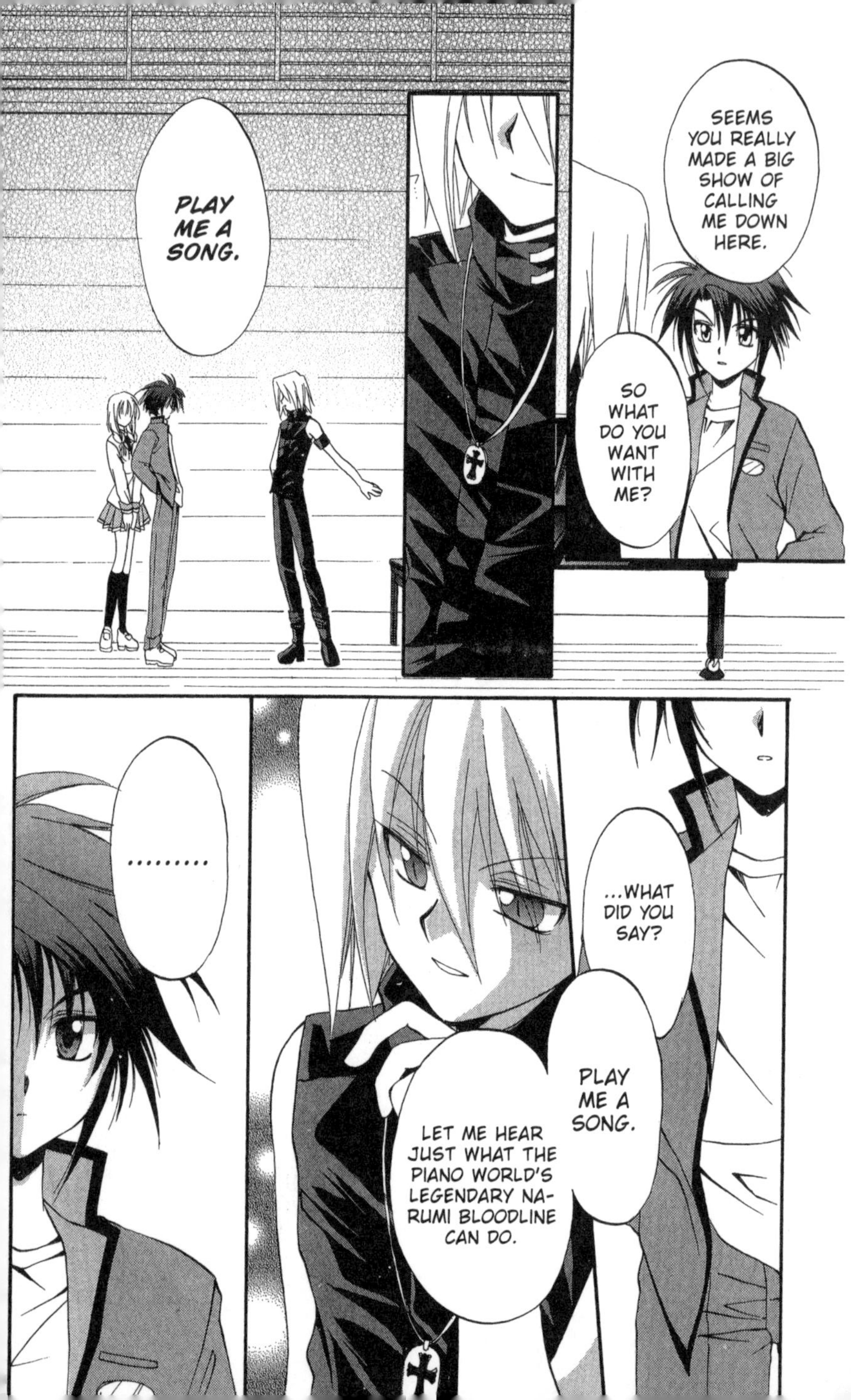
SEEMS YOU REALLY MADE A BIG SHOW OF CALLING ME DOWN HERE.
SO WHAT DO YOU WANT WITH ME?
PLAY ME A SONG.
...WHAT DID YOU SAY?
PLAY ME A SONG.
LET ME HEAR JUST WHAT THE PIANO WORLD'S LEGENDARY NA-RUMI BLOODLINE CAN DO.
....

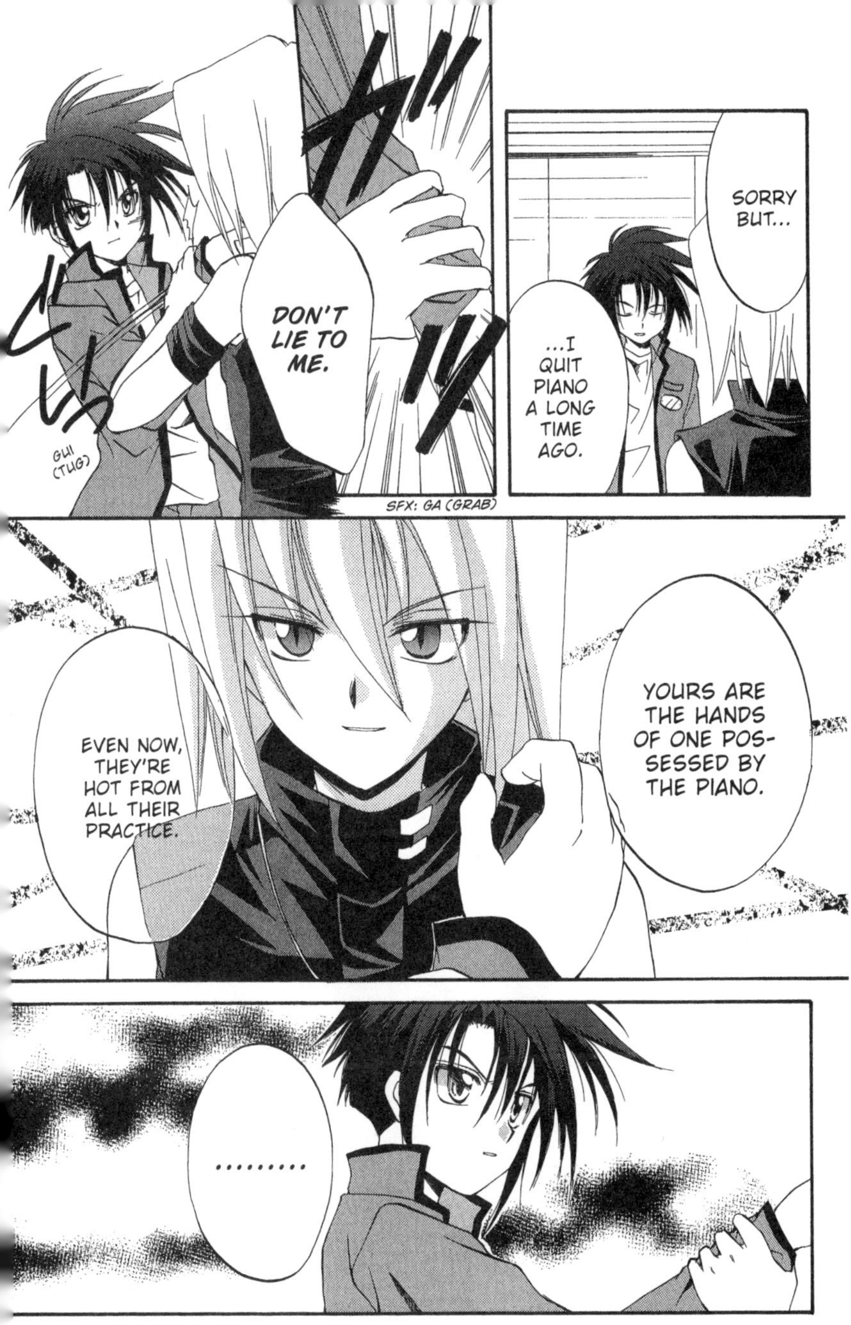
SORRY BUT...
...I QUIT PIANO A LONG TIME AGO.
DON'T LIE TO ME.
SFX: GA (GRAB)
GUI (TUG)
YOURS ARE THE HANDS OF ONE POS-SESSED BY THE PIANO.
EVEN NOW, THEY'RE HOT FROM ALL THEIR PRACTICE.
....

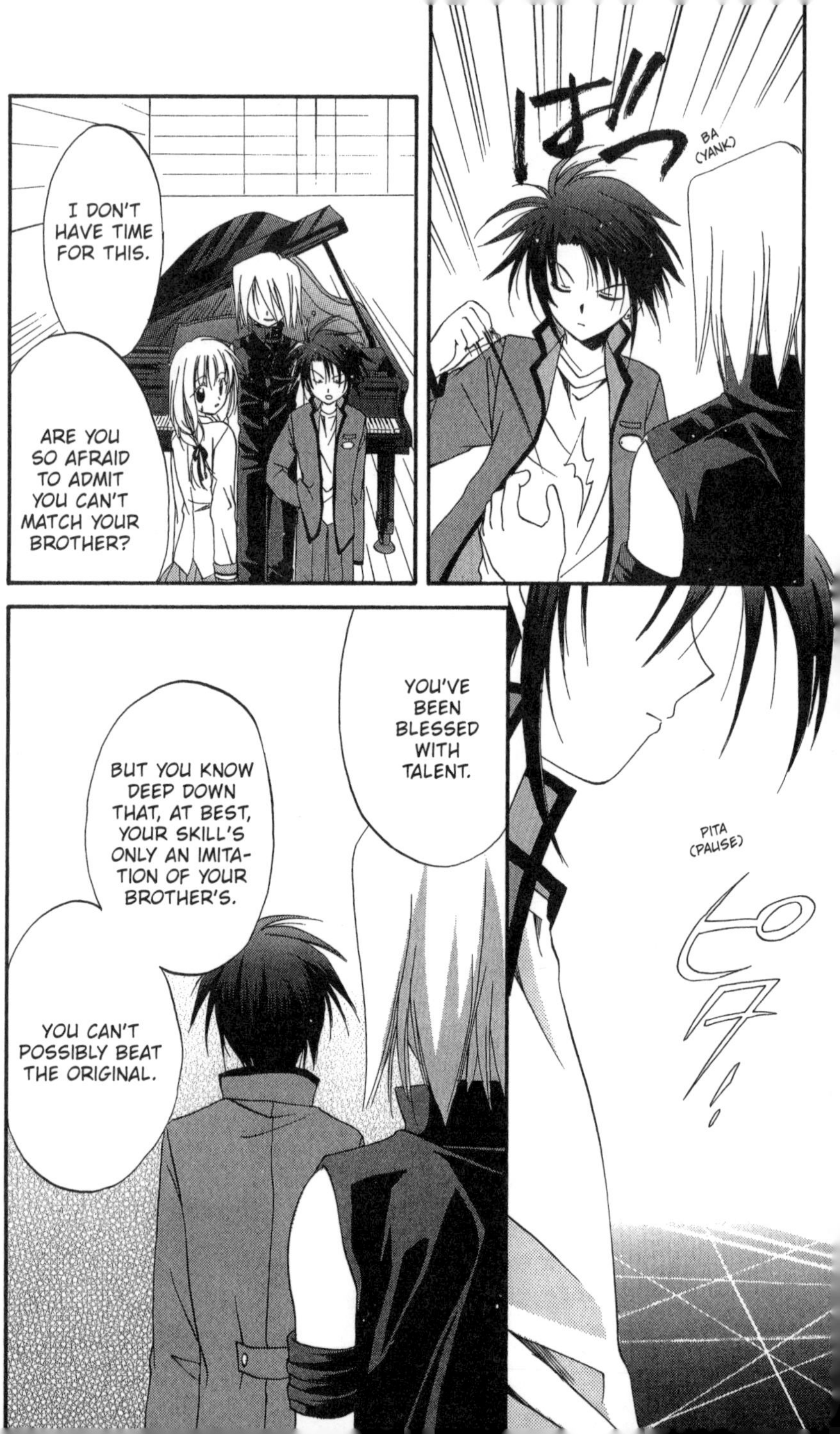
BA (YANK)
I DON'T HAVE TIME FOR THIS.
ARE YOU SO AFRAID TO ADMIT YOU CAN'T MATCH YOUR BROTHER?
PITA (PAUSE)
YOU'VE BEEN BLESSED WITH TALENT.
BUT YOU KNOW DEEP DOWN THAT, AT BEST, YOUR SKILL'S ONLY AN IMITATION OF YOUR BROTHER'S.
YOU CAN'T POSSIBLY BEAT THE ORIGINAL.

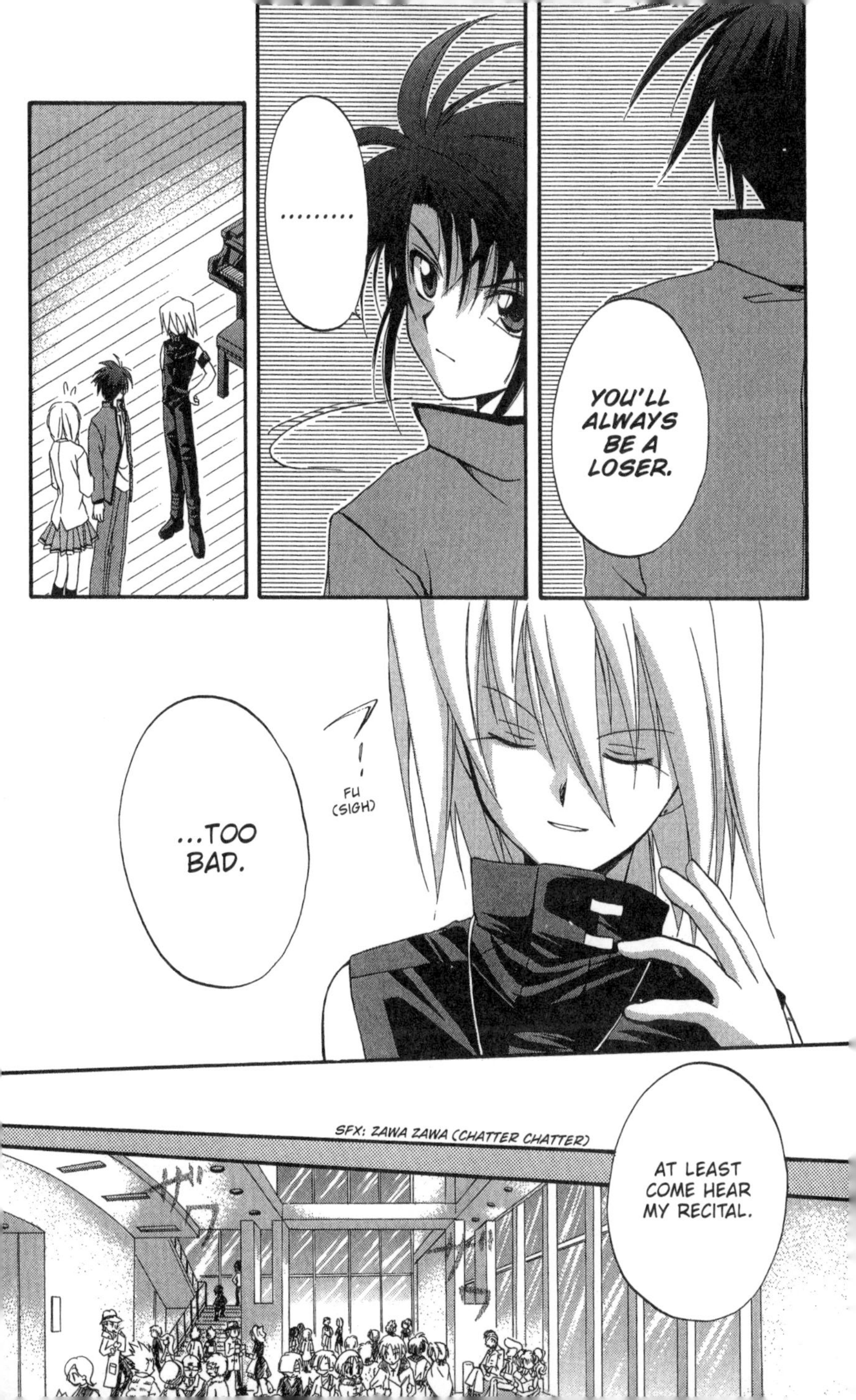
YOU'LL ALWAYS BE A LOSER.
....
FU (SIGH)
...TOO BAD.
AT LEAST COME HEAR MY RECITAL.
SFX: ZAWA ZAWA (CHATTER CHATTER)

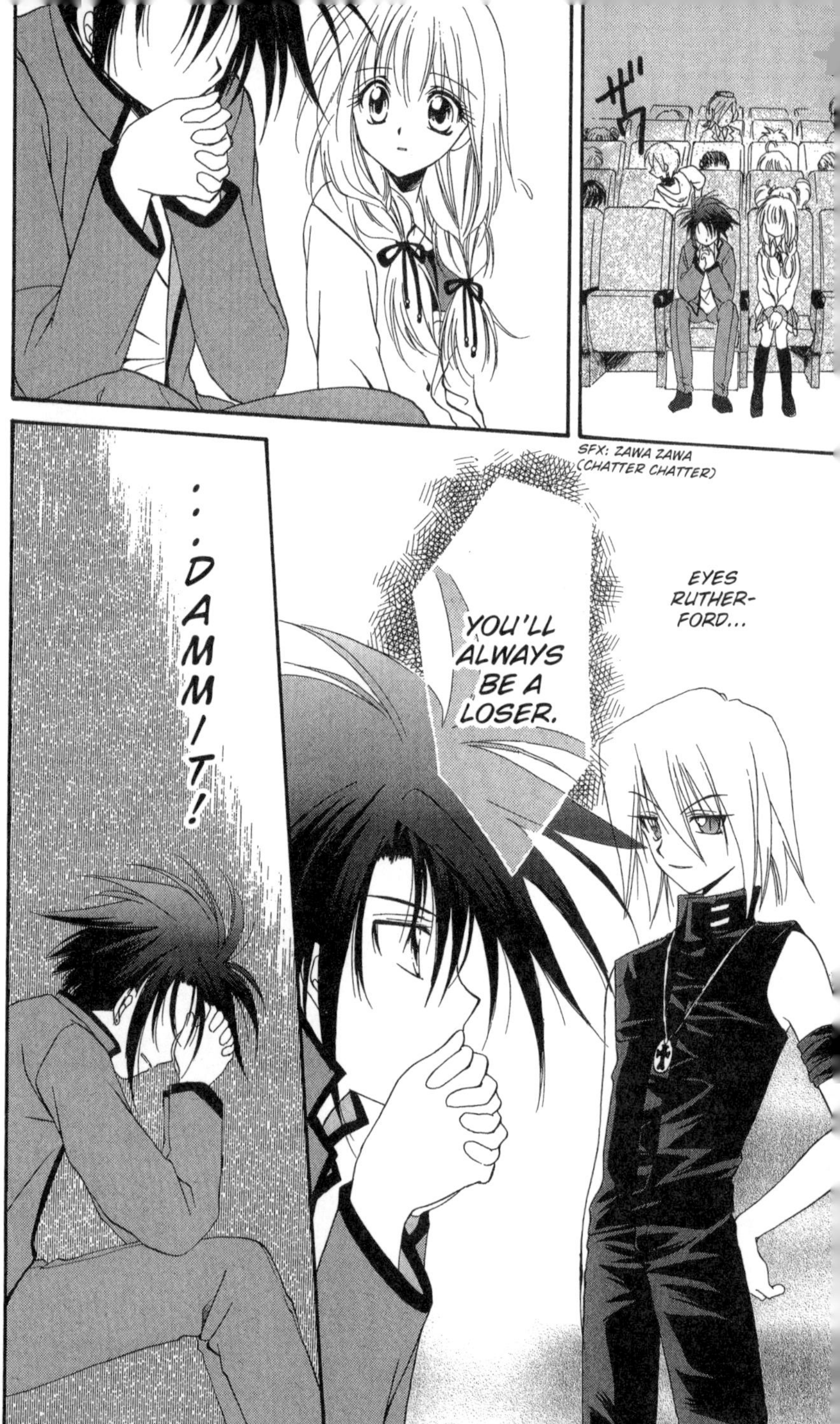
SFX: ZAWA ZAWA (CHATTER CHATTER)
EYES RUTHERFORD...
YOU'LL ALWAYS BE A LOSER.
...DAMMIT!

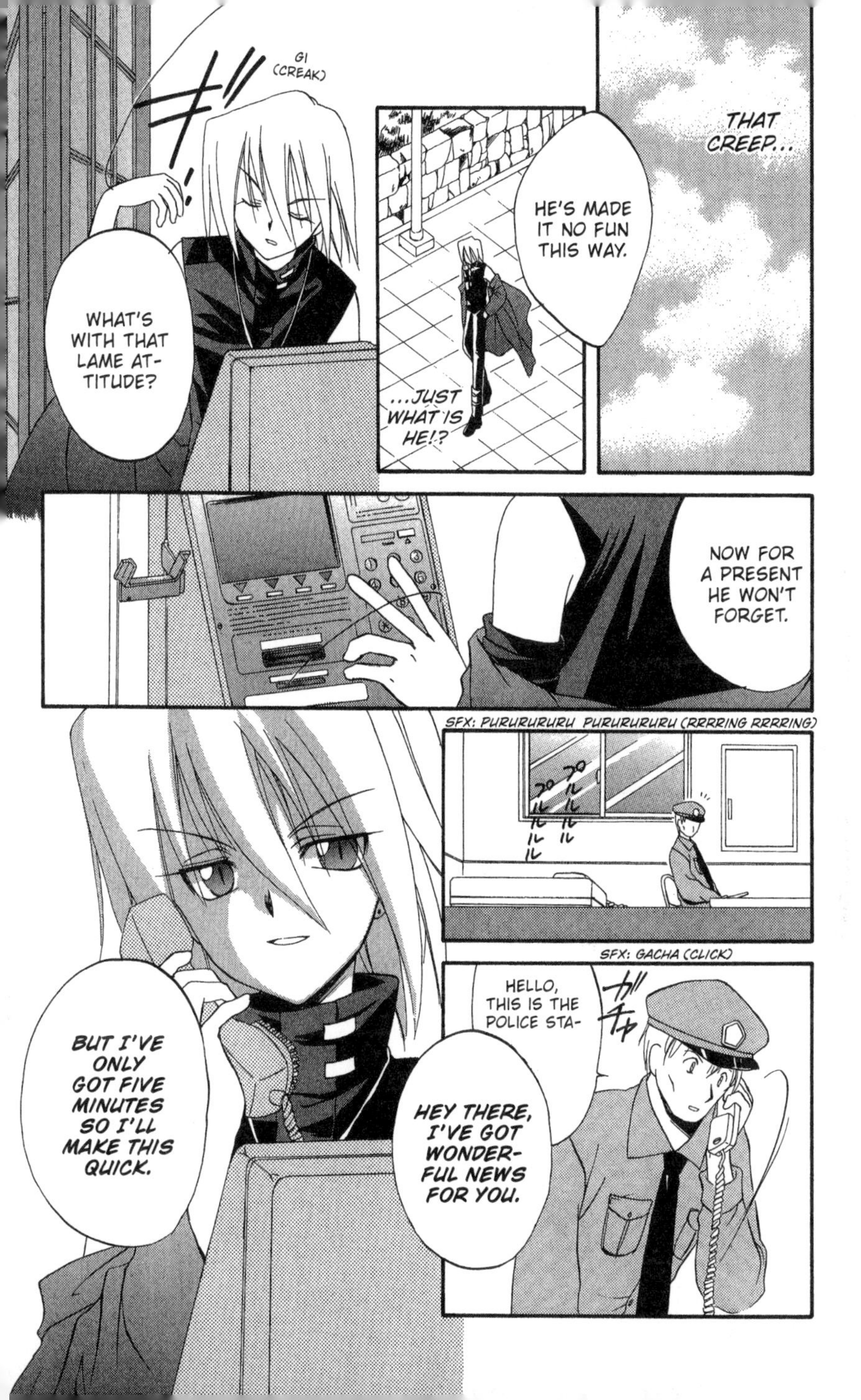
THAT CREEP...
HE'S MADE IT NO FUN THIS WAY.
...JUST WHAT IS HE!?
GI (CREAK)
WHAT'S WITH THAT LAME AT-TITUDE?
NOW FOR A PRESENT HE WON'T FORGET.
SFX: PURURURURU PURURURURU (RRRRING RRRRING)
SFX: GACHA (CLICK)
HELLO, THIS IS THE POLICE STA-
HEY THERE, I'VE GOT WONDER-FUL NEWS FOR YOU.
BUT I'VE ONLY GOT FIVE MINUTES SO I'LL MAKE THIS QUICK.

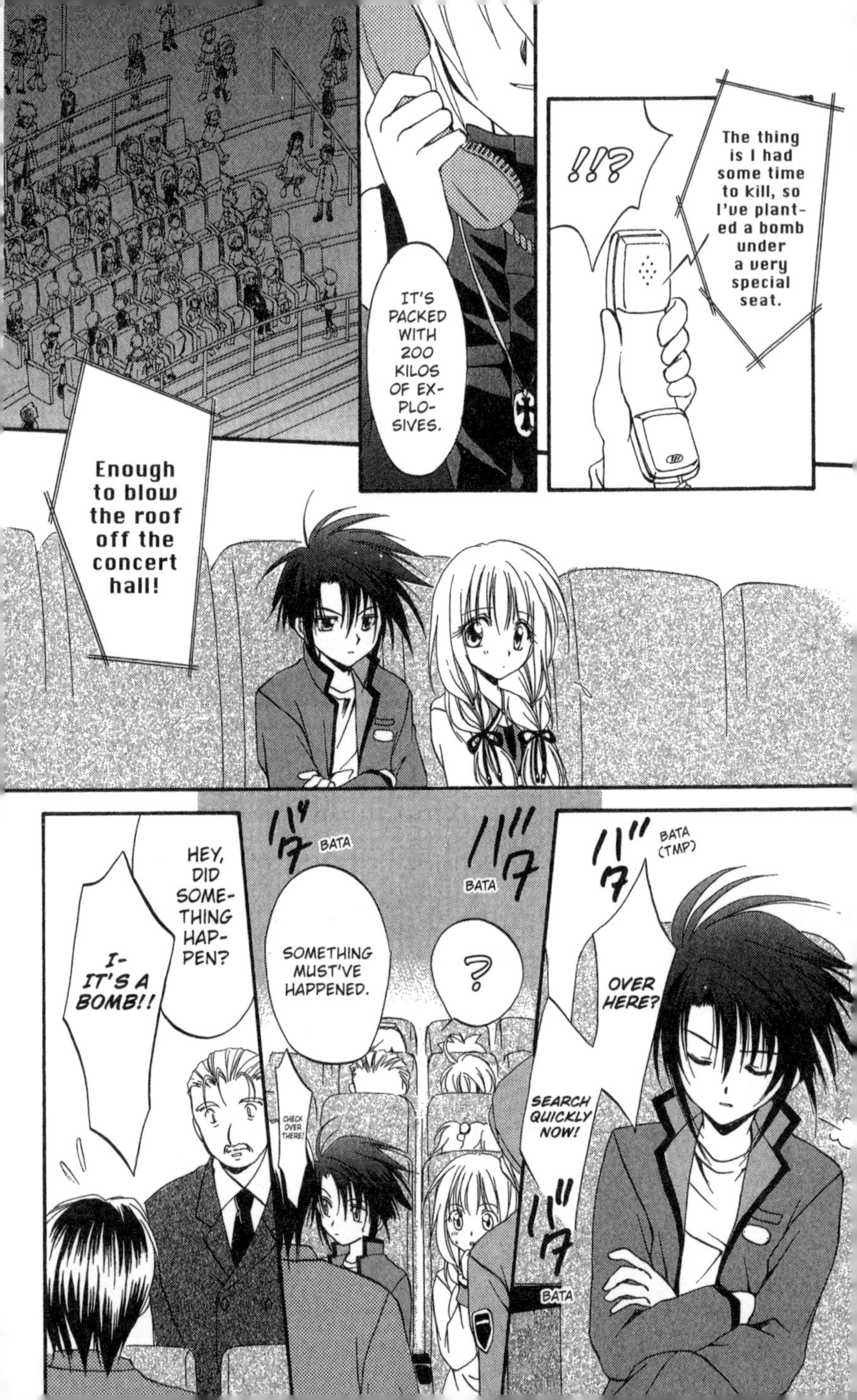
!!?
The thing is I had some time to kill, so I've planted a bomb under a very special seat.
IT'S PACKED WITH 200 KILOS OF EXPLOSIVES.
Enough to blow the roof off the concert hall!
バタ
BATA (TMP)
OVER HERE?
SEARCH QUICKLY NOW!
バタ
BATA
バタ
BATA
?
バタ
BATA
SOMETHING MUST'VE HAPPENED.
CHECK OVER THERE!
HEY, DID SOMETHING HAPPEN?
I- IT'S A BOMB!!

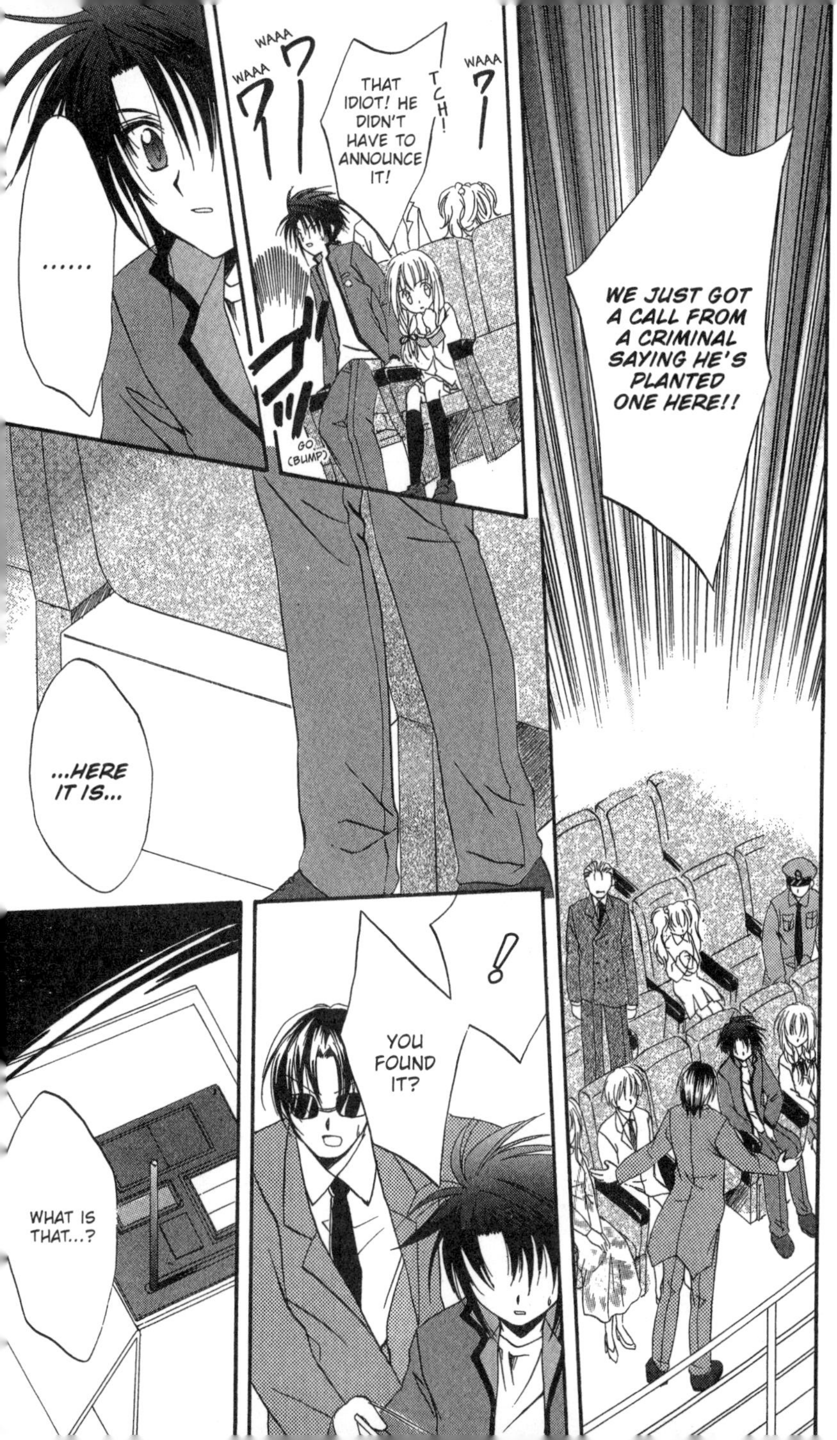
WE JUST GOT A CALL FROM A CRIMINAL SAYING HE'S PLANTED ONE HERE!!
WAAA
WAAA
WAAA
TCH!
THAT IDIOT! HE DIDN'T HAVE TO ANNOUNCE IT!
GO (BUMP)
......
...HERE IT IS...
!
YOU FOUND IT?
WHAT IS THAT...?

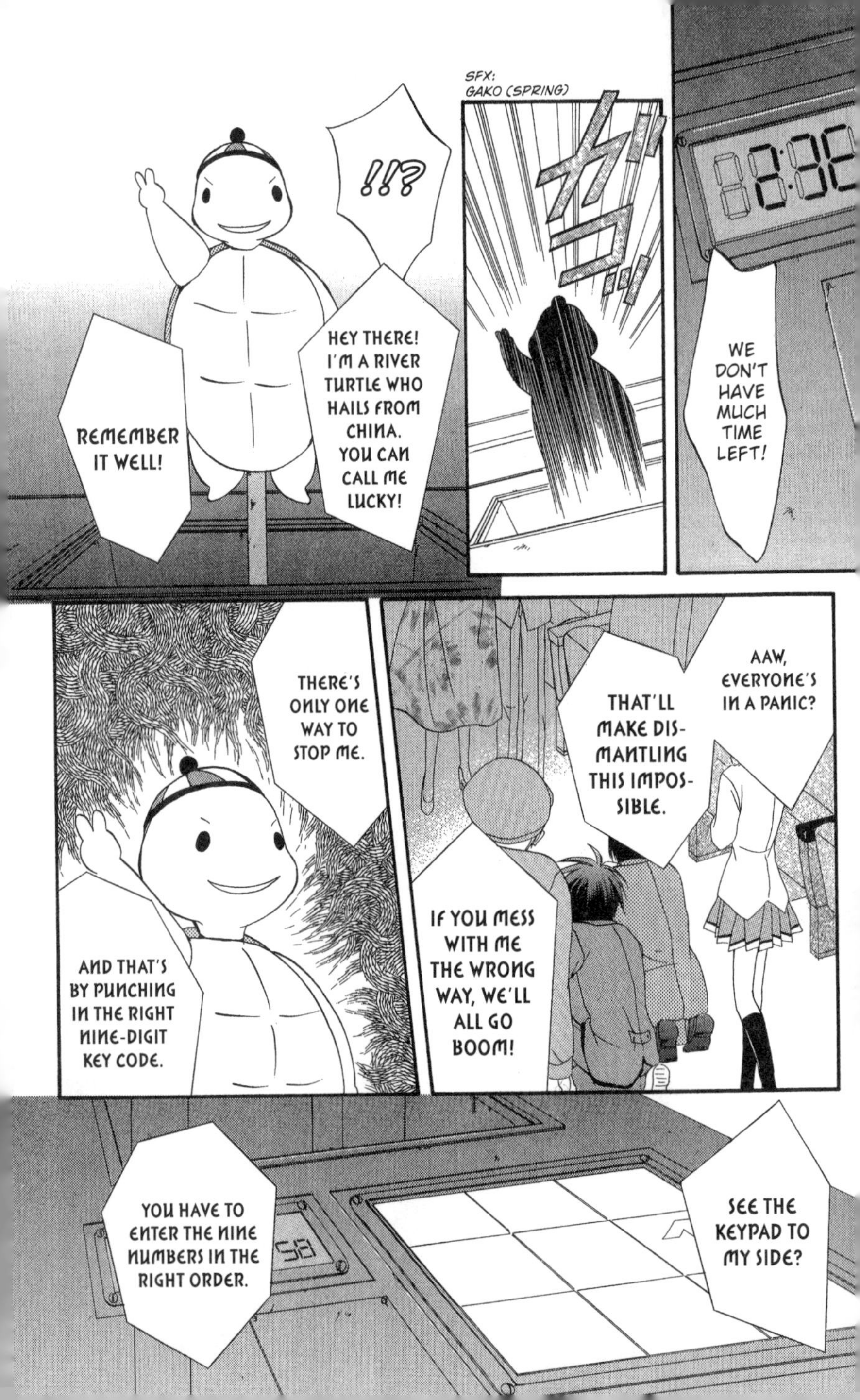
WE DON'T HAVE MUCH TIME LEFT!
SFX: GAKO (SPRING)
!!?
HEY THERE! I'M A RIVER TURTLE WHO HAILS FROM CHINA. YOU CAN CALL ME LUCKY!
REMEMBER IT WELL!
AAW, EVERYONE'S IN A PANIC?
THAT'LL MAKE DIS-MANTLING THIS IMPOS-SIBLE.
IF YOU MESS WITH ME THE WRONG WAY, WE'LL ALL GO BOOM!
THERE'S ONLY ONE WAY TO STOP ME.
AND THAT'S BY PUNCHING IN THE RIGHT NINE-DIGIT KEY CODE.
SEE THE KEYPAD TO MY SIDE?
YOU HAVE TO ENTER THE NINE NUMBERS IN THE RIGHT ORDER.

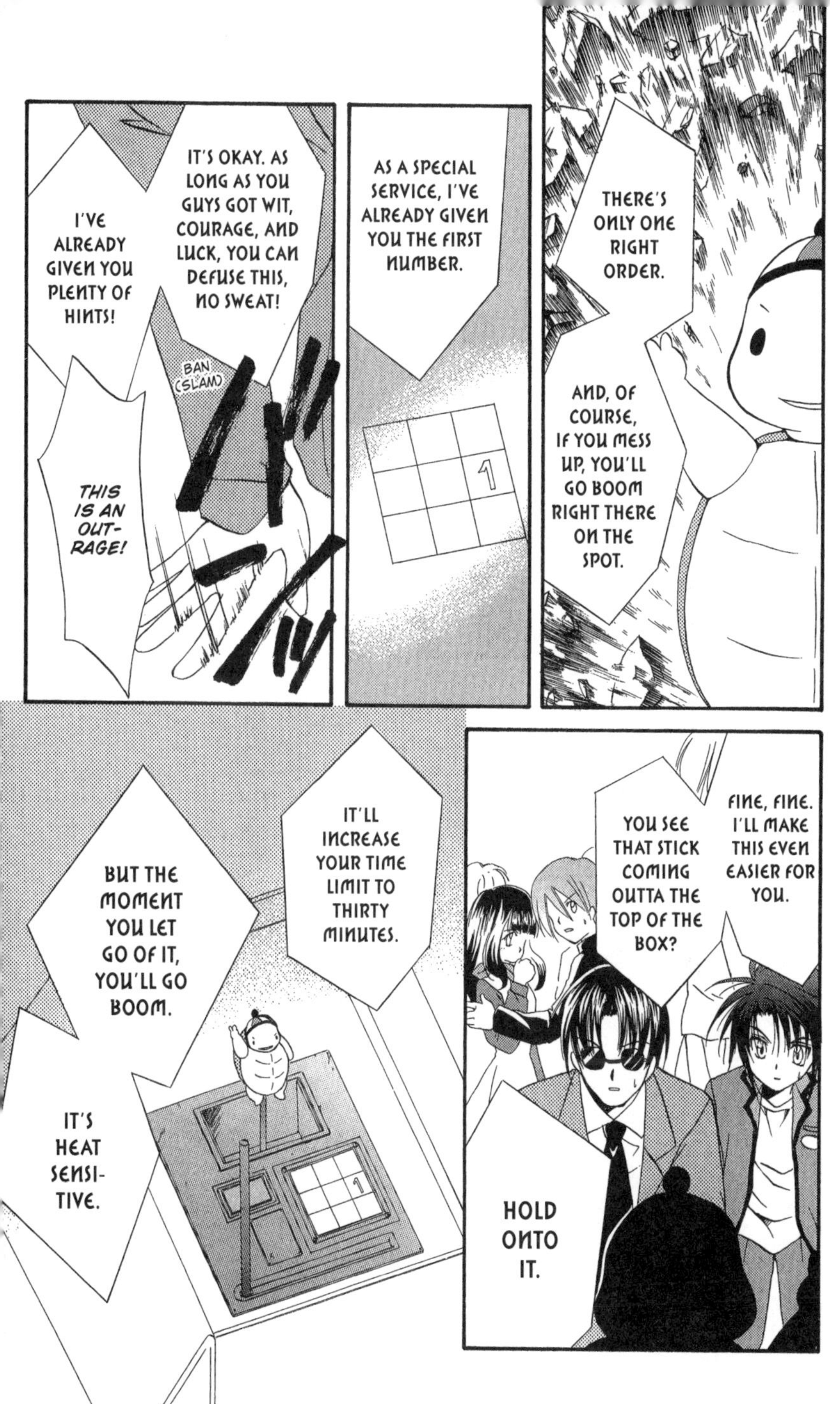
THERE'S ONLY ONE RIGHT ORDER.
AND, OF COURSE, IF YOU MESS UP, YOU'LL GO BOOM RIGHT THERE ON THE SPOT.
AS A SPECIAL SERVICE, I'VE ALREADY GIVEN YOU THE FIRST NUMBER.
IT'S OKAY. AS LONG AS YOU GUYS GOT WIT, COURAGE, AND LUCK, YOU CAN DEFUSE THIS, NO SWEAT!
I'VE ALREADY GIVEN YOU PLENTY OF HINTS!
BAN (SLAM)
THIS IS AN OUT-RAGE!
FINE, FINE. I'LL MAKE THIS EVEN EASIER FOR YOU.
YOU SEE THAT STICK COMING OUTTA THE TOP OF THE BOX?
HOLD ONTO IT.
IT'LL INCREASE YOUR TIME LIMIT TO THIRTY MINUTES.
BUT THE MOMENT YOU LET GO OF IT, YOU'LL GO BOOM.
IT'S HEAT SENSITIVE.

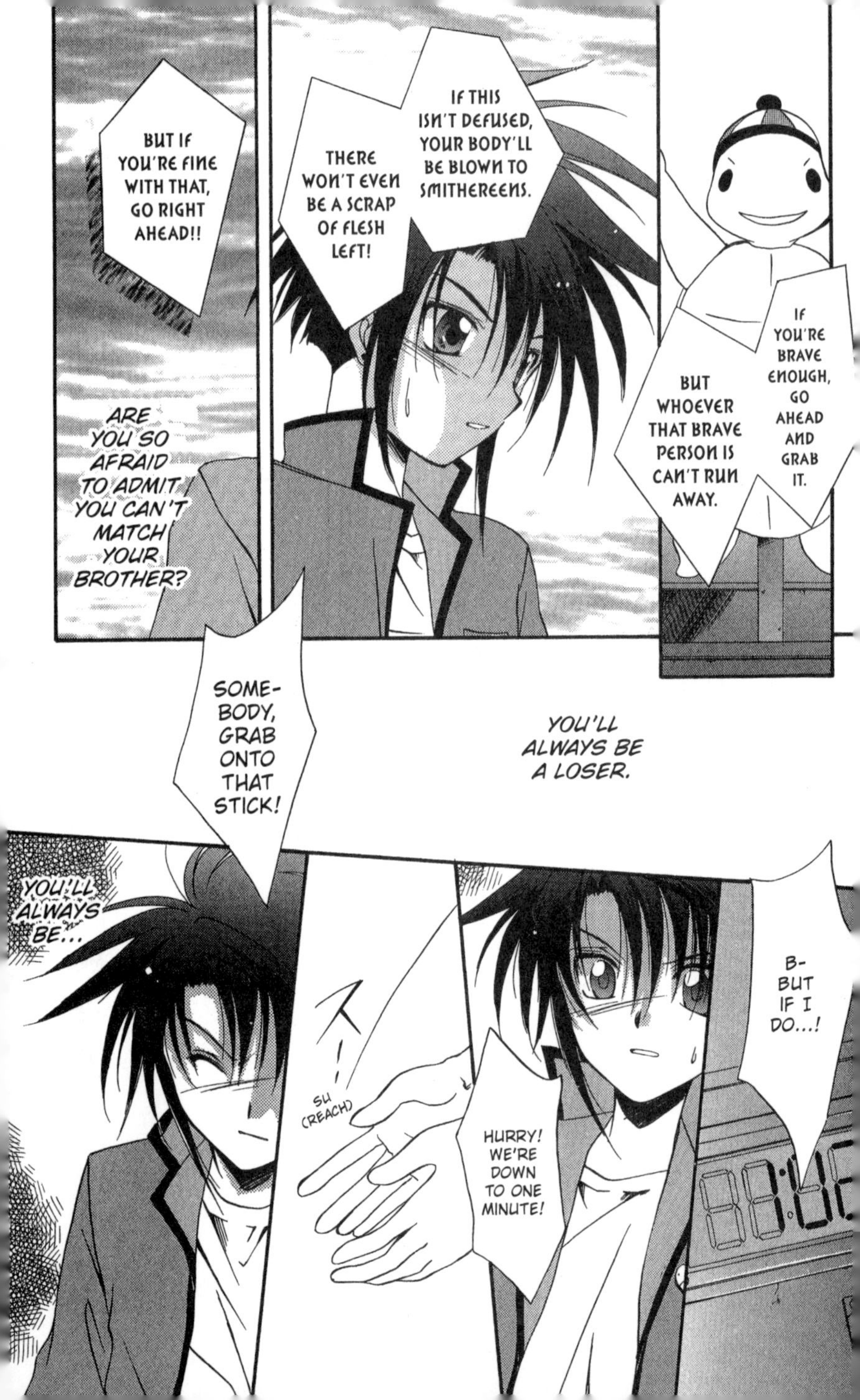
IF YOU'RE BRAVE ENOUGH, GO AHEAD AND GRAB IT.
BUT WHOEVER THAT BRAVE PERSON IS CAN'T RUN AWAY.
IF THIS ISN'T DEFUSED, YOUR BODY'LL BE BLOWN TO SMITHEREENS.
THERE WON'T EVEN BE A SCRAP OF FLESH LEFT!
BUT IF YOU'RE FINE WITH THAT, GO RIGHT AHEAD!!
ARE YOU SO AFRAID TO ADMIT YOU CAN'T MATCH YOUR BROTHER?
YOU'LL ALWAYS BE A LOSER.
SOME-BODY, GRAB ONTO THAT STICK!
B-BUT IF I DO...!
HURRY! WE'RE DOWN TO ONE MINUTE!
SU (REACH)
YOU'LL ALWAYS BE...

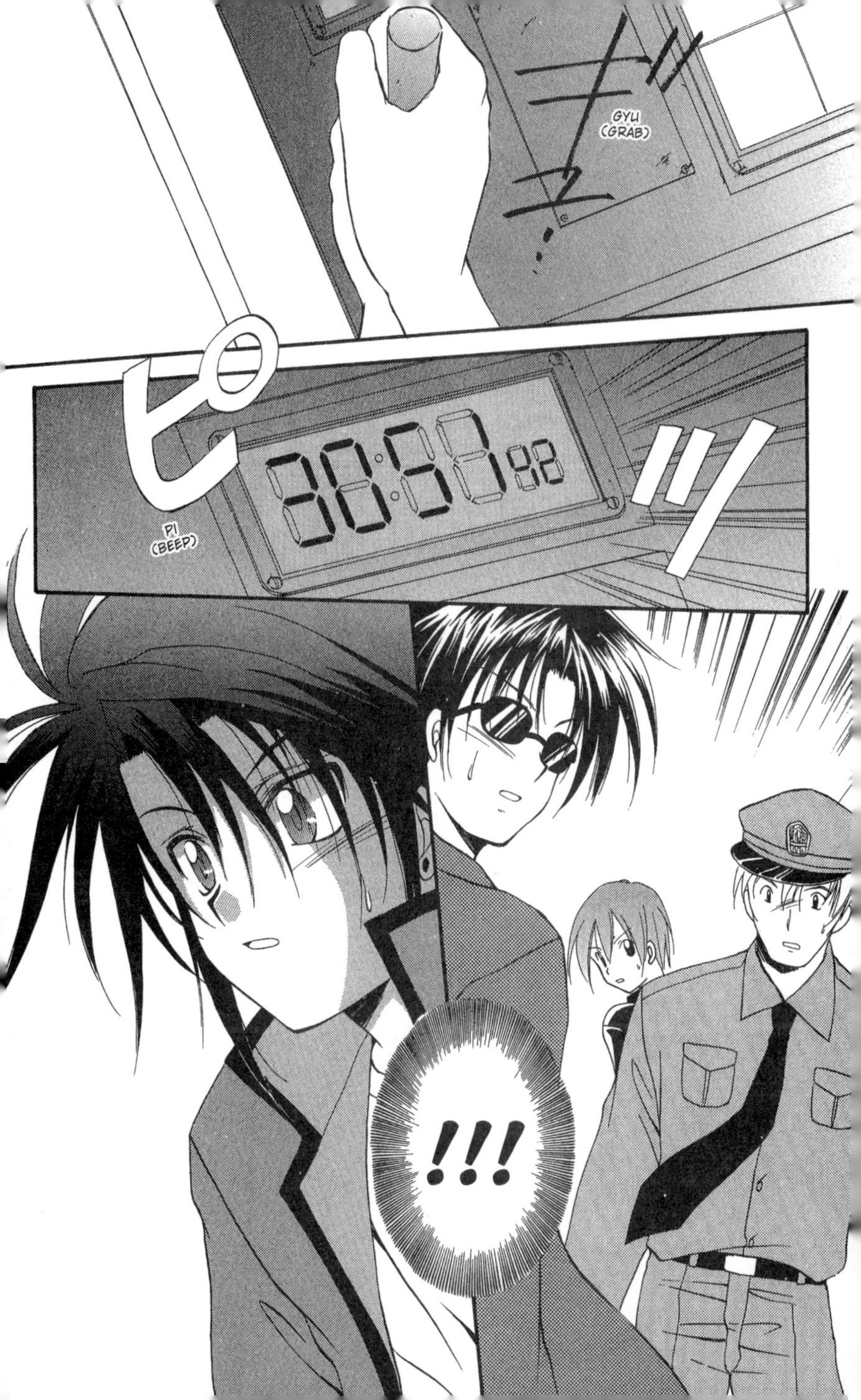
GYU
(GRAB)
PI
(BEEP)
!!!

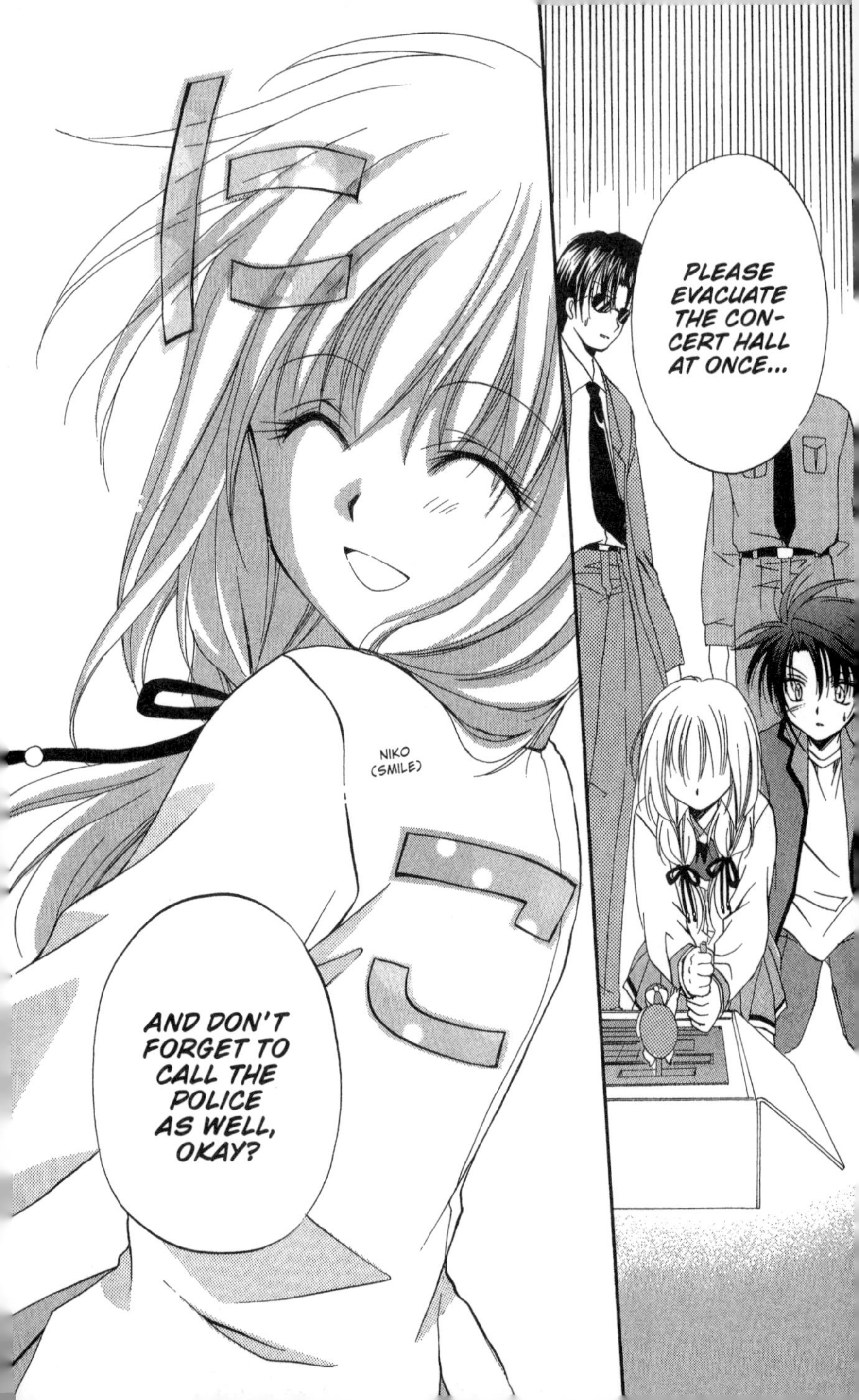
PLEASE EVACUATE THE CON- CERT HALL AT ONCE...
NIKO (SMILE)
AND DON'T FORGET TO CALL THE POLICE AS WELL, OKAY?

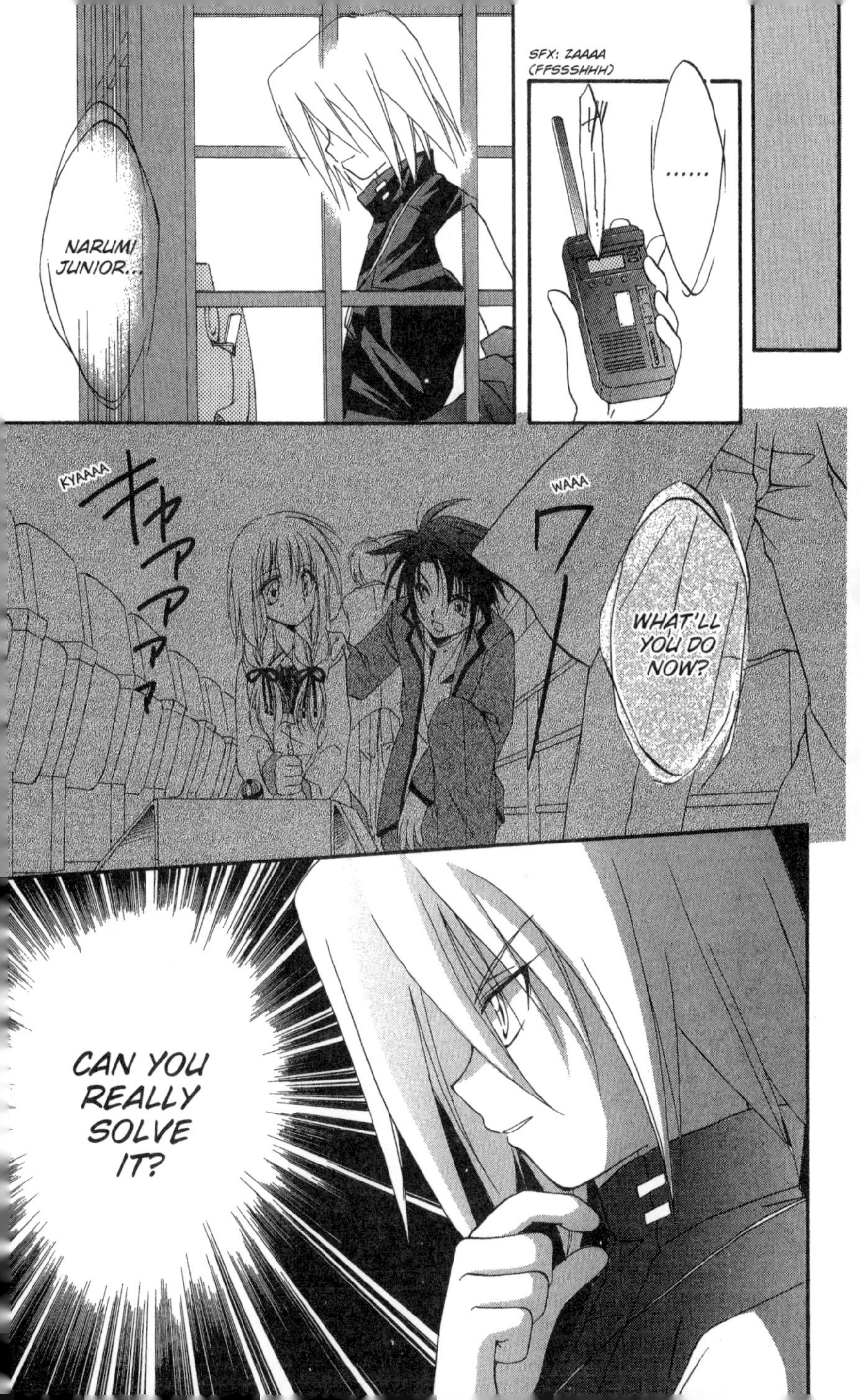
SFX: ZAAAA (FFSSSHHH)
......
NARUMI JUNIOR...
WHAT'LL YOU DO NOW?
WAAA
ワー
KYAAAA
キャアアア
CAN YOU REALLY SOLVE IT?

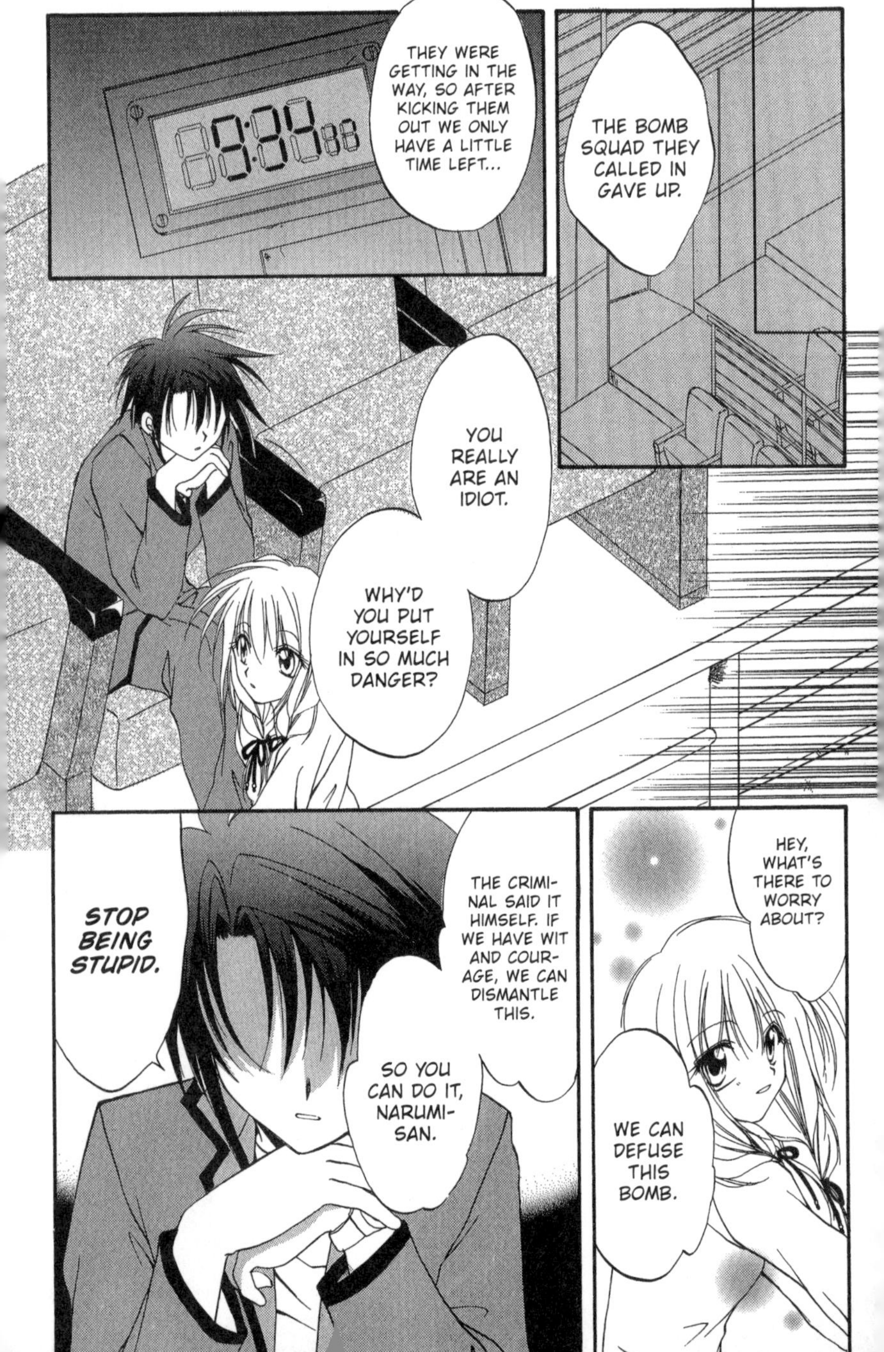
THE BOMB SQUAD THEY CALLED IN GAVE UP.
THEY WERE GETTING IN THE WAY, SO AFTER KICKING THEM OUT WE ONLY HAVE A LITTLE TIME LEFT...
YOU REALLY ARE AN IDIOT.
WHY'D YOU PUT YOURSELF IN SO MUCH DANGER?
HEY, WHAT'S THERE TO WORRY ABOUT?
WE CAN DEFUSE THIS BOMB.
THE CRIMINAL SAID IT HIMSELF. IF WE HAVE WIT AND COURAGE, WE CAN DISMANTLE THIS.
SO YOU CAN DO IT, NARUMI-SAN.
STOP BEING STUPID.

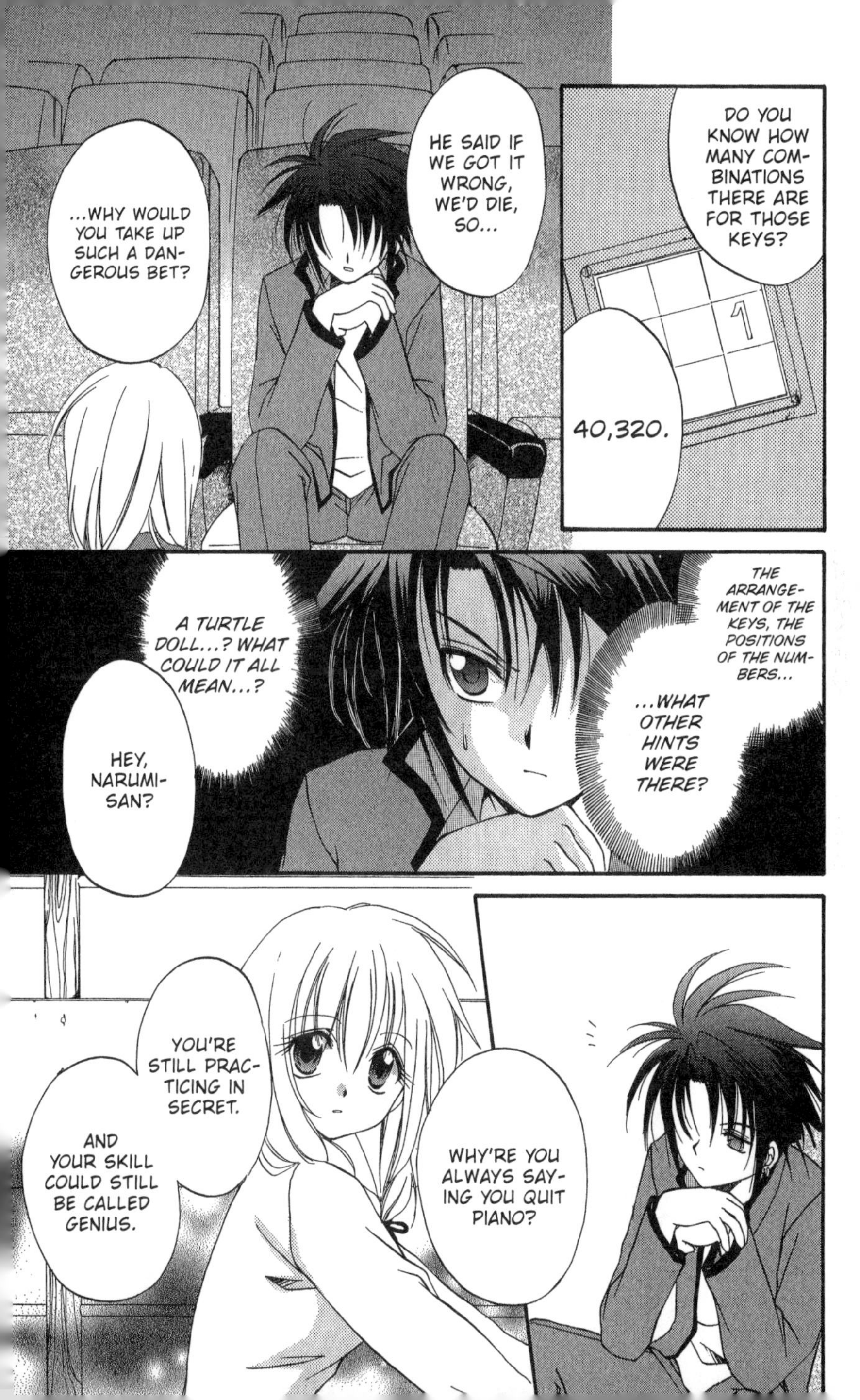
DO YOU KNOW HOW MANY COMBINATIONS THERE ARE FOR THOSE KEYS?
40,320.
HE SAID IF WE GOT IT WRONG, WE'D DIE, SO...
...WHY WOULD YOU TAKE UP SUCH A DANGEROUS BET?
THE ARRANGEMENT OF THE KEYS, THE POSITIONS OF THE NUMBERS...
...WHAT OTHER HINTS WERE THERE?
A TURTLE DOLL...? WHAT COULD IT ALL MEAN...?
HEY, NARUMI-SAN?
YOU'RE STILL PRACTICING IN SECRET.
AND YOUR SKILL COULD STILL BE CALLED GENIUS.
WHY'RE YOU ALWAYS SAYING YOU QUIT PIANO?

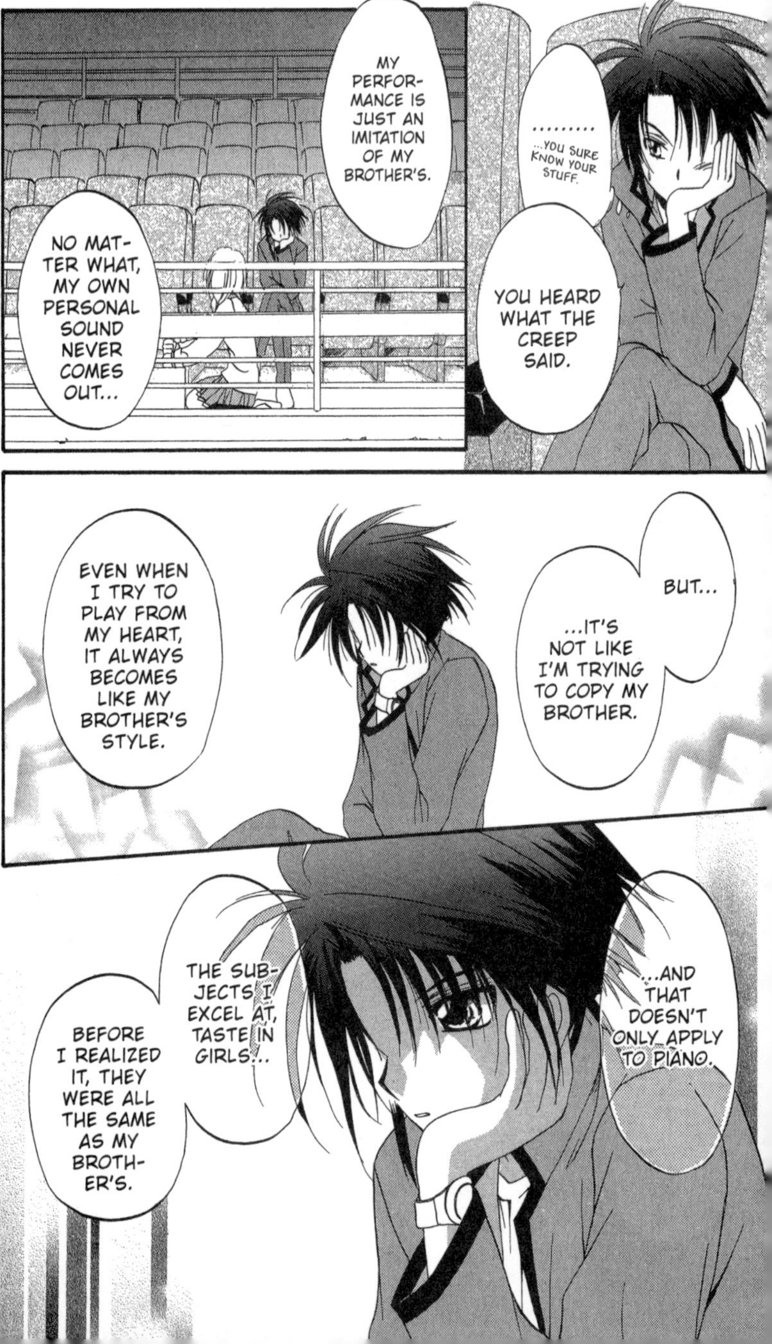
....
...YOU SURE KNOW YOUR STUFF.
YOU HEARD WHAT THE CREEP SAID.
MY PERFORMANCE IS JUST AN IMITATION OF MY BROTHER'S.
NO MATTER WHAT, MY OWN PERSONAL SOUND NEVER COMES OUT...
BUT...
...IT'S NOT LIKE I'M TRYING TO COPY MY BROTHER.
EVEN WHEN I TRY TO PLAY FROM MY HEART, IT ALWAYS BECOMES LIKE MY BROTHER'S STYLE.
...AND THAT DOESN'T ONLY APPLY TO PIANO.
THE SUBJECTS I EXCEL AT, TASTE IN GIRLS...
BEFORE I REALIZED IT, THEY WERE ALL THE SAME AS MY BROTHER'S.

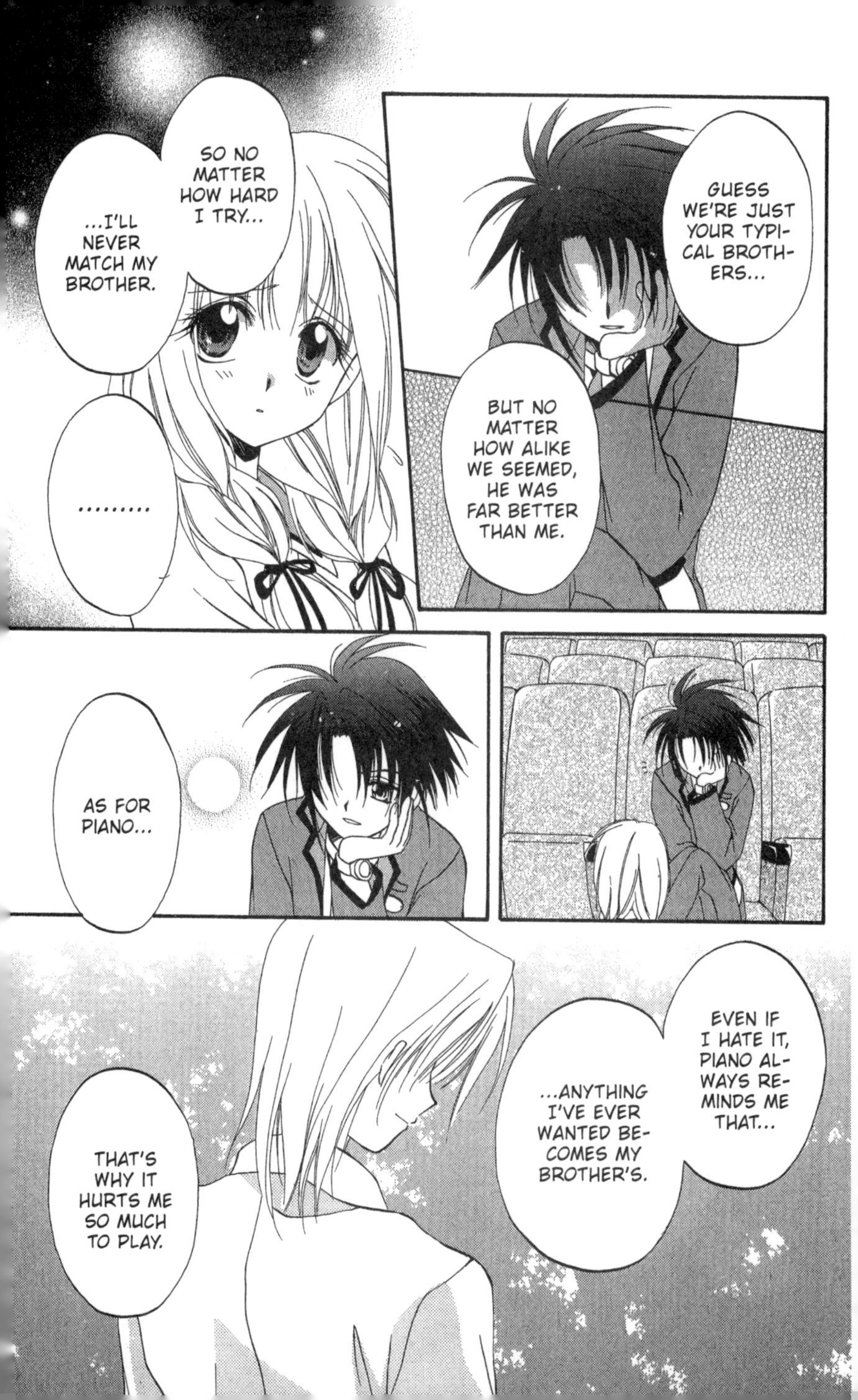

GUESS WE'RE JUST YOUR TYPICAL BROTHERS...
BUT NO MATTER HOW ALIKE WE SEEMED, HE WAS FAR BETTER THAN ME.
SO NO MATTER HOW HARD I TRY...
...I'LL NEVER MATCH MY BROTHER.
....
AS FOR PIANO...
EVEN IF I HATE IT, PIANO ALWAYS REMINDS ME THAT...
...ANYTHING I'VE EVER WANTED BECOMES MY BROTHER'S.
THAT'S WHY IT HURTS ME SO MUCH TO PLAY.

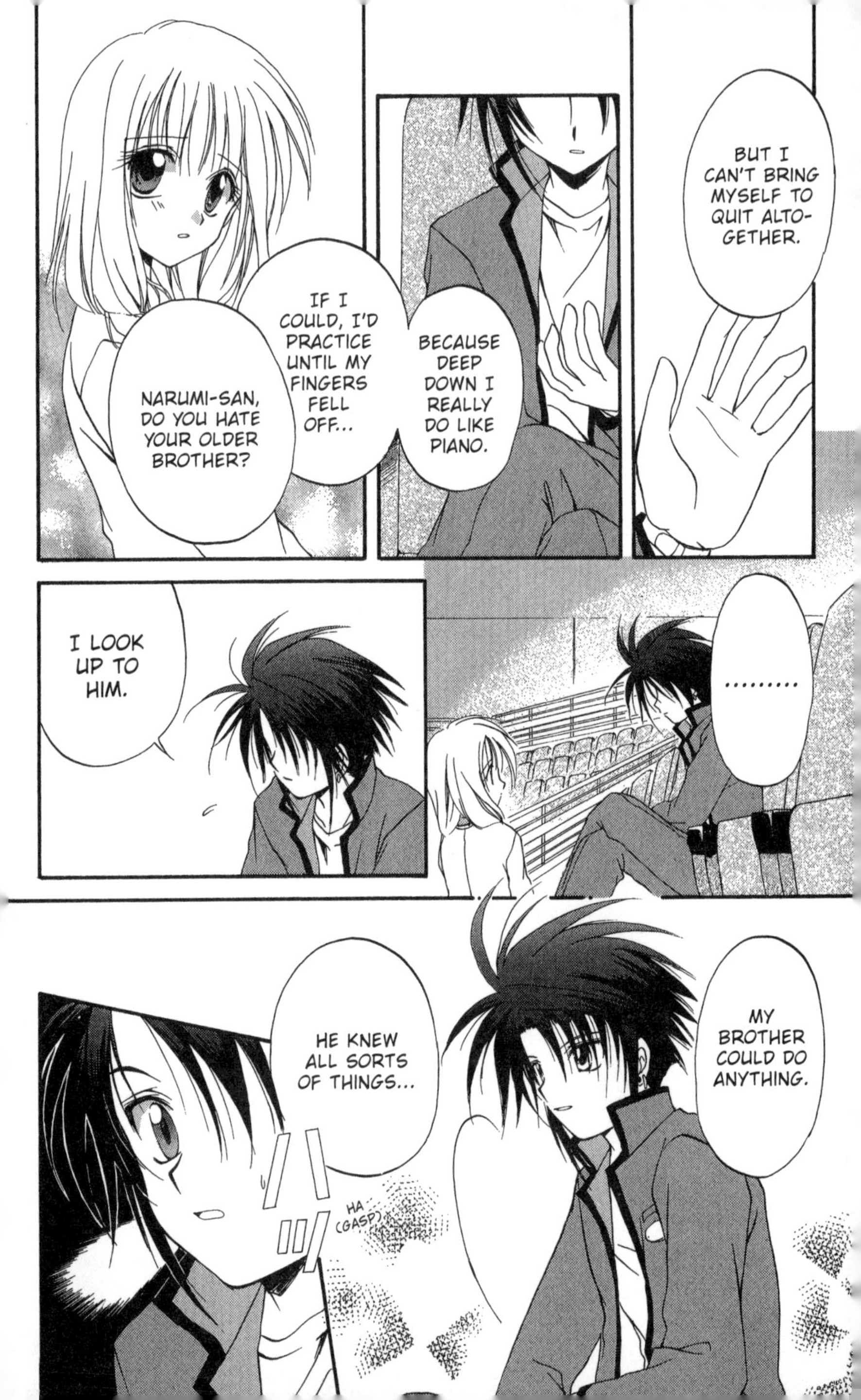
BUT I CAN'T BRING MYSELF TO QUIT ALTO-GETHER.
BECAUSE DEEP DOWN I REALLY DO LIKE PIANO.
IF I COULD, I'D PRACTICE UNTIL MY FINGERS FELL OFF...
NARUMI-SAN, DO YOU HATE YOUR OLDER BROTHER?
....
I LOOK UP TO HIM.
MY BROTHER COULD DO ANYTHING.
HE KNEW ALL SORTS OF THINGS...
HA (GASP)

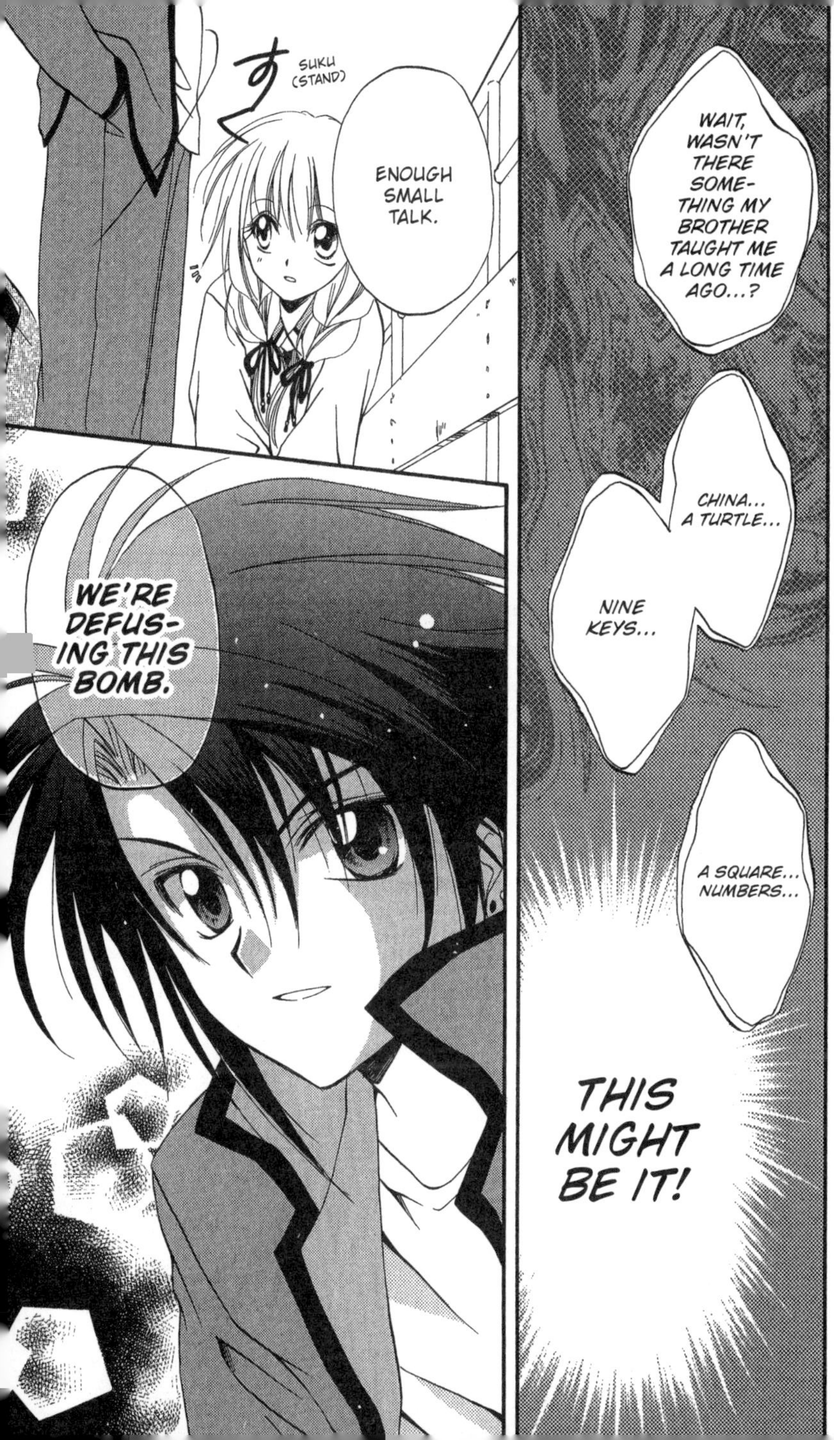
WAIT, WASN'T THERE SOMETHING MY BROTHER TAUGHT ME A LONG TIME AGO...?
CHINA... A TURTLE...
NINE KEYS...
A SQUARE... NUMBERS...
THIS MIGHT BE IT!
ENOUGH SMALL TALK.
す
SUKU (STAND)
WE'RE DEFUSING THIS BOMB.

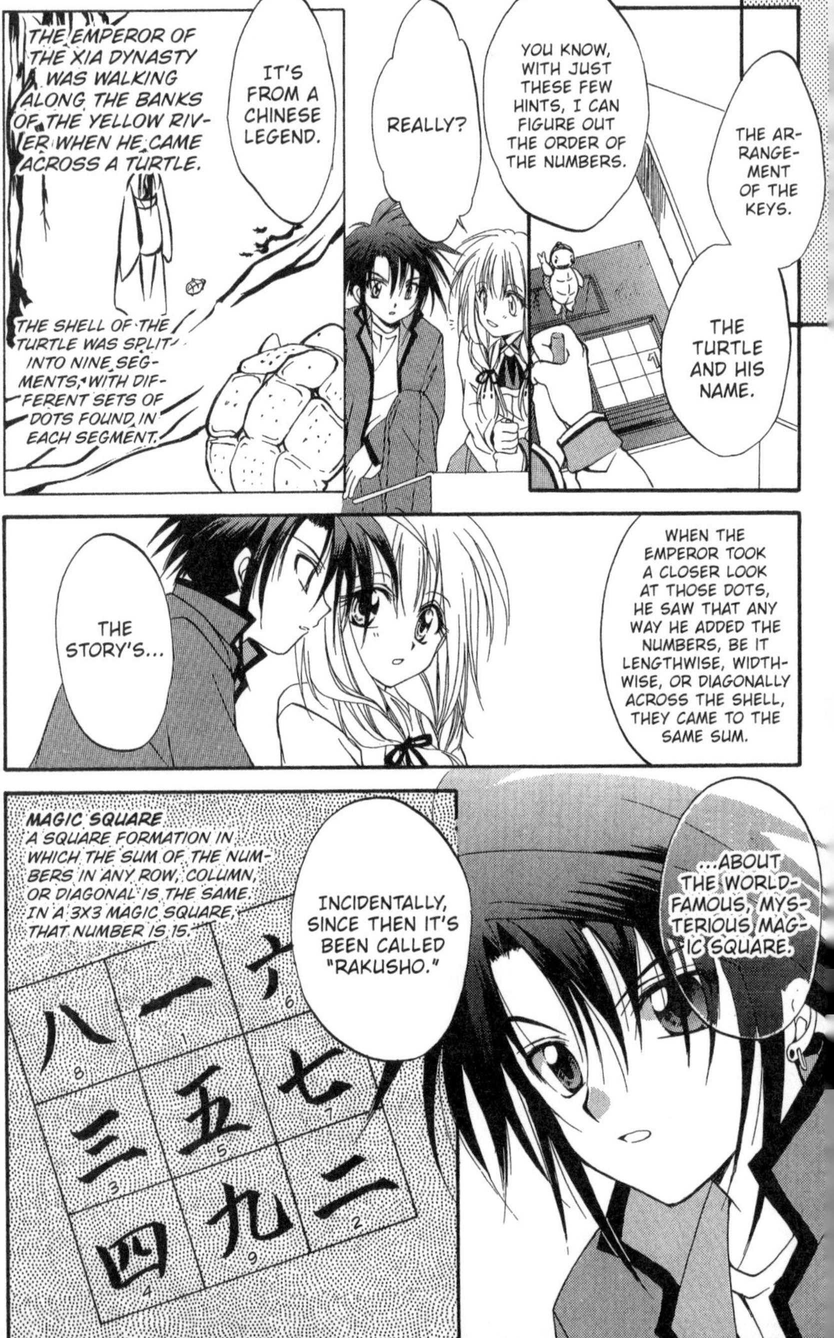

YOU KNOW, WITH JUST THESE FEW HINTS, I CAN FIGURE OUT THE ORDER OF THE NUMBERS.
THE ARRANGEMENT OF THE KEYS.
THE TURTLE AND HIS NAME.
REALLY?
IT'S FROM A CHINESE LEGEND.
THE EMPEROR OF THE XIA DYNASTY WAS WALKING ALONG THE BANKS OF THE YELLOW RIVER WHEN HE CAME ACROSS A TURTLE.
THE SHELL OF THE TURTLE WAS SPLIT INTO NINE SEGMENTS, WITH DIFFERENT SETS OF DOTS FOUND IN EACH SEGMENT.
WHEN THE EMPEROR TOOK A CLOSER LOOK AT THOSE DOTS, HE SAW THAT ANY WAY HE ADDED THE NUMBERS, BE IT LENGTHWISE, WIDTHWISE, OR DIAGONALLY ACROSS THE SHELL, THEY CAME TO THE SAME SUM.
THE STORY'S...
...ABOUT THE WORLD-FAMOUS, MYSTERIOUS MAGIC SQUARE.
INCIDENTALLY, SINCE THEN IT'S BEEN CALLED "RAKUSHO."
MAGIC SQUARE
A SQUARE FORMATION IN WHICH THE SUM OF THE NUMBERS IN ANY ROW, COLUMN, OR DIAGONAL IS THE SAME. IN A 3X3 MAGIC SQUARE, THAT NUMBER IS 15.
六 6
一 1
八 8
七 7
五 5
三 3
二 2
九 9
四 4

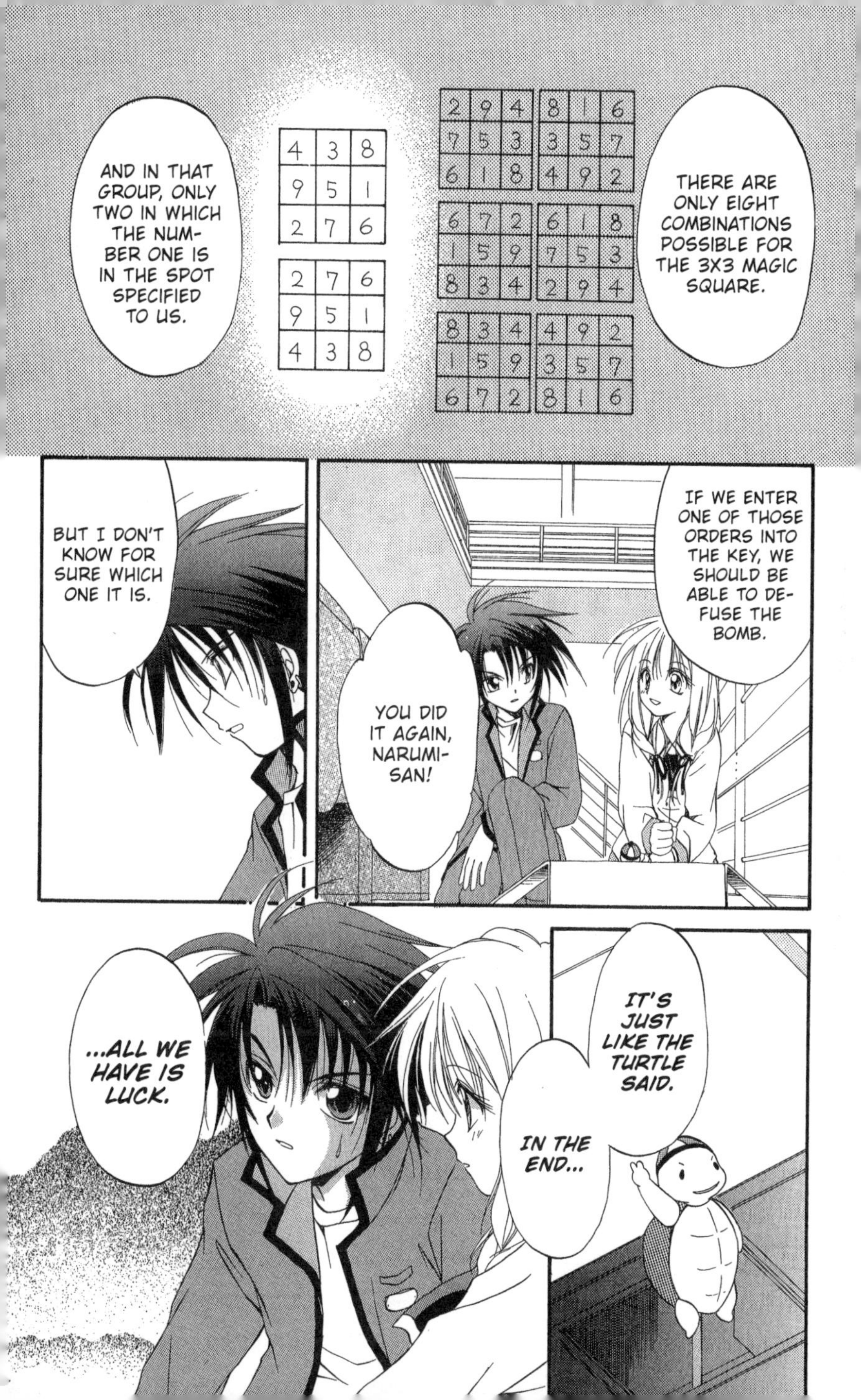
THERE ARE ONLY EIGHT COMBINATIONS POSSIBLE FOR THE 3X3 MAGIC SQUARE.
8 1 6 / 3 5 7 / 4 9 2
2 9 4 / 7 5 3 / 6 1 8
6 1 8 / 7 5 3 / 2 9 4
6 7 2 / 1 5 9 / 8 3 4
4 9 2 / 3 5 7 / 8 1 6
8 3 4 / 1 5 9 / 6 7 2
4 3 8 / 9 5 1 / 2 7 6
2 7 6 / 9 5 1 / 4 3 8
AND IN THAT GROUP, ONLY TWO IN WHICH THE NUMBER ONE IS IN THE SPOT SPECIFIED TO US.
IF WE ENTER ONE OF THOSE ORDERS INTO THE KEY, WE SHOULD BE ABLE TO DEFUSE THE BOMB.
YOU DID IT AGAIN, NARUMI-SAN!
BUT I DON'T KNOW FOR SURE WHICH ONE IT IS.
IT'S JUST LIKE THE TURTLE SAID.
IN THE END...
...ALL WE HAVE IS LUCK.

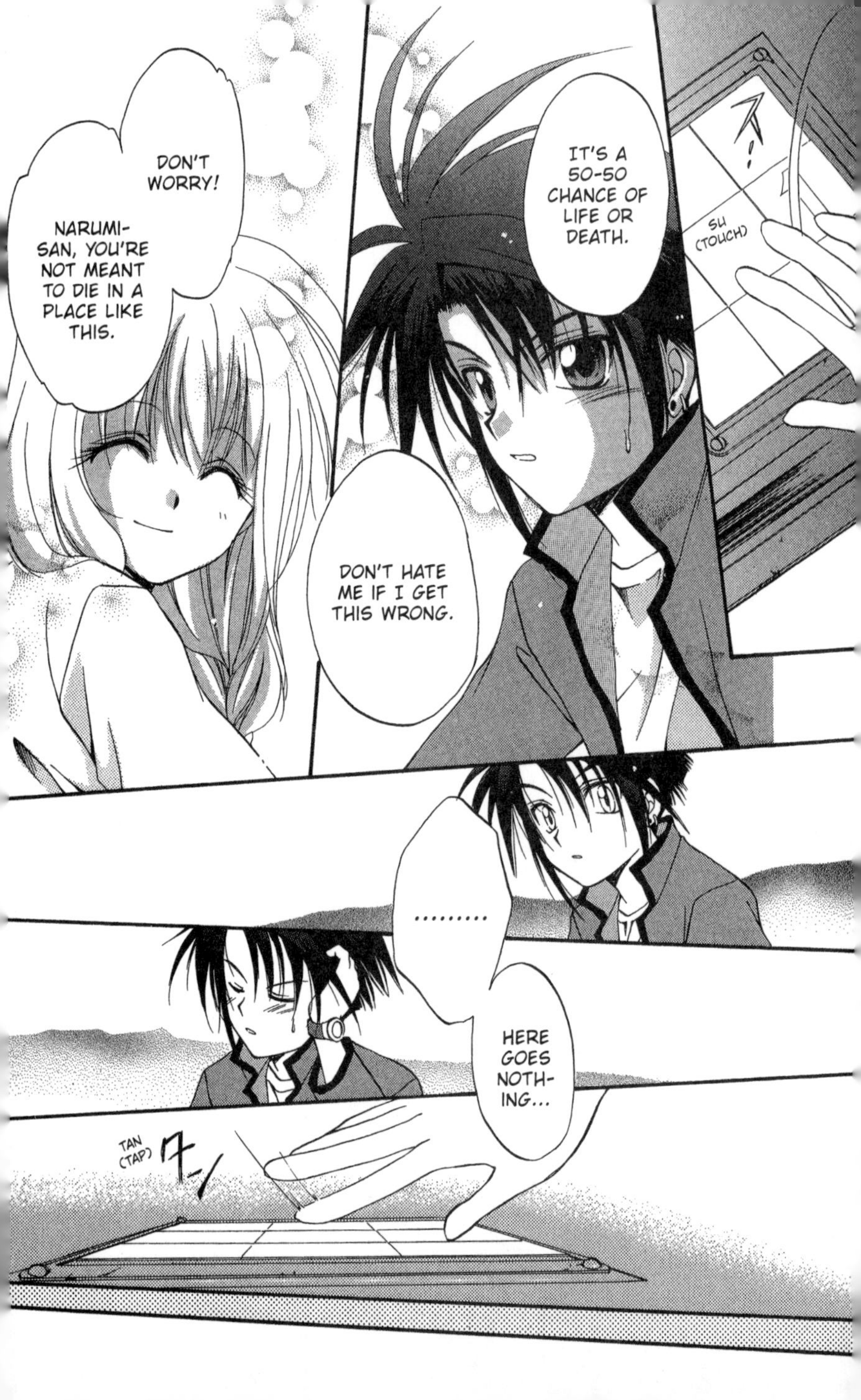
SU (TOUCH)
IT'S A 50-50 CHANCE OF LIFE OR DEATH.
DON'T HATE ME IF I GET THIS WRONG.
DON'T WORRY!
NARUMI-SAN, YOU'RE NOT MEANT TO DIE IN A PLACE LIKE THIS.
....
HERE GOES NOTH-ING...
TAN (TAP)

SFX: SHIIN (SILENCE)

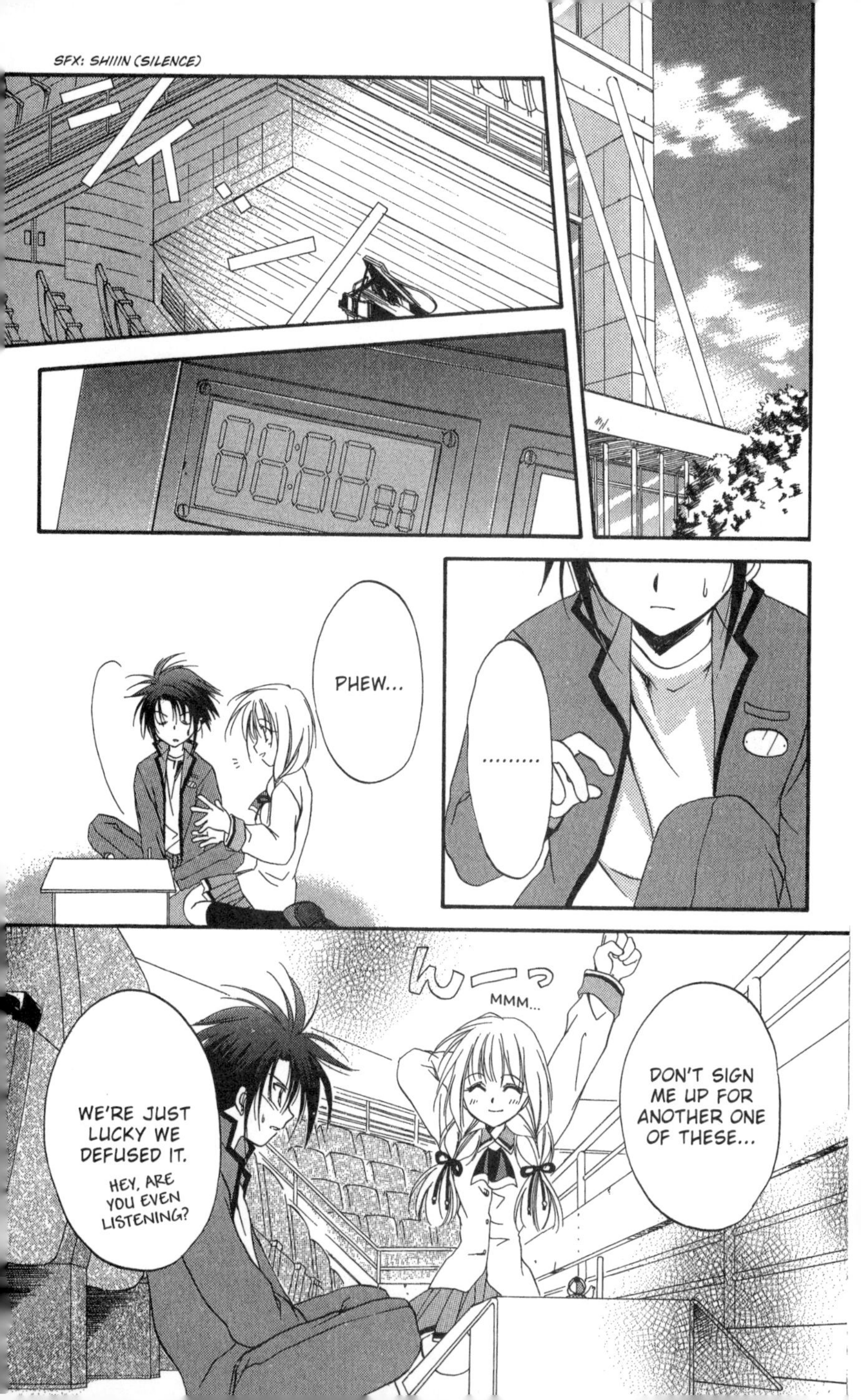
....
PHEW...
DON'T SIGN ME UP FOR ANOTHER ONE OF THESE...
んーっ
MMM...
WE'RE JUST LUCKY WE DEFUSED IT.
HEY, ARE YOU EVEN LISTENING?

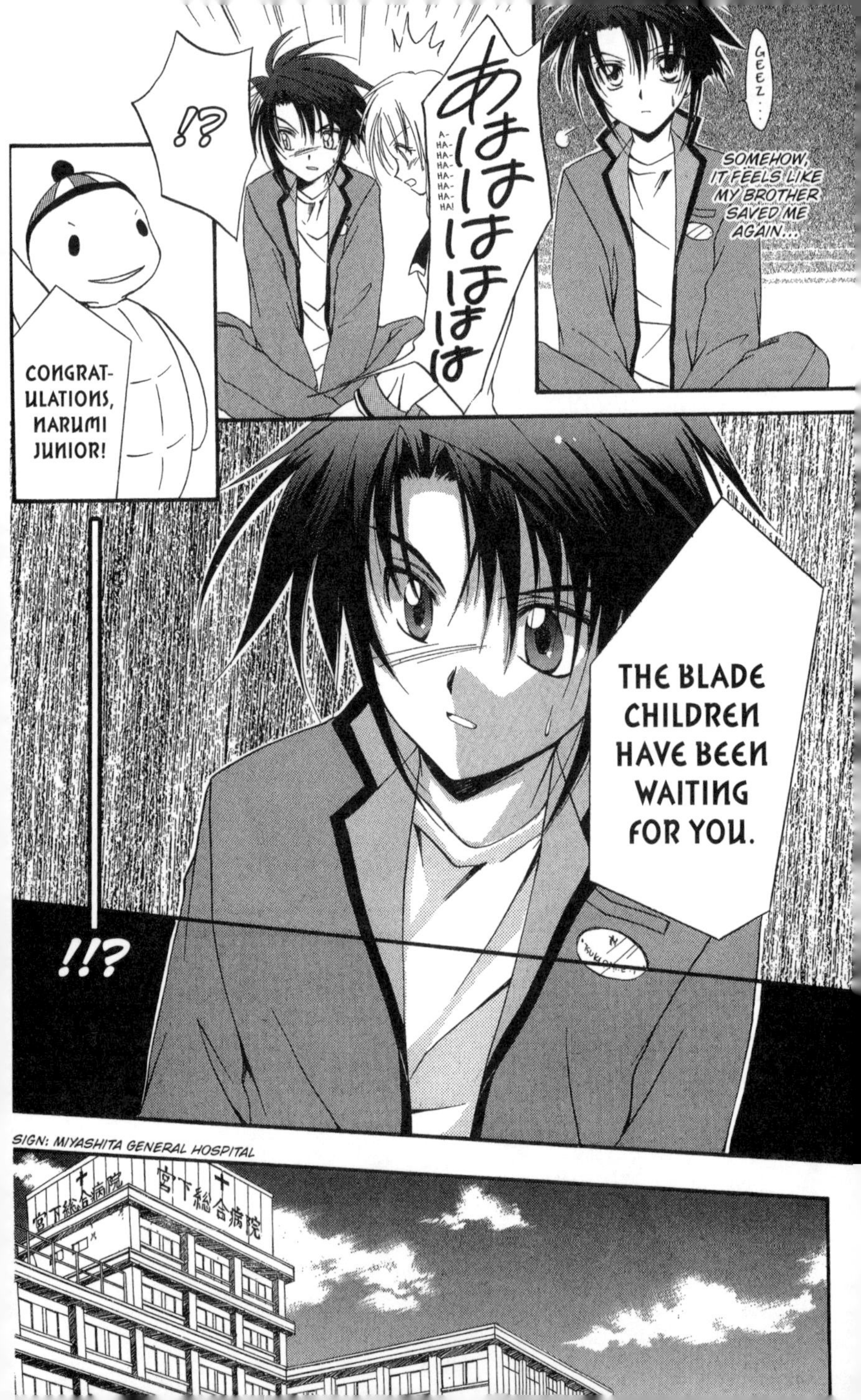
GEEZ...
SOMEHOW, IT FEELS LIKE MY BROTHER SAVED ME AGAIN...
あはははははは
A-HA-HA-HA-HA-HA-HA!
!?
CONGRAT-ULATIONS, NARUMI JUNIOR!
THE BLADE CHILDREN HAVE BEEN WAITING FOR YOU.
!!?
SIGN: MIYASHITA GENERAL HOSPITAL
宮下総合病院
宮下総合病院

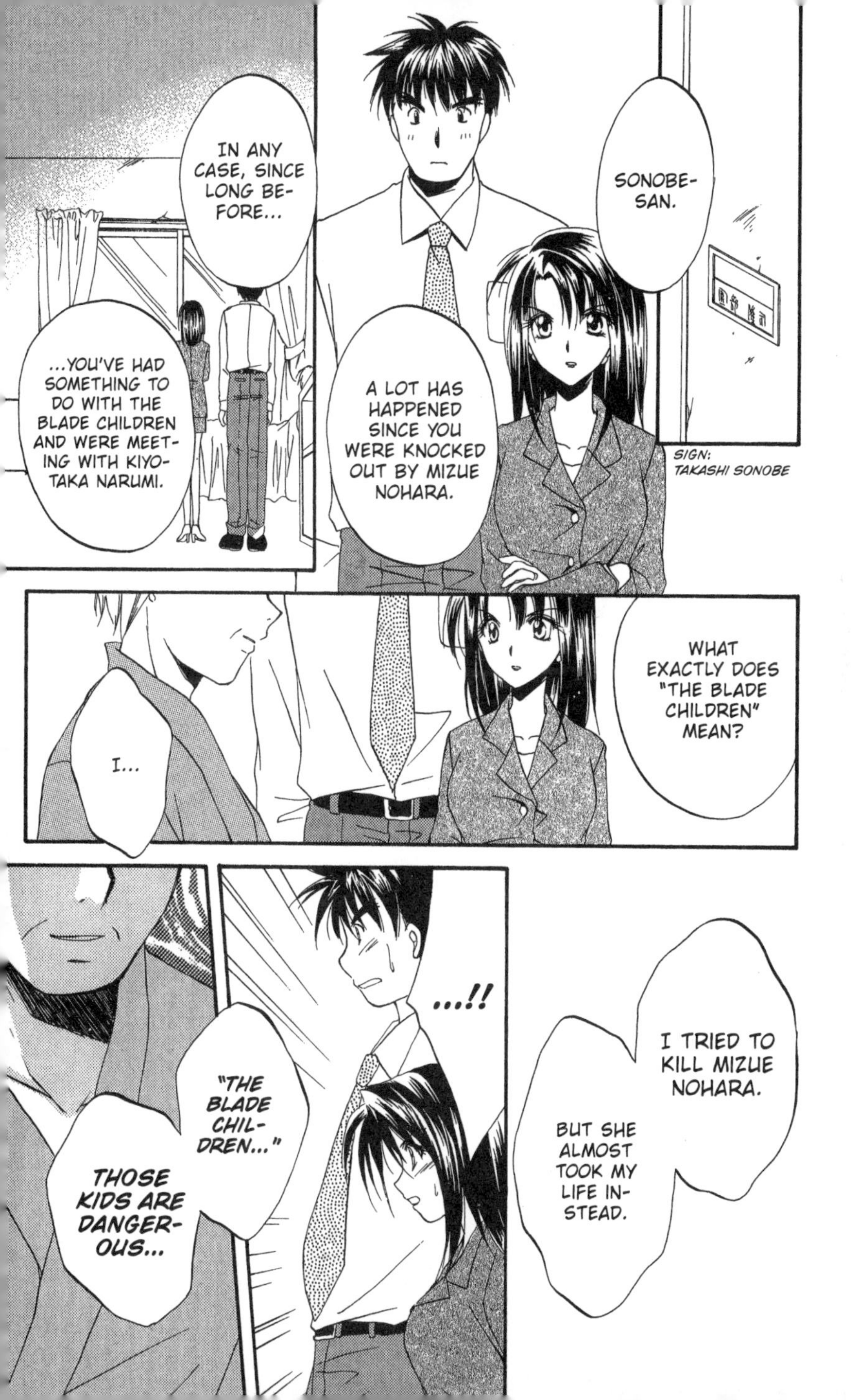
SONOBE-SAN.
SIGN: TAKASHI SONOBE
A LOT HAS HAPPENED SINCE YOU WERE KNOCKED OUT BY MIZUE NOHARA.
IN ANY CASE, SINCE LONG BEFORE...
...YOU'VE HAD SOMETHING TO DO WITH THE BLADE CHILDREN AND WERE MEETING WITH KIYOTAKA NARUMI.
WHAT EXACTLY DOES "THE BLADE CHILDREN" MEAN?
I...
I TRIED TO KILL MIZUE NOHARA.
BUT SHE ALMOST TOOK MY LIFE INSTEAD.
...!!
"THE BLADE CHILDREN..."
THOSE KIDS ARE DANGEROUS...

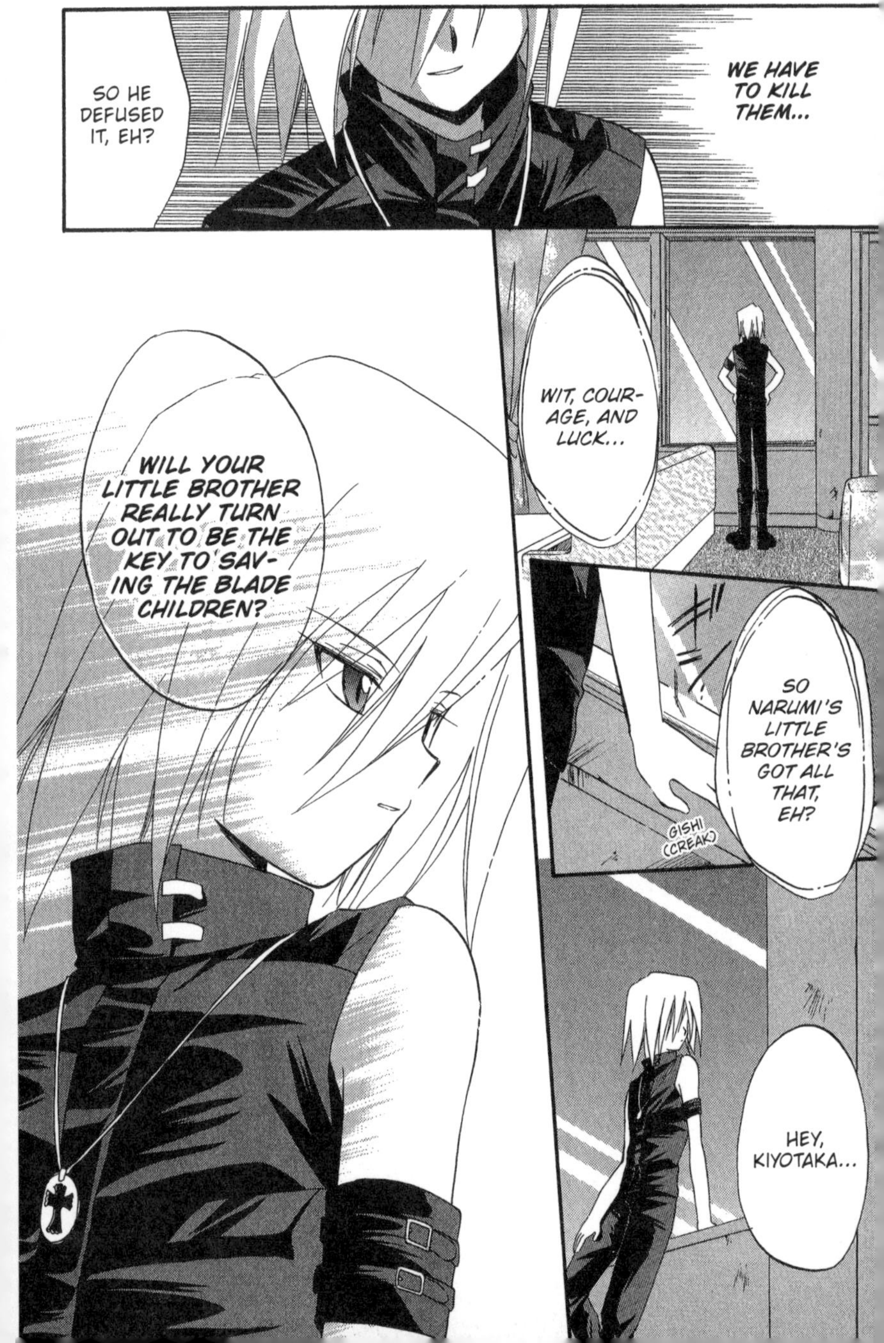
WE HAVE TO KILL THEM...
SO HE DEFUSED IT, EH?
WIT, COURAGE, AND LUCK...
SO NARUMI'S LITTLE BROTHER'S GOT ALL THAT, EH?
GISHI (CREAK)
HEY, KIYOTAKA...
WILL YOUR LITTLE BROTHER REALLY TURN OUT TO BE THE KEY TO SAVING THE BLADE CHILDREN?

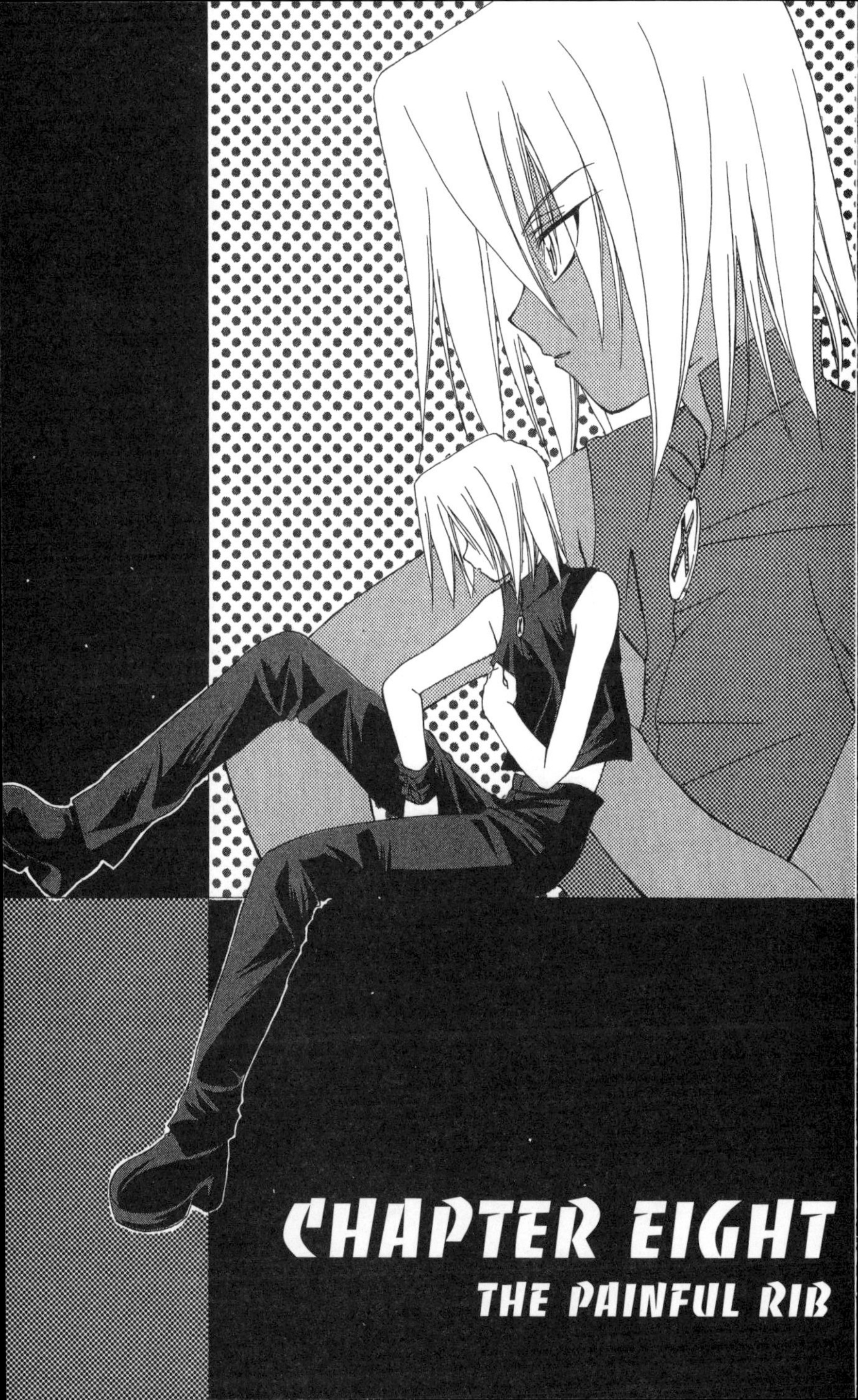
CHAPTER EIGHT
THE PAINFUL RIB

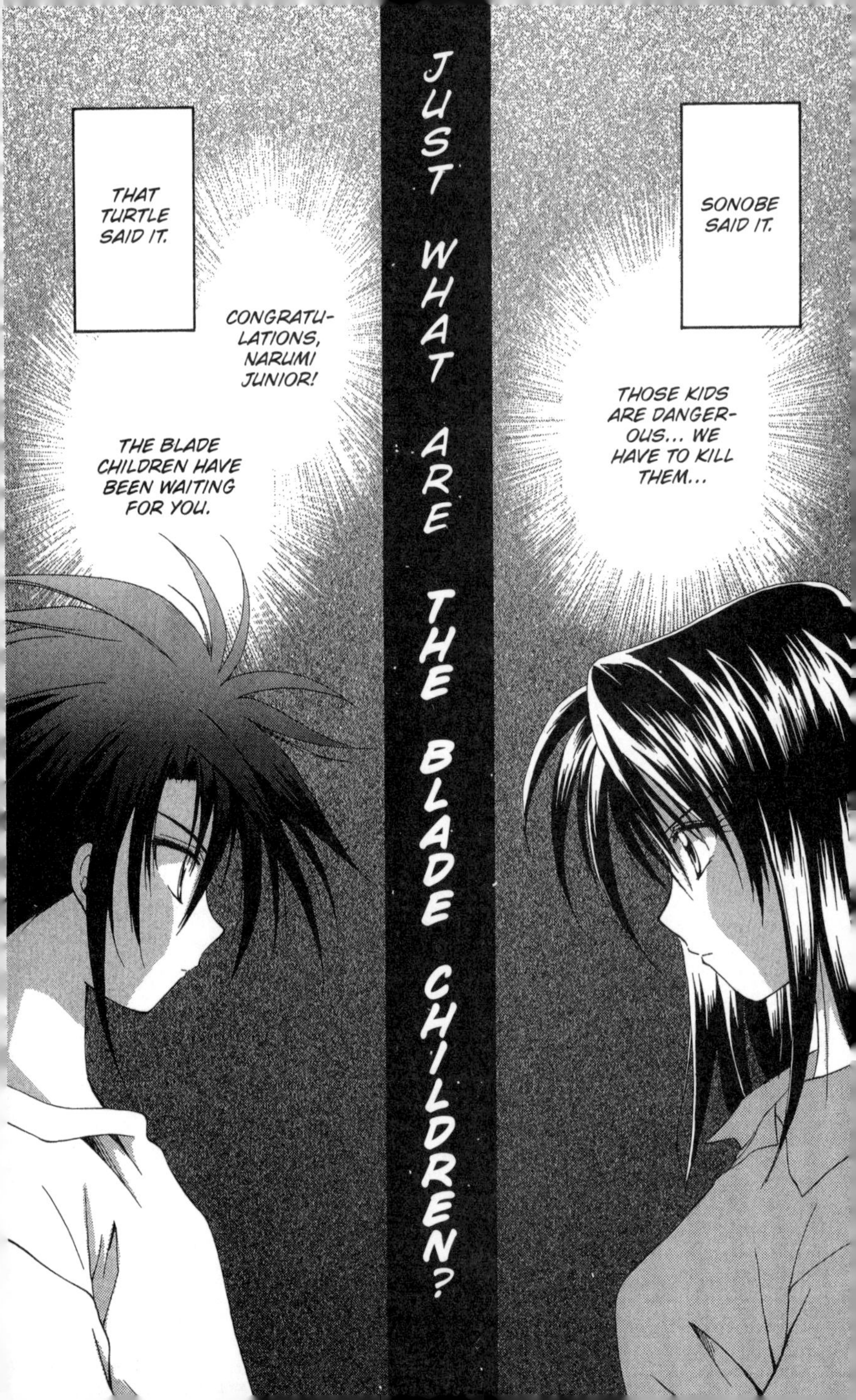
SONOBE SAID IT.
THOSE KIDS ARE DANGER-OUS... WE HAVE TO KILL THEM...
THAT TURTLE SAID IT.
CONGRATU-LATIONS, NARUMI JUNIOR!
THE BLADE CHILDREN HAVE BEEN WAITING FOR YOU.
JUST WHAT ARE THE BLADE CHILDREN?

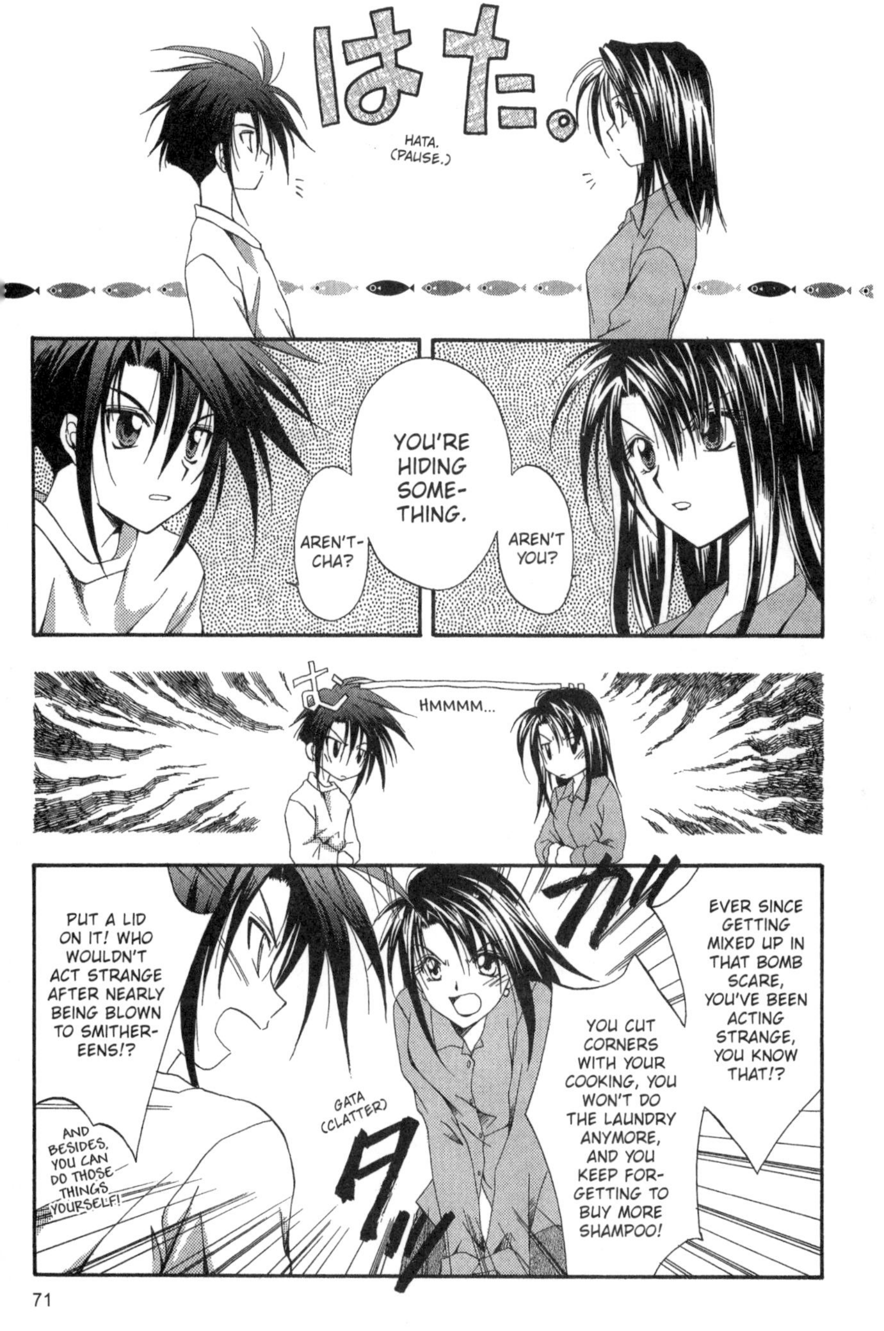
はた。
HATA. (PAUSE.)
YOU'RE HIDING SOMETHING.
AREN'T YOU?
AREN'T-CHA?
む
HMMMM...
EVER SINCE GETTING MIXED UP IN THAT BOMB SCARE, YOU'VE BEEN ACTING STRANGE, YOU KNOW THAT!?
YOU CUT CORNERS WITH YOUR COOKING, YOU WON'T DO THE LAUNDRY ANYMORE, AND YOU KEEP FOR-GETTING TO BUY MORE SHAMPOO!
カッ
GATA (CLATTER)
タッ
PUT A LID ON IT! WHO WOULDN'T ACT STRANGE AFTER NEARLY BEING BLOWN TO SMITHER-EENS!?
AND BESIDES, YOU CAN DO THOSE THINGS YOURSELF!

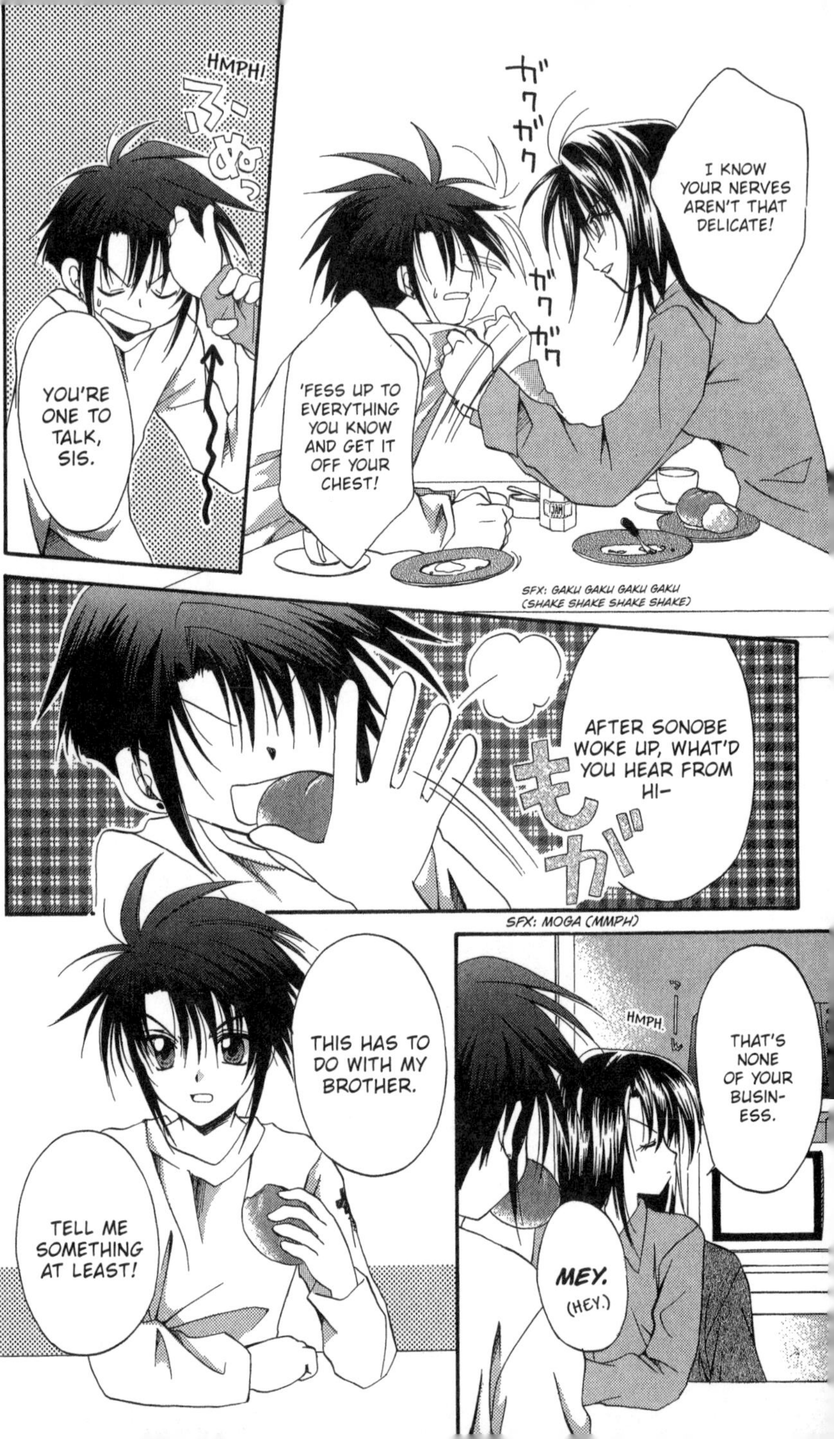
I KNOW YOUR NERVES AREN'T THAT DELICATE!
ガクガク ガクガク
'FESS UP TO EVERYTHING YOU KNOW AND GET IT OFF YOUR CHEST!
HMPH!
ふーぬっ
YOU'RE ONE TO TALK, SIS.
SFX: GAKU GAKU GAKU GAKU (SHAKE SHAKE SHAKE SHAKE)
AFTER SONOBE WOKE UP, WHAT'D YOU HEAR FROM HI-
もガ
SFX: MOGA (MMPH)
HMPH.
THAT'S NONE OF YOUR BUSIN- ESS.
MEY. (HEY.)
THIS HAS TO DO WITH MY BROTHER.
TELL ME SOMETHING AT LEAST!

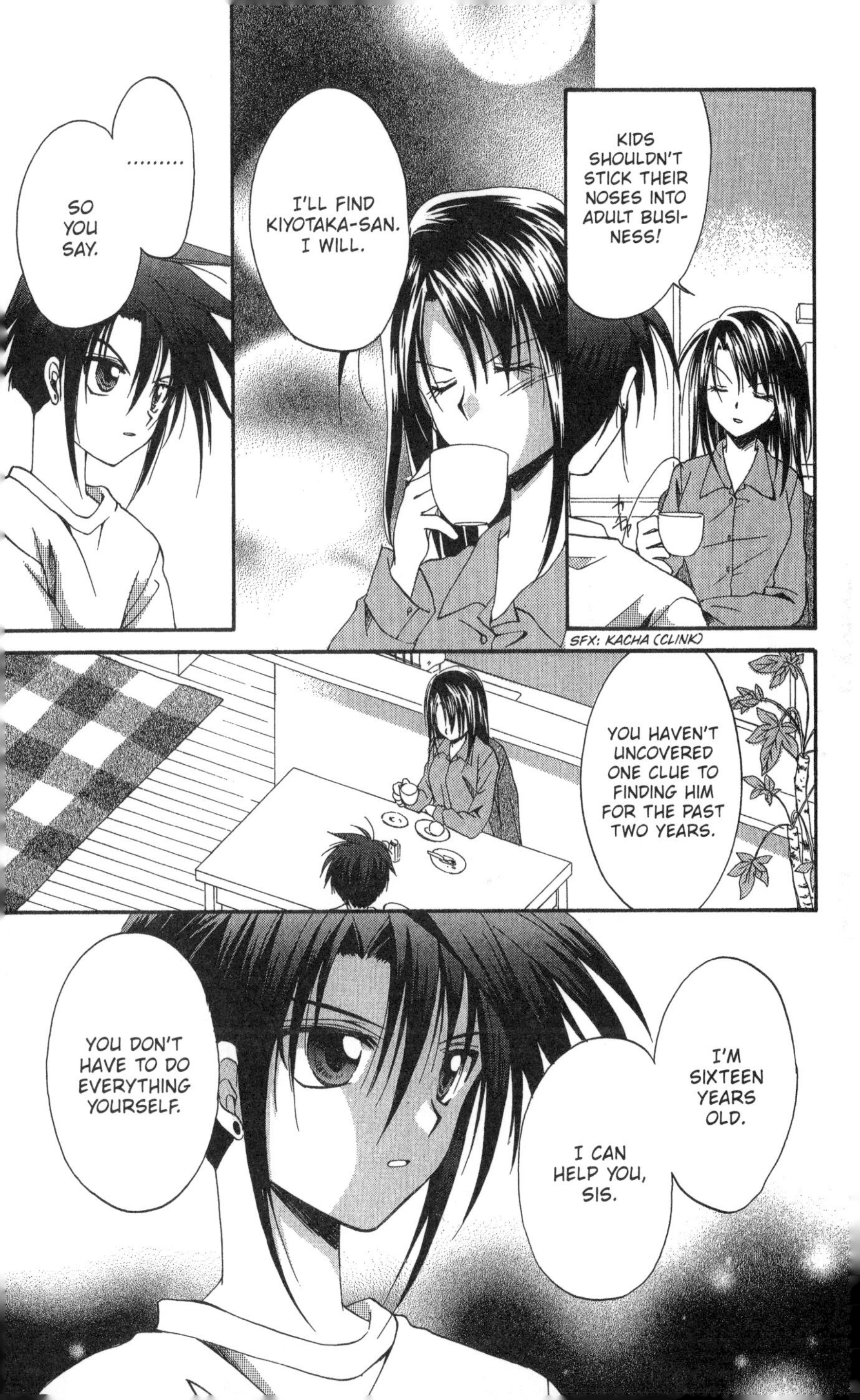
KIDS SHOULDN'T STICK THEIR NOSES INTO ADULT BUSINESS!
SFX: KACHA (CLINK)
I'LL FIND KIYOTAKA-SAN. I WILL.
....
SO YOU SAY.
YOU HAVEN'T UNCOVERED ONE CLUE TO FINDING HIM FOR THE PAST TWO YEARS.
I'M SIXTEEN YEARS OLD.
I CAN HELP YOU, SIS.
YOU DON'T HAVE TO DO EVERYTHING YOURSELF.

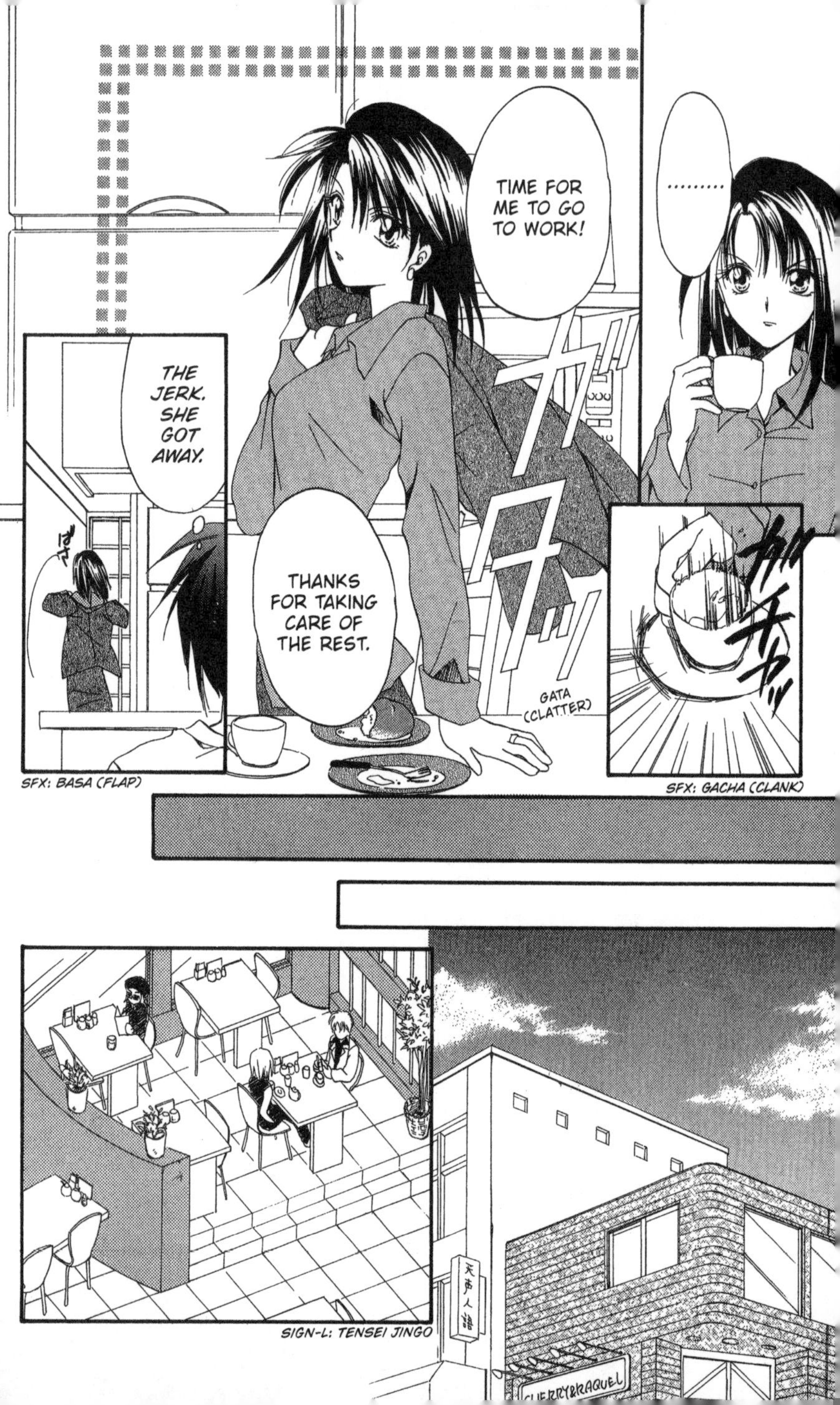
....
SFX: GACHA (CLANK)
TIME FOR ME TO GO TO WORK!
THANKS FOR TAKING CARE OF THE REST.
GATA (CLATTER)
THE JERK. SHE GOT AWAY.
SFX: BASA (FLAP)
CHERRY&RAQUEL
SIGN-L: TENSEI JINGO

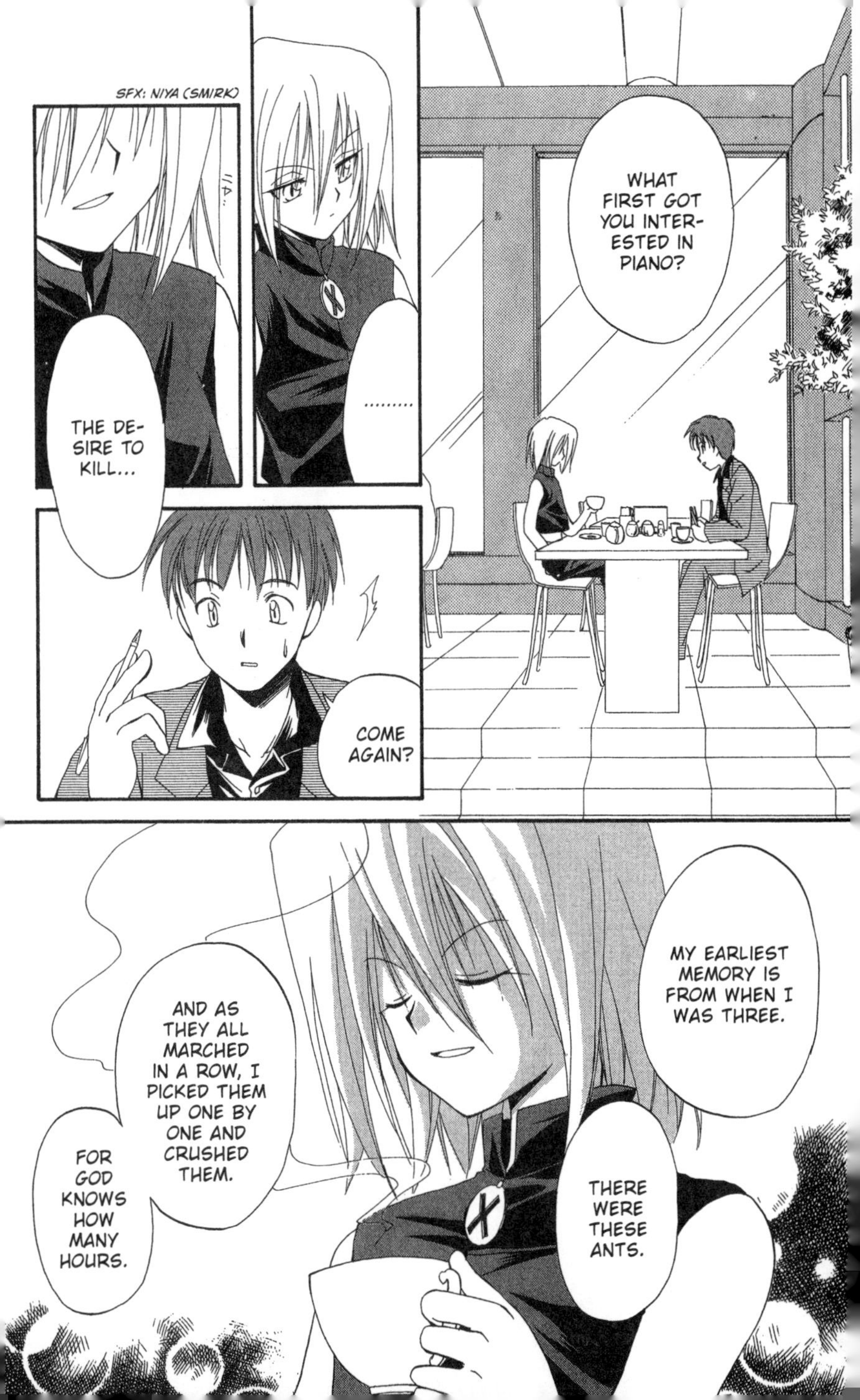
WHAT FIRST GOT YOU INTER-ESTED IN PIANO?
....
SFX: NIYA (SMIRK)
ニヤ..
THE DE-SIRE TO KILL...
COME AGAIN?
MY EARLIEST MEMORY IS FROM WHEN I WAS THREE.
THERE WERE THESE ANTS.
AND AS THEY ALL MARCHED IN A ROW, I PICKED THEM UP ONE BY ONE AND CRUSHED THEM.
FOR GOD KNOWS HOW MANY HOURS.

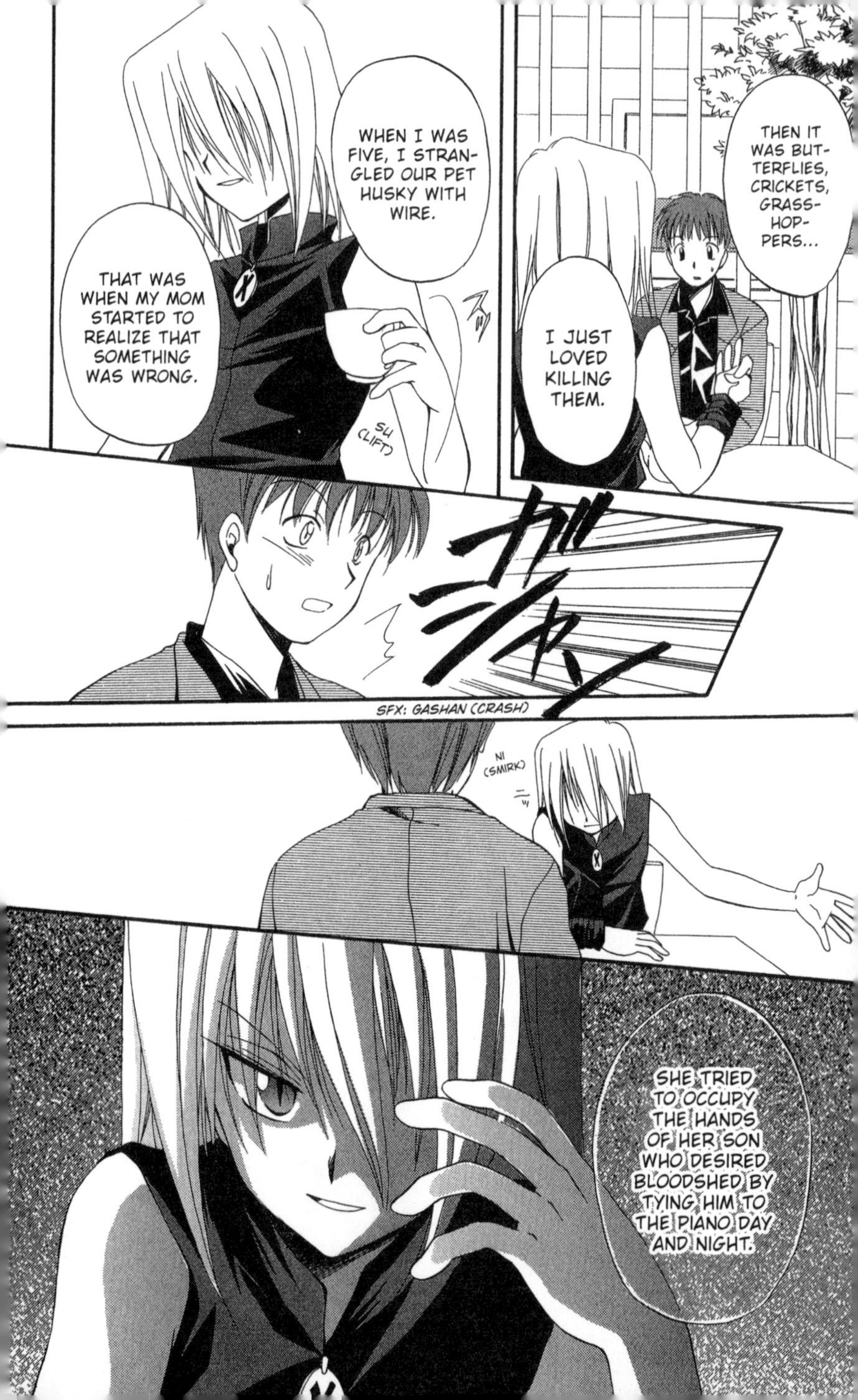

THEN IT WAS BUTTERFLIES, CRICKETS, GRASSHOPPERS...
I JUST LOVED KILLING THEM.
WHEN I WAS FIVE, I STRANGLED OUR PET HUSKY WITH WIRE.
THAT WAS WHEN MY MOM STARTED TO REALIZE THAT SOMETHING WAS WRONG.
SU (LIFT)
SFX: GASHAN (CRASH)
NI (SMIRK)
SHE TRIED TO OCCUPY THE HANDS OF HER SON WHO DESIRED BLOODSHED BY TYING HIM TO THE PIANO DAY AND NIGHT.

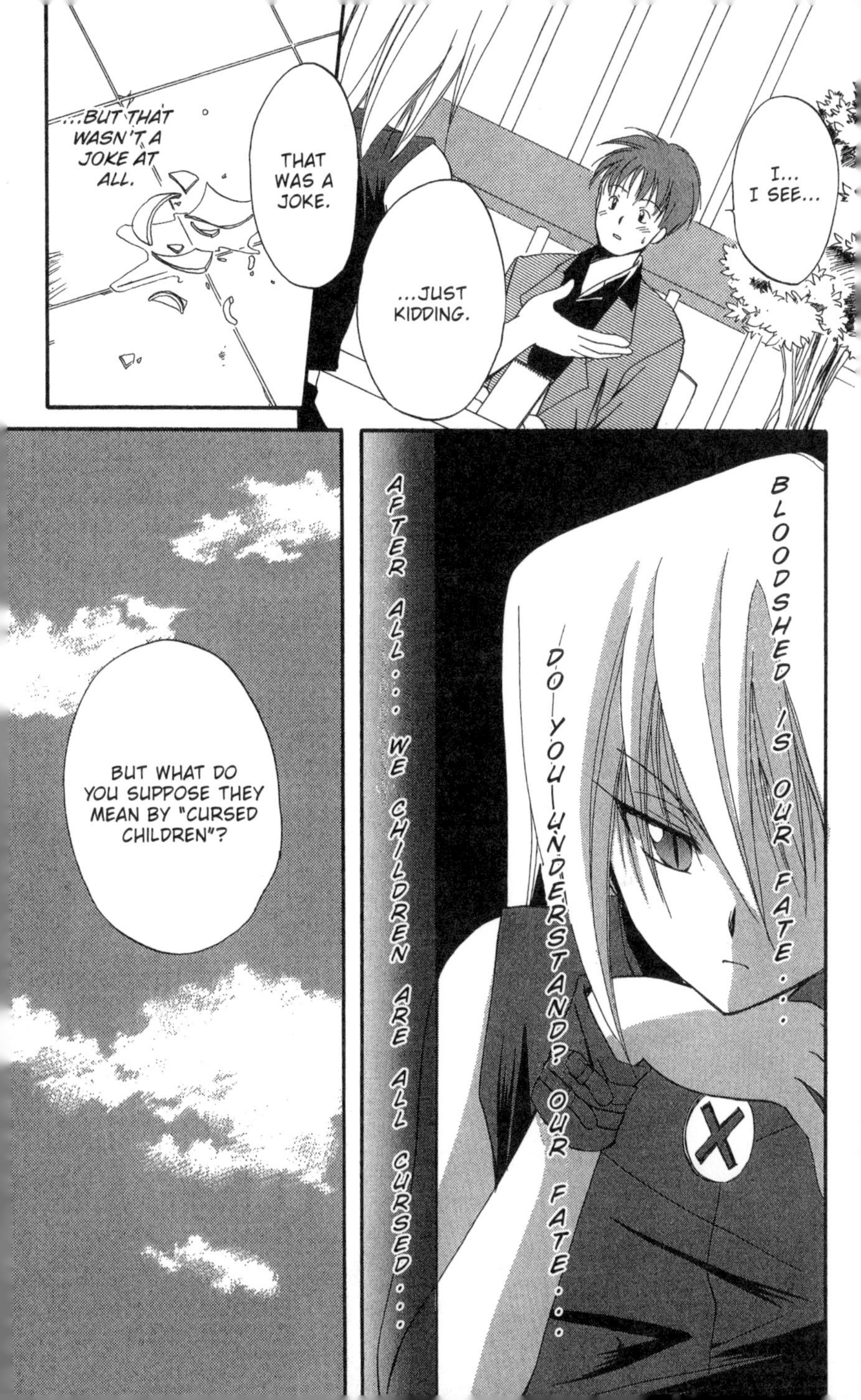
I... I SEE...
THAT WAS A JOKE.
...JUST KIDDING.
...BUT THAT WASN'T A JOKE AT ALL.
BLOODSHED IS OUR FATE...
DO YOU UNDERSTAND? OUR FATE...
AFTER ALL... WE CHILDREN ARE ALL CURSED...
BUT WHAT DO YOU SUPPOSE THEY MEAN BY "CURSED CHILDREN"?

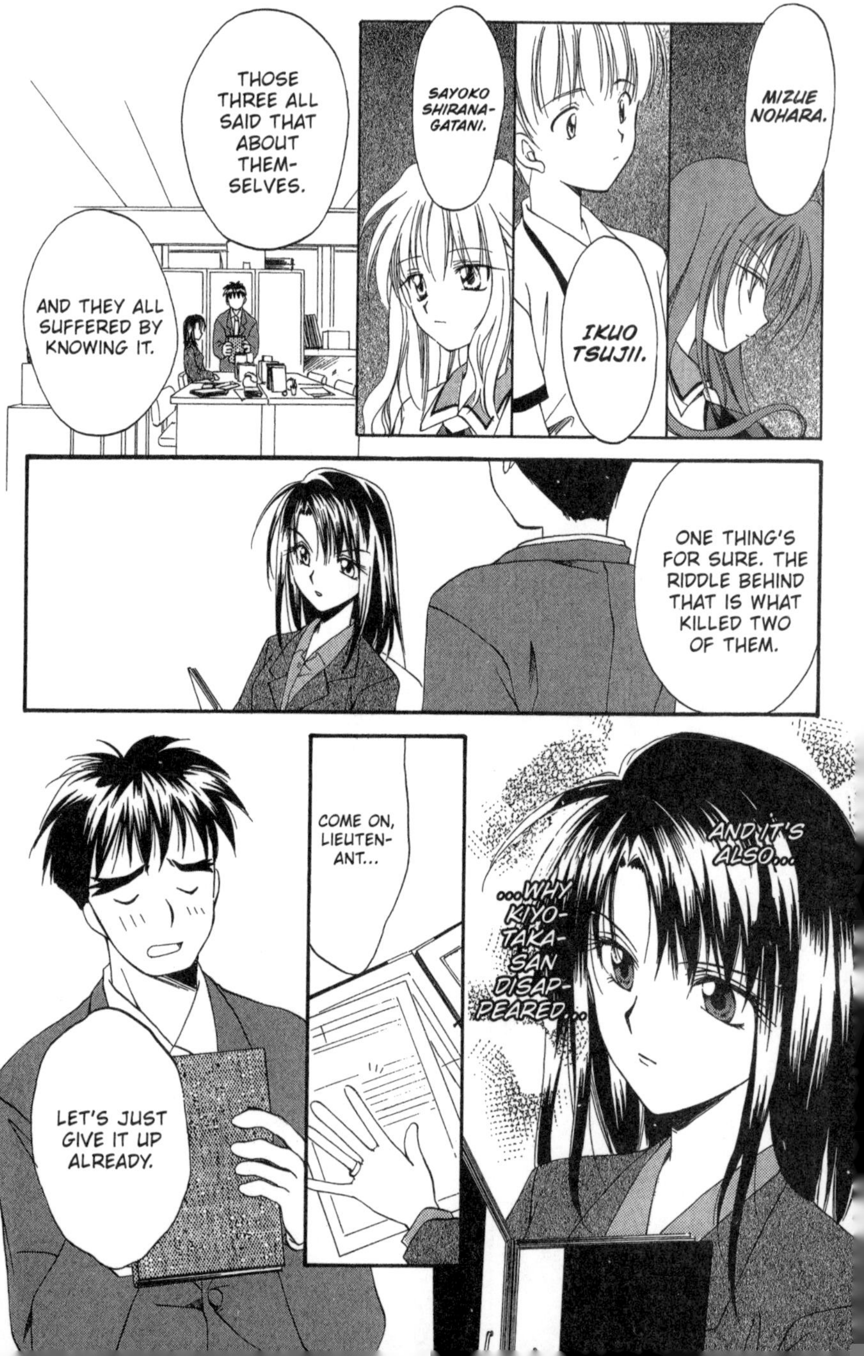
MIZUE NOHARA.
IKUO TSUJII.
SAYOKO SHIRANA-GATANI.
THOSE THREE ALL SAID THAT ABOUT THEM-SELVES.
AND THEY ALL SUFFERED BY KNOWING IT.
ONE THING'S FOR SURE. THE RIDDLE BEHIND THAT IS WHAT KILLED TWO OF THEM.
AND IT'S ALSO...
...WHY KIYO-TAKA-SAN DISAP-PEARED...
COME ON, LIEUTEN-ANT...
LET'S JUST GIVE IT UP ALREADY.

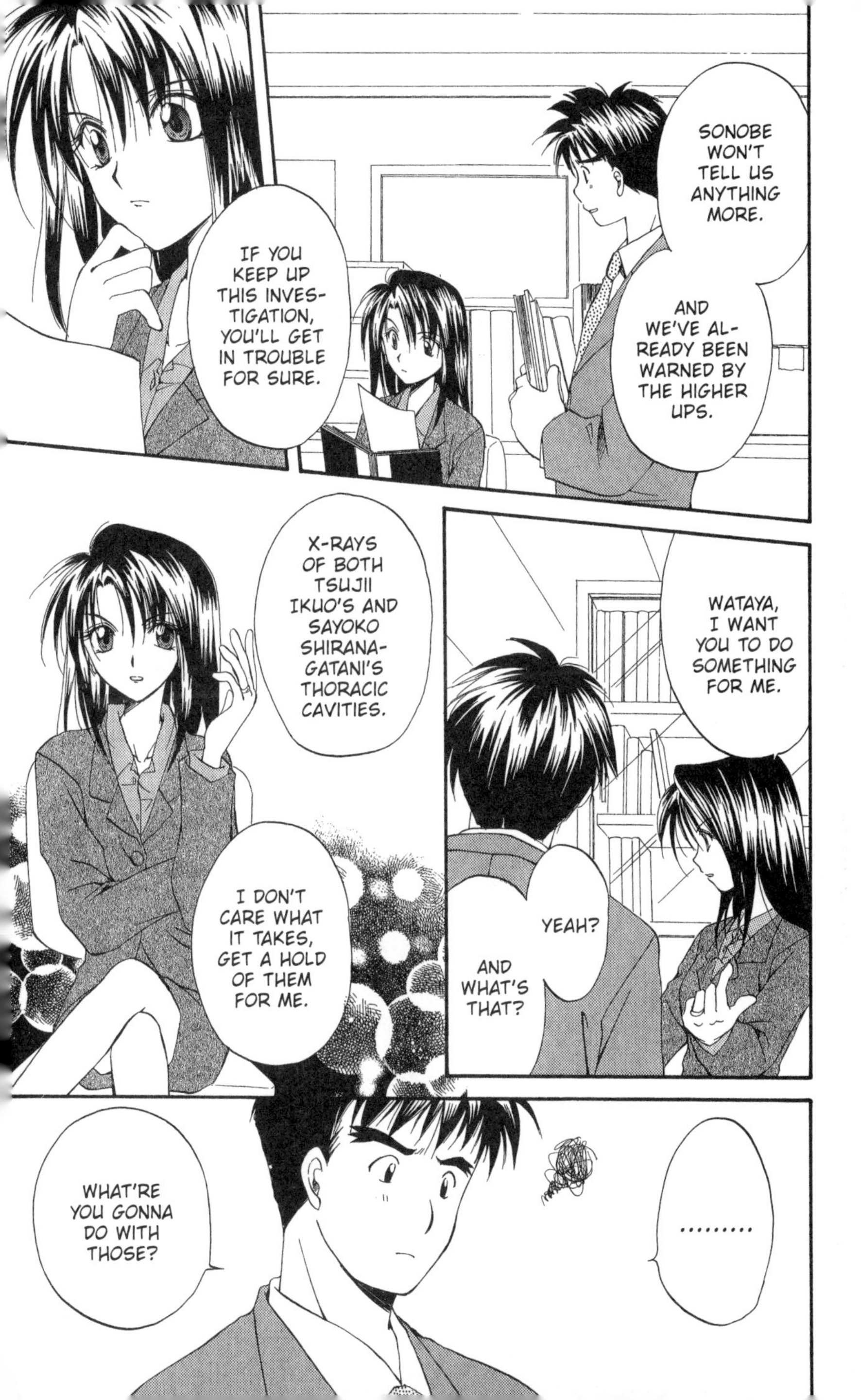
SONOBE WON'T TELL US ANYTHING MORE.
AND WE'VE ALREADY BEEN WARNED BY THE HIGHER UPS.
IF YOU KEEP UP THIS INVESTIGATION, YOU'LL GET IN TROUBLE FOR SURE.
WATAYA, I WANT YOU TO DO SOMETHING FOR ME.
YEAH?
AND WHAT'S THAT?
X-RAYS OF BOTH TSUJII IKUO'S AND SAYOKO SHIRANAGATANI'S THORACIC CAVITIES.
I DON'T CARE WHAT IT TAKES, GET A HOLD OF THEM FOR ME.
....
WHAT'RE YOU GONNA DO WITH THOSE?

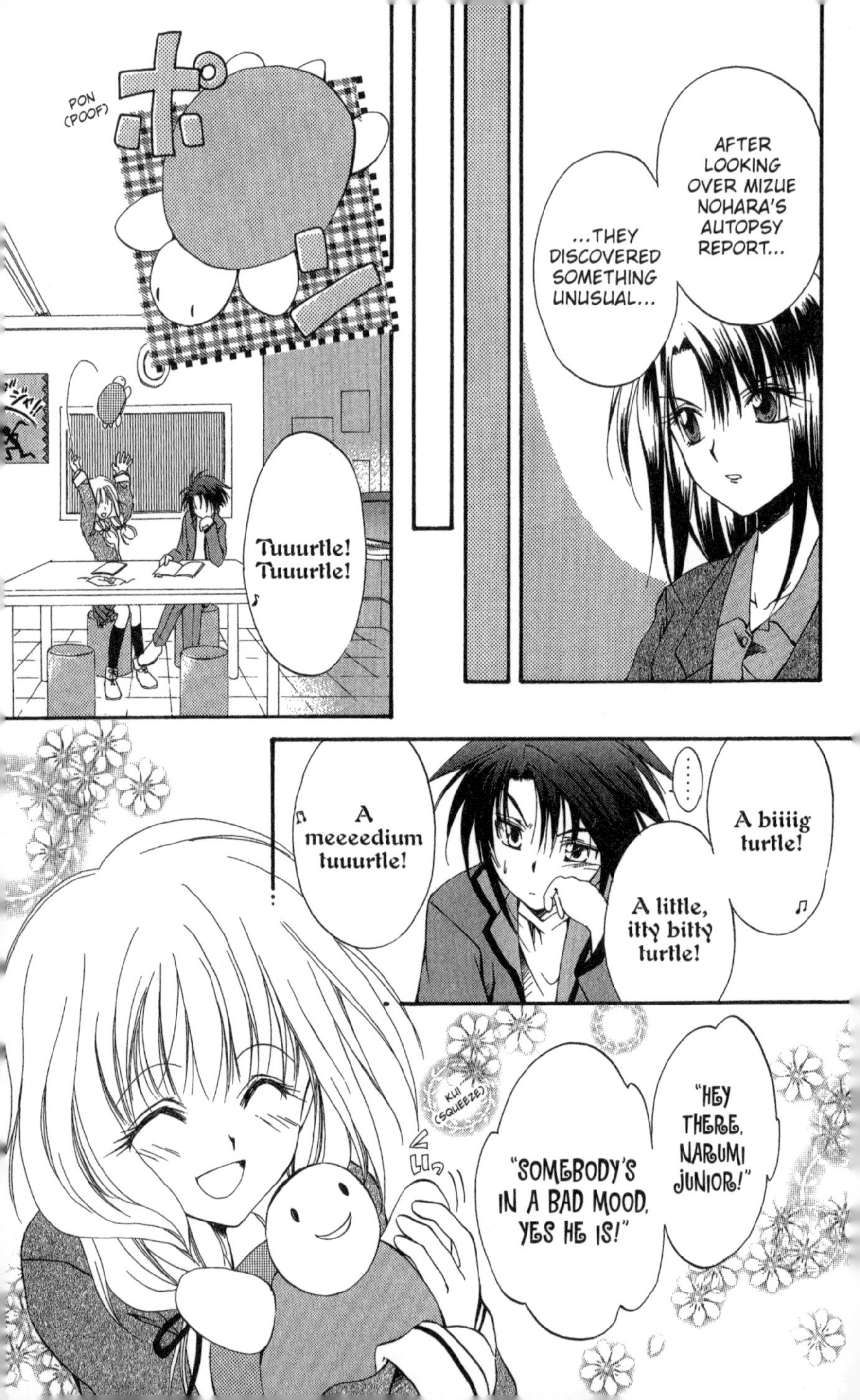
AFTER LOOKING OVER MIZUE NOHARA'S AUTOPSY REPORT...
...THEY DISCOVERED SOMETHING UNUSUAL...
PON (POOF)
Tuuurtle! Tuuurtle!
A biiiig turtle!
......
A little, itty bitty turtle!
A meeeedium tuuurtle!
"HEY THERE, NARUMI JUNIOR!"
"SOMEBODY'S IN A BAD MOOD, YES HE IS!"
KUI (SQUEEZE)

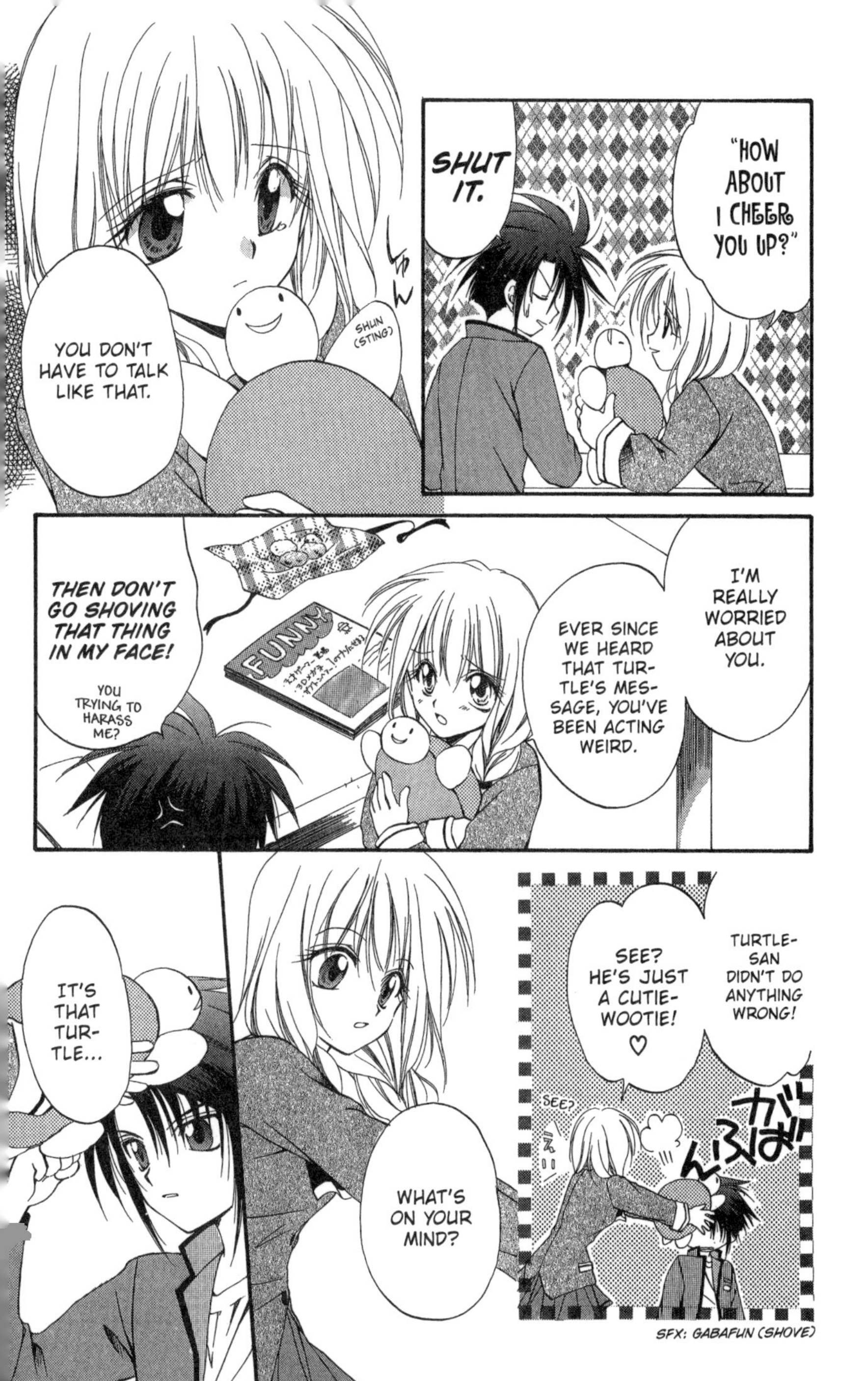
"HOW ABOUT I CHEER YOU UP?"
SHUT IT.
しゅん
SHUN (STING)
YOU DON'T HAVE TO TALK LIKE THAT.
I'M REALLY WORRIED ABOUT YOU.
EVER SINCE WE HEARD THAT TUR-TLE'S MES-SAGE, YOU'VE BEEN ACTING WEIRD.
THEN DON'T GO SHOVING THAT THING IN MY FACE!
YOU TRYING TO HARASS ME?
FUNNY
TURTLE-SAN DIDN'T DO ANYTHING WRONG!
SEE? HE'S JUST A CUTIE-WOOTIE! ♡
SEE?
がばふん
WHAT'S ON YOUR MIND?
IT'S THAT TUR-TLE...
SFX: GABAFUN (SHOVE)

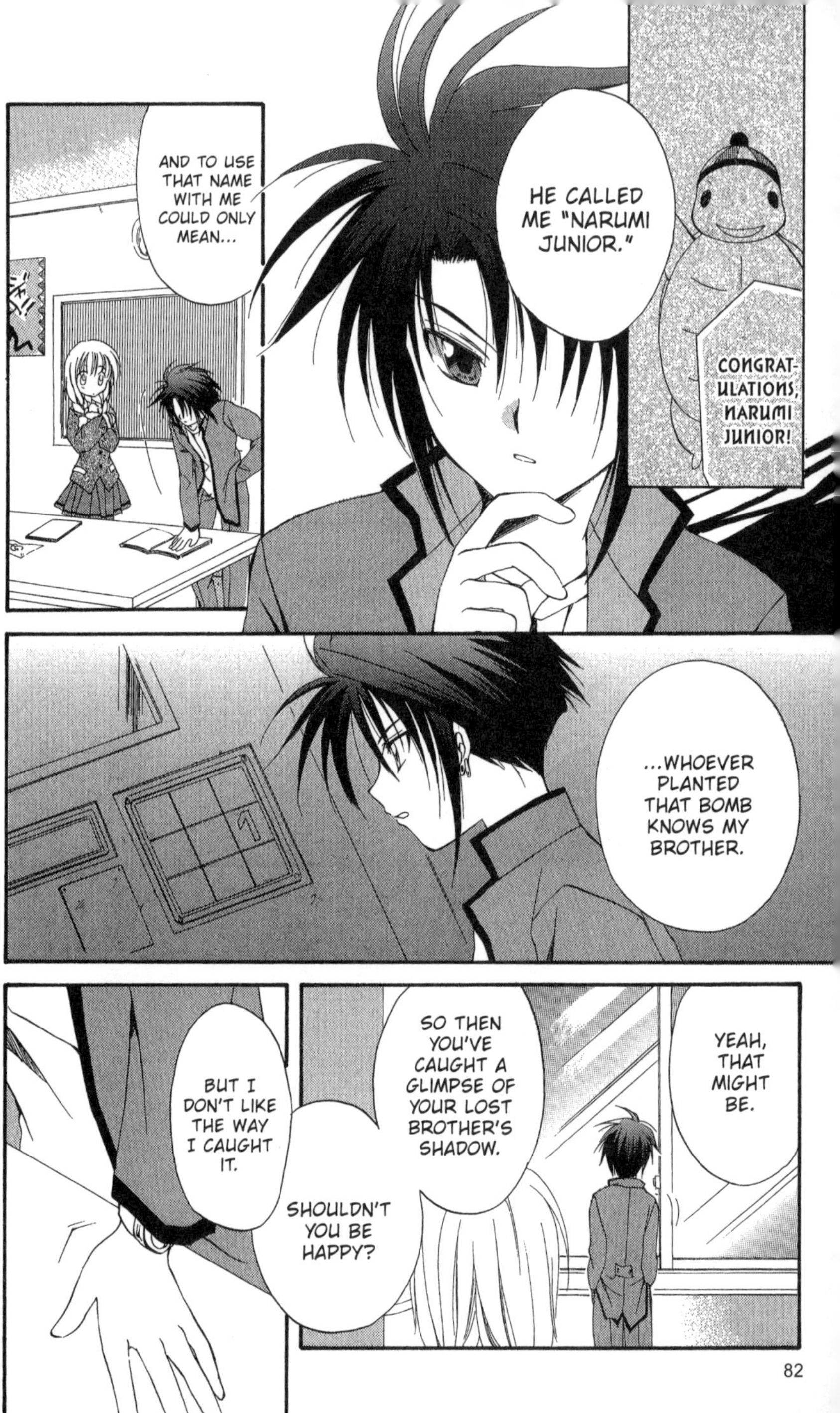
CONGRAT-ULATIONS, NARUMI JUNIOR!
HE CALLED ME "NARUMI JUNIOR."
AND TO USE THAT NAME WITH ME COULD ONLY MEAN...
...WHOEVER PLANTED THAT BOMB KNOWS MY BROTHER.
SO THEN YOU'VE CAUGHT A GLIMPSE OF YOUR LOST BROTHER'S SHADOW.
YEAH, THAT MIGHT BE.
SHOULDN'T YOU BE HAPPY?
BUT I DON'T LIKE THE WAY I CAUGHT IT.

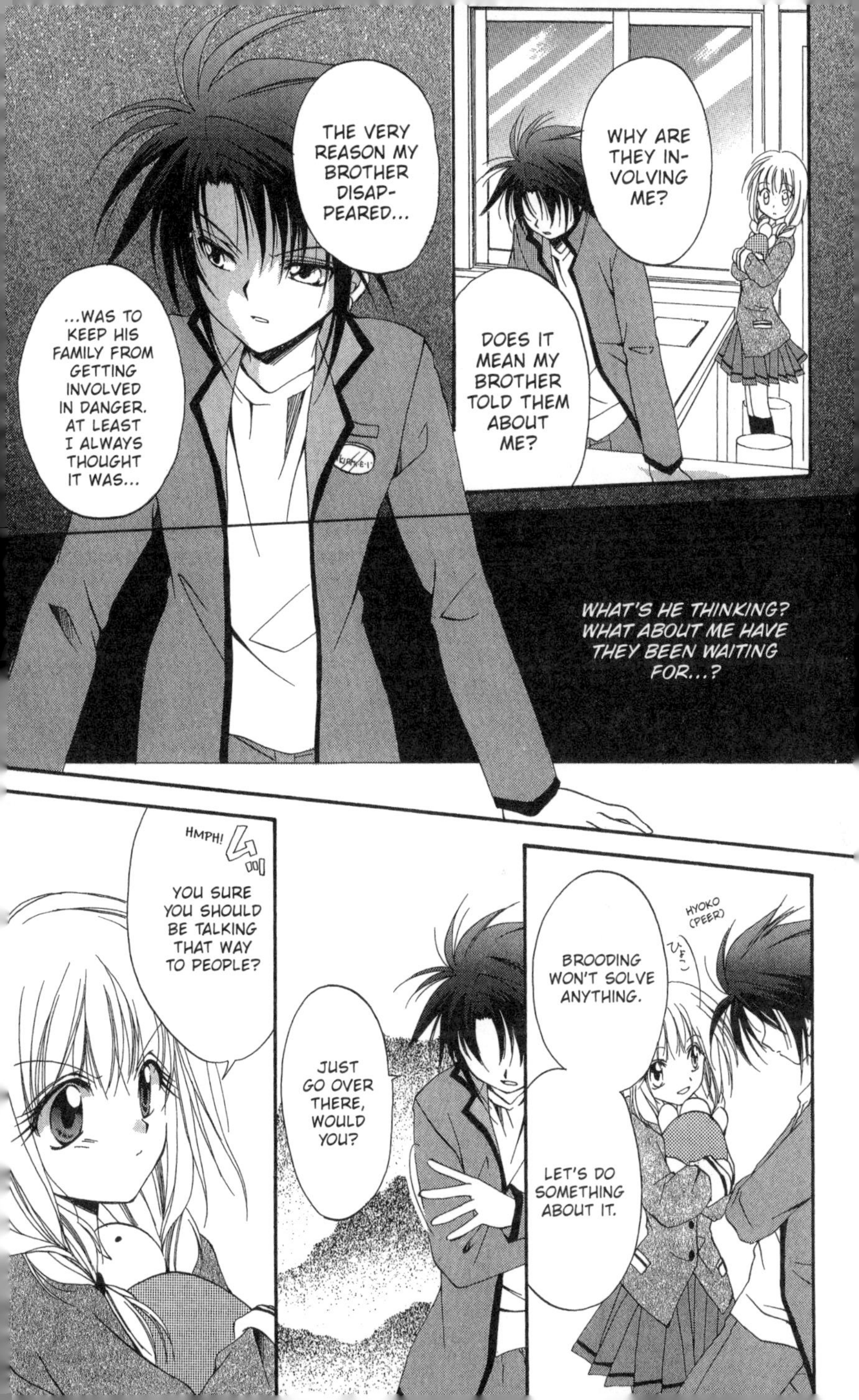
WHY ARE THEY INVOLVING ME?
DOES IT MEAN MY BROTHER TOLD THEM ABOUT ME?
THE VERY REASON MY BROTHER DISAPPEARED...
...WAS TO KEEP HIS FAMILY FROM GETTING INVOLVED IN DANGER. AT LEAST I ALWAYS THOUGHT IT WAS...
WHAT'S HE THINKING? WHAT ABOUT ME HAVE THEY BEEN WAITING FOR...?
HYOKO (PEER)
BROODING WON'T SOLVE ANYTHING.
LET'S DO SOMETHING ABOUT IT.
JUST GO OVER THERE, WOULD YOU?
HMPH!
YOU SURE YOU SHOULD BE TALKING THAT WAY TO PEOPLE?

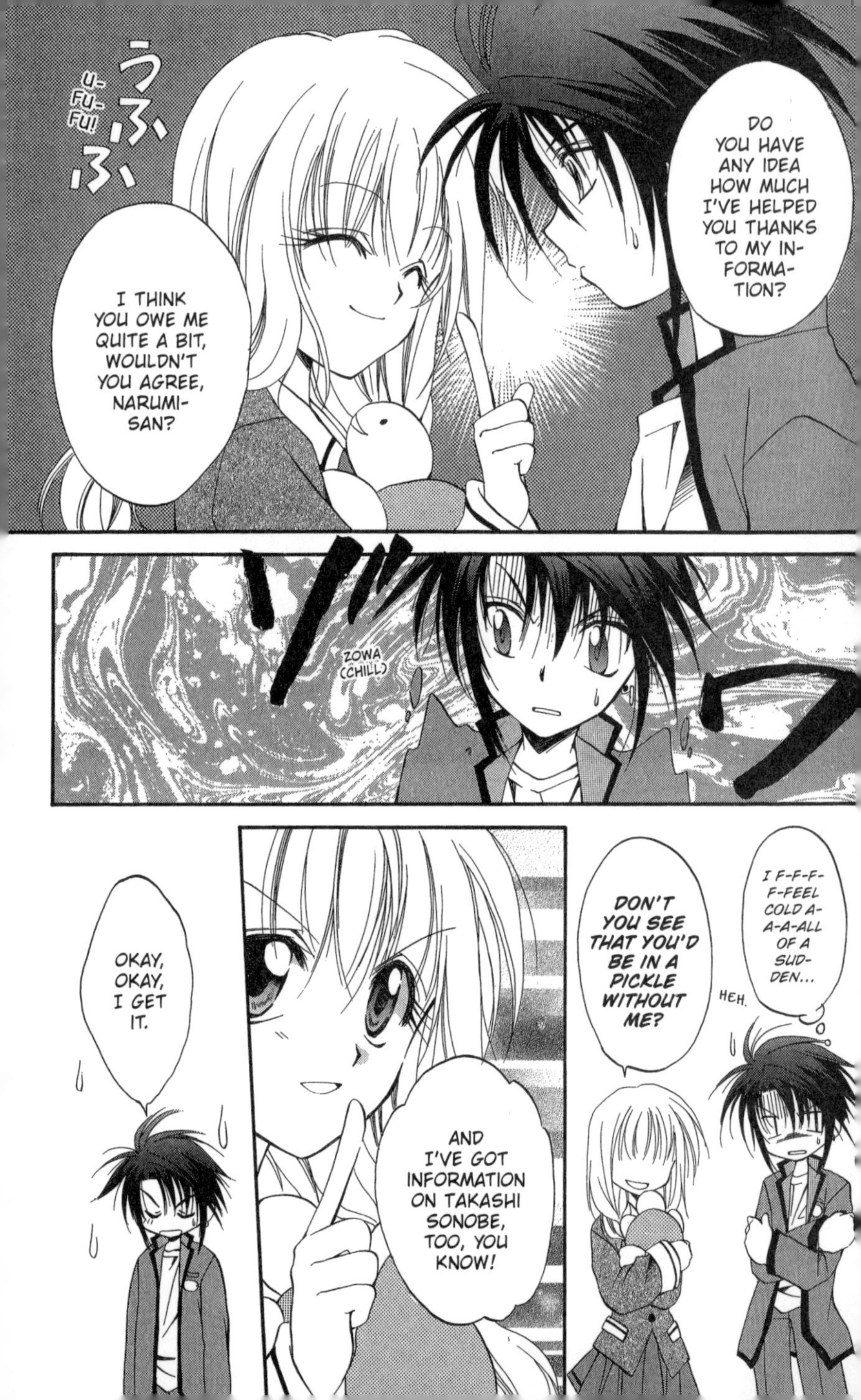
DO YOU HAVE ANY IDEA HOW MUCH I'VE HELPED YOU THANKS TO MY INFORMATION?
うふふ
U-FU-FU!
I THINK YOU OWE ME QUITE A BIT, WOULDN'T YOU AGREE, NARUMI-SAN?
ZOWA (CHILL)
I F-F-F-F-FEEL COLD A-A-A-ALL OF A SUDDEN...
HEH.
DON'T YOU SEE THAT YOU'D BE IN A PICKLE WITHOUT ME?
AND I'VE GOT INFORMATION ON TAKASHI SONOBE, TOO, YOU KNOW!
OKAY, OKAY, I GET IT.

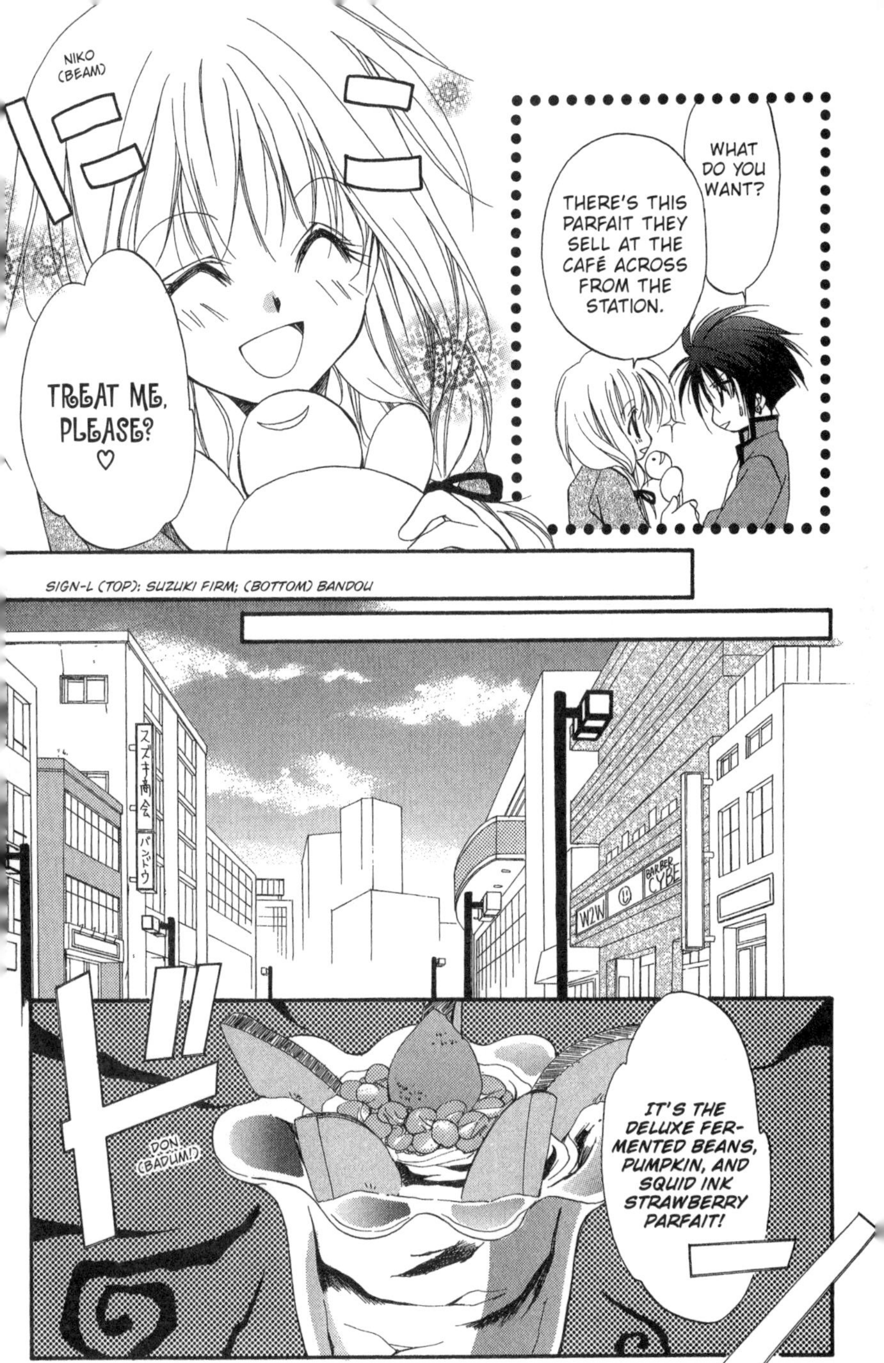
WHAT DO YOU WANT?
THERE'S THIS PARFAIT THEY SELL AT THE CAFÉ ACROSS FROM THE STATION.
NIKO (BEAM)
TREAT ME, PLEASE? ♡
SIGN-L (TOP): SUZUKI FIRM; (BOTTOM) BANDOU
スズキ商会
バンドウ
BARBER CYBE
W2W
IT'S THE DELUXE FERMENTED BEANS, PUMPKIN, AND SQUID INK STRAWBERRY PARFAIT!
DON (BADUM!)

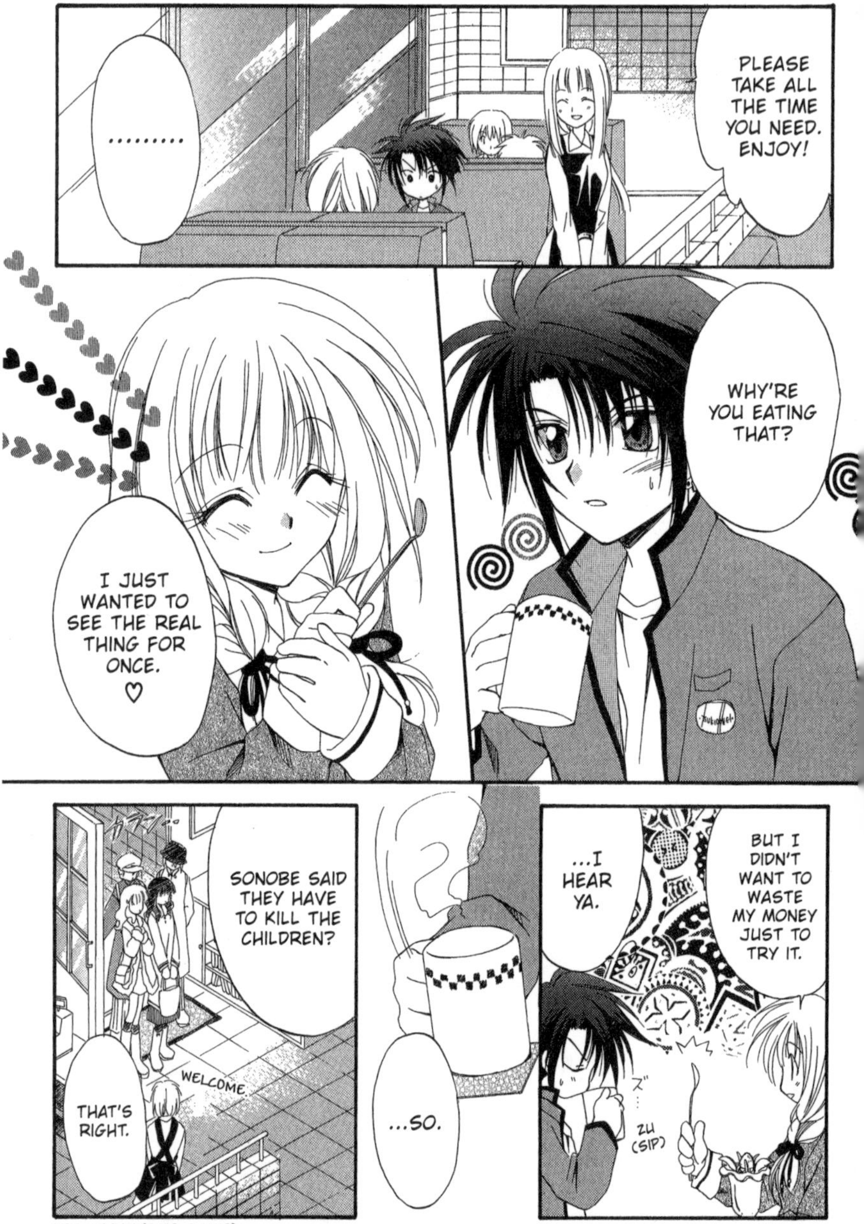
PLEASE TAKE ALL THE TIME YOU NEED. ENJOY!
....
WHY'RE YOU EATING THAT?
I JUST WANTED TO SEE THE REAL THING FOR ONCE. ♡
BUT I DIDN'T WANT TO WASTE MY MONEY JUST TO TRY IT.
...I HEAR YA.
ZU (SIP)
...SO.
SONOBE SAID THEY HAVE TO KILL THE CHILDREN?
WELCOME.
THAT'S RIGHT.

SFX: KARAN (DING-A-LING)

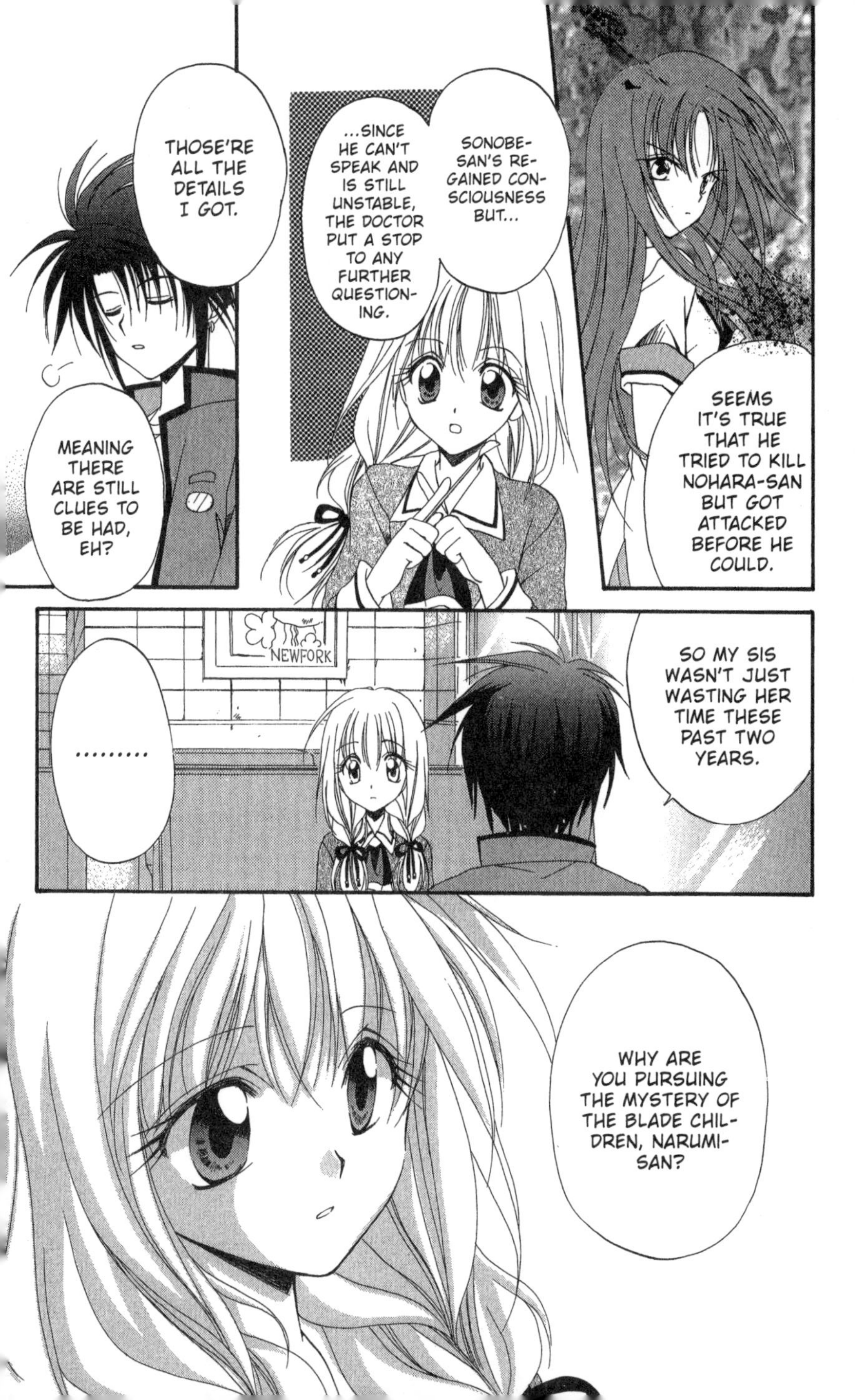
SEEMS IT'S TRUE THAT HE TRIED TO KILL NOHARA-SAN BUT GOT ATTACKED BEFORE HE COULD.
SONOBE-SAN'S REGAINED CONSCIOUSNESS BUT...
...SINCE HE CAN'T SPEAK AND IS STILL UNSTABLE, THE DOCTOR PUT A STOP TO ANY FURTHER QUESTIONING.
THOSE'RE ALL THE DETAILS I GOT.
MEANING THERE ARE STILL CLUES TO BE HAD, EH?
SO MY SIS WASN'T JUST WASTING HER TIME THESE PAST TWO YEARS.
NEWFORK
....
WHY ARE YOU PURSUING THE MYSTERY OF THE BLADE CHILDREN, NARUMI-SAN?

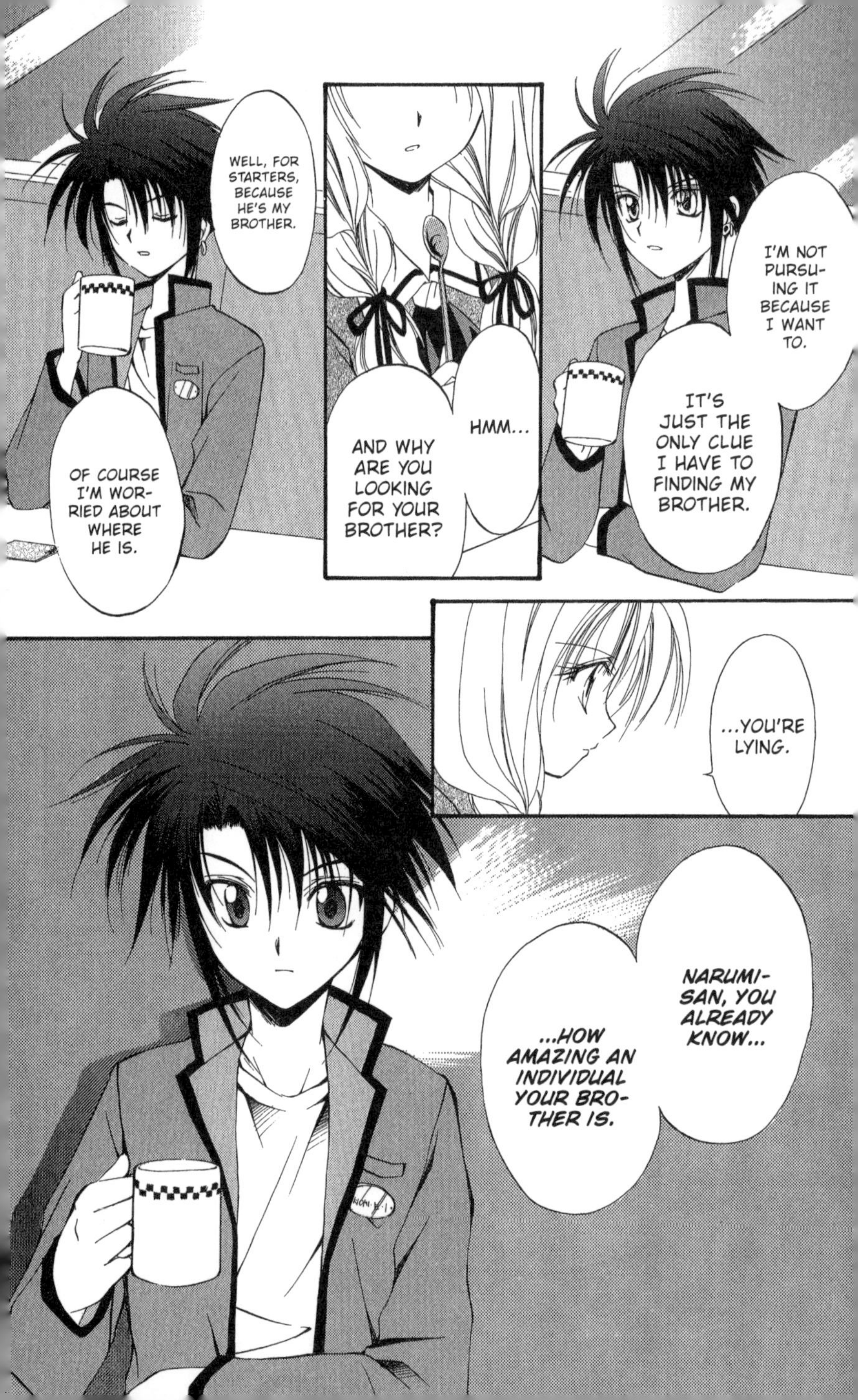
I'M NOT PURSUING IT BECAUSE I WANT TO.
IT'S JUST THE ONLY CLUE I HAVE TO FINDING MY BROTHER.
HMM...
AND WHY ARE YOU LOOKING FOR YOUR BROTHER?
WELL, FOR STARTERS, BECAUSE HE'S MY BROTHER.
OF COURSE I'M WORRIED ABOUT WHERE HE IS.
...YOU'RE LYING.
NARUMI-SAN, YOU ALREADY KNOW...
...HOW AMAZING AN INDIVIDUAL YOUR BROTHER IS.

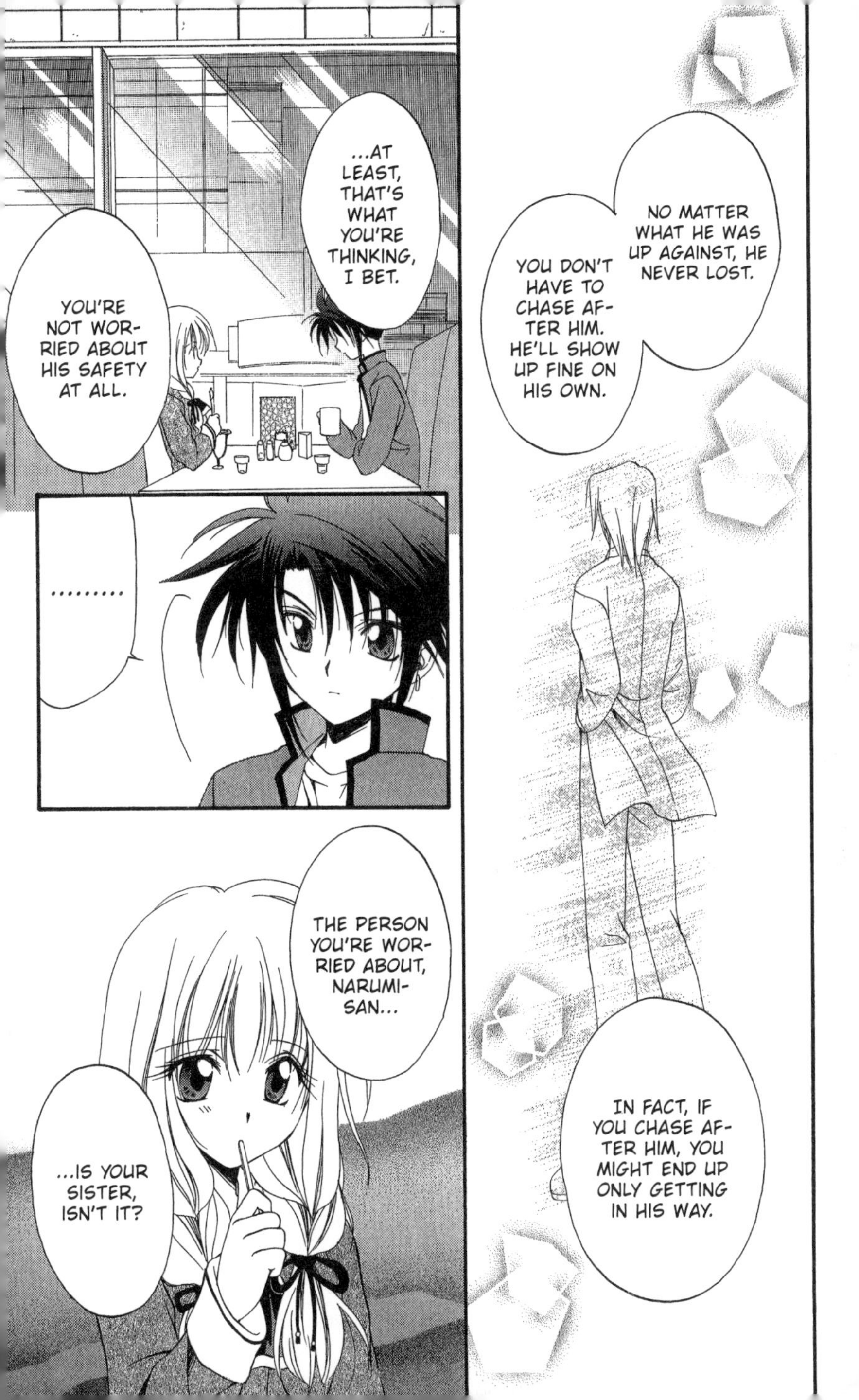
NO MATTER WHAT HE WAS UP AGAINST, HE NEVER LOST.
YOU DON'T HAVE TO CHASE AF-TER HIM. HE'LL SHOW UP FINE ON HIS OWN.
IN FACT, IF YOU CHASE AF-TER HIM, YOU MIGHT END UP ONLY GETTING IN HIS WAY.
...AT LEAST, THAT'S WHAT YOU'RE THINKING, I BET.
YOU'RE NOT WOR-RIED ABOUT HIS SAFETY AT ALL.
....
THE PERSON YOU'RE WOR-RIED ABOUT, NARUMI-SAN...
...IS YOUR SISTER, ISN'T IT?

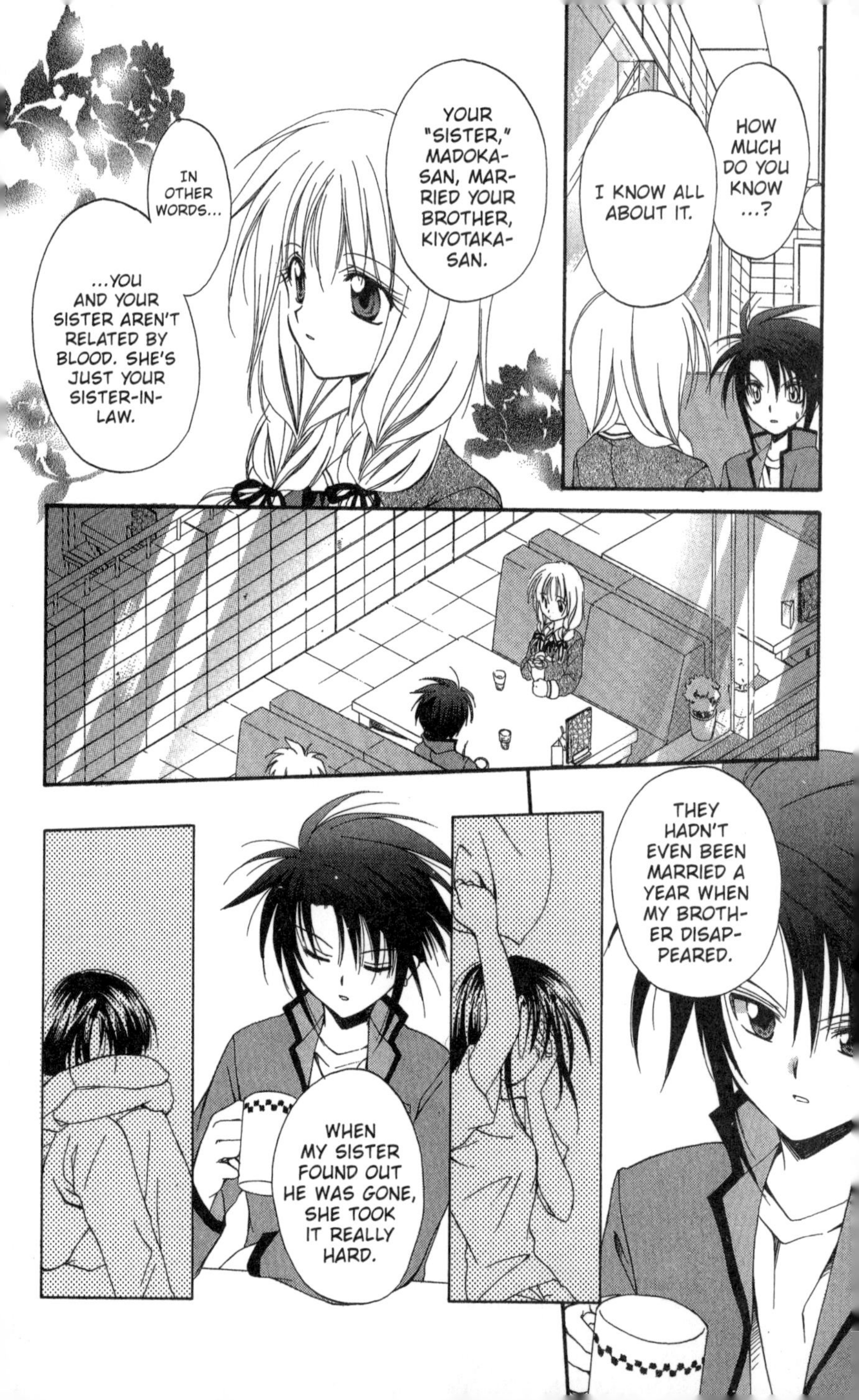
HOW MUCH DO YOU KNOW ...?
I KNOW ALL ABOUT IT.
YOUR "SISTER," MADOKA-SAN, MARRIED YOUR BROTHER, KIYOTAKA-SAN.
IN OTHER WORDS...
...YOU AND YOUR SISTER AREN'T RELATED BY BLOOD. SHE'S JUST YOUR SISTER-IN-LAW.
THEY HADN'T EVEN BEEN MARRIED A YEAR WHEN MY BROTHER DISAPPEARED.
WHEN MY SISTER FOUND OUT HE WAS GONE, SHE TOOK IT REALLY HARD.

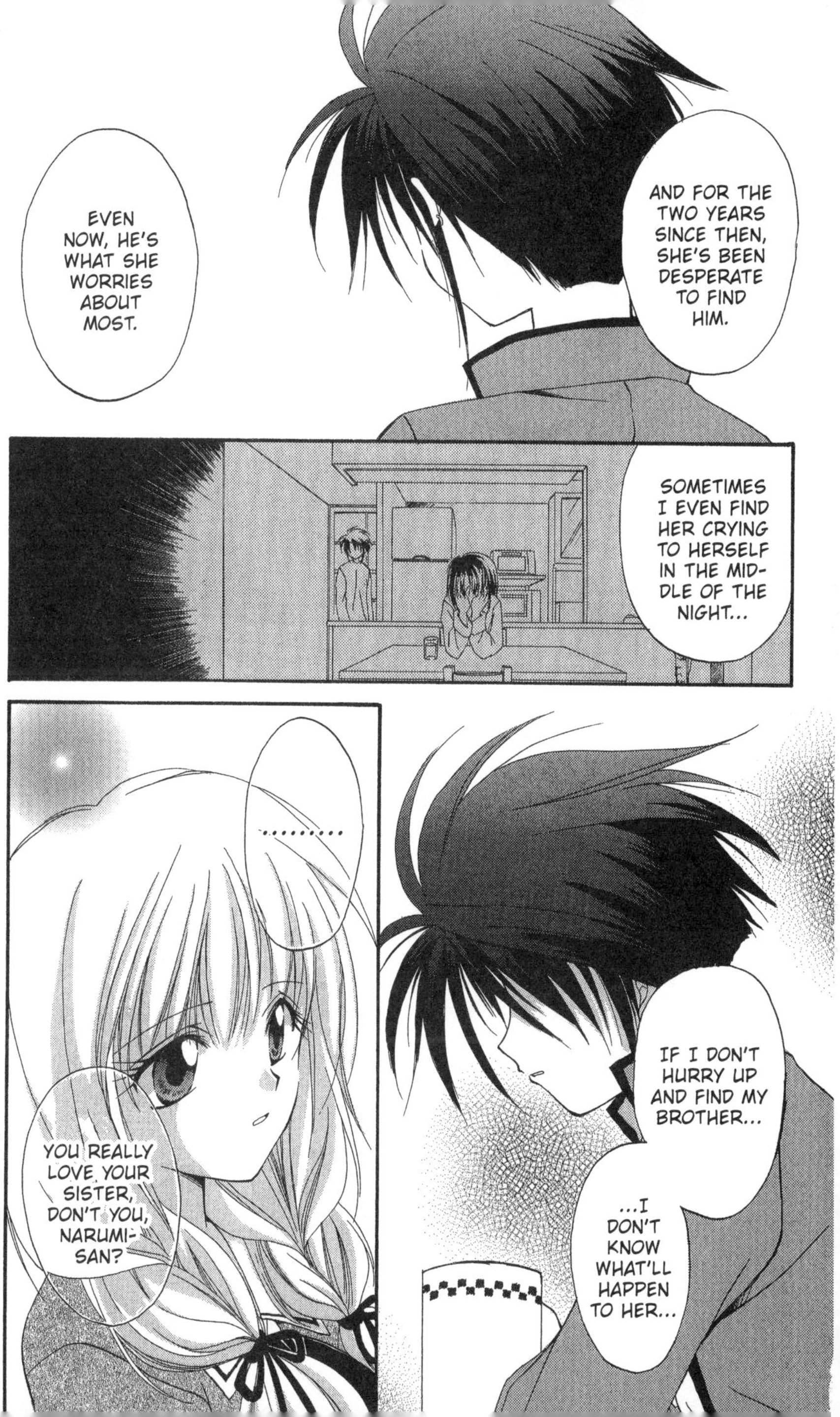
AND FOR THE TWO YEARS SINCE THEN, SHE'S BEEN DESPERATE TO FIND HIM.
EVEN NOW, HE'S WHAT SHE WORRIES ABOUT MOST.
SOMETIMES I EVEN FIND HER CRYING TO HERSELF IN THE MID-DLE OF THE NIGHT...
IF I DON'T HURRY UP AND FIND MY BROTHER...
...I DON'T KNOW WHAT'LL HAPPEN TO HER...
....
YOU REALLY LOVE YOUR SISTER, DON'T YOU, NARUMI-SAN?

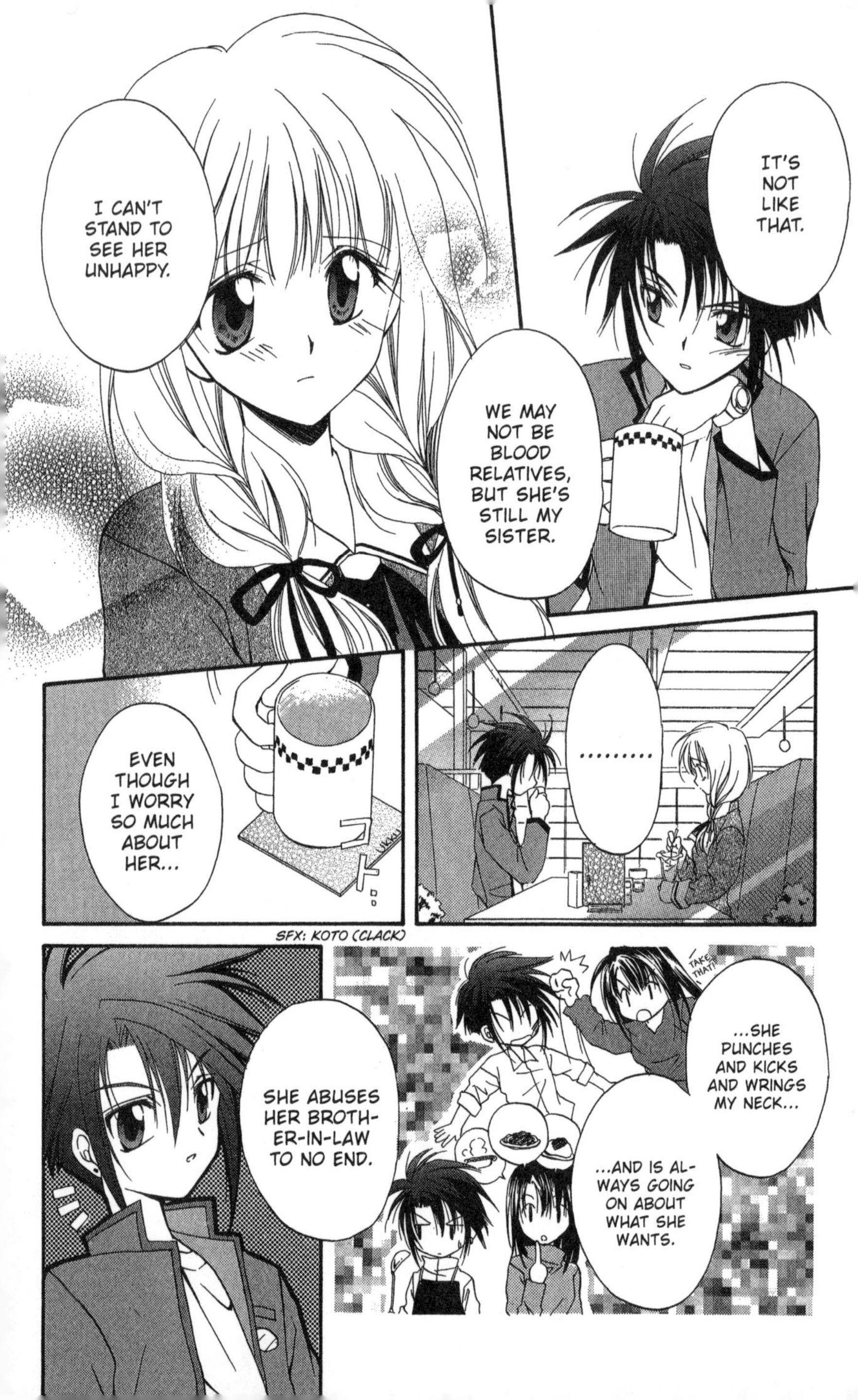
IT'S NOT LIKE THAT.
WE MAY NOT BE BLOOD RELATIVES, BUT SHE'S STILL MY SISTER.
I CAN'T STAND TO SEE HER UNHAPPY.
....
EVEN THOUGH I WORRY SO MUCH ABOUT HER...
SFX: KOTO (CLACK)
TAKE THAT!
...SHE PUNCHES AND KICKS AND WRINGS MY NECK...
...AND IS AL-WAYS GOING ON ABOUT WHAT SHE WANTS.
SHE ABUSES HER BROTH-ER-IN-LAW TO NO END.

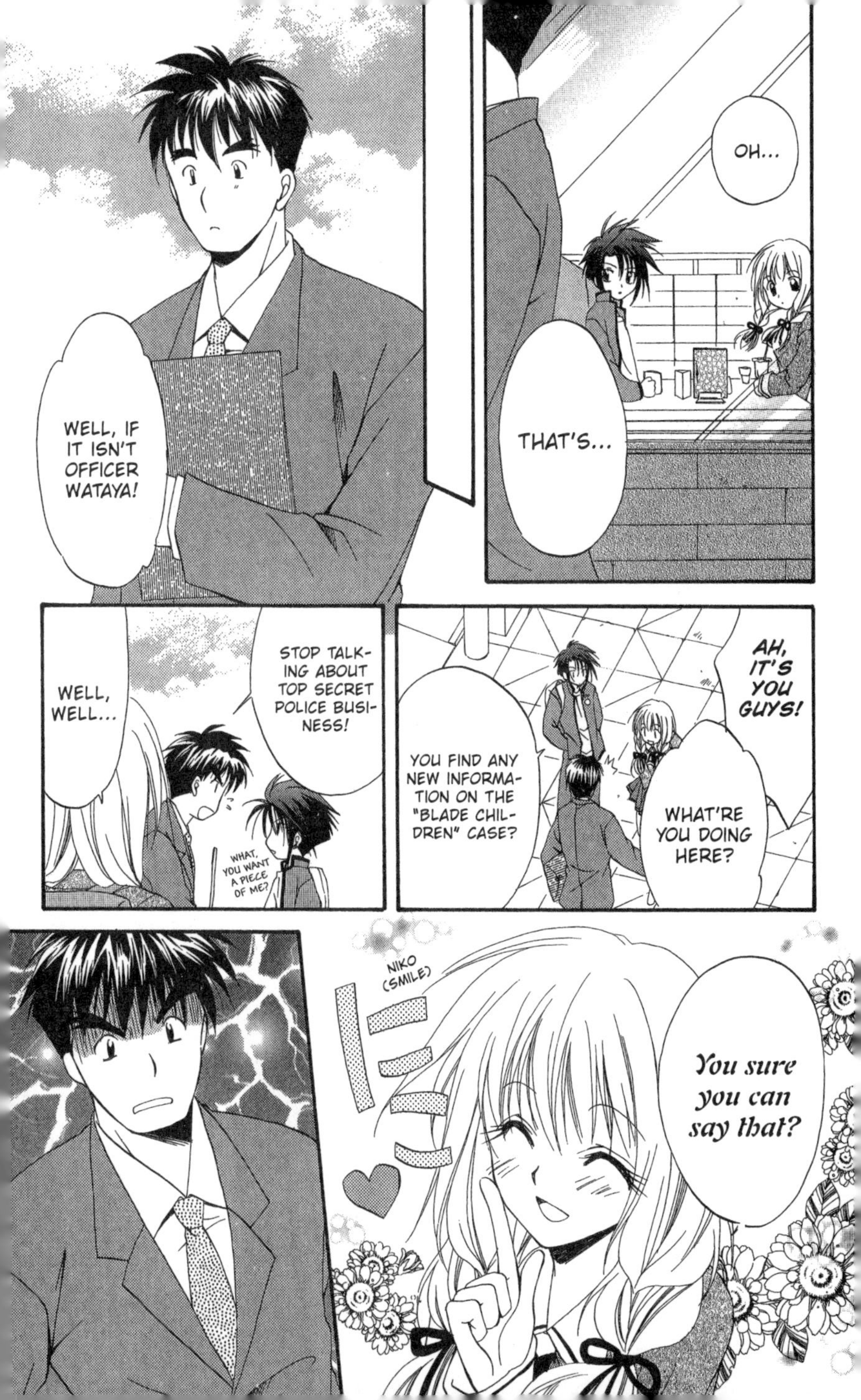
OH...
THAT'S...
WELL, IF IT ISN'T OFFICER WATAYA!
AH, IT'S YOU GUYS!
WHAT'RE YOU DOING HERE?
YOU FIND ANY NEW INFORMATION ON THE "BLADE CHILDREN" CASE?
STOP TALKING ABOUT TOP SECRET POLICE BUSINESS!
WELL, WELL...
WHAT, YOU WANT A PIECE OF ME?
NIKO (SMILE)
You sure you can say that?

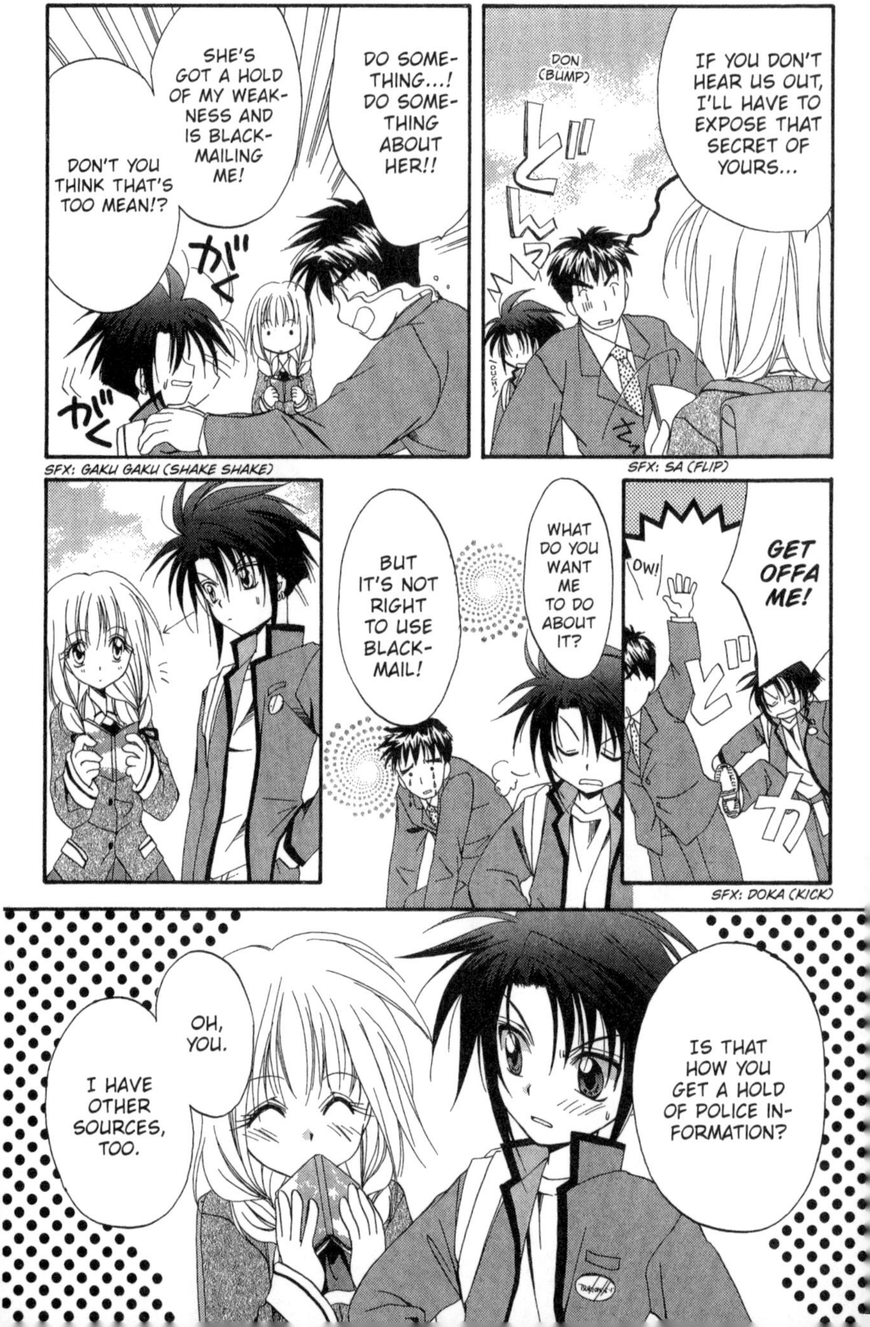
IF YOU DON'T HEAR US OUT, I'LL HAVE TO EXPOSE THAT SECRET OF YOURS...
DON (BUMP)
OUCH!
SFX: SA (FLIP)
DO SOMETHING...! DO SOMETHING ABOUT HER!!
SHE'S GOT A HOLD OF MY WEAKNESS AND IS BLACKMAILING ME!
DON'T YOU THINK THAT'S TOO MEAN!?
SFX: GAKU GAKU (SHAKE SHAKE)
GET OFFA ME!
OW!
SFX: DOKA (KICK)
WHAT DO YOU WANT ME TO DO ABOUT IT?
BUT IT'S NOT RIGHT TO USE BLACKMAIL!
IS THAT HOW YOU GET A HOLD OF POLICE INFORMATION?
OH, YOU.
I HAVE OTHER SOURCES, TOO.

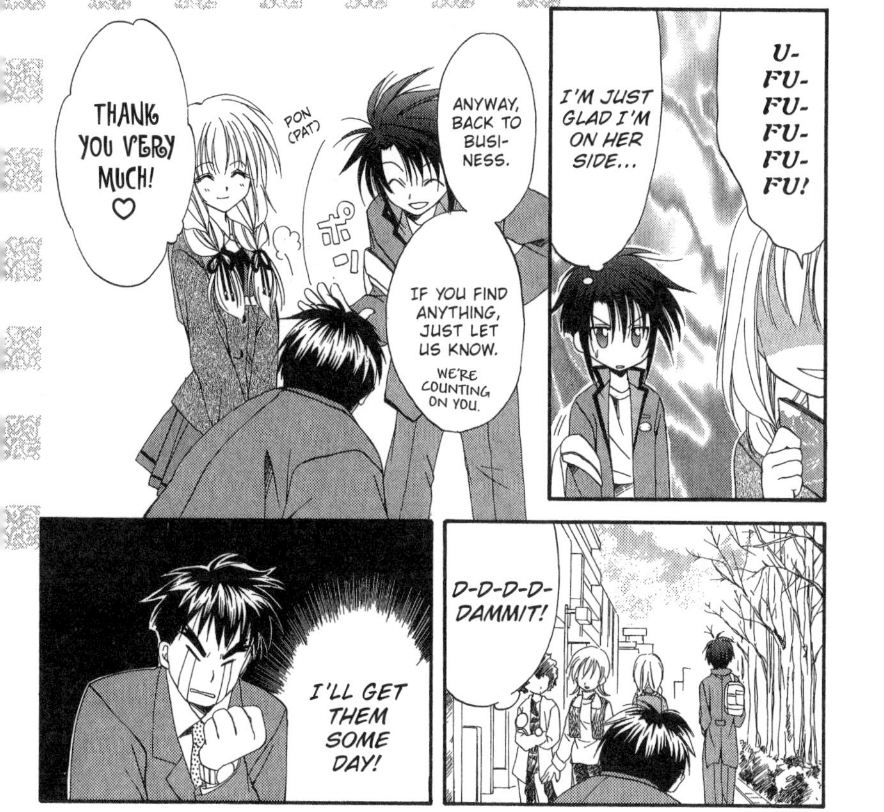
U-FU-FU-FU-FU-FU!
I'M JUST GLAD I'M ON HER SIDE...
ANYWAY, BACK TO BUSI-NESS.
IF YOU FIND ANYTHING, JUST LET US KNOW.
WE'RE COUNTING ON YOU.
PON (PAT)
ポン
THANK YOU VERY MUCH! ♡
D-D-D-D-DAMMIT!
I'LL GET THEM SOME DAY!

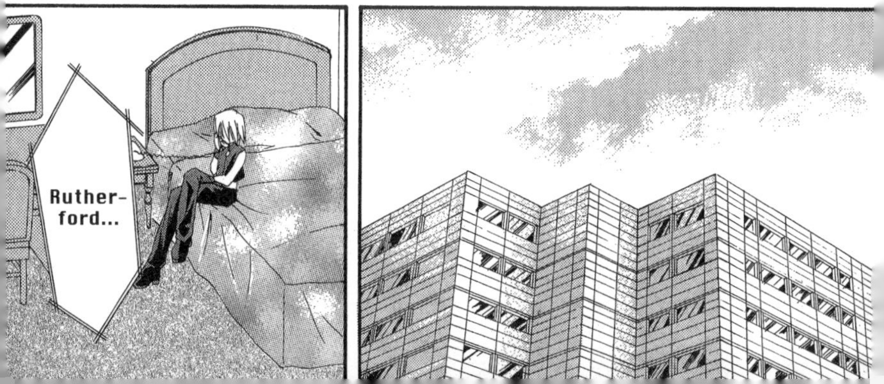
Ruther-ford...

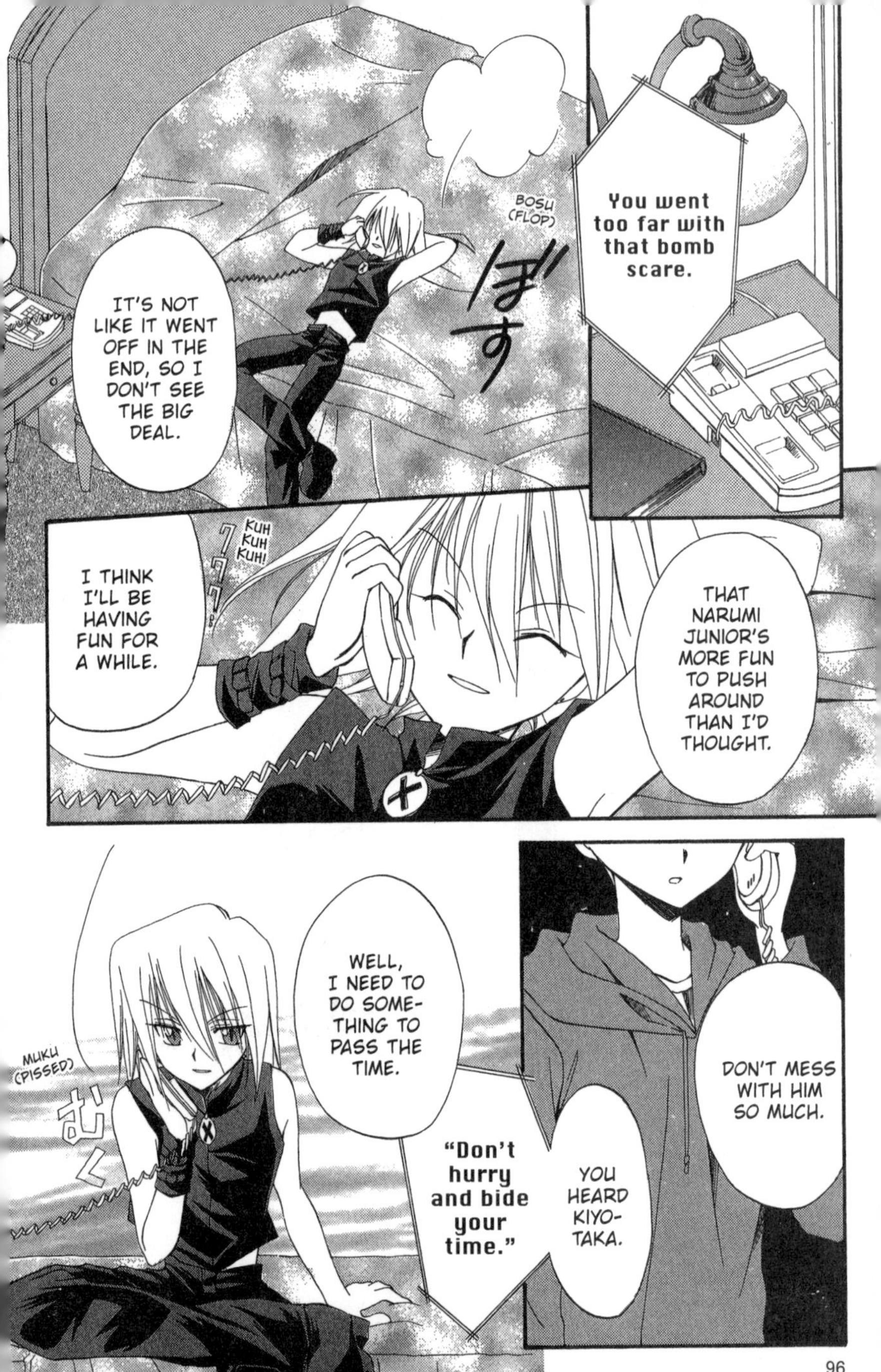
You went too far with that bomb scare.
BOSU (FLOP)
ぼす
IT'S NOT LIKE IT WENT OFF IN THE END, SO I DON'T SEE THE BIG DEAL.
THAT NARUMI JUNIOR'S MORE FUN TO PUSH AROUND THAN I'D THOUGHT.
KUH KUH KUH!
I THINK I'LL BE HAVING FUN FOR A WHILE.
DON'T MESS WITH HIM SO MUCH.
YOU HEARD KIYOTAKA.
"Don't hurry and bide your time."
WELL, I NEED TO DO SOMETHING TO PASS THE TIME.
MUKU (PISSED)
むく

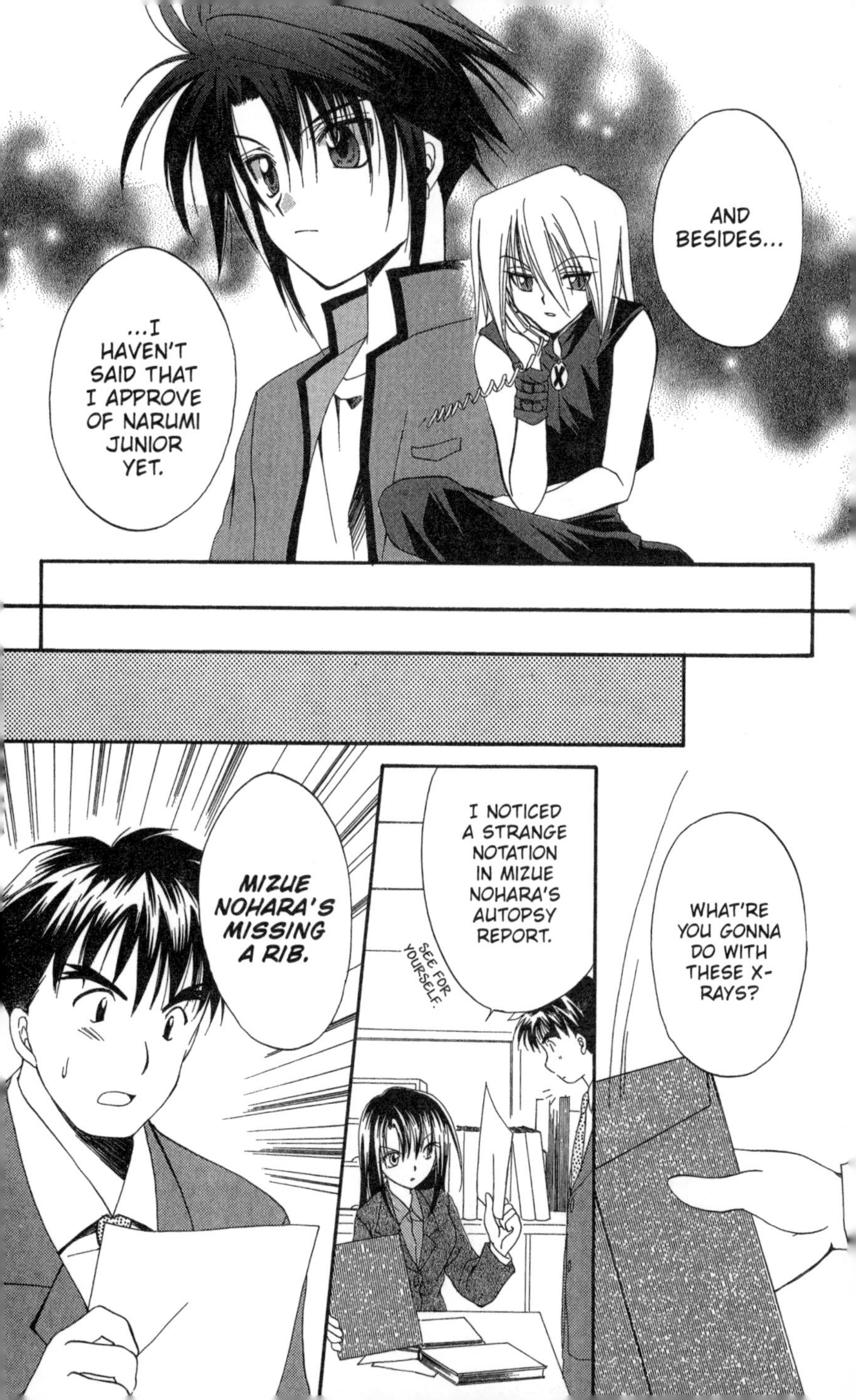
AND BESIDES...
...I HAVEN'T SAID THAT I APPROVE OF NARUMI JUNIOR YET.
WHAT'RE YOU GONNA DO WITH THESE X-RAYS?
I NOTICED A STRANGE NOTATION IN MIZUE NOHARA'S AUTOPSY REPORT.
SEE FOR YOURSELF.
MIZUE NOHARA'S MISSING A RIB.

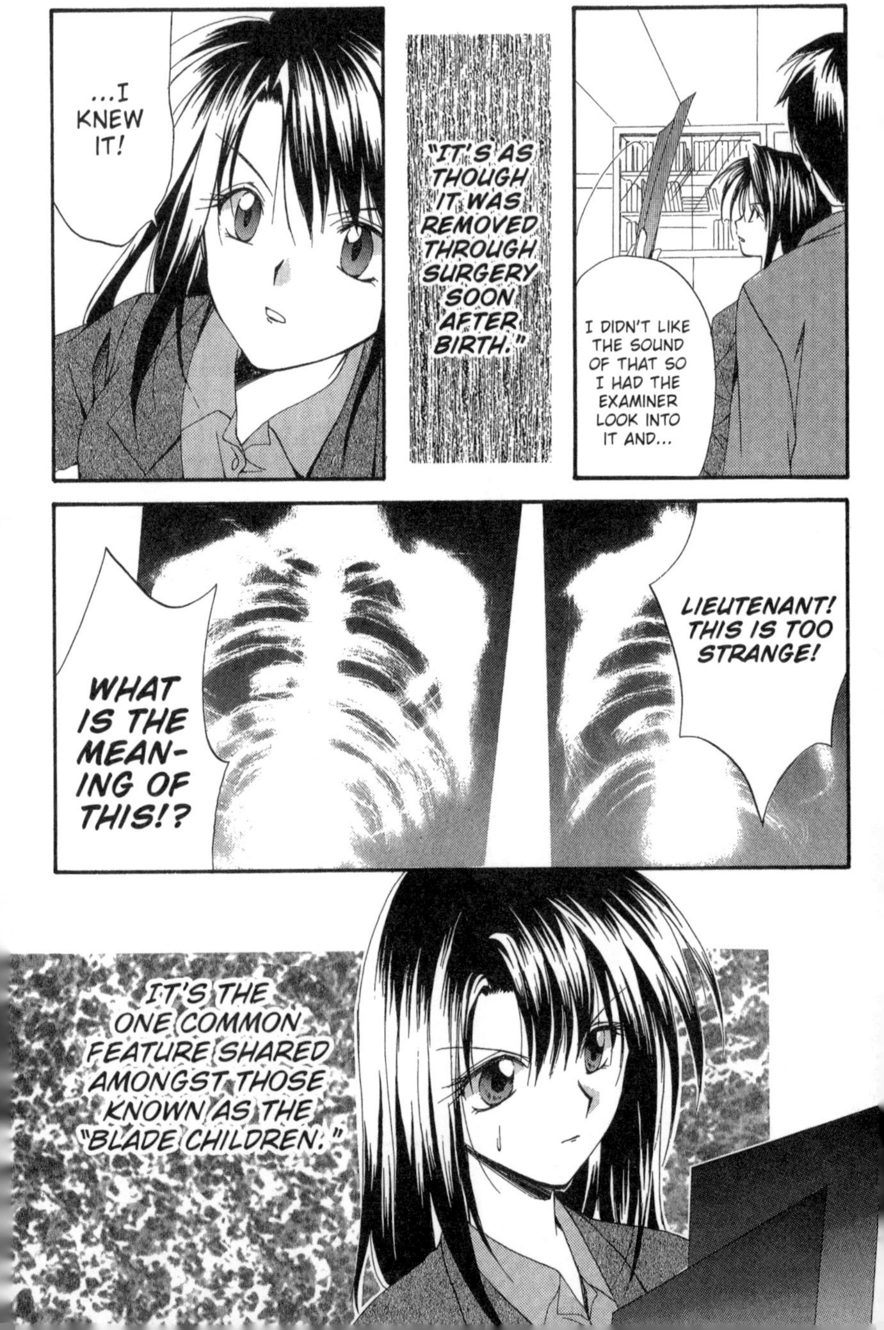
I DIDN'T LIKE THE SOUND OF THAT SO I HAD THE EXAMINER LOOK INTO IT AND...
"IT'S AS THOUGH IT WAS REMOVED THROUGH SURGERY SOON AFTER BIRTH."
...I KNEW IT!
LIEUTENANT! THIS IS TOO STRANGE!
WHAT IS THE MEAN-ING OF THIS!?
IT'S THE ONE COMMON FEATURE SHARED AMONGST THOSE KNOWN AS THE "BLADE CHILDREN."

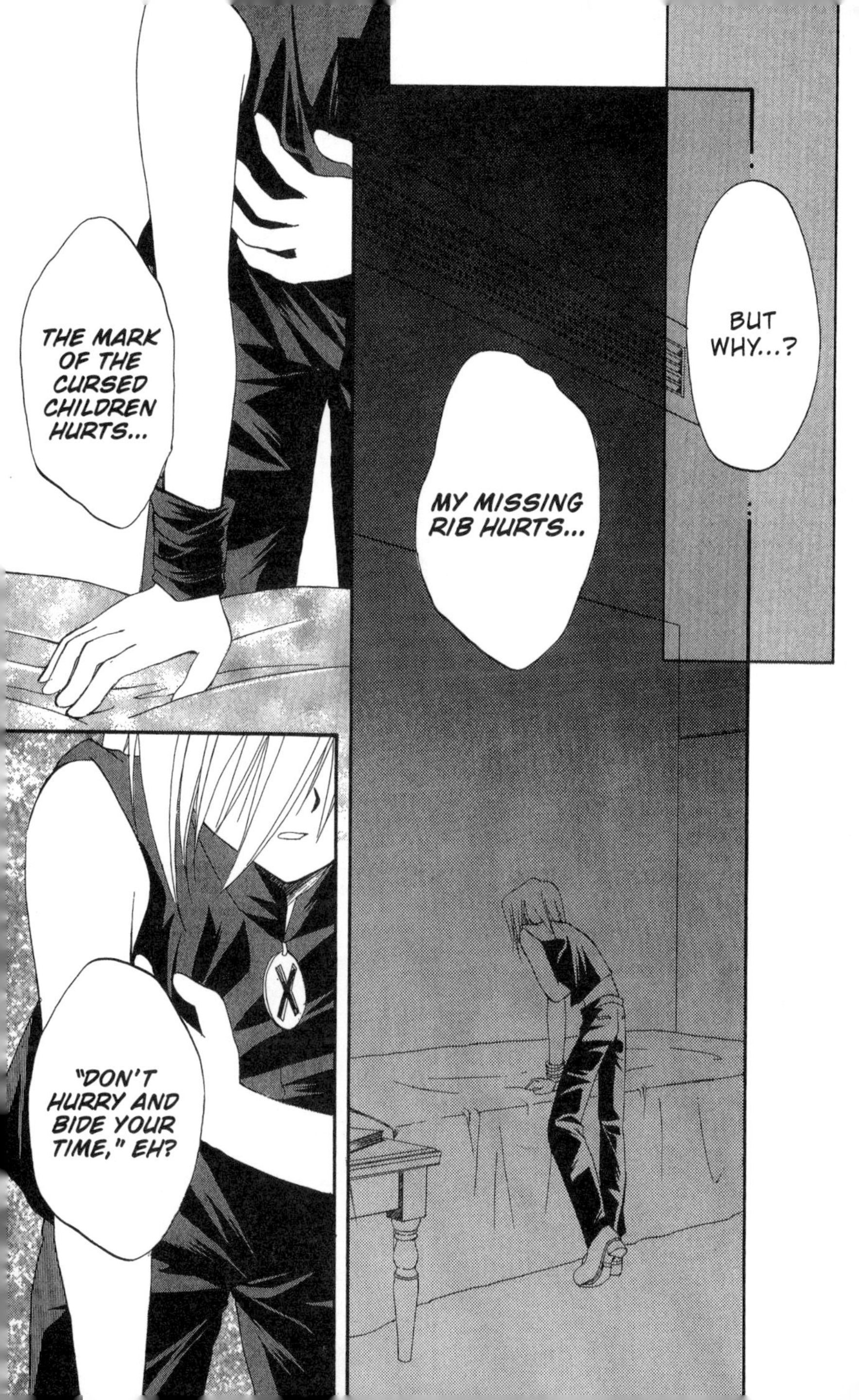
BUT WHY...?
MY MISSING RIB HURTS...
THE MARK OF THE CURSED CHILDREN HURTS...
"DON'T HURRY AND BIDE YOUR TIME," EH?

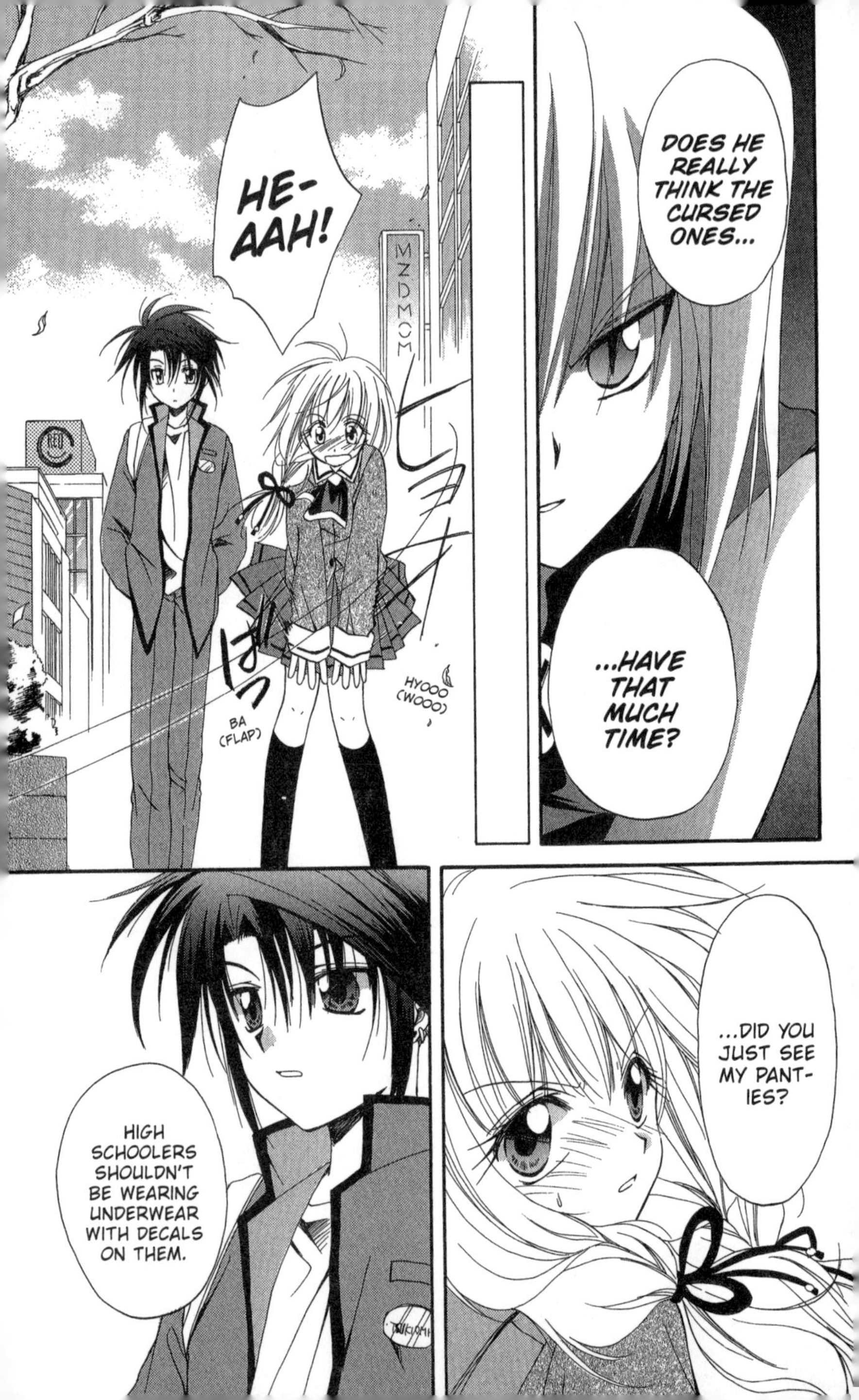
DOES HE REALLY THINK THE CURSED ONES...
...HAVE THAT MUCH TIME?
HE-AAH!
HYOOO (WOOO)
BA (FLAP)
...DID YOU JUST SEE MY PANT-IES?
HIGH SCHOOLERS SHOULDN'T BE WEARING UNDERWEAR WITH DECALS ON THEM.

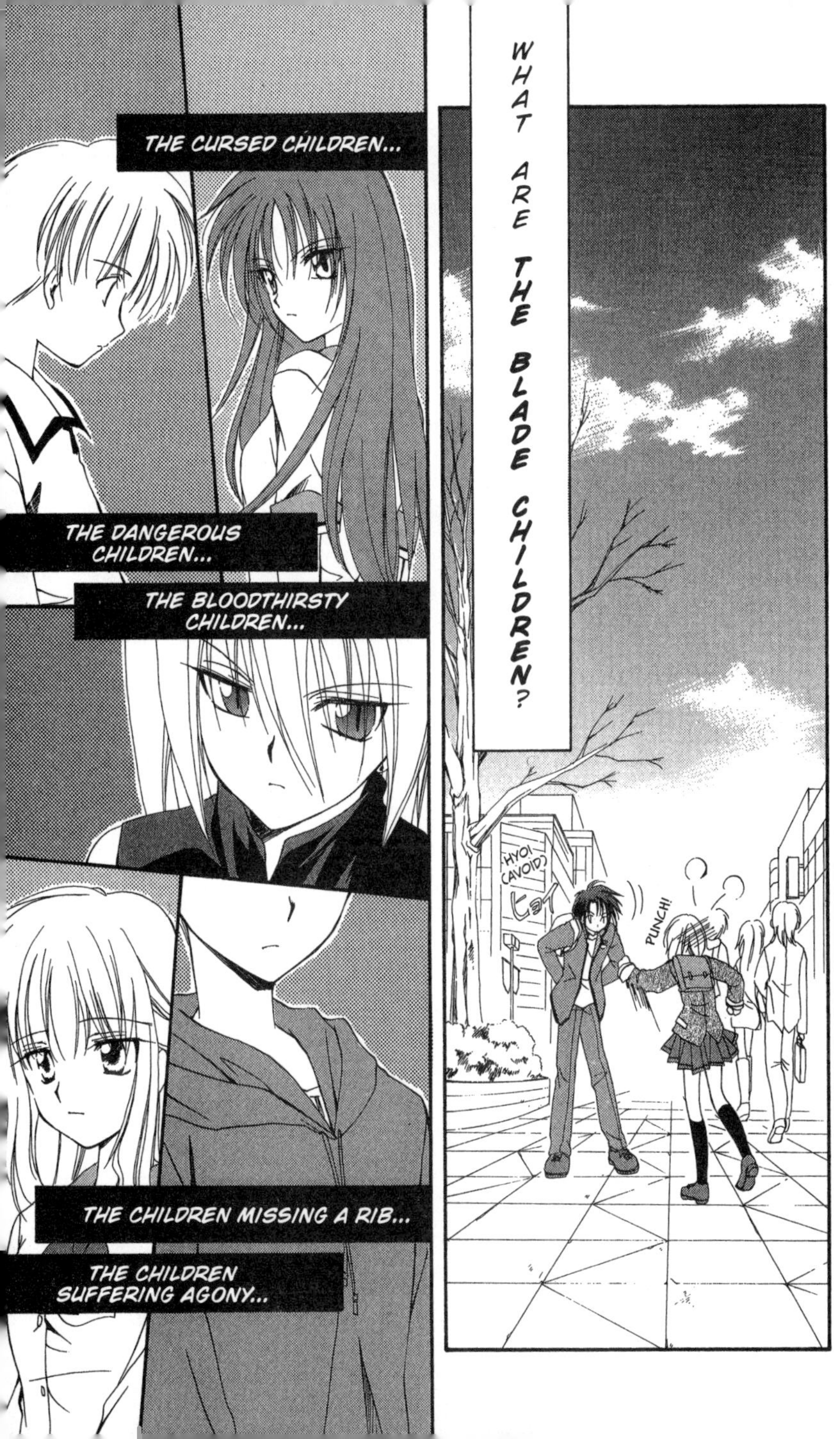
WHAT ARE THE BLADE CHILDREN?
HYOI (AVOID)
ヒョイ
PUNCH!
THE CURSED CHILDREN...
THE DANGEROUS CHILDREN...
THE BLOODTHIRSTY CHILDREN...
THE CHILDREN MISSING A RIB...
THE CHILDREN SUFFERING AGONY...

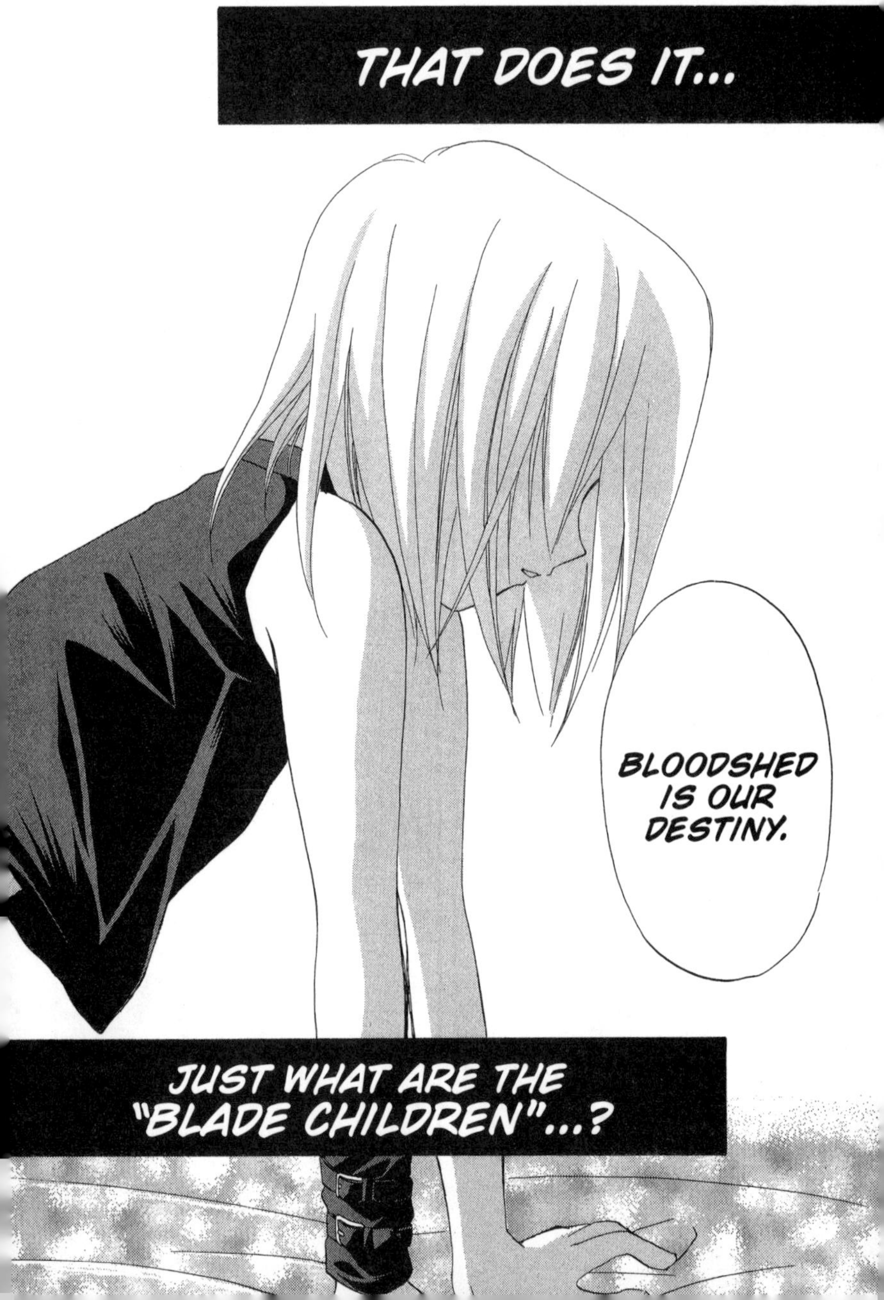
THAT DOES IT...
BLOODSHED IS OUR DESTINY.
JUST WHAT ARE THE "BLADE CHILDREN"...?

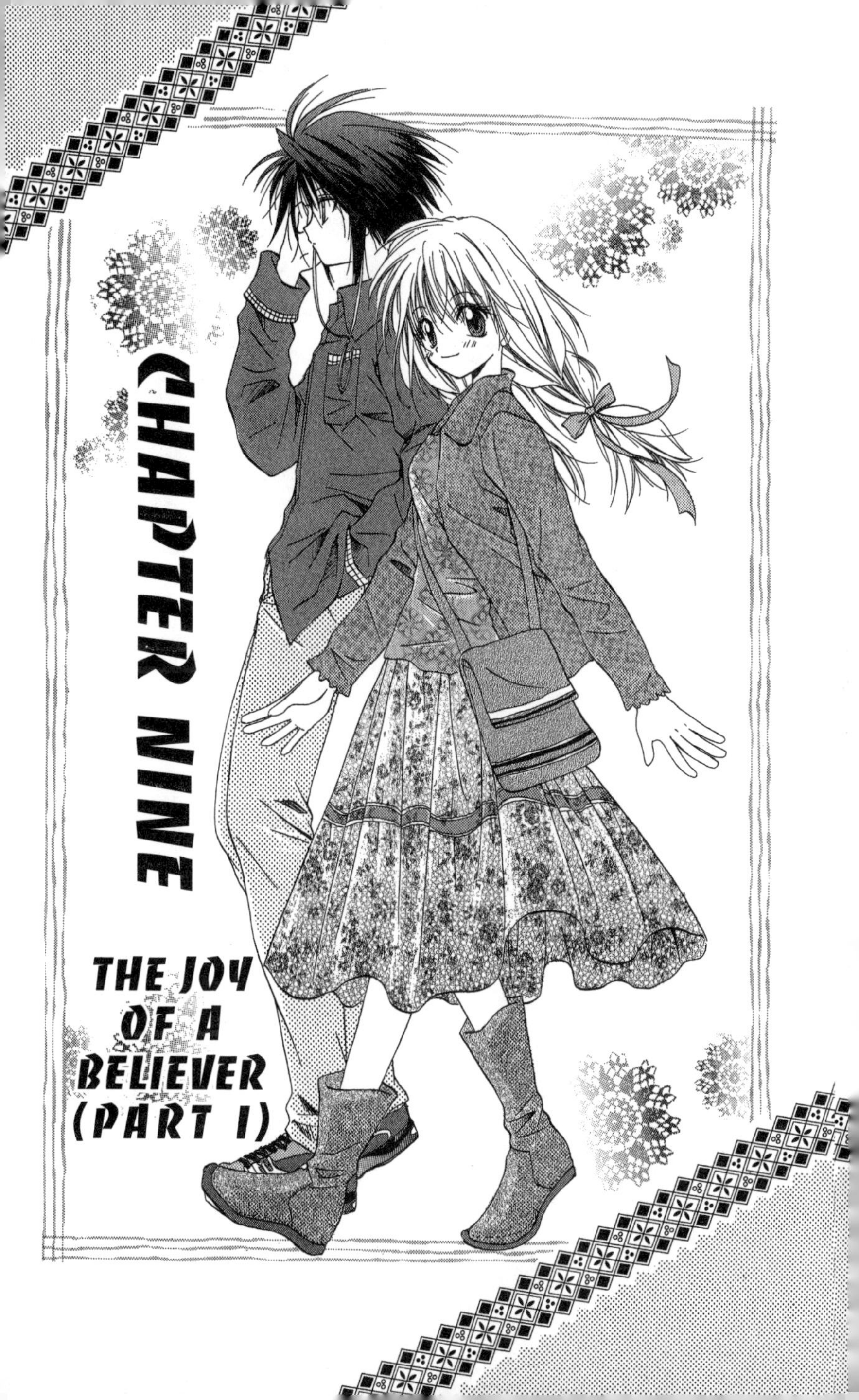
CHAPTER NINE
THE JOY OF A BELIEVER (PART 1)

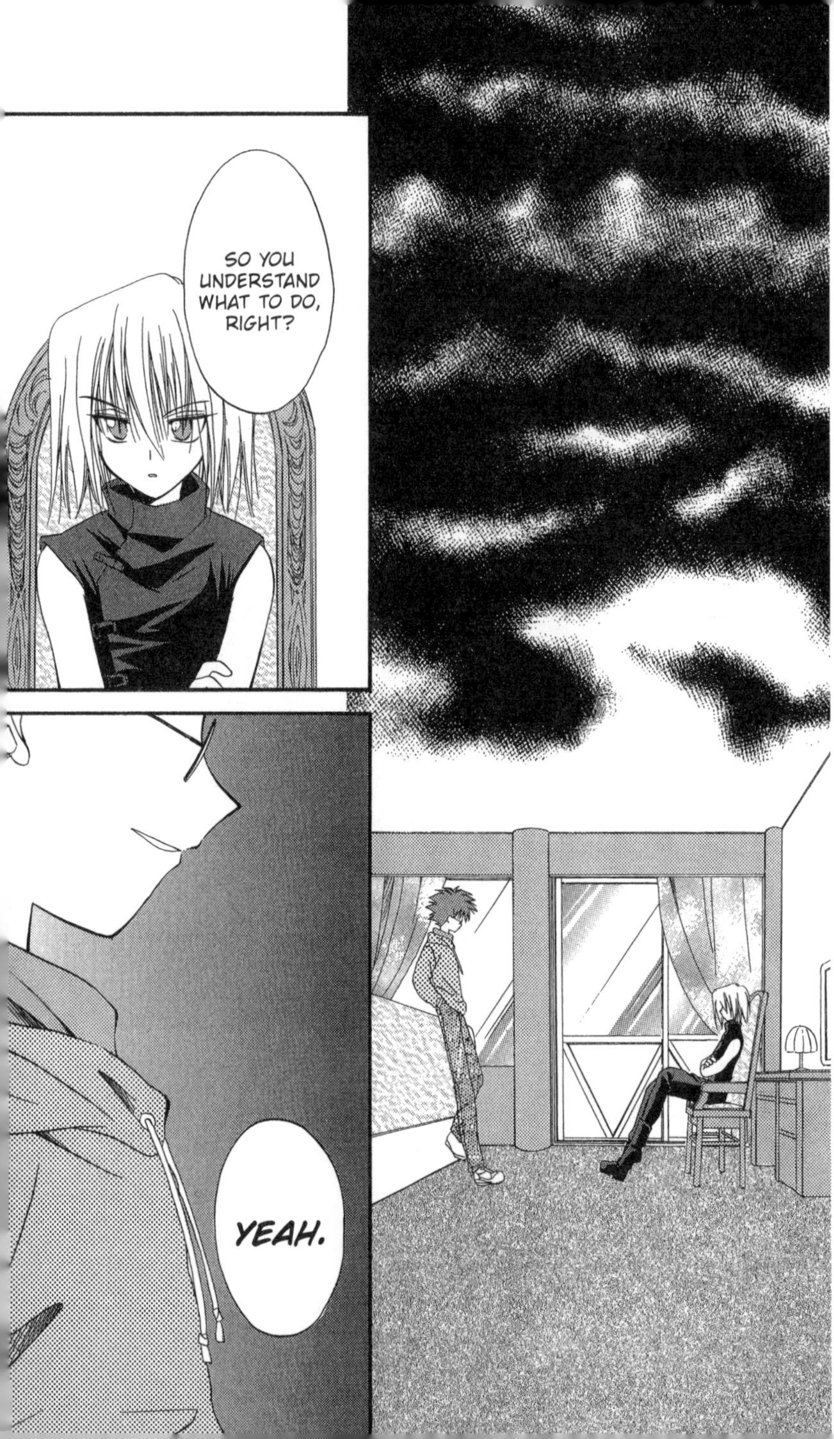
SO YOU UNDERSTAND WHAT TO DO, RIGHT?
YEAH.

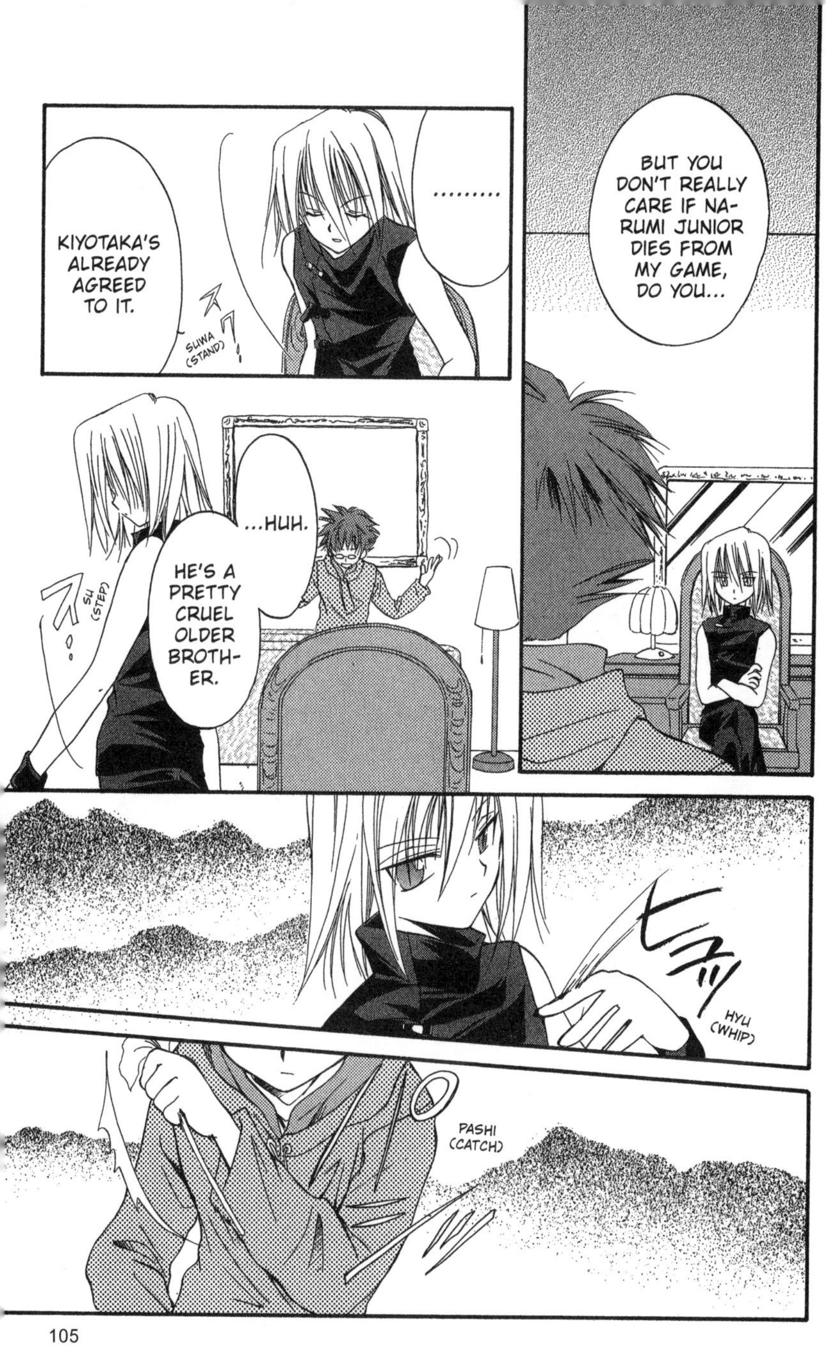
BUT YOU DON'T REALLY CARE IF NA-RUMI JUNIOR DIES FROM MY GAME, DO YOU...
....
KIYOTAKA'S ALREADY AGREED TO IT.
SUWA (STAND)
...HUH.
HE'S A PRETTY CRUEL OLDER BROTH-ER.
SU (STEP)
HYU (WHIP)
PASHI (CATCH)

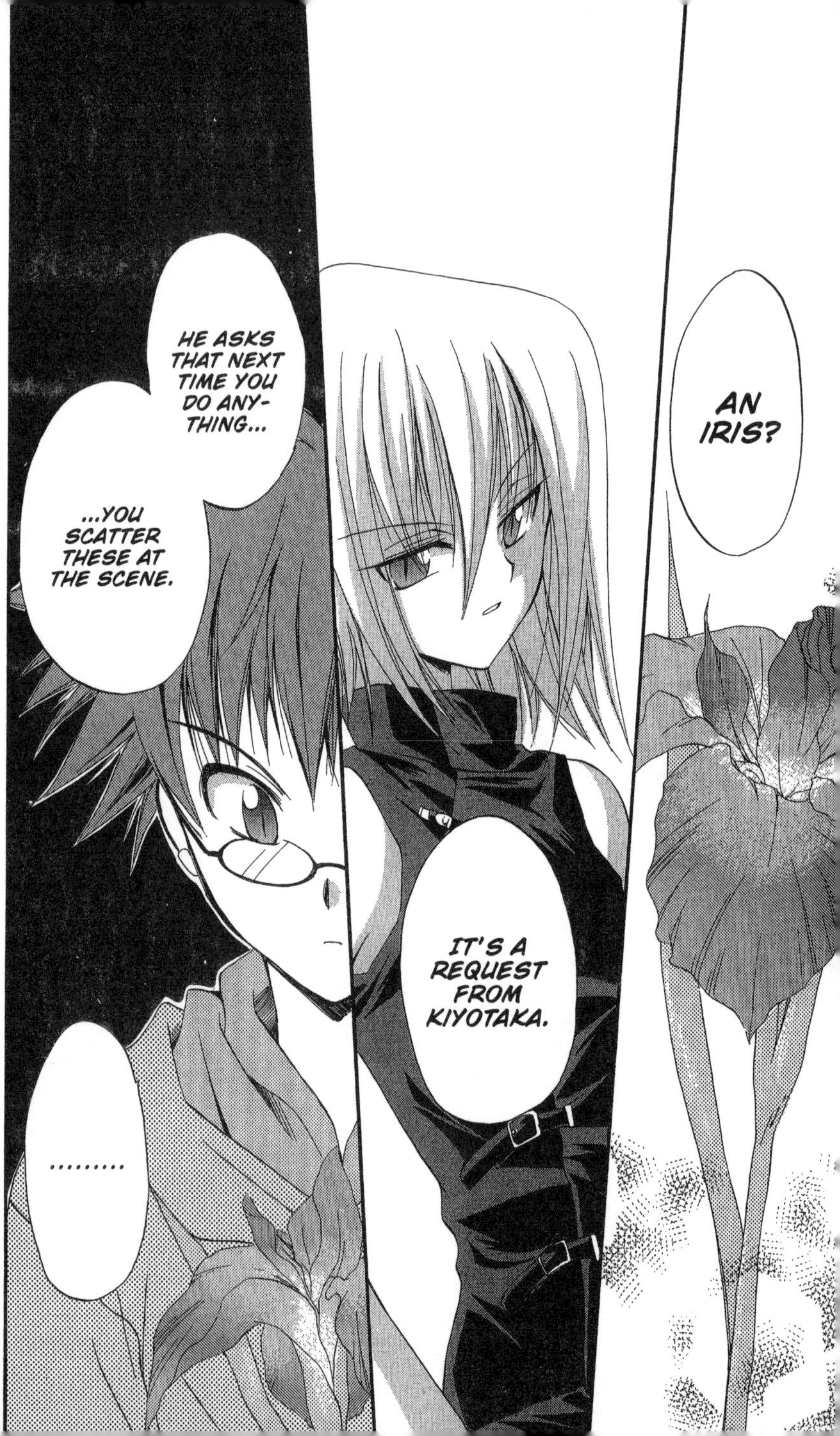
AN IRIS?
IT'S A REQUEST FROM KIYOTAKA.
HE ASKS THAT NEXT TIME YOU DO ANY-THING...
...YOU SCATTER THESE AT THE SCENE.
....

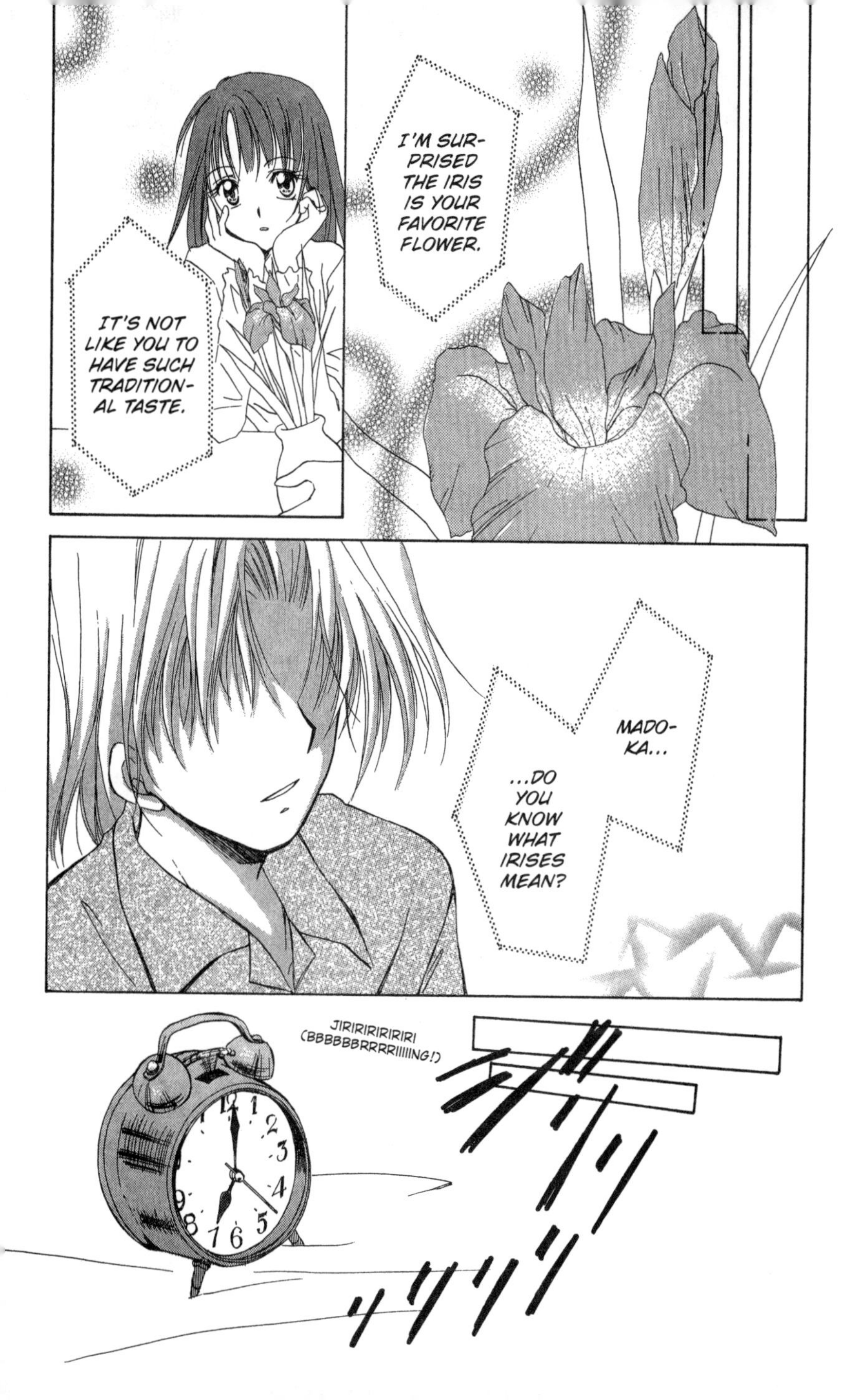
I'M SURPRISED THE IRIS IS YOUR FAVORITE FLOWER.
IT'S NOT LIKE YOU TO HAVE SUCH TRADITIONAL TASTE.
MADOKA...
...DO YOU KNOW WHAT IRISES MEAN?
JIRIRIRIRIRIRI
(BBBBBBRRRRRIIIIIING!)

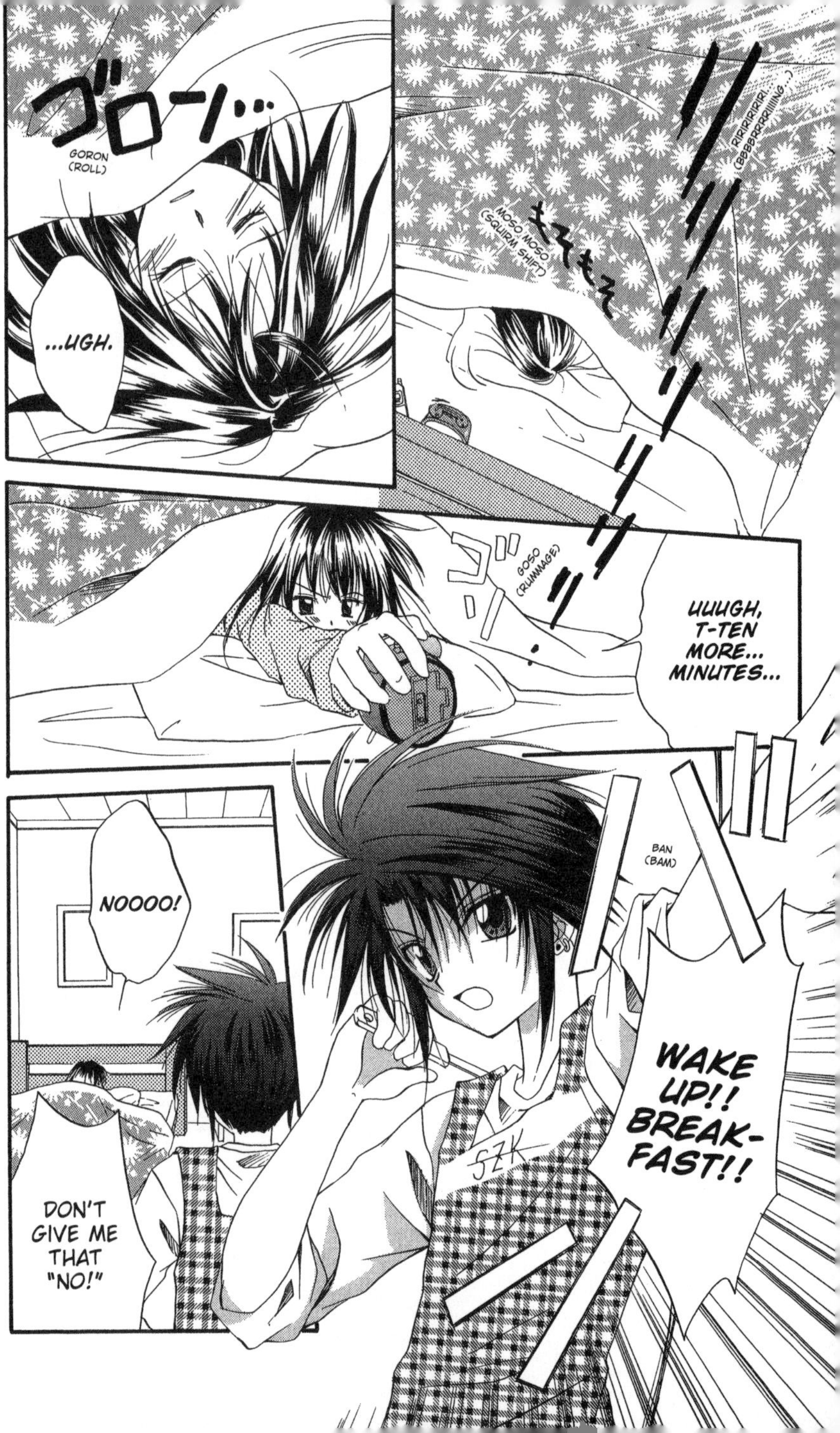

RIRIRIRIRIRI (BBBBRRRRIIIIING...)
MOSO MOSO (SQUIRM SHIFT)
GORON (ROLL)
...UGH.
GOSO (RUMMAGE)
UUUGH, T-TEN MORE... MINUTES...
BAN (BAM)
WAKE UP!! BREAK-FAST!!
SZK
NOOOO!
DON'T GIVE ME THAT "NO!"

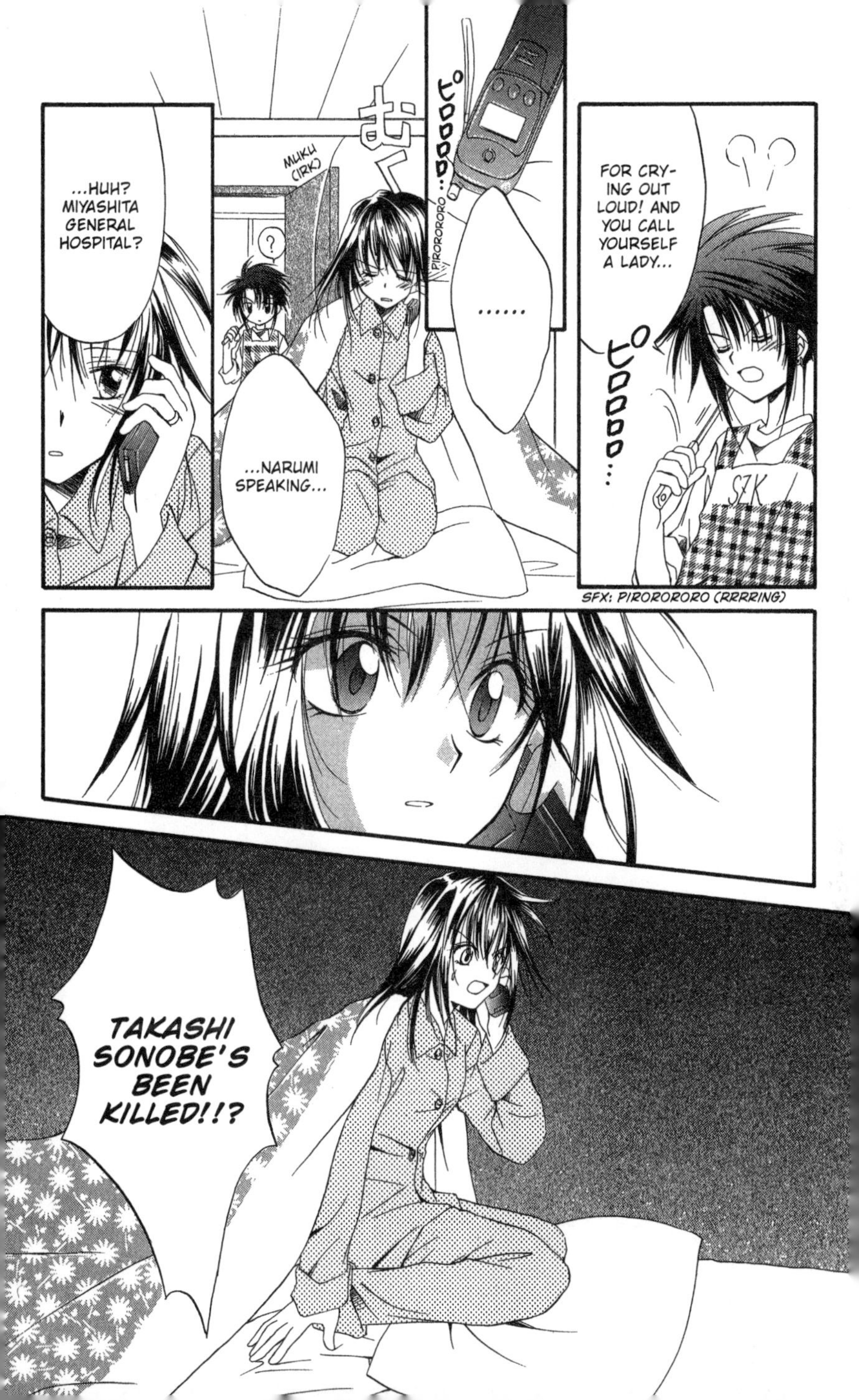
FOR CRY-ING OUT LOUD! AND YOU CALL YOURSELF A LADY...
PIROROROR
......
MUKU (IRK)
...NARUMI SPEAKING...
...HUH? MIYASHITA GENERAL HOSPITAL?
SFX: PIROROROR (RRRING)
TAKASHI SONOBE'S BEEN KILLED!!?

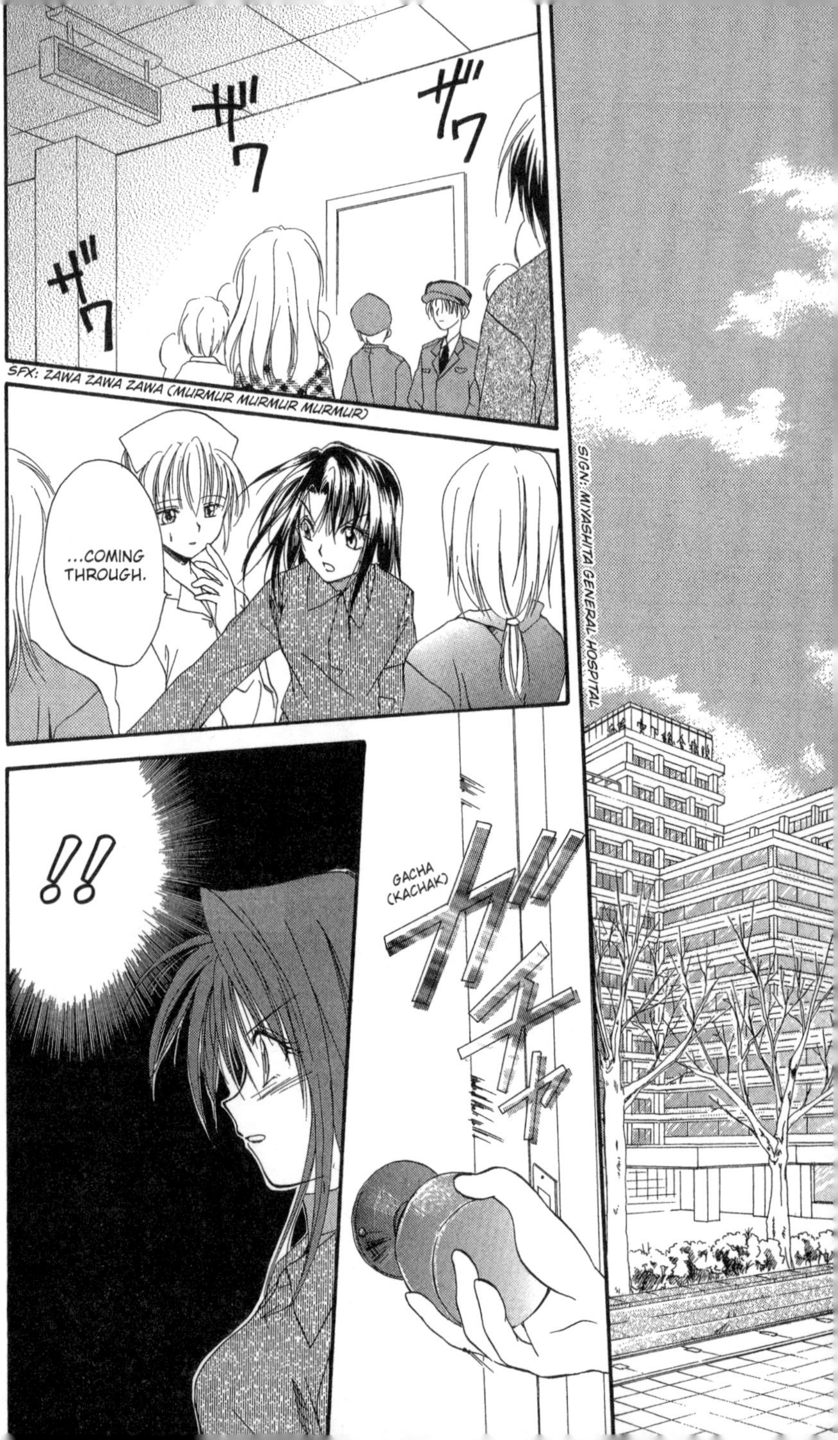
SIGN: MIYASHITA GENERAL HOSPITAL
ザワ
ザワ
ザワ
SFX: ZAWA ZAWA ZAWA (MURMUR MURMUR MURMUR)
...COMING THROUGH.
ガチャ
GACHA (KACHAK)
!!

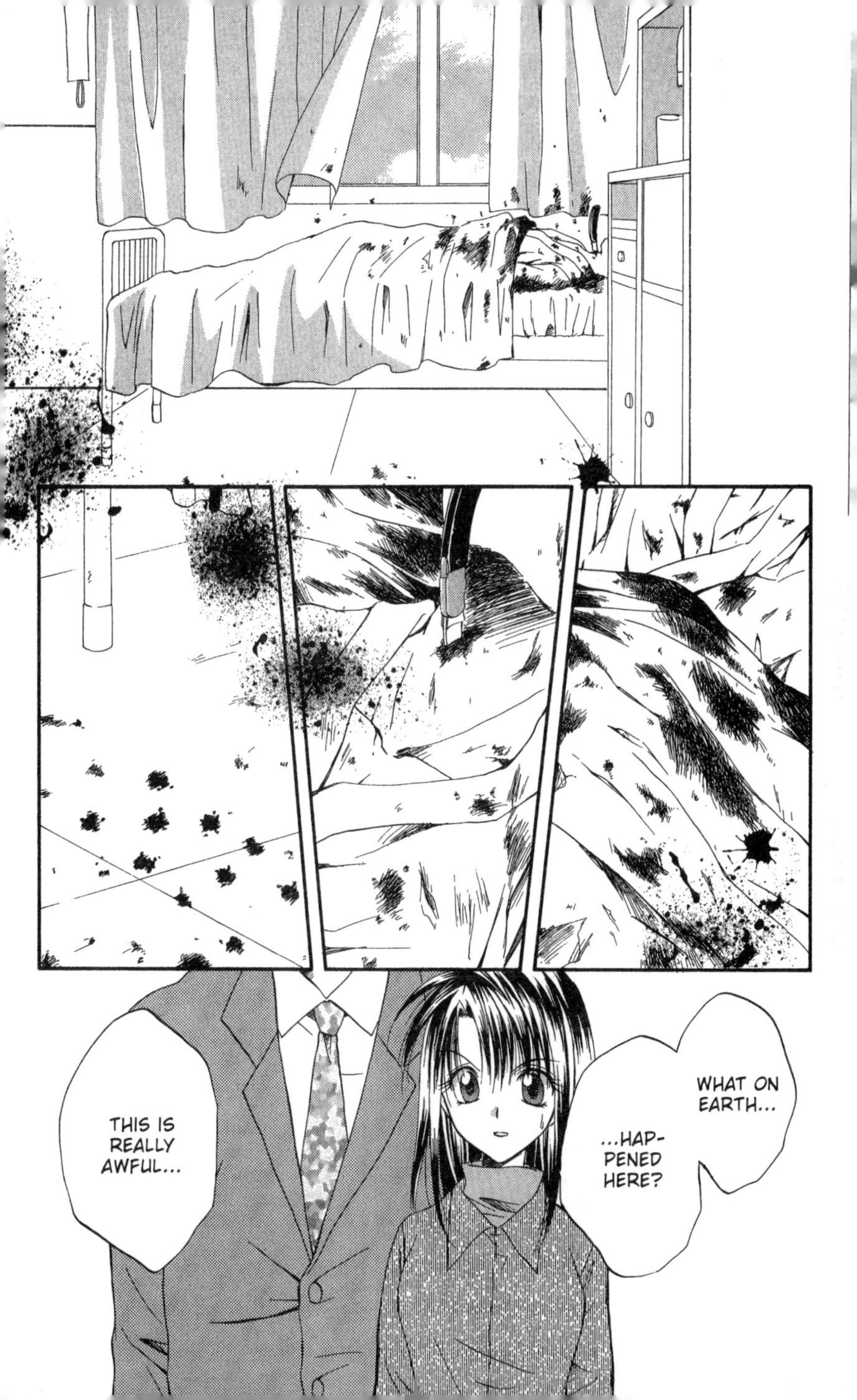
WHAT ON EARTH...
...HAP-PENED HERE?
THIS IS REALLY AWFUL...

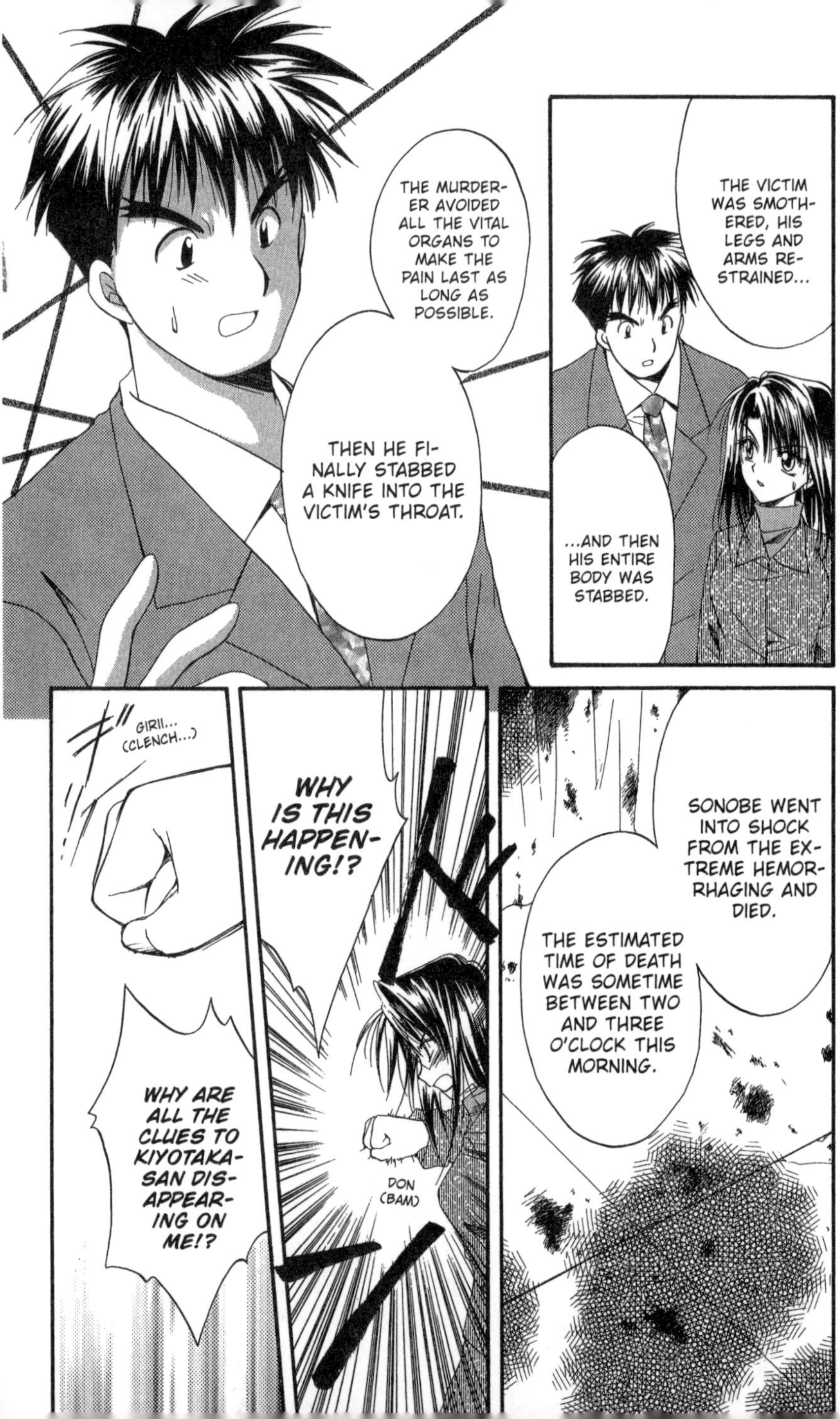
THE VICTIM WAS SMOTHERED, HIS LEGS AND ARMS RESTRAINED...
...AND THEN HIS ENTIRE BODY WAS STABBED.
THE MURDERER AVOIDED ALL THE VITAL ORGANS TO MAKE THE PAIN LAST AS LONG AS POSSIBLE.
THEN HE FINALLY STABBED A KNIFE INTO THE VICTIM'S THROAT.
SONOBE WENT INTO SHOCK FROM THE EXTREME HEMORRHAGING AND DIED.
THE ESTIMATED TIME OF DEATH WAS SOMETIME BETWEEN TWO AND THREE O'CLOCK THIS MORNING.
WHY IS THIS HAPPENING!?
DON (BAM)
GIRII... (CLENCH...)
WHY ARE ALL THE CLUES TO KIYOTAKA-SAN DISAPPEARING ON ME!?

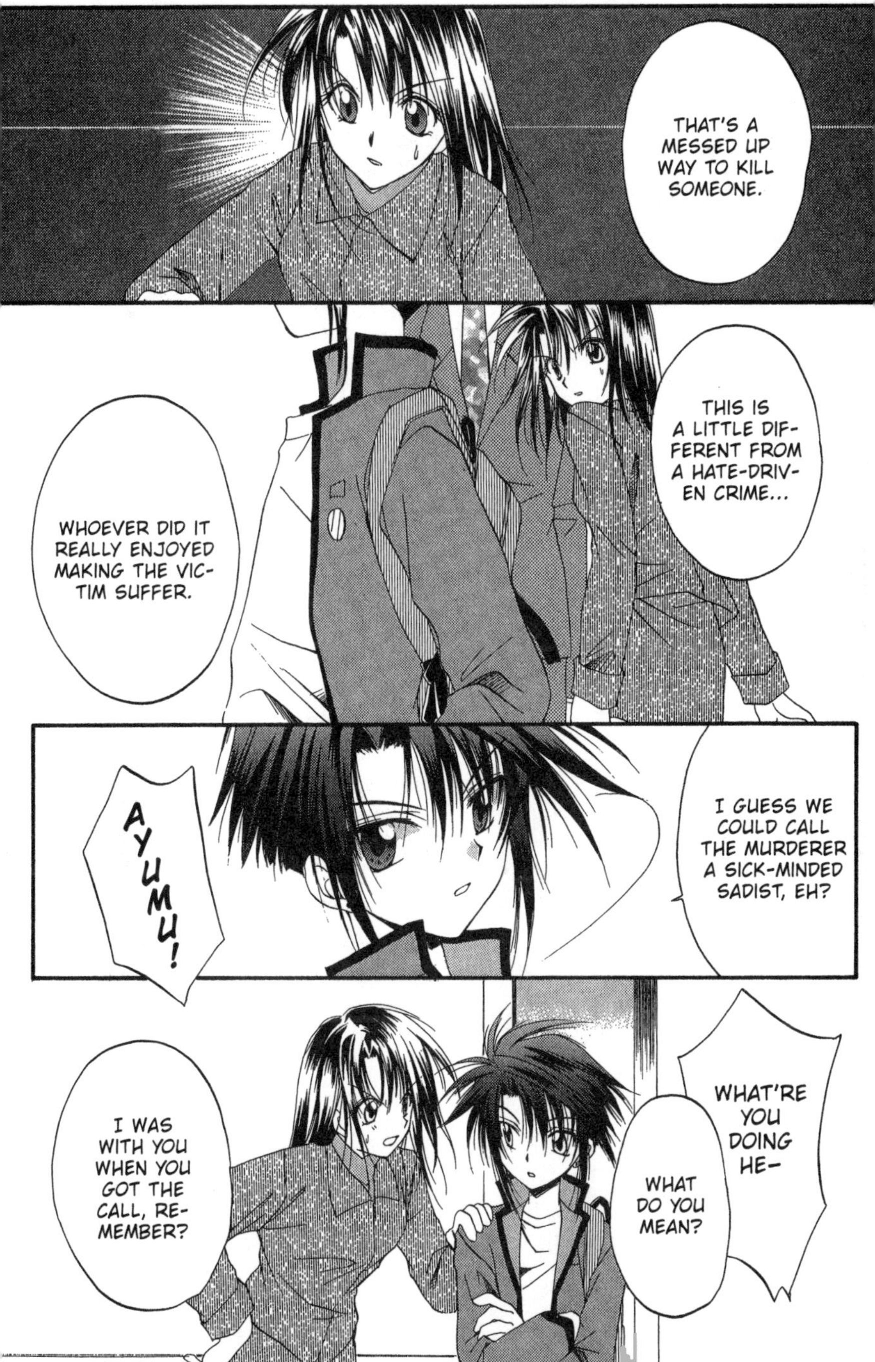
THAT'S A MESSED UP WAY TO KILL SOMEONE.
THIS IS A LITTLE DIF-FERENT FROM A HATE-DRIV-EN CRIME...
WHOEVER DID IT REALLY ENJOYED MAKING THE VIC-TIM SUFFER.
I GUESS WE COULD CALL THE MURDERER A SICK-MINDED SADIST, EH?
AYUMU!
WHAT'RE YOU DOING HE-
WHAT DO YOU MEAN?
I WAS WITH YOU WHEN YOU GOT THE CALL, RE-MEMBER?

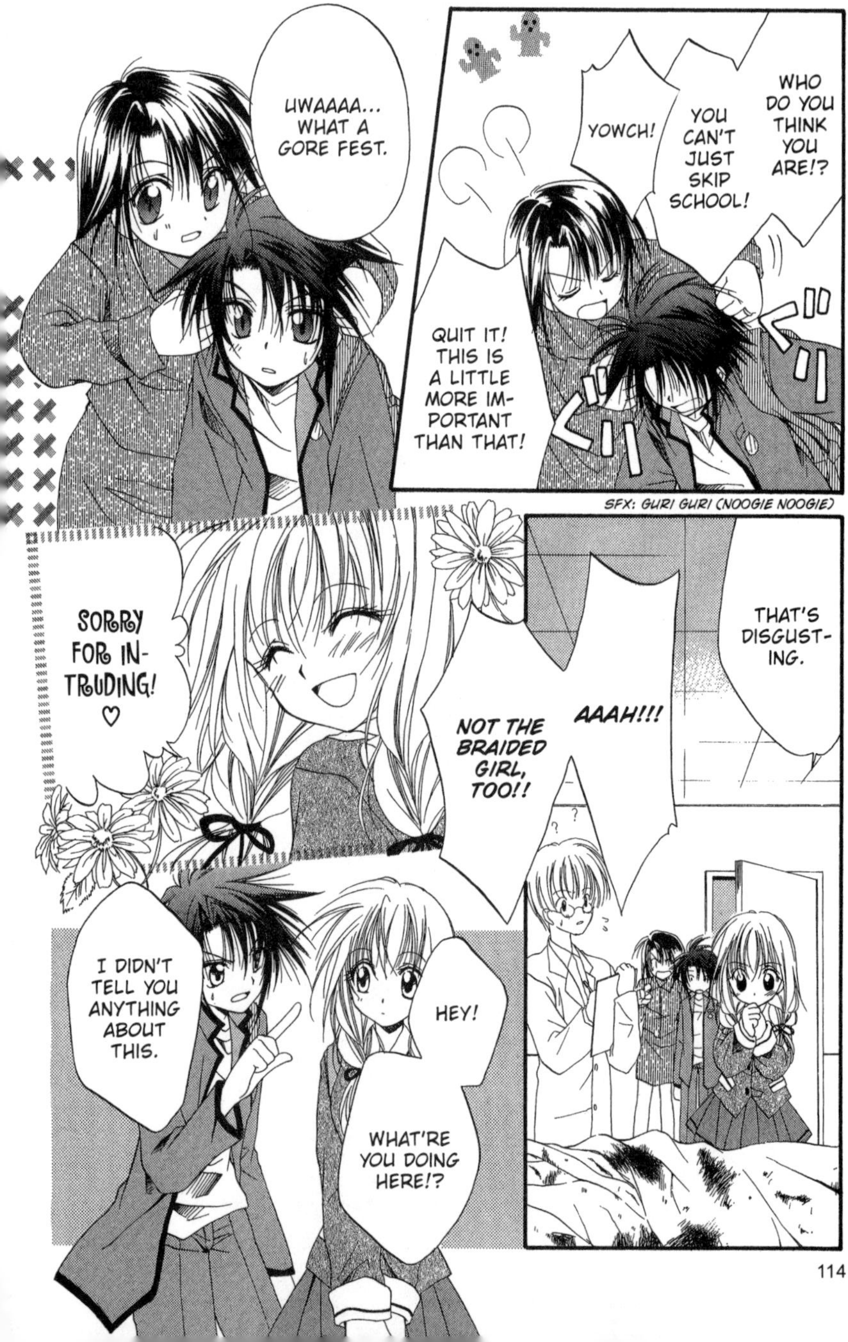

WHO DO YOU THINK YOU ARE!?
YOU CAN'T JUST SKIP SCHOOL!
YOWCH!
QUIT IT! THIS IS A LITTLE MORE IM-PORTANT THAN THAT!
SFX: GURI GURI (NOOGIE NOOGIE)
UWAAAA... WHAT A GORE FEST.
THAT'S DISGUST-ING.
AAAH!!!
NOT THE BRAIDED GIRL, TOO!!
SORRY FOR IN-TRUDING! ♡
HEY!
WHAT'RE YOU DOING HERE!?
I DIDN'T TELL YOU ANYTHING ABOUT THIS.

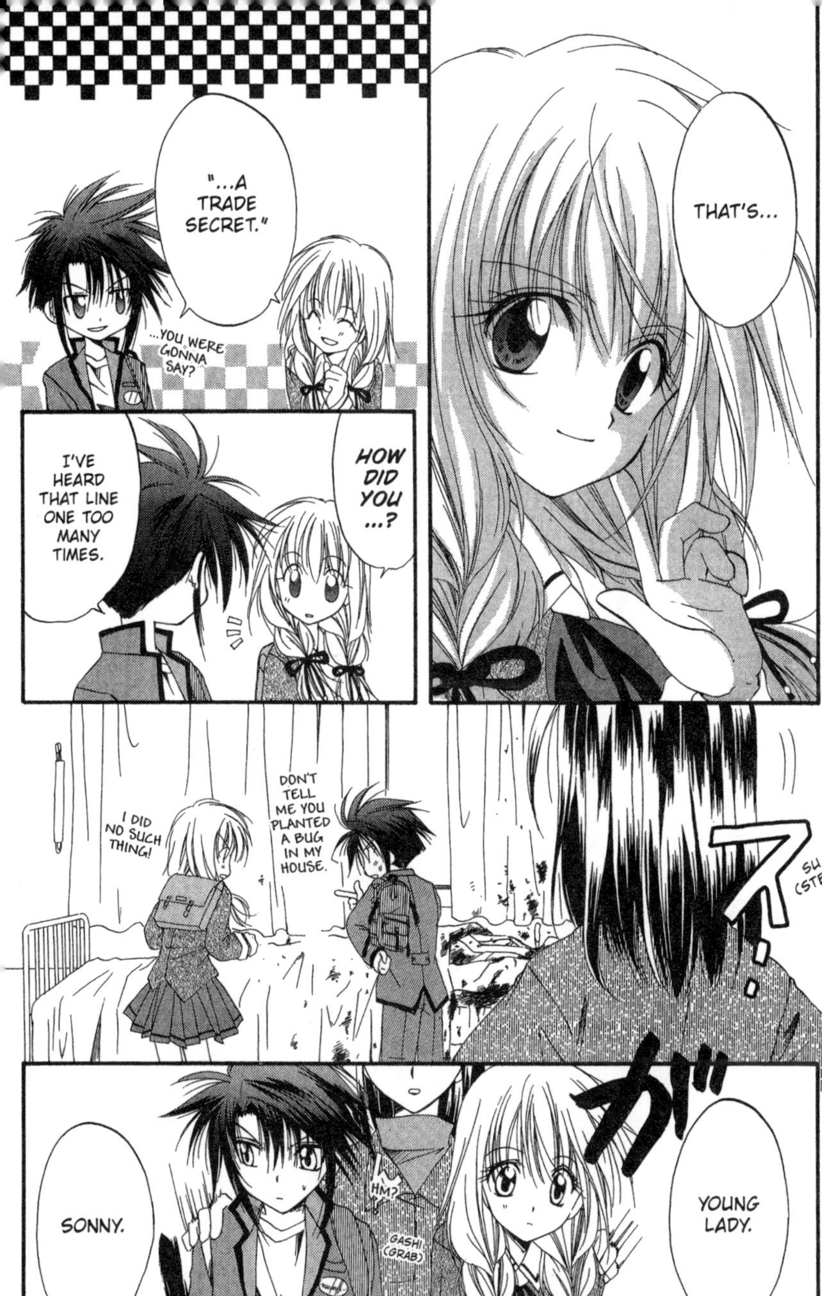
THAT'S...
"...A TRADE SECRET."
...YOU WERE GONNA SAY?
HOW DID YOU ...?
I'VE HEARD THAT LINE ONE TOO MANY TIMES.
ス
SU (STEP)
DON'T TELL ME YOU PLANTED A BUG IN MY HOUSE.
I DID NO SUCH THING!
ガ
YOUNG LADY.
HM?
GASHI (GRAB)
SONNY.

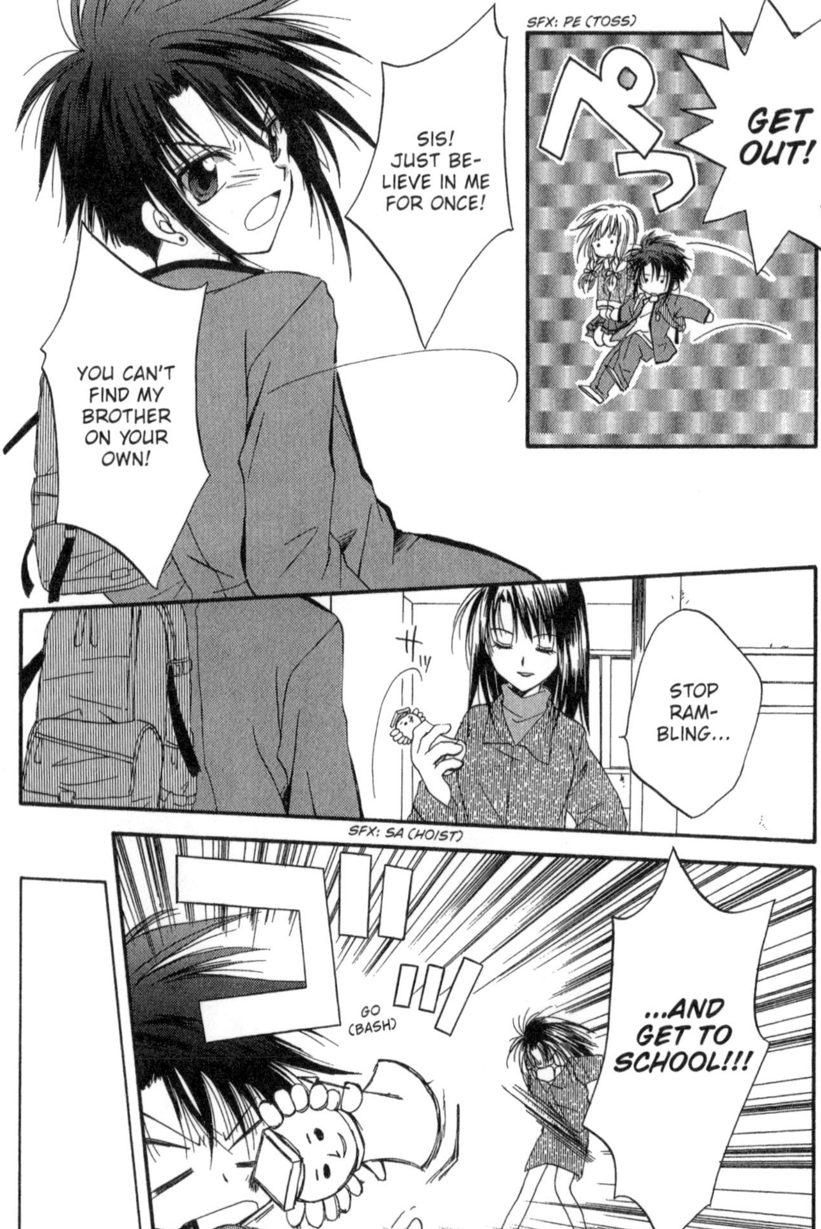
SFX: PE (TOSS)
GET OUT!
SIS! JUST BE-LIEVE IN ME FOR ONCE!
YOU CAN'T FIND MY BROTHER ON YOUR OWN!
STOP RAM-BLING...
SFX: SA (HOIST)
...AND GET TO SCHOOL!!!
GO (BASH)

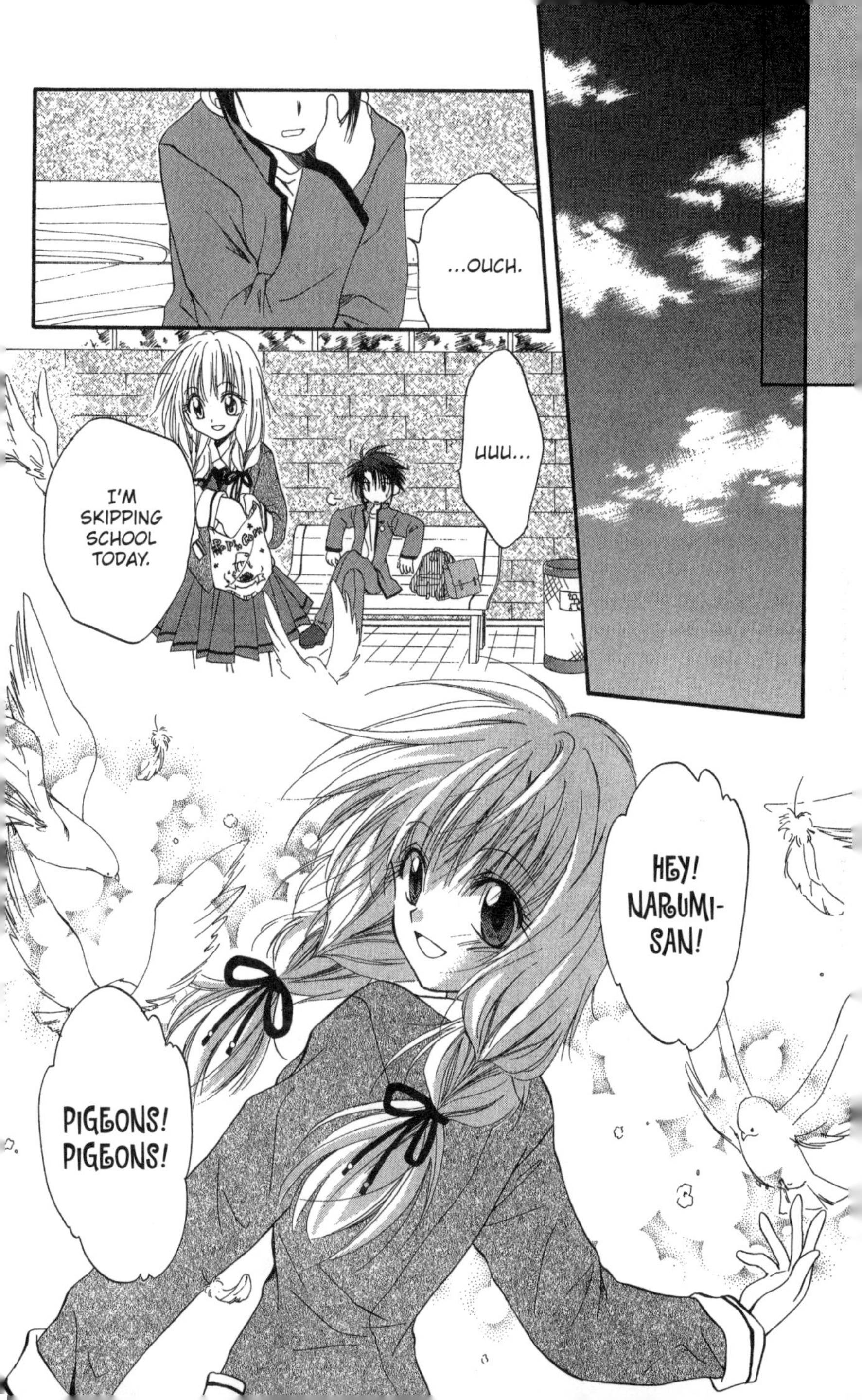
...OUCH.
UUU...
I'M SKIPPING SCHOOL TODAY.
HEY! NARUMI-SAN!
PIGEONS! PIGEONS!

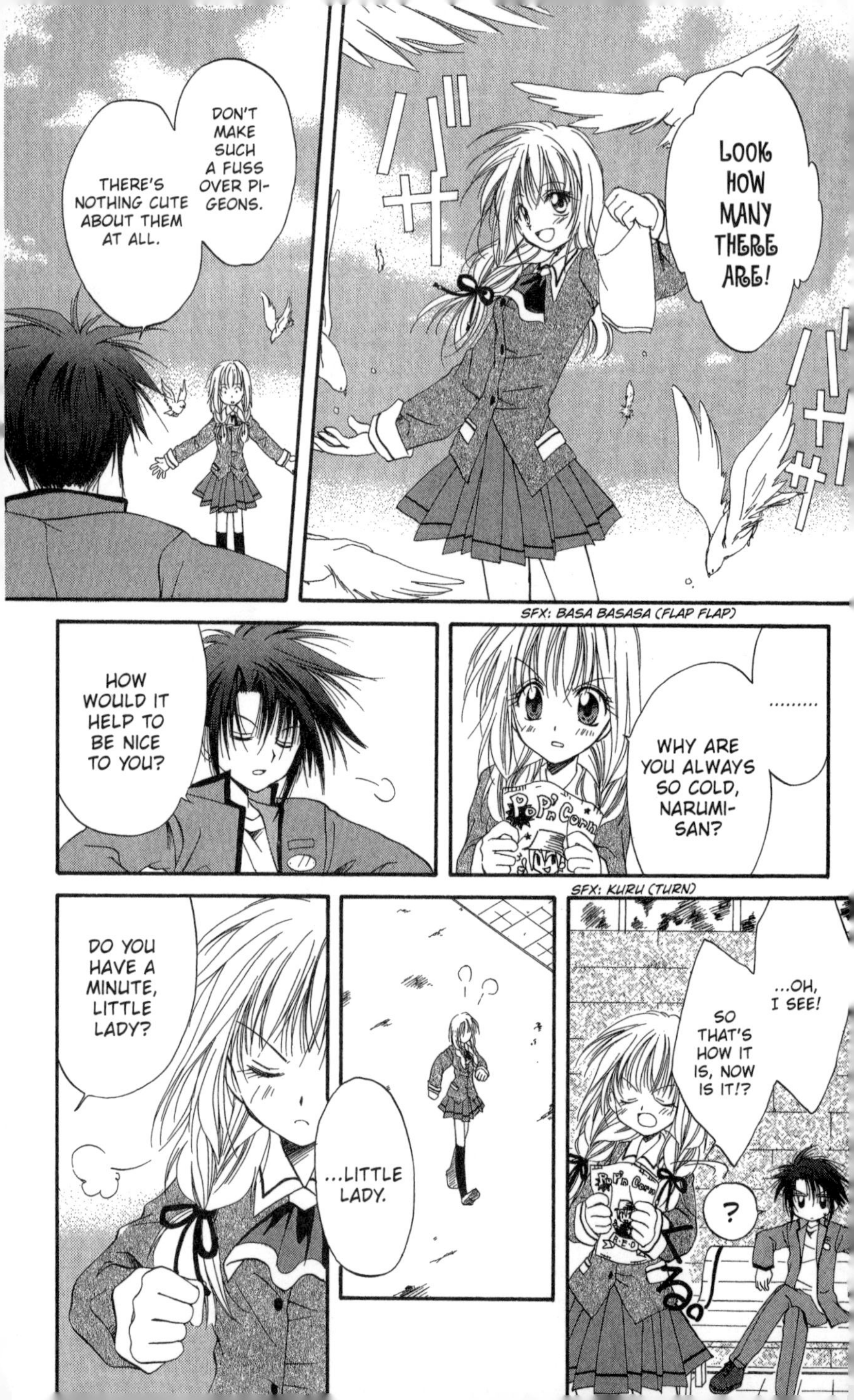
LOOK HOW MANY THERE ARE!
DON'T MAKE SUCH A FUSS OVER PI-GEONS.
THERE'S NOTHING CUTE ABOUT THEM AT ALL.
SFX: BASA BASASA (FLAP FLAP)
....
WHY ARE YOU ALWAYS SO COLD, NARUMI-SAN?
HOW WOULD IT HELP TO BE NICE TO YOU?
SFX: KURU (TURN)
...OH, I SEE!
SO THAT'S HOW IT IS, NOW IS IT!?
?
...LITTLE LADY.
DO YOU HAVE A MINUTE, LITTLE LADY?

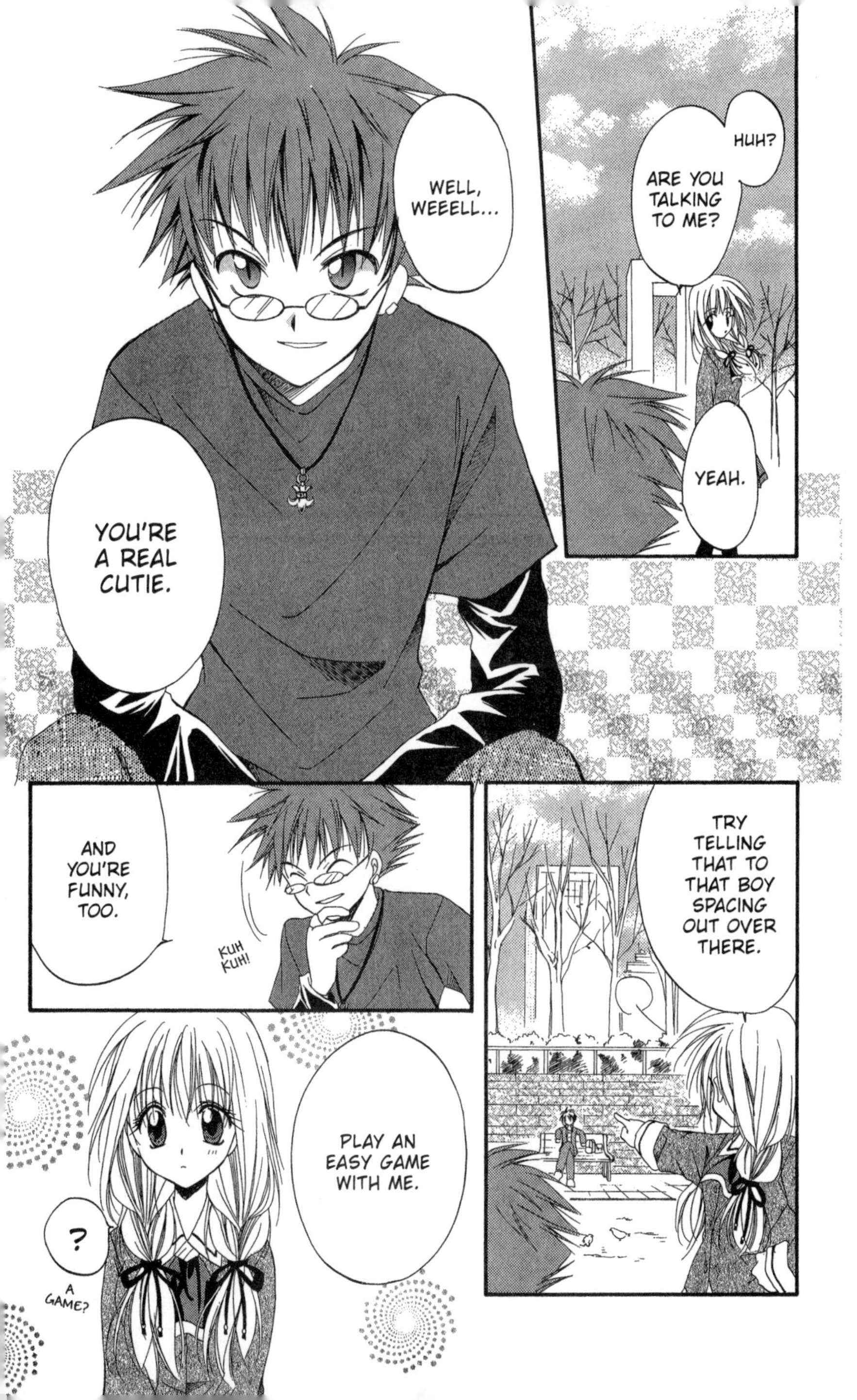
HUH?
ARE YOU TALKING TO ME?
YEAH.
WELL, WEEELL...
YOU'RE A REAL CUTIE.
TRY TELLING THAT TO THAT BOY SPACING OUT OVER THERE.
AND YOU'RE FUNNY, TOO.
KUH KUH!
PLAY AN EASY GAME WITH ME.
?
A GAME?

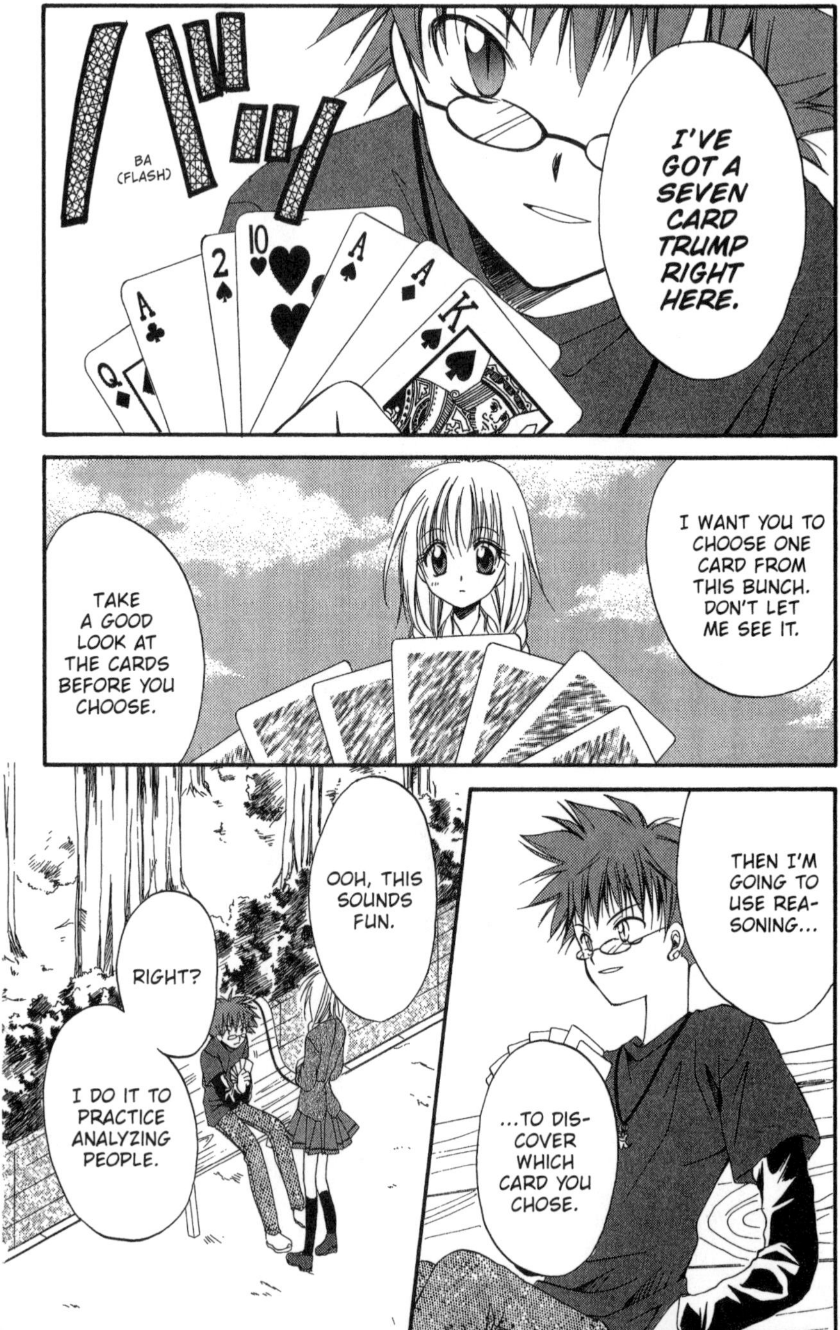
I'VE GOT A SEVEN CARD TRUMP RIGHT HERE.
BA (FLASH)
I WANT YOU TO CHOOSE ONE CARD FROM THIS BUNCH. DON'T LET ME SEE IT.
TAKE A GOOD LOOK AT THE CARDS BEFORE YOU CHOOSE.
THEN I'M GOING TO USE REA-SONING...
...TO DIS-COVER WHICH CARD YOU CHOSE.
OOH, THIS SOUNDS FUN.
RIGHT?
I DO IT TO PRACTICE ANALYZING PEOPLE.

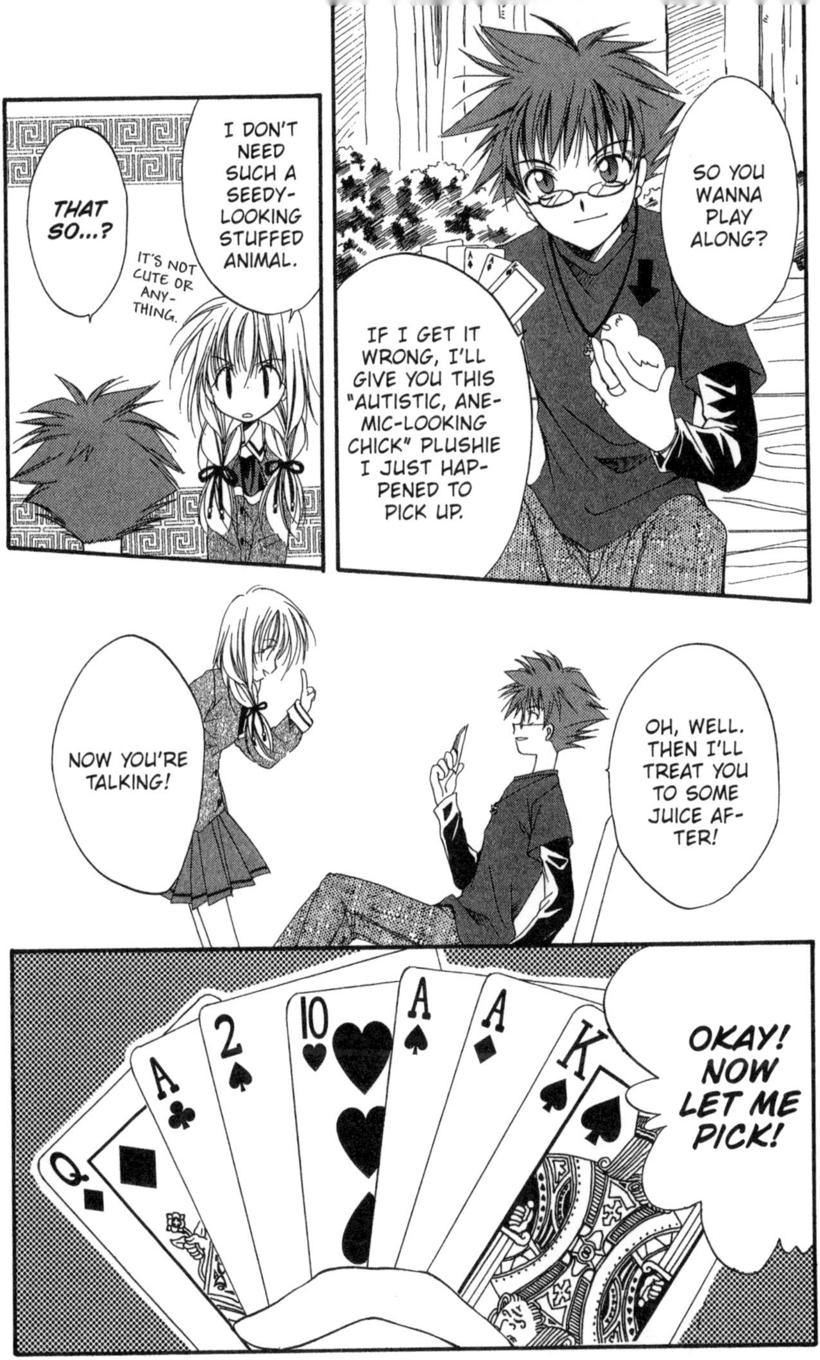
SO YOU WANNA PLAY ALONG?
IF I GET IT WRONG, I'LL GIVE YOU THIS "AUTISTIC, ANEMIC-LOOKING CHICK" PLUSHIE I JUST HAPPENED TO PICK UP.
I DON'T NEED SUCH A SEEDY-LOOKING STUFFED ANIMAL.
IT'S NOT CUTE OR ANYTHING.
THAT SO...?
OH, WELL. THEN I'LL TREAT YOU TO SOME JUICE AFTER!
NOW YOU'RE TALKING!
OKAY! NOW LET ME PICK!

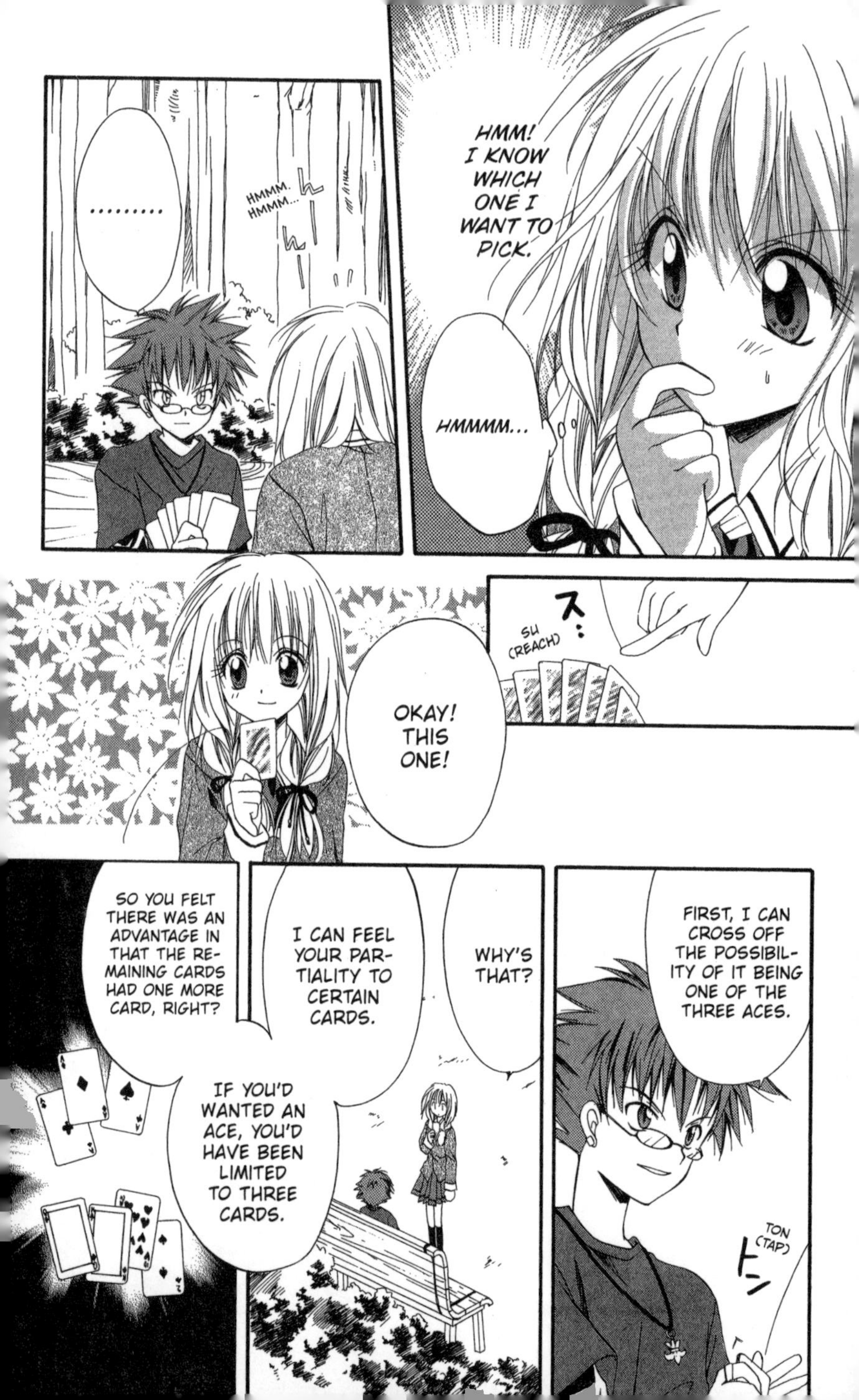
HMM! I KNOW WHICH ONE I WANT TO PICK.
HMMMM...
HMMM. HMMM...
....
ス
SU (REACH)
OKAY! THIS ONE!
FIRST, I CAN CROSS OFF THE POSSIBIL- ITY OF IT BEING ONE OF THE THREE ACES.
トン
TON (TAP)
WHY'S THAT?
I CAN FEEL YOUR PAR- TIALITY TO CERTAIN CARDS.
SO YOU FELT THERE WAS AN ADVANTAGE IN THAT THE RE- MAINING CARDS HAD ONE MORE CARD, RIGHT?
IF YOU'D WANTED AN ACE, YOU'D HAVE BEEN LIMITED TO THREE CARDS.

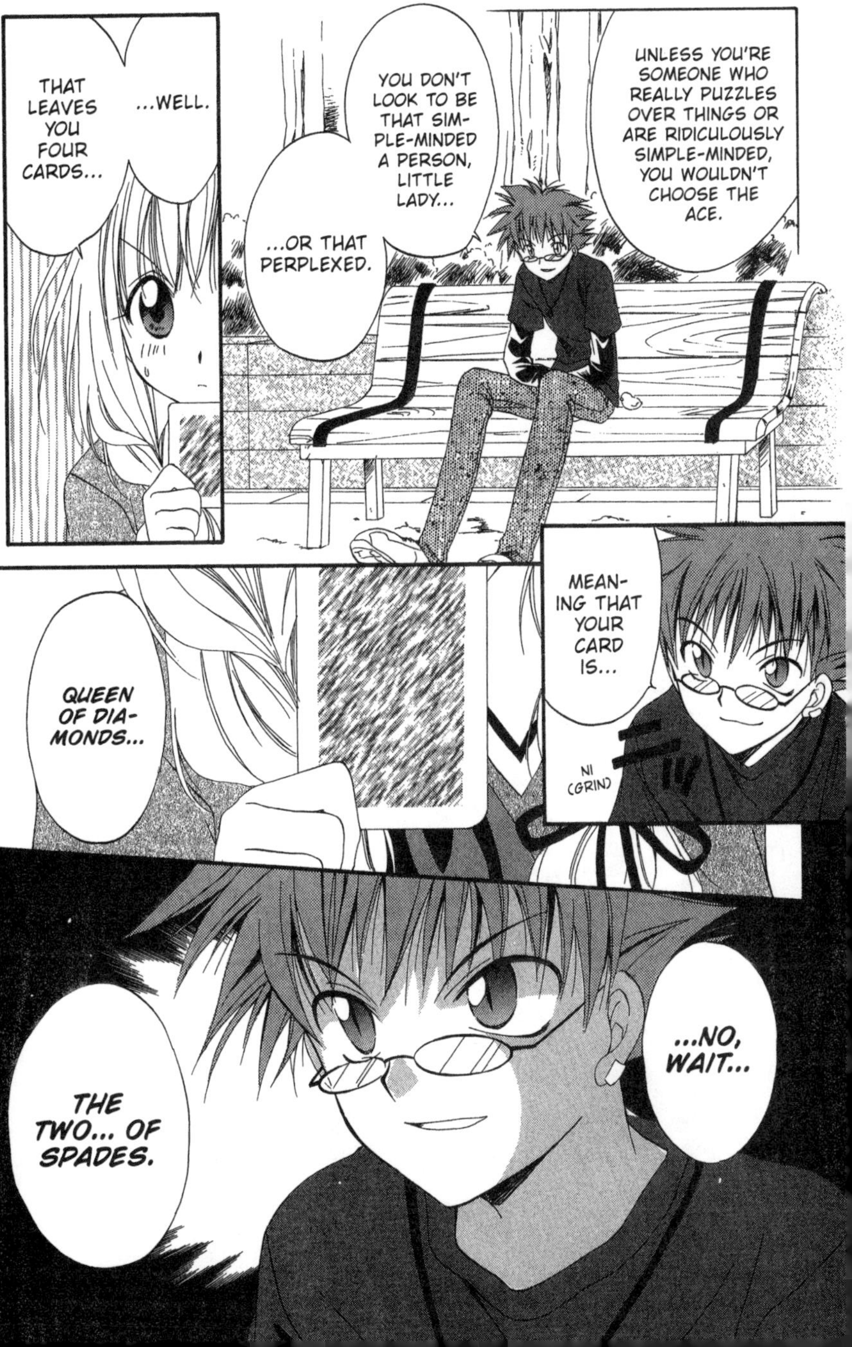
UNLESS YOU'RE SOMEONE WHO REALLY PUZZLES OVER THINGS OR ARE RIDICULOUSLY SIMPLE-MINDED, YOU WOULDN'T CHOOSE THE ACE.
YOU DON'T LOOK TO BE THAT SIM-PLE-MINDED A PERSON, LITTLE LADY...
...OR THAT PERPLEXED.
...WELL.
THAT LEAVES YOU FOUR CARDS...
MEAN-ING THAT YOUR CARD IS...
NI (GRIN)
QUEEN OF DIA-MONDS...
...NO, WAIT...
THE TWO... OF SPADES.

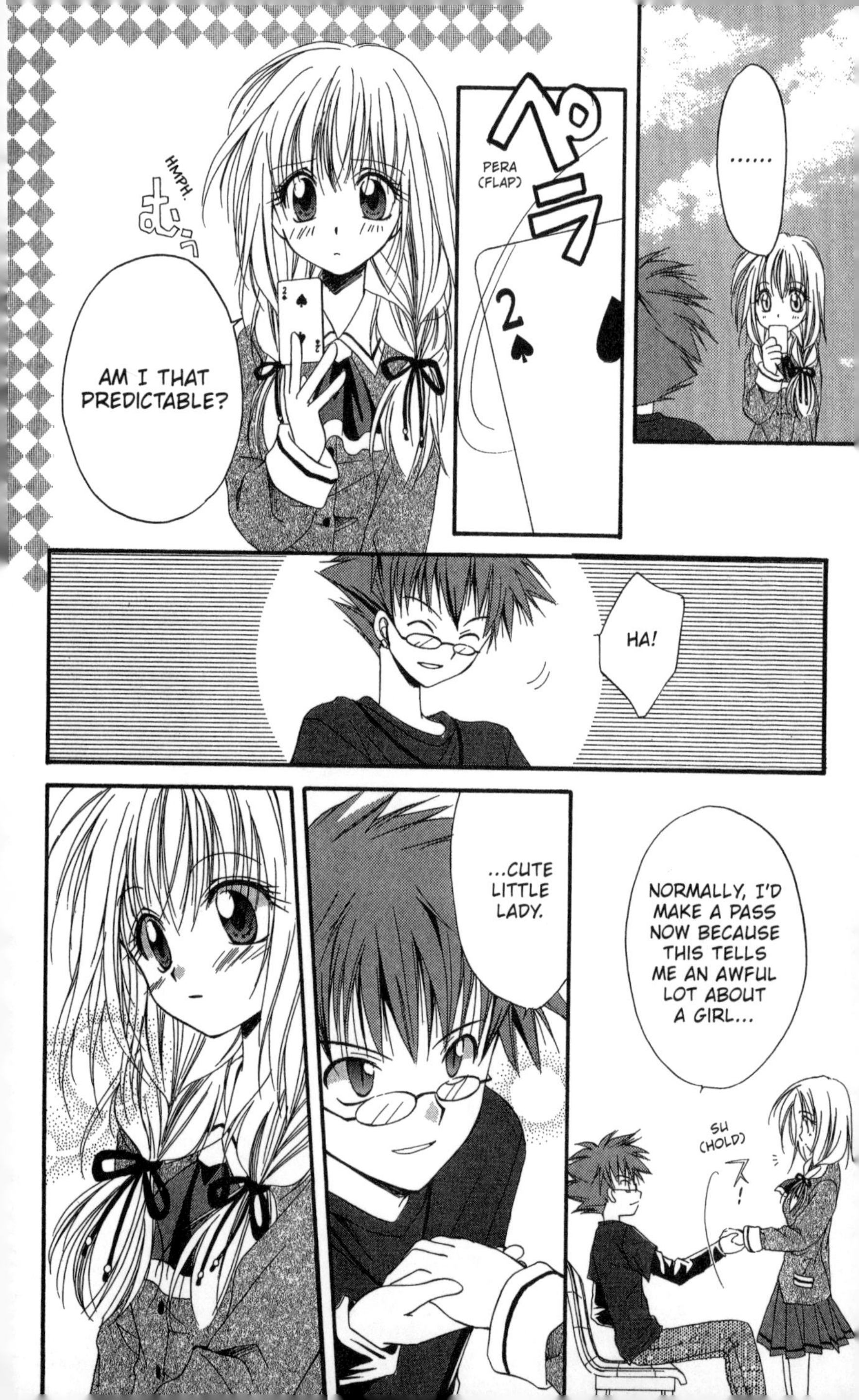
......
ペラ
PERA (FLAP)
むぅ
HMPH.
AM I THAT PREDICTABLE?
HA!
NORMALLY, I'D MAKE A PASS NOW BECAUSE THIS TELLS ME AN AWFUL LOT ABOUT A GIRL...
ス!
SU (HOLD)
...CUTE LITTLE LADY.

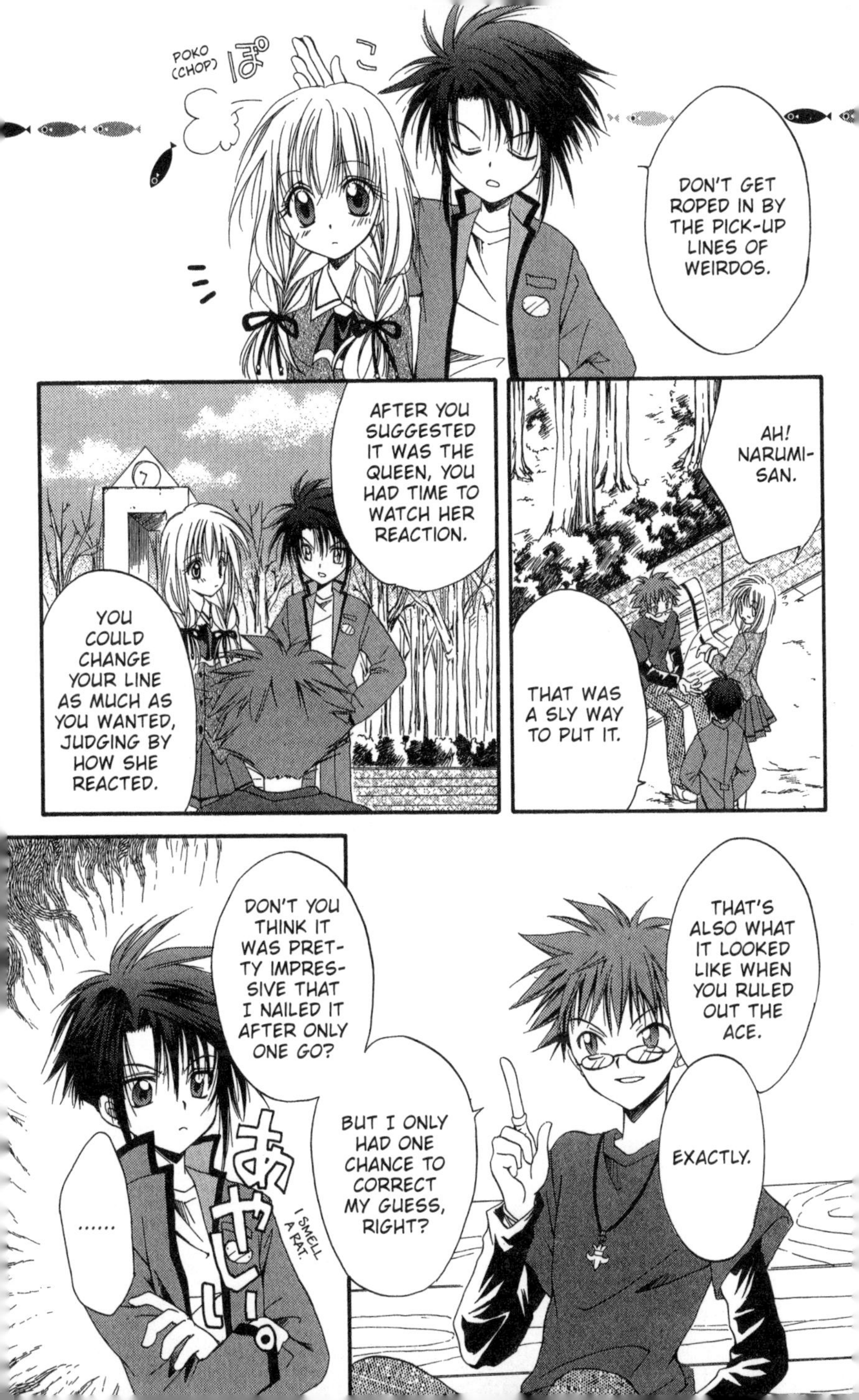
POKO (CHOP)
DON'T GET ROPED IN BY THE PICK-UP LINES OF WEIRDOS.
AH! NARUMI-SAN.
THAT WAS A SLY WAY TO PUT IT.
AFTER YOU SUGGESTED IT WAS THE QUEEN, YOU HAD TIME TO WATCH HER REACTION.
YOU COULD CHANGE YOUR LINE AS MUCH AS YOU WANTED, JUDGING BY HOW SHE REACTED.
THAT'S ALSO WHAT IT LOOKED LIKE WHEN YOU RULED OUT THE ACE.
EXACTLY.
DON'T YOU THINK IT WAS PRETTY IMPRESSIVE THAT I NAILED IT AFTER ONLY ONE GO?
BUT I ONLY HAD ONE CHANCE TO CORRECT MY GUESS, RIGHT?
I SMELL A RAT.
......

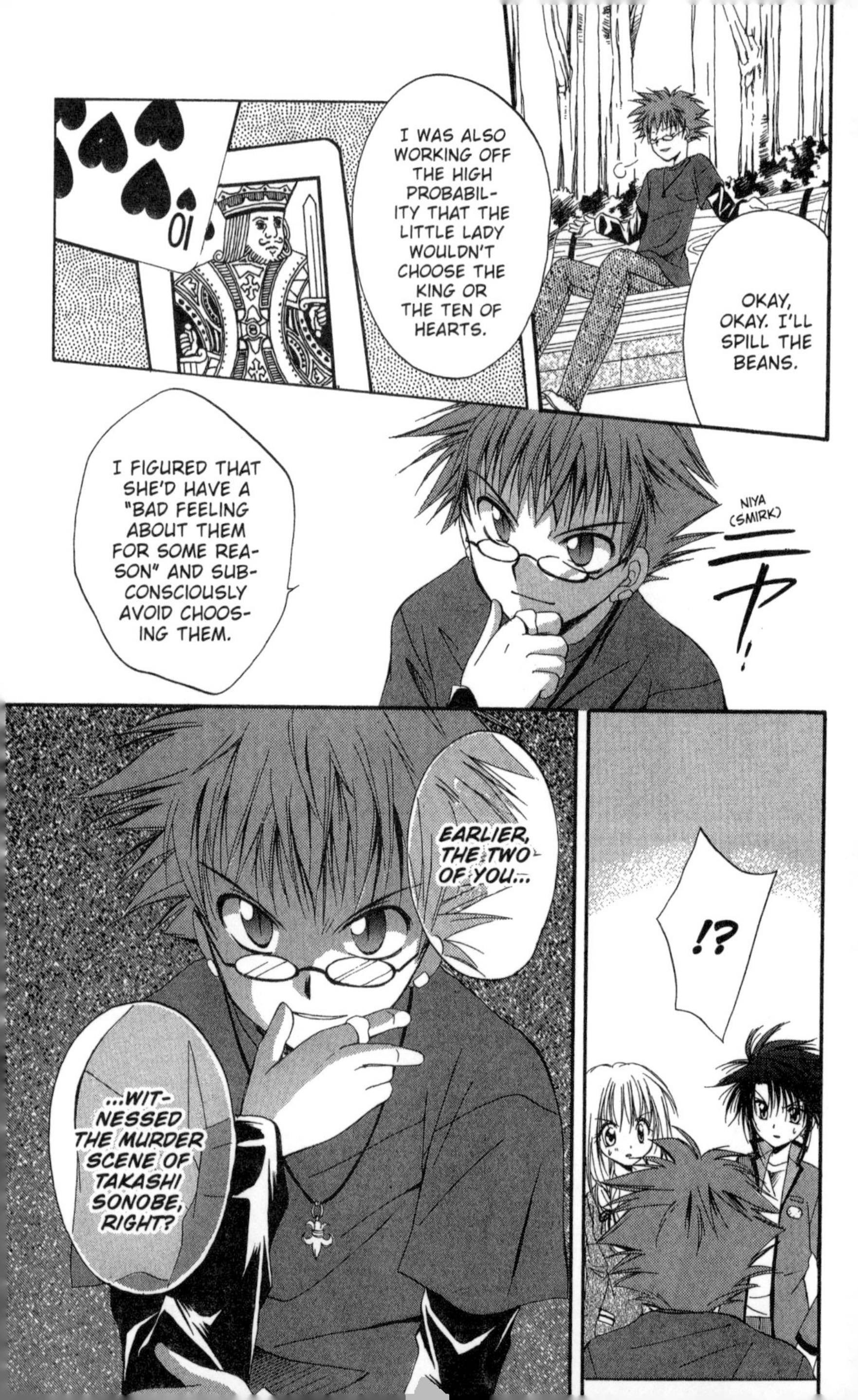
OKAY, OKAY. I'LL SPILL THE BEANS.
I WAS ALSO WORKING OFF THE HIGH PROBABIL-ITY THAT THE LITTLE LADY WOULDN'T CHOOSE THE KING OR THE TEN OF HEARTS.
NIYA (SMIRK)
I FIGURED THAT SHE'D HAVE A "BAD FEELING ABOUT THEM FOR SOME REA-SON" AND SUB-CONSCIOUSLY AVOID CHOOS-ING THEM.
!?
EARLIER, THE TWO OF YOU...
...WIT-NESSED THE MURDER SCENE OF TAKASHI SONOBE, RIGHT?

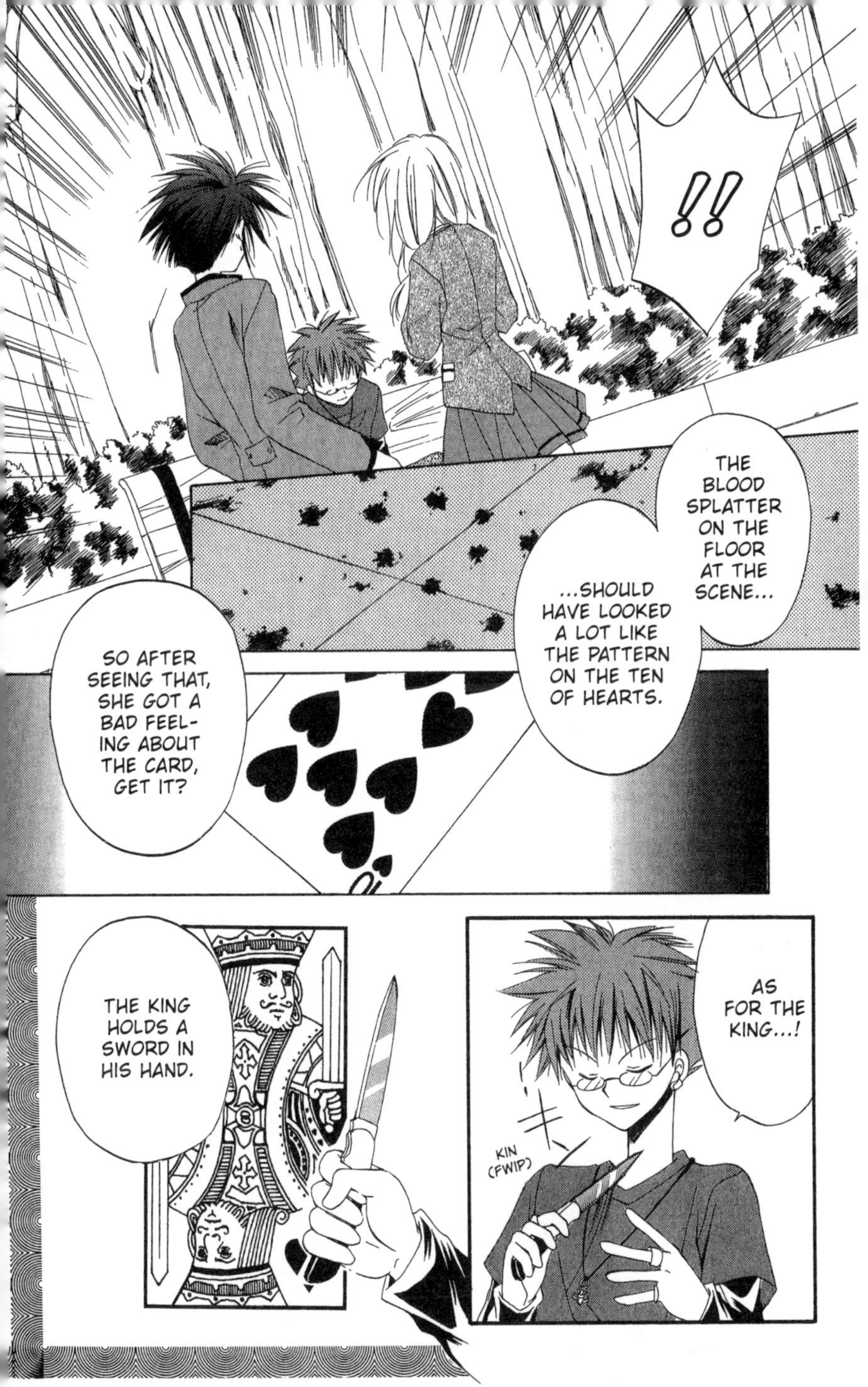
!!
THE BLOOD SPLATTER ON THE FLOOR AT THE SCENE...
...SHOULD HAVE LOOKED A LOT LIKE THE PATTERN ON THE TEN OF HEARTS.
SO AFTER SEEING THAT, SHE GOT A BAD FEEL-ING ABOUT THE CARD, GET IT?
AS FOR THE KING...!
KIN (FWIP)
THE KING HOLDS A SWORD IN HIS HAND.

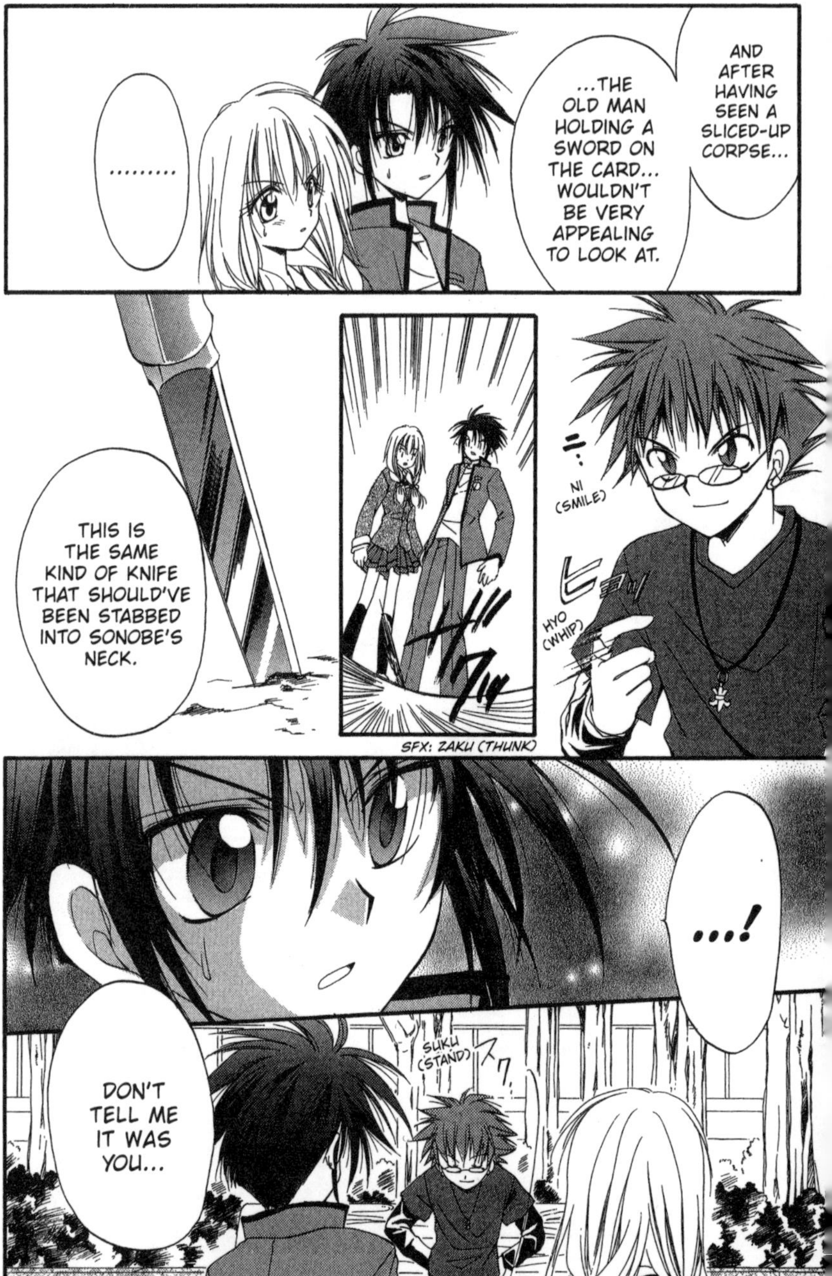
AND AFTER HAVING SEEN A SLICED-UP CORPSE...
...THE OLD MAN HOLDING A SWORD ON THE CARD... WOULDN'T BE VERY APPEALING TO LOOK AT.
....
NI (SMILE)
HYO (WHIP)
SFX: ZAKU (THUNK)
THIS IS THE SAME KIND OF KNIFE THAT SHOULD'VE BEEN STABBED INTO SONOBE'S NECK.
...!
SUKU (STAND)
DON'T TELL ME IT WAS YOU...

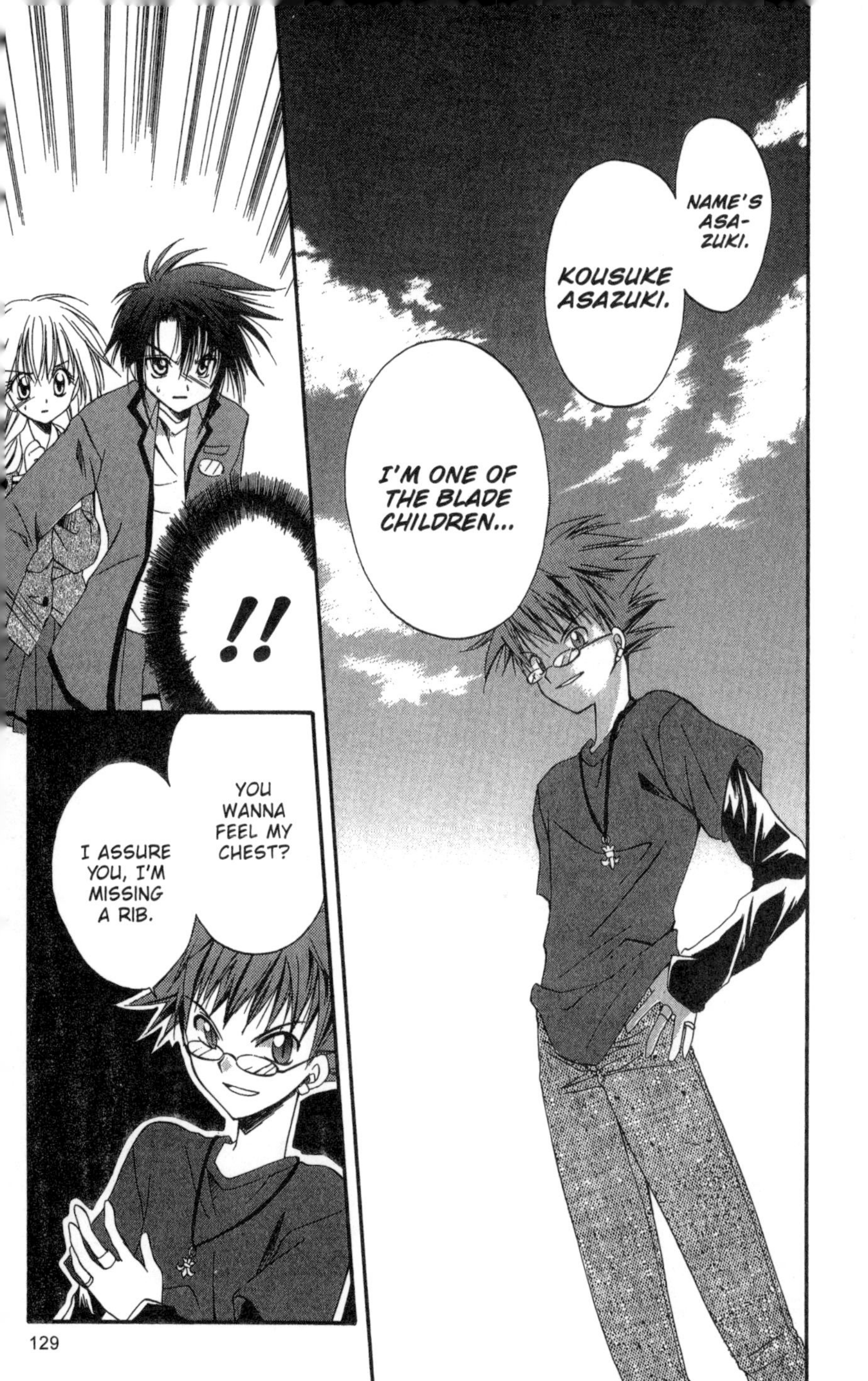
NAME'S ASA-ZUKI.
KOUSUKE ASAZUKI.
I'M ONE OF THE BLADE CHILDREN...
!!
YOU WANNA FEEL MY CHEST?
I ASSURE YOU, I'M MISSING A RIB.

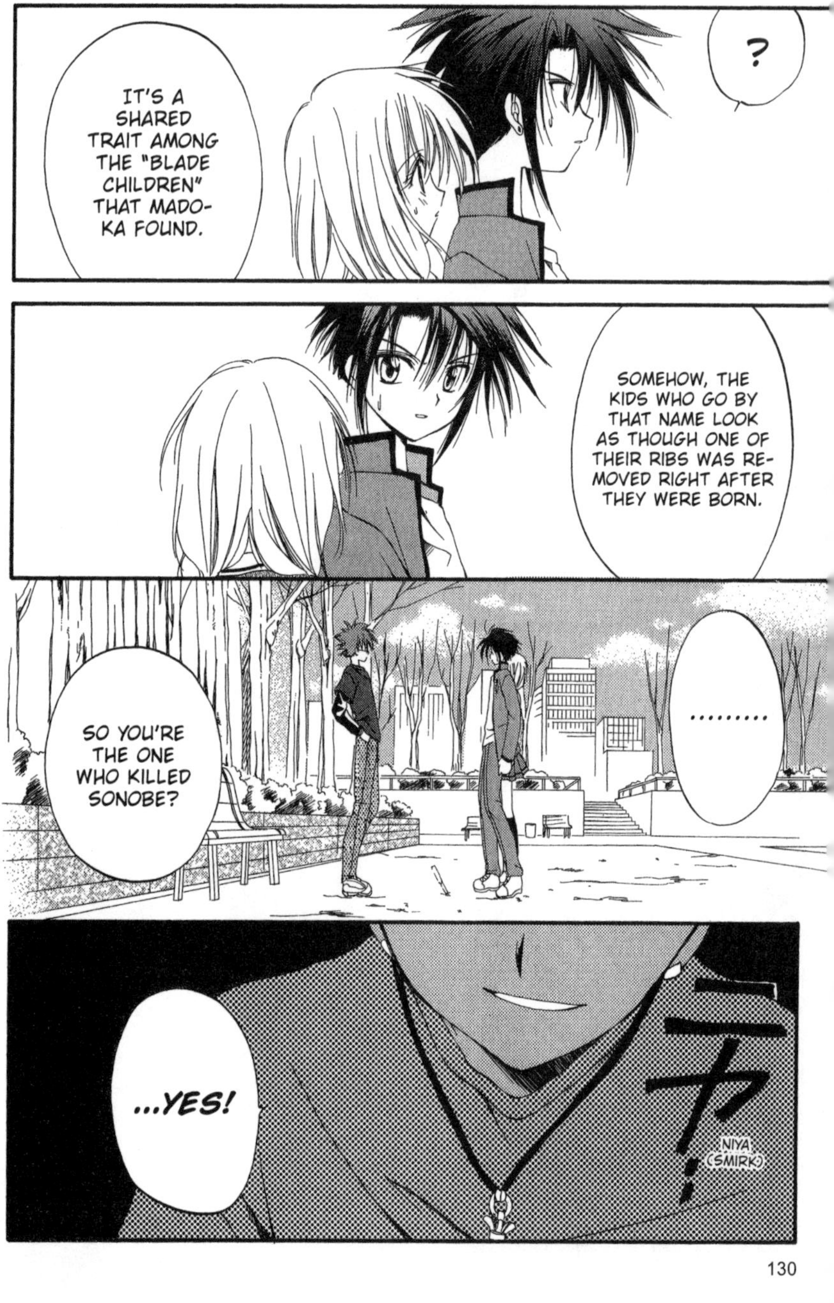
?
IT'S A SHARED TRAIT AMONG THE "BLADE CHILDREN" THAT MADO-KA FOUND.
SOMEHOW, THE KIDS WHO GO BY THAT NAME LOOK AS THOUGH ONE OF THEIR RIBS WAS RE-MOVED RIGHT AFTER THEY WERE BORN.
....
SO YOU'RE THE ONE WHO KILLED SONOBE?
NIYA (SMIRK)
...YES!

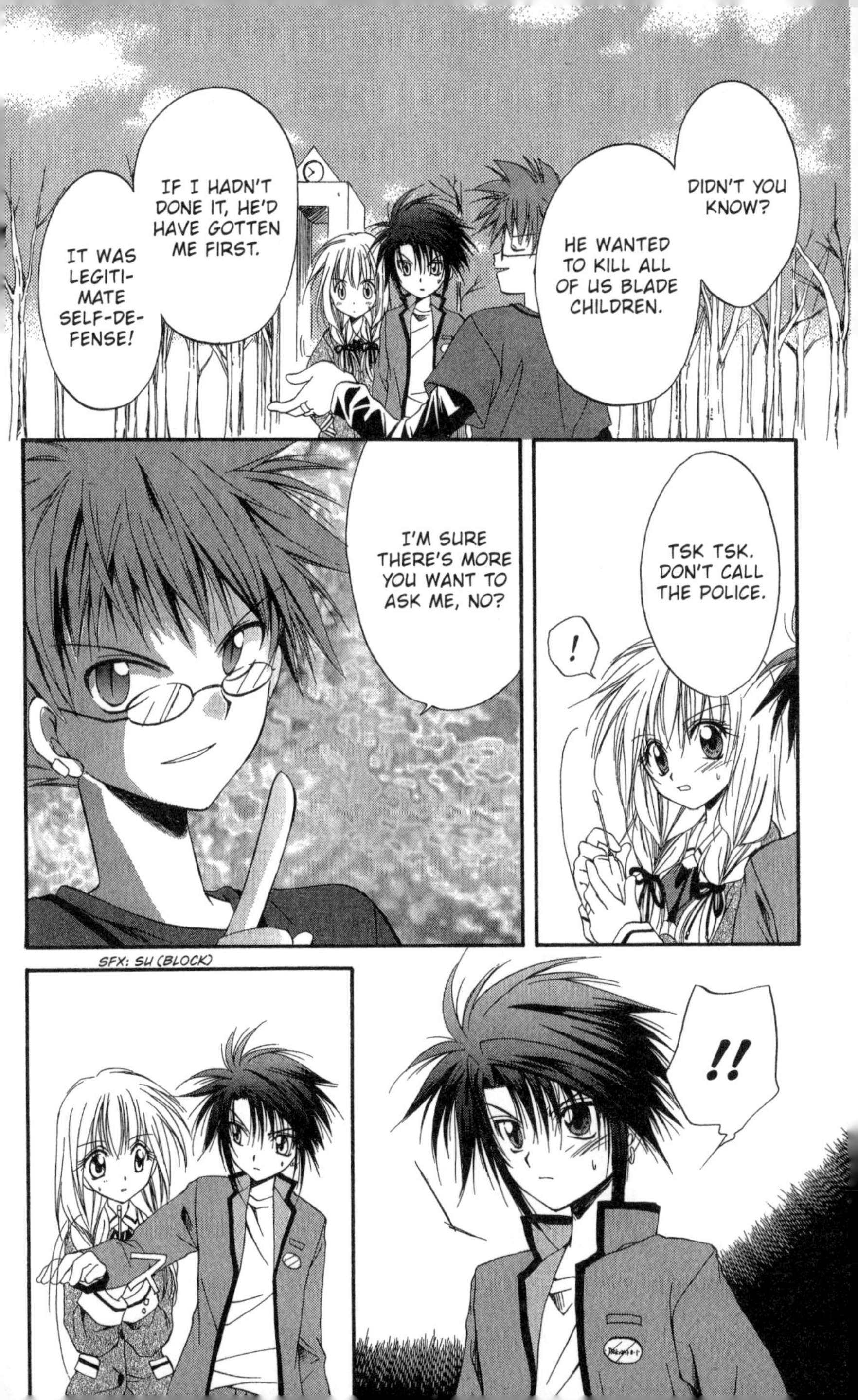
DIDN'T YOU KNOW?
HE WANTED TO KILL ALL OF US BLADE CHILDREN.
IF I HADN'T DONE IT, HE'D HAVE GOTTEN ME FIRST.
IT WAS LEGITIMATE SELF-DEFENSE!
TSK TSK. DON'T CALL THE POLICE.
!
I'M SURE THERE'S MORE YOU WANT TO ASK ME, NO?
SFX: SU (BLOCK)
!!

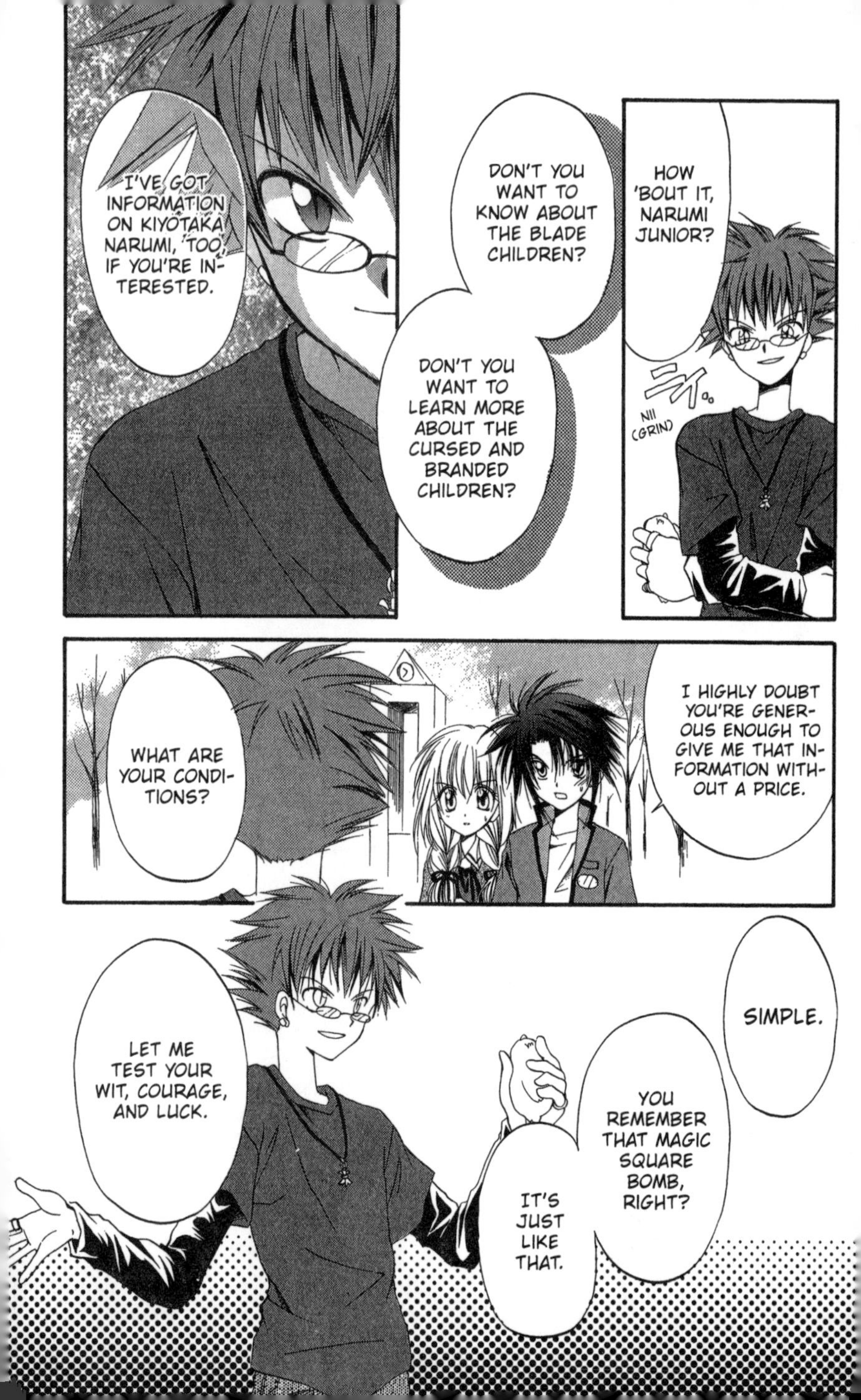
HOW 'BOUT IT, NARUMI JUNIOR?
NII (GRIN)
DON'T YOU WANT TO KNOW ABOUT THE BLADE CHILDREN?
DON'T YOU WANT TO LEARN MORE ABOUT THE CURSED AND BRANDED CHILDREN?
I'VE GOT INFORMATION ON KIYOTAKA NARUMI, TOO, IF YOU'RE INTERESTED.
I HIGHLY DOUBT YOU'RE GENEROUS ENOUGH TO GIVE ME THAT INFORMATION WITHOUT A PRICE.
WHAT ARE YOUR CONDITIONS?
SIMPLE.
YOU REMEMBER THAT MAGIC SQUARE BOMB, RIGHT?
IT'S JUST LIKE THAT.
LET ME TEST YOUR WIT, COURAGE, AND LUCK.

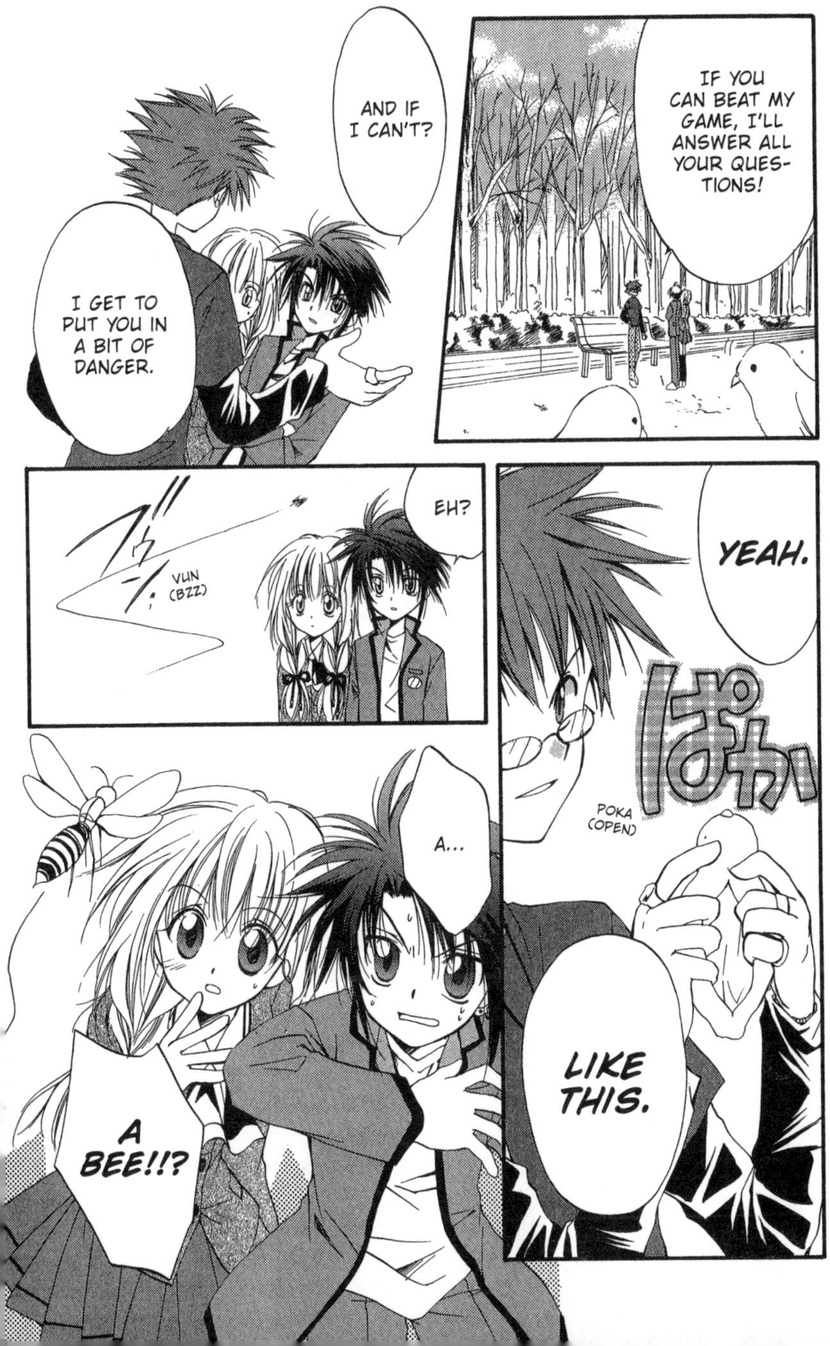

IF YOU CAN BEAT MY GAME, I'LL ANSWER ALL YOUR QUESTIONS!
AND IF I CAN'T?
I GET TO PUT YOU IN A BIT OF DANGER.
YEAH.
POKA (OPEN)
LIKE THIS.
EH?
VUN (BZZ)
A...
A BEE!!?

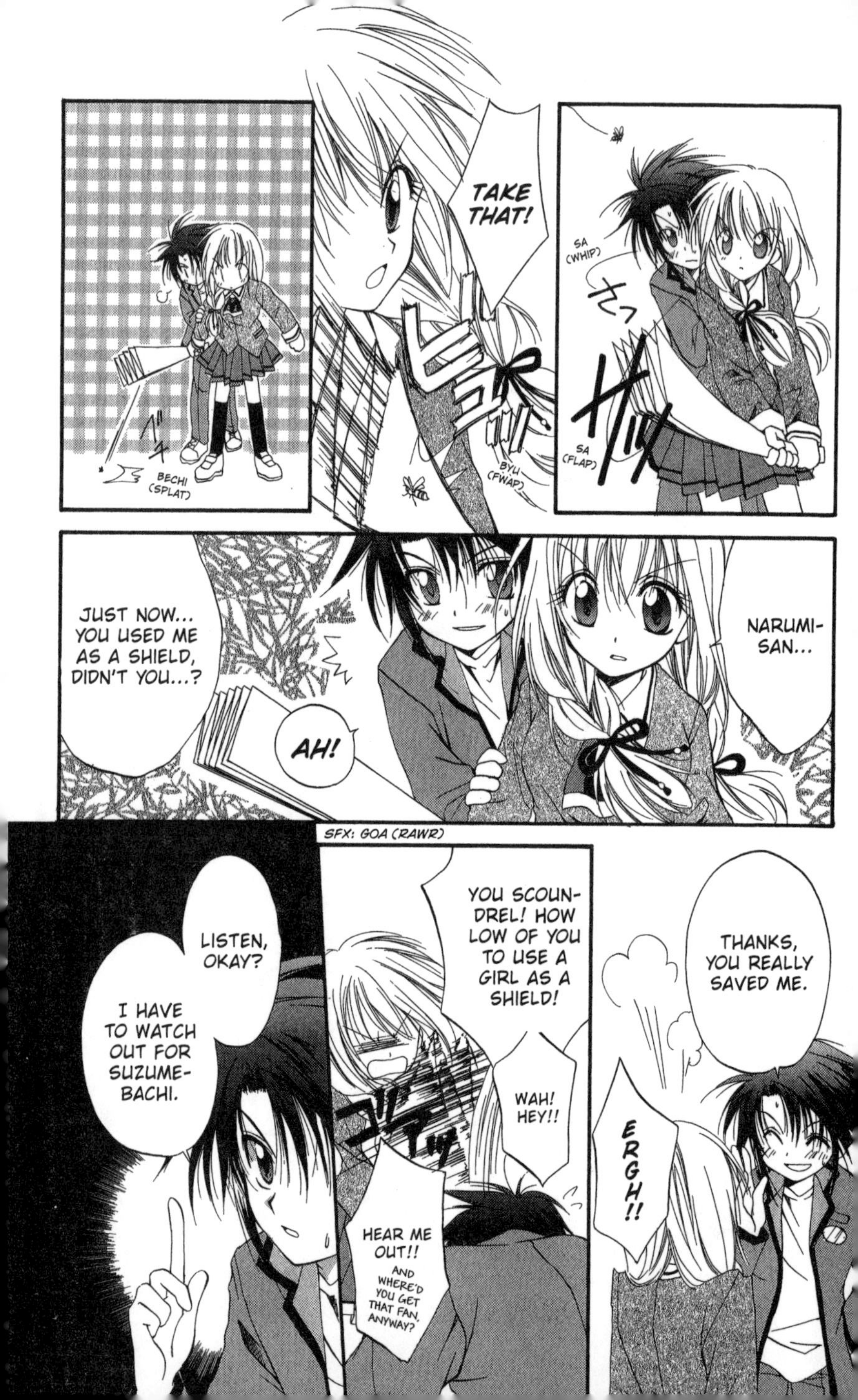

SA (WHIP)
さっ
SA (FLAP)
TAKE THAT!
BYU (FWAP)
BECHI (SPLAT)
NARUMI-SAN...
JUST NOW... YOU USED ME AS A SHIELD, DIDN'T YOU...?
AH!
SFX: GOA (RAWR)
THANKS, YOU REALLY SAVED ME.
ERGH!!
YOU SCOUNDREL! HOW LOW OF YOU TO USE A GIRL AS A SHIELD!
WAH! HEY!!
HEAR ME OUT!!
AND WHERE'D YOU GET THAT FAN, ANYWAY?
LISTEN, OKAY?
I HAVE TO WATCH OUT FOR SUZUME-BACHI.

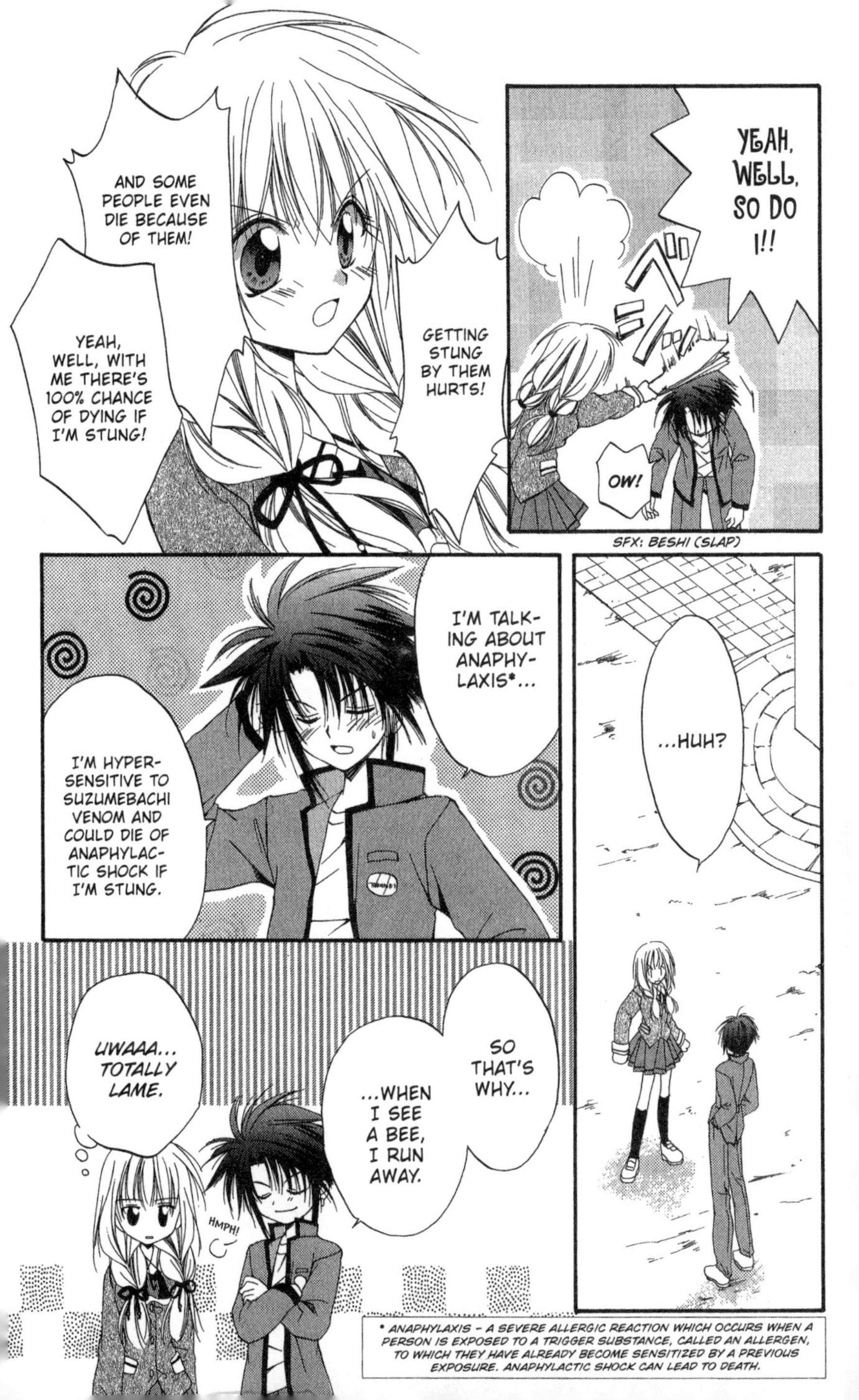
YEAH, WELL, SO DO I!!
OW!
SFX: BESHI (SLAP)
GETTING STUNG BY THEM HURTS!
AND SOME PEOPLE EVEN DIE BECAUSE OF THEM!
YEAH, WELL, WITH ME THERE'S 100% CHANCE OF DYING IF I'M STUNG!
...HUH?
I'M TALK-ING ABOUT ANAPHY-LAXIS*...
I'M HYPER-SENSITIVE TO SUZUMEBACHI VENOM AND COULD DIE OF ANAPHYLAC-TIC SHOCK IF I'M STUNG.
SO THAT'S WHY...
...WHEN I SEE A BEE, I RUN AWAY.
HMPH!
UWAAA... TOTALLY LAME.

* ANAPHYLAXIS - A SEVERE ALLERGIC REACTION WHICH OCCURS WHEN A PERSON IS EXPOSED TO A TRIGGER SUBSTANCE, CALLED AN ALLERGEN, TO WHICH THEY HAVE ALREADY BECOME SENSITIZED BY A PREVIOUS EXPOSURE. ANAPHYLACTIC SHOCK CAN LEAD TO DEATH.

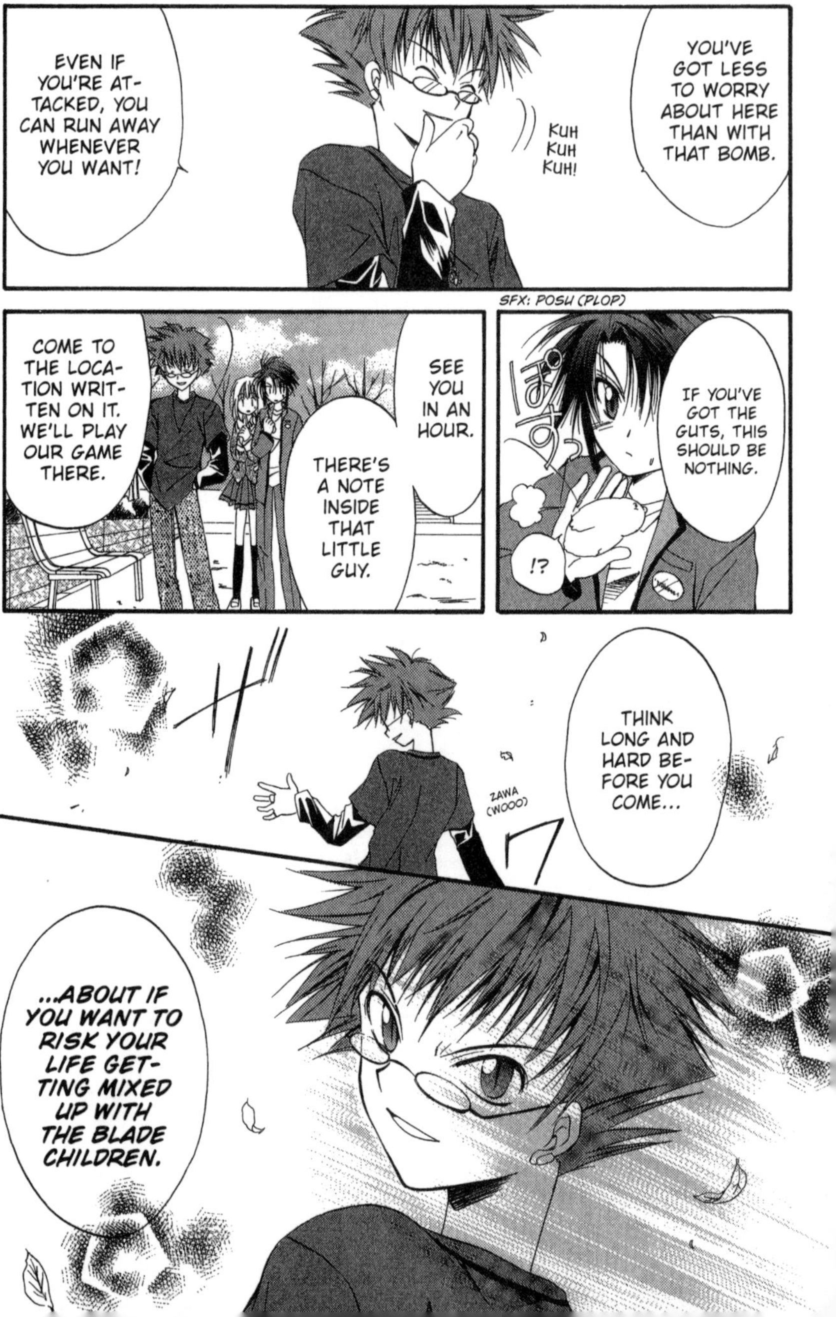
YOU'VE GOT LESS TO WORRY ABOUT HERE THAN WITH THAT BOMB.
KUH KUH KUH!
EVEN IF YOU'RE AT-TACKED, YOU CAN RUN AWAY WHENEVER YOU WANT!
SFX: POSU (PLOP)
IF YOU'VE GOT THE GUTS, THIS SHOULD BE NOTHING.
!?
SEE YOU IN AN HOUR.
THERE'S A NOTE INSIDE THAT LITTLE GUY.
COME TO THE LOCA-TION WRIT-TEN ON IT. WE'LL PLAY OUR GAME THERE.
THINK LONG AND HARD BE-FORE YOU COME...
ZAWA (WOOO)
...ABOUT IF YOU WANT TO RISK YOUR LIFE GET-TING MIXED UP WITH THE BLADE CHILDREN.

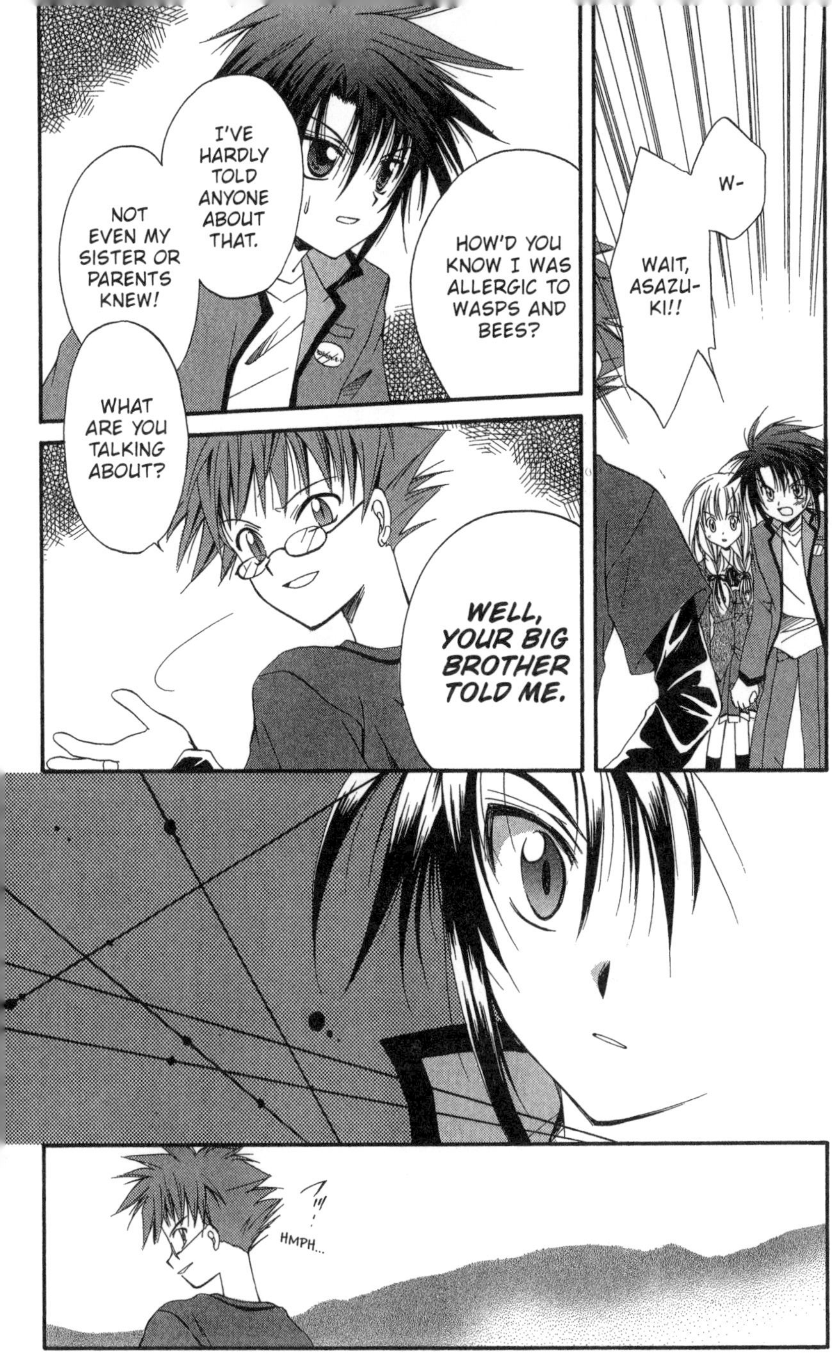
W-
WAIT, ASAZUKI!!
HOW'D YOU KNOW I WAS ALLERGIC TO WASPS AND BEES?
I'VE HARDLY TOLD ANYONE ABOUT THAT.
NOT EVEN MY SISTER OR PARENTS KNEW!
WHAT ARE YOU TALKING ABOUT?
WELL, YOUR BIG BROTHER TOLD ME.
HMPH...

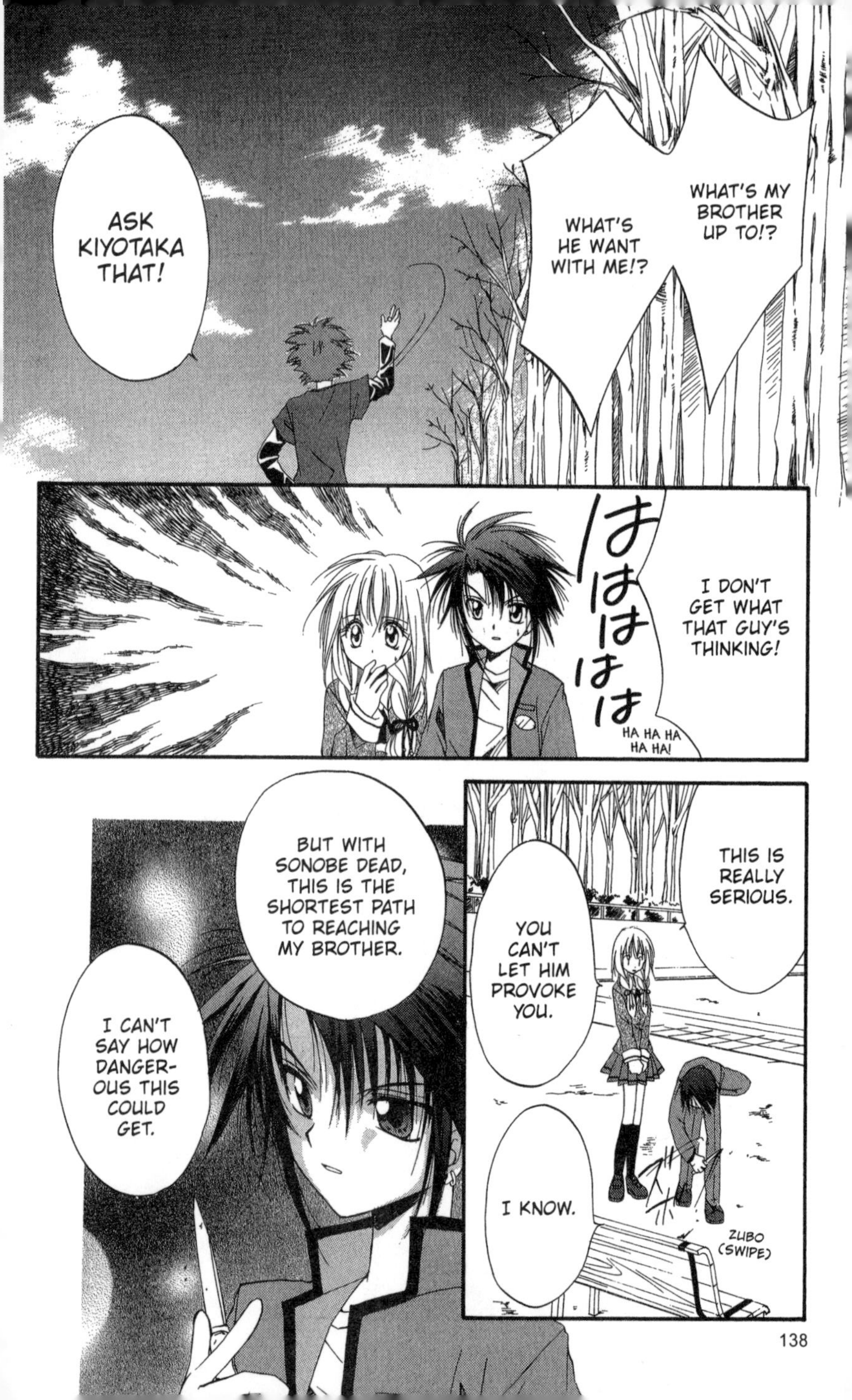
WHAT'S MY BROTHER UP TO!?
WHAT'S HE WANT WITH ME!?
ASK KIYOTAKA THAT!
I DON'T GET WHAT THAT GUY'S THINKING!
ははははは
HA HA HA HA HA!
THIS IS REALLY SERIOUS.
YOU CAN'T LET HIM PROVOKE YOU.
I KNOW.
ZUBO (SWIPE)
BUT WITH SONOBE DEAD, THIS IS THE SHORTEST PATH TO REACHING MY BROTHER.
I CAN'T SAY HOW DANGER-OUS THIS COULD GET.

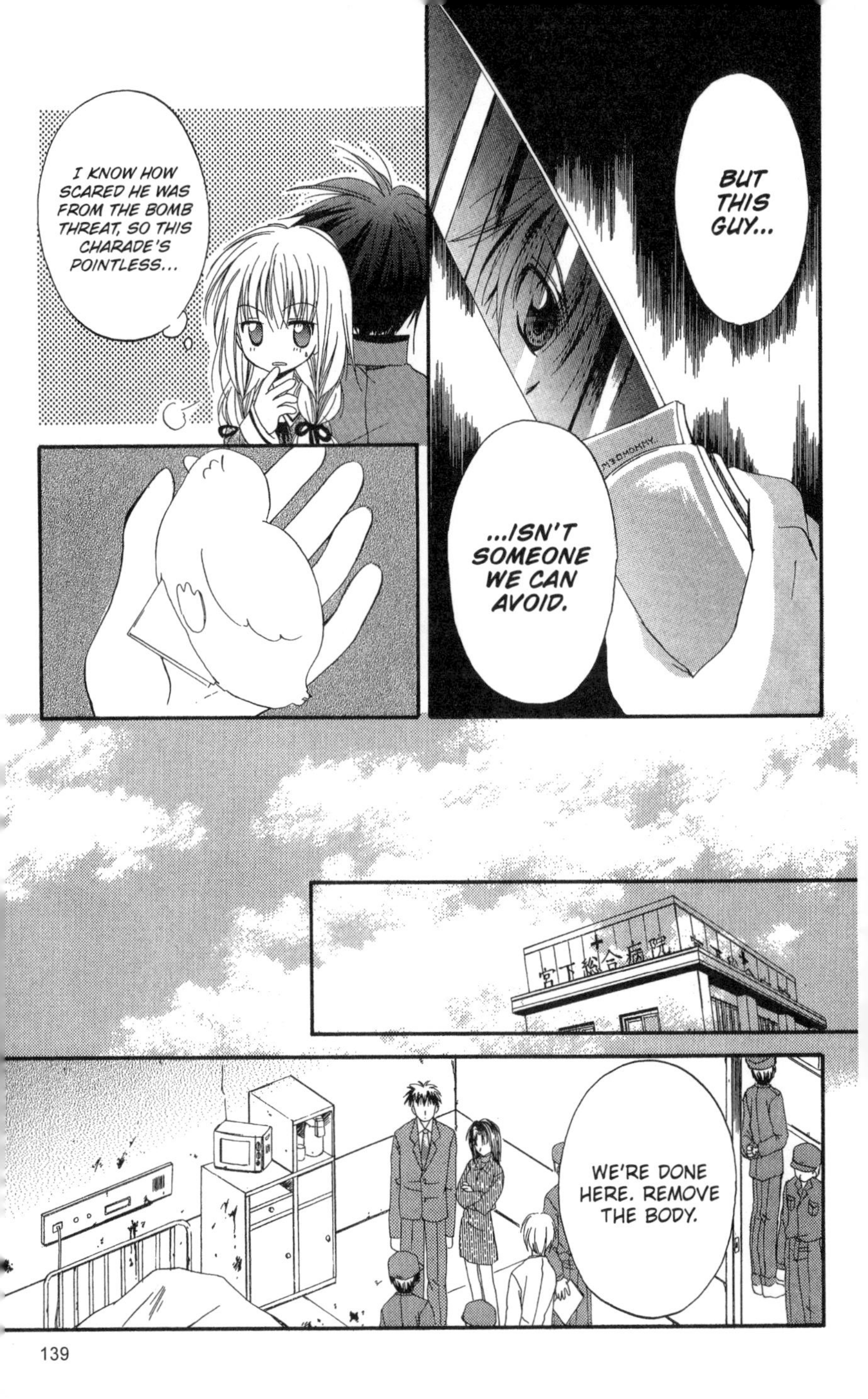
BUT THIS GUY...
...ISN'T SOMEONE WE CAN AVOID.
I KNOW HOW SCARED HE WAS FROM THE BOMB THREAT, SO THIS CHARADE'S POINTLESS...
宮下総合病院
WE'RE DONE HERE. REMOVE THE BODY.

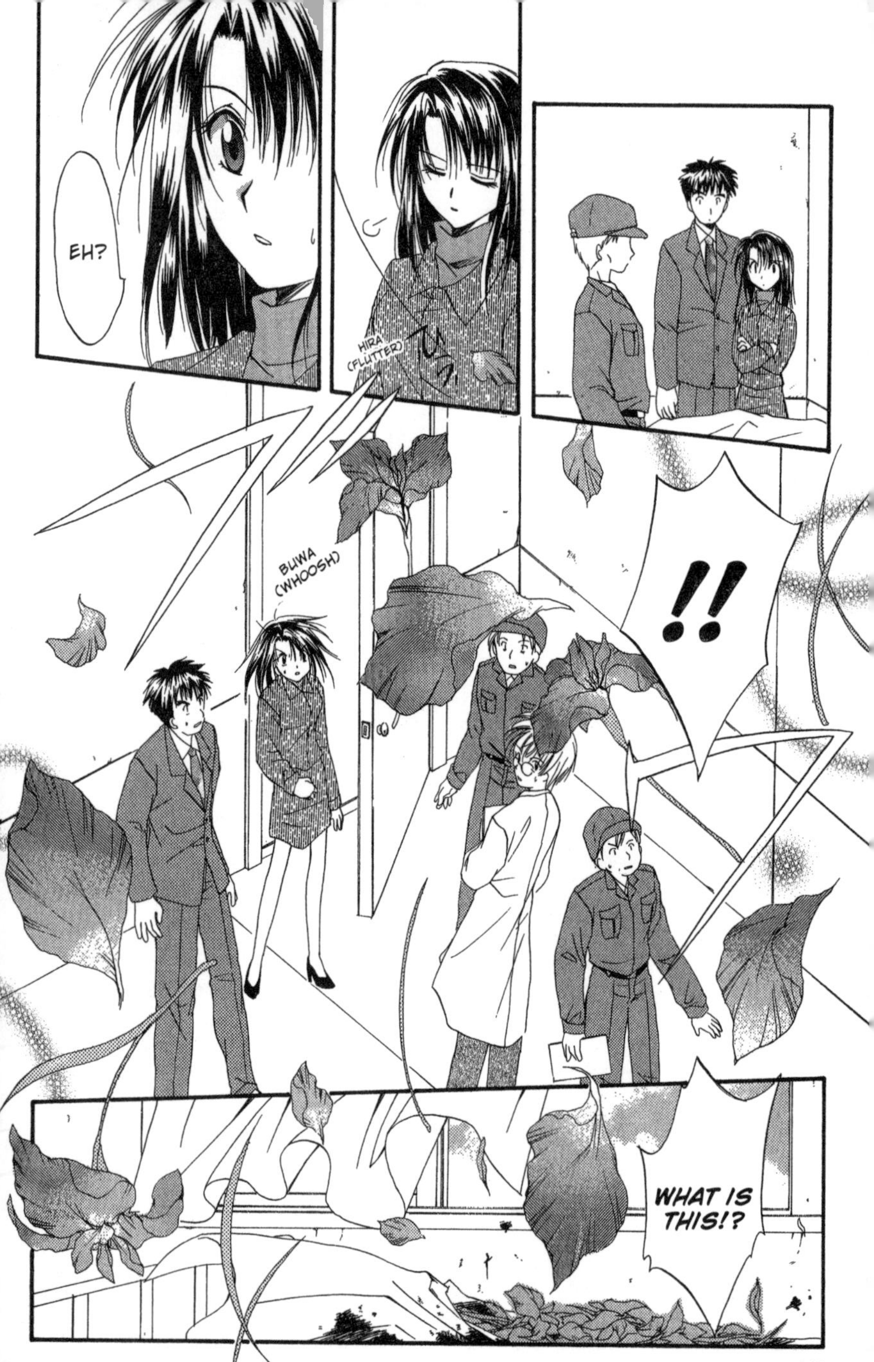
HIRA (FLUTTER)
EH?
!!
BUWA (WHOOSH)
WHAT IS THIS!?

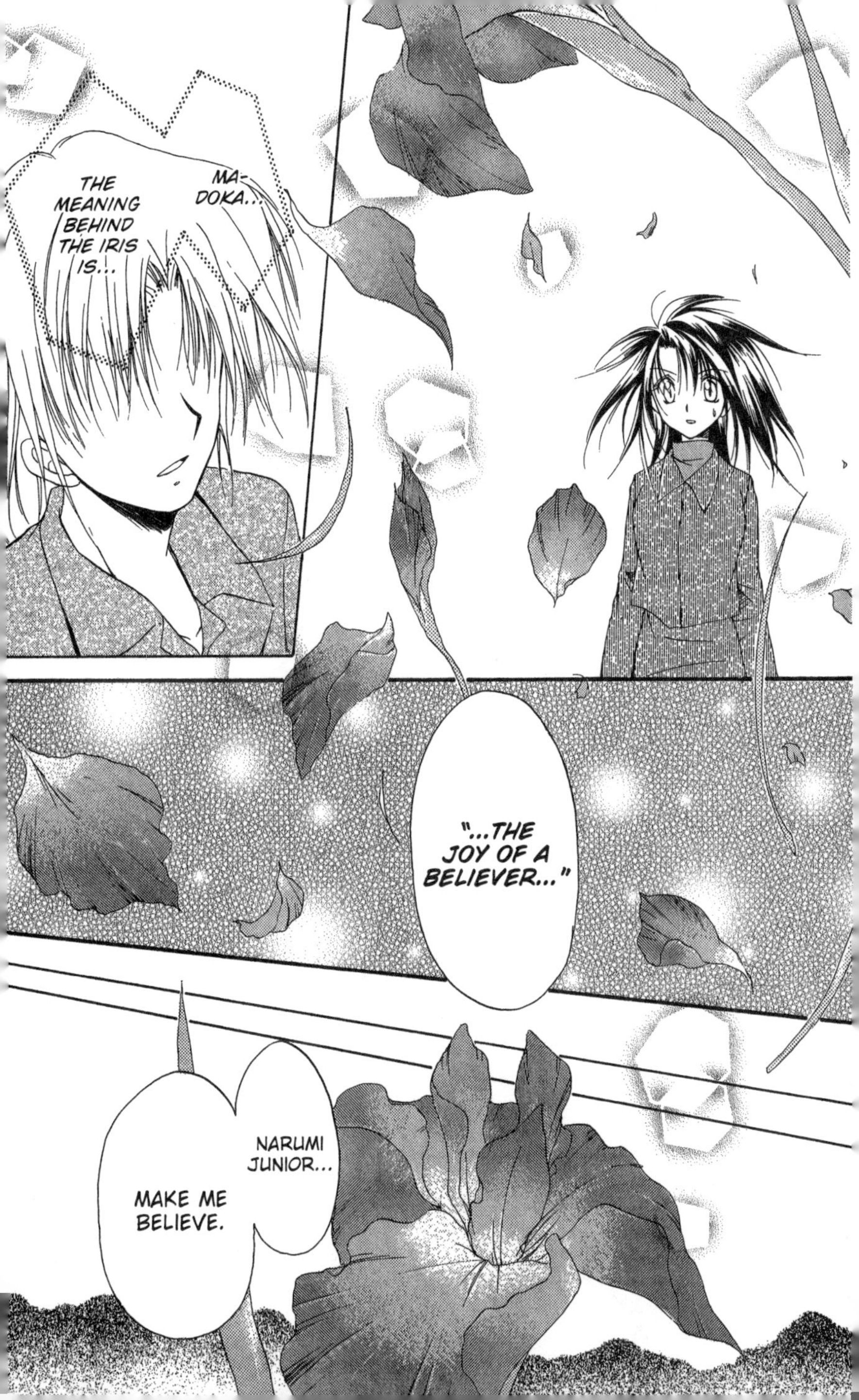
MA-DOKA...
THE MEANING BEHIND THE IRIS IS...
"...THE JOY OF A BELIEVER..."
NARUMI JUNIOR...
MAKE ME BELIEVE.

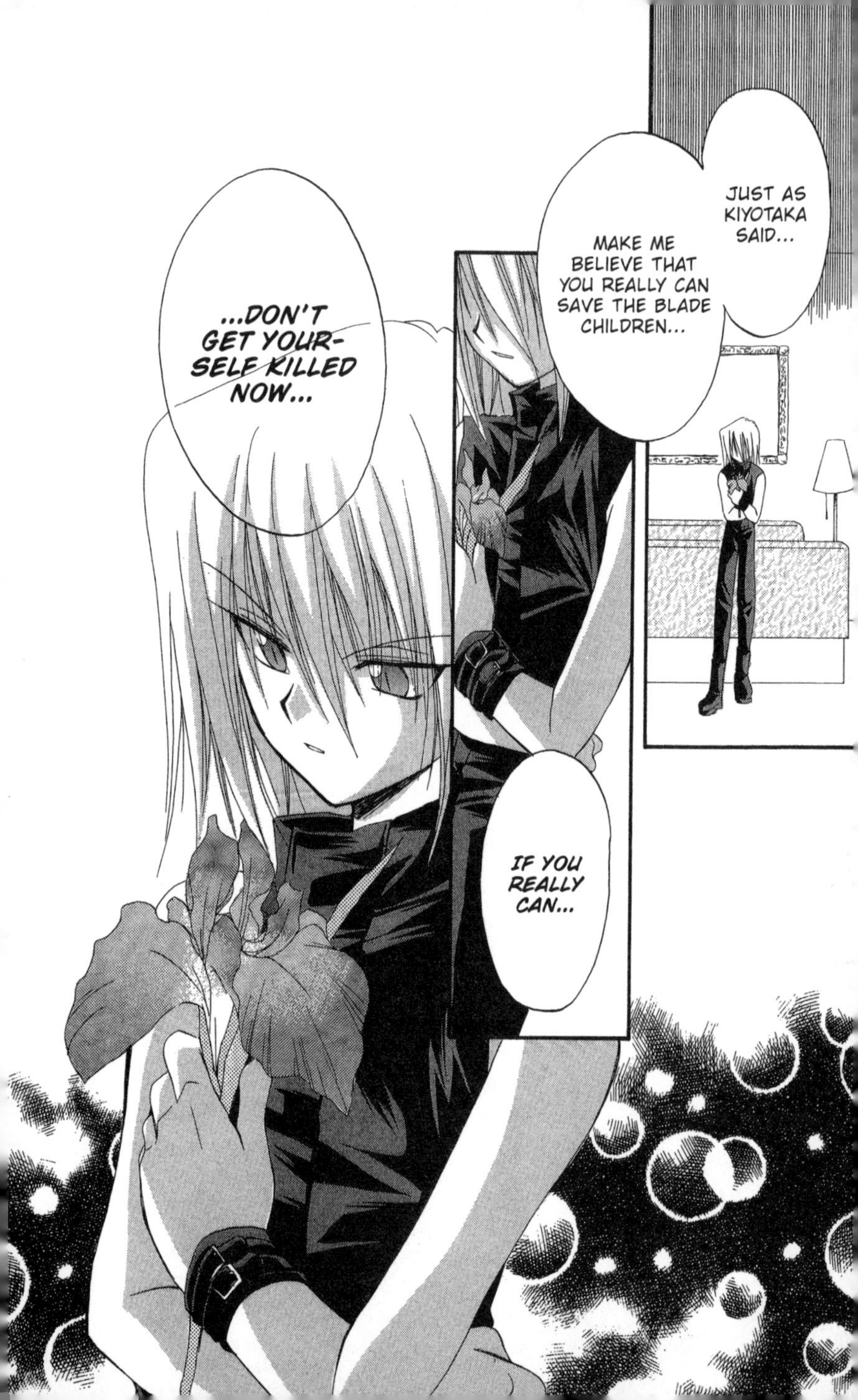
JUST AS KIYOTAKA SAID...
MAKE ME BELIEVE THAT YOU REALLY CAN SAVE THE BLADE CHILDREN...
IF YOU REALLY CAN...
...DON'T GET YOURSELF KILLED NOW...

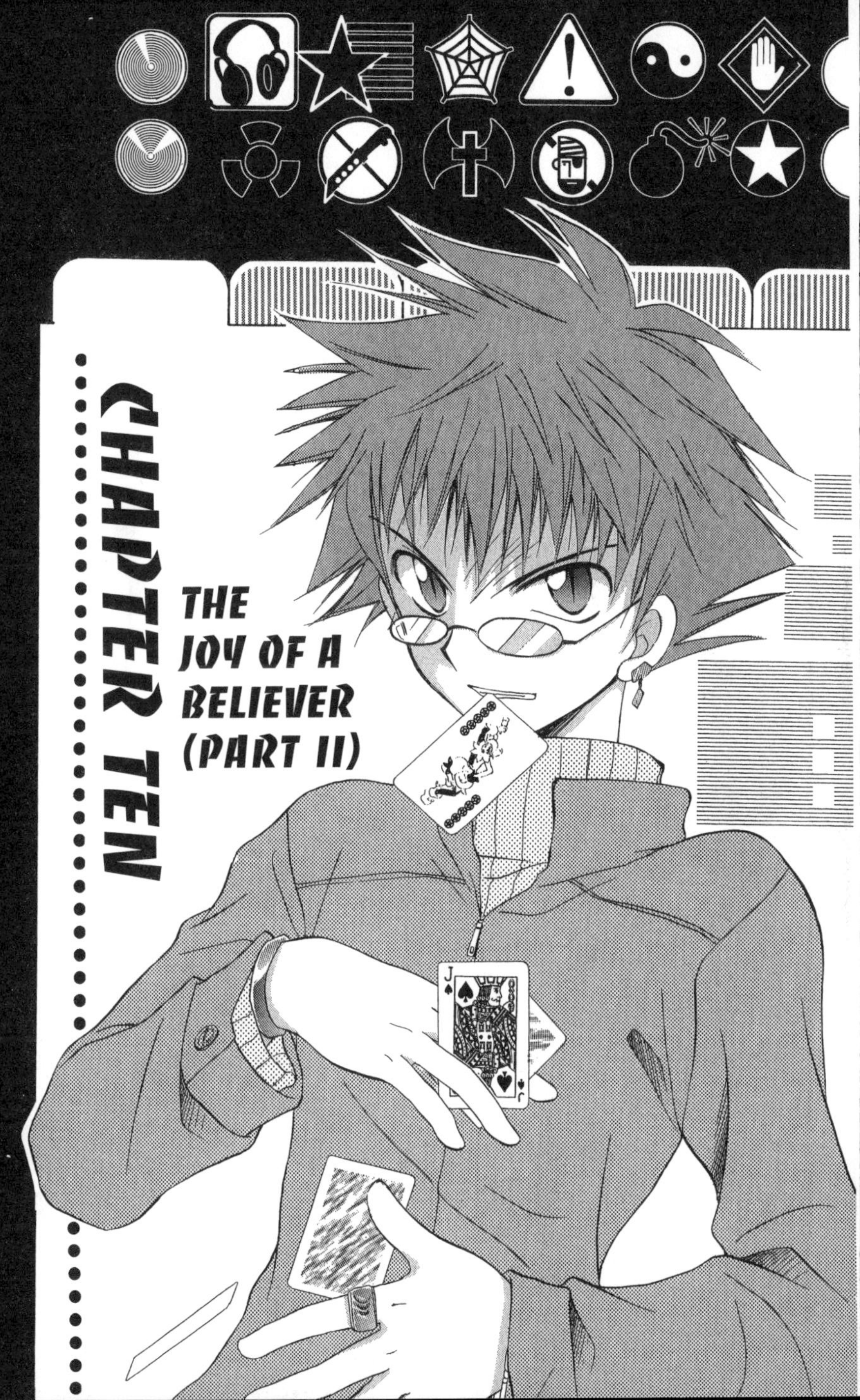
CHAPTER TEN
THE JOY OF A BELIEVER (PART II)

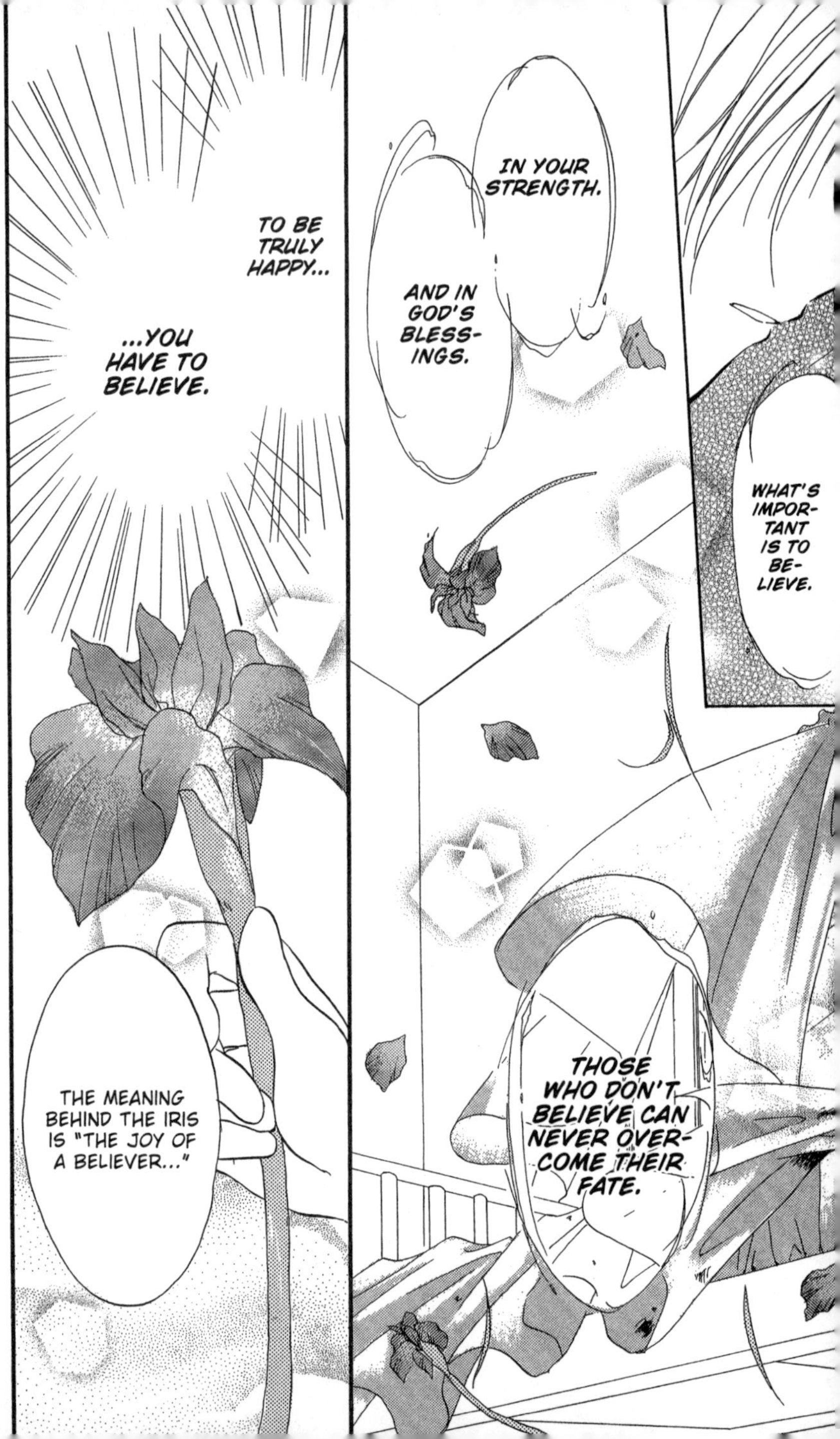
WHAT'S IMPORTANT IS TO BELIEVE.
IN YOUR STRENGTH.
AND IN GOD'S BLESSINGS.
THOSE WHO DON'T BELIEVE CAN NEVER OVERCOME THEIR FATE.
TO BE TRULY HAPPY...
...YOU HAVE TO BELIEVE.
THE MEANING BEHIND THE IRIS IS "THE JOY OF A BELIEVER..."

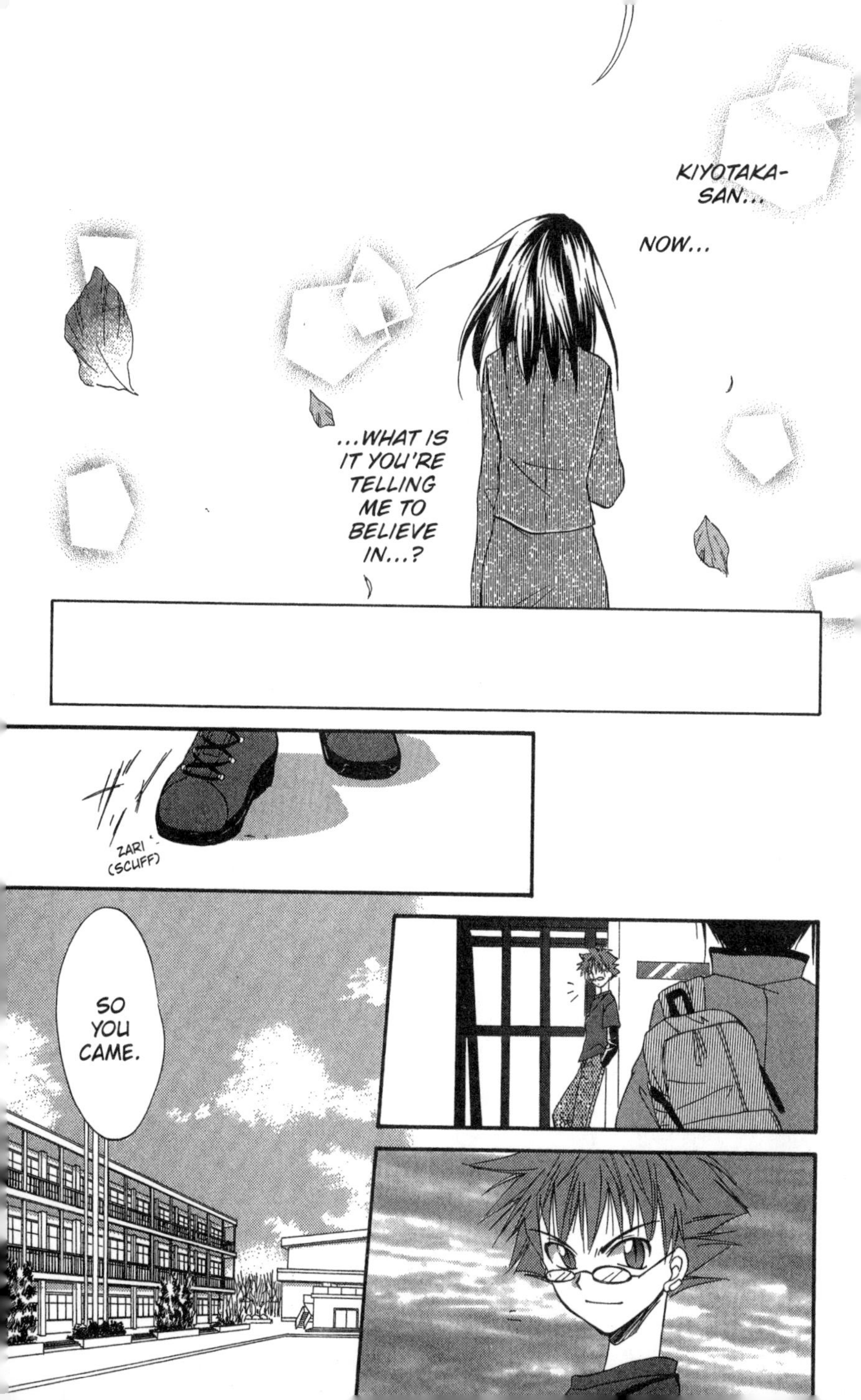
KIYOTAKA-SAN...
NOW...
...WHAT IS IT YOU'RE TELLING ME TO BELIEVE IN...?
ZARI (SCUFF)
SO YOU CAME.

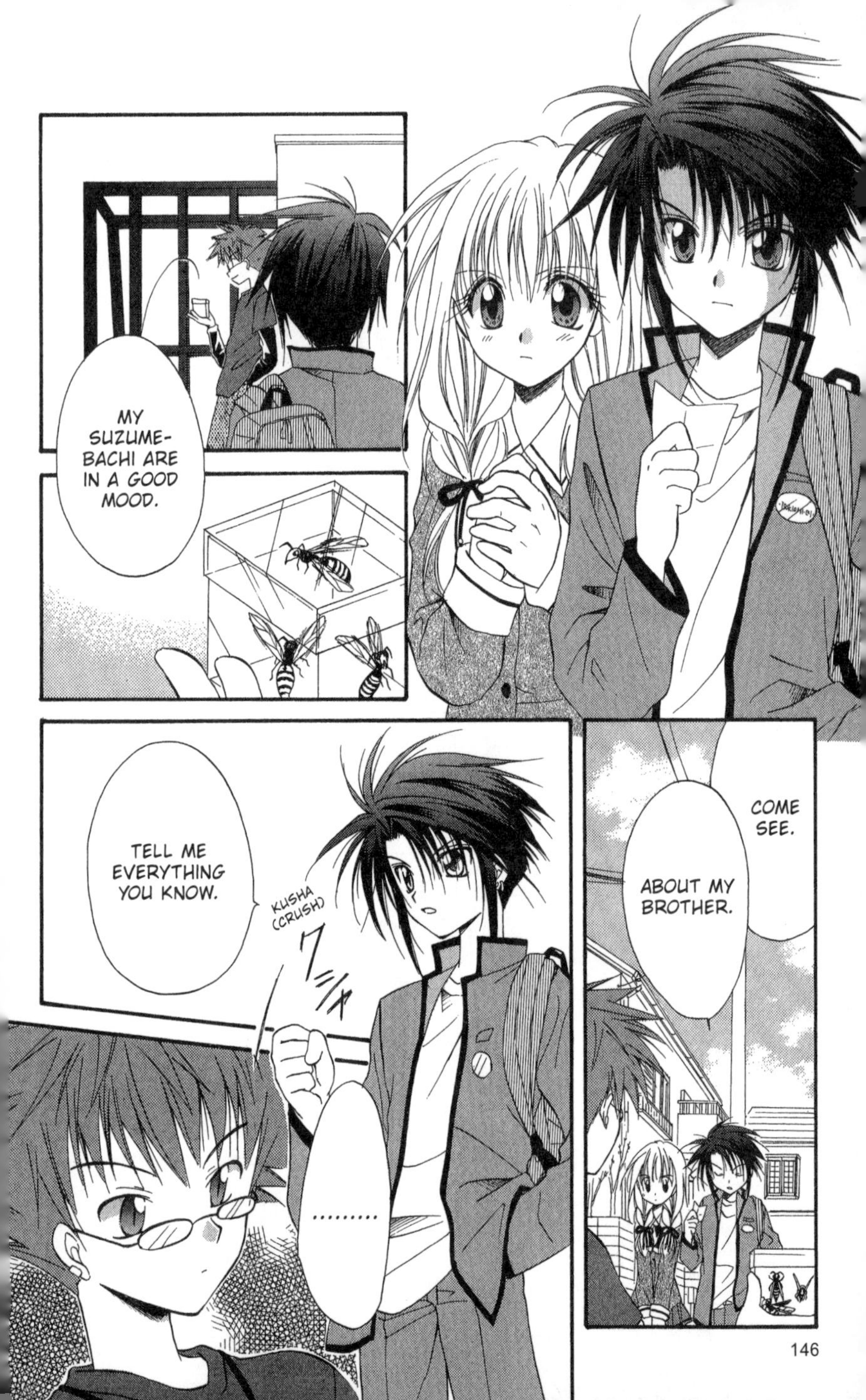

MY SUZUME-BACHI ARE IN A GOOD MOOD.
COME SEE.
ABOUT MY BROTHER.
TELL ME EVERYTHING YOU KNOW.
KUSHA (CRUSH)
....

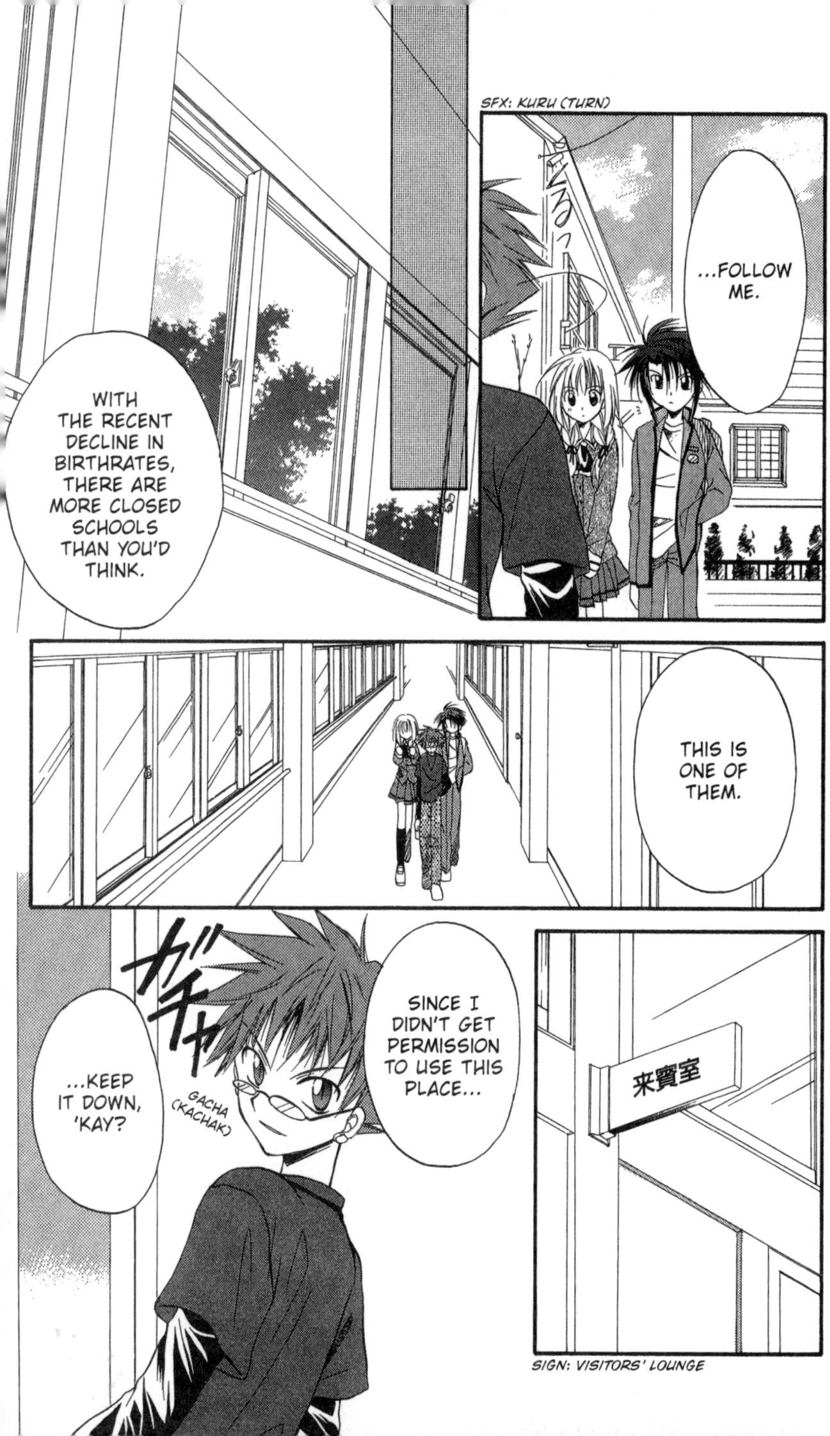
SFX: KURU (TURN)
...FOLLOW ME.
WITH THE RECENT DECLINE IN BIRTHRATES, THERE ARE MORE CLOSED SCHOOLS THAN YOU'D THINK.
THIS IS ONE OF THEM.
来賓室
SIGN: VISITORS' LOUNGE
SINCE I DIDN'T GET PERMISSION TO USE THIS PLACE...
GACHA (KACHAK)
...KEEP IT DOWN, 'KAY?

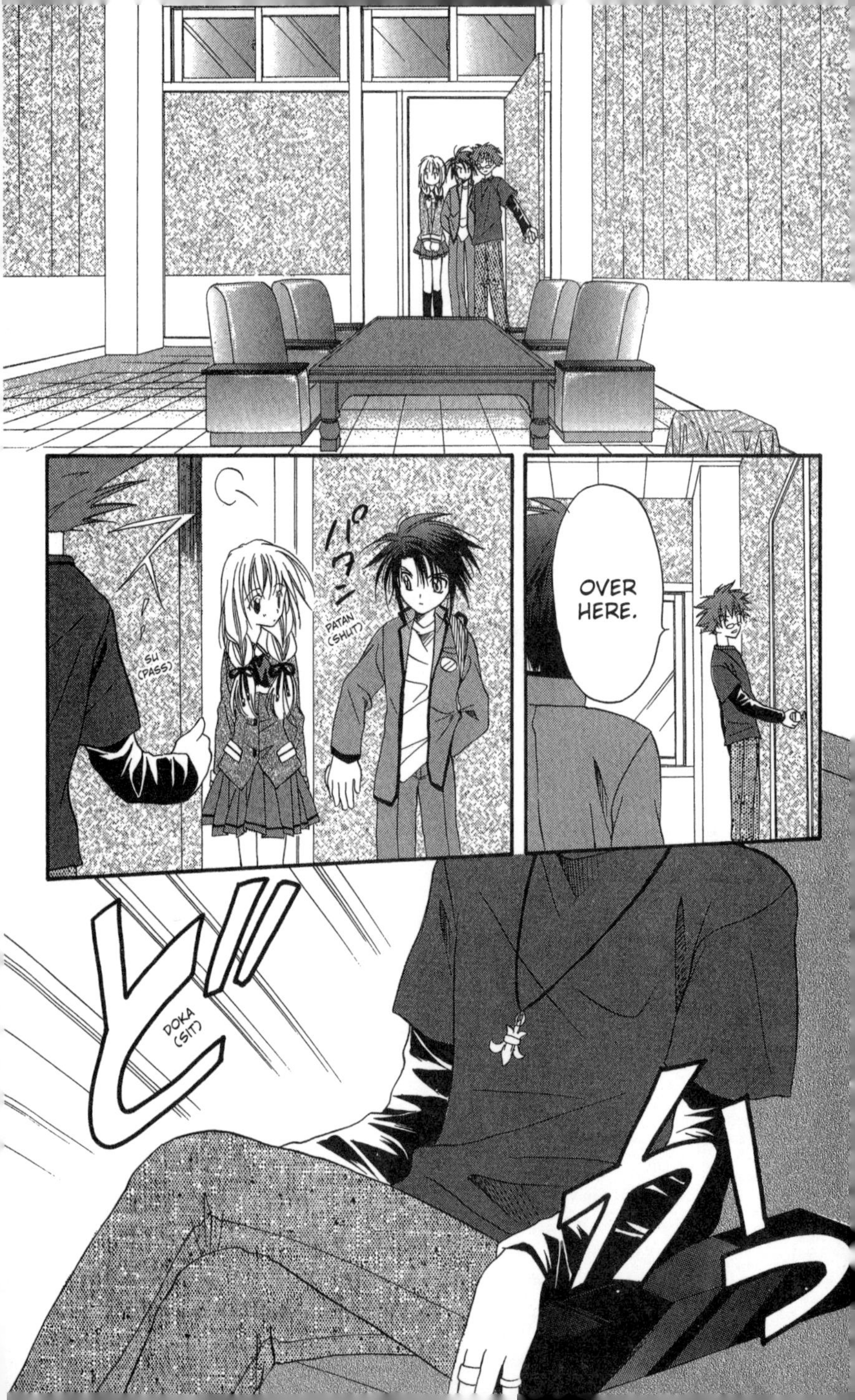
OVER HERE.
PATAN (SHUT)
SU (PASS)
DOKA (SIT)

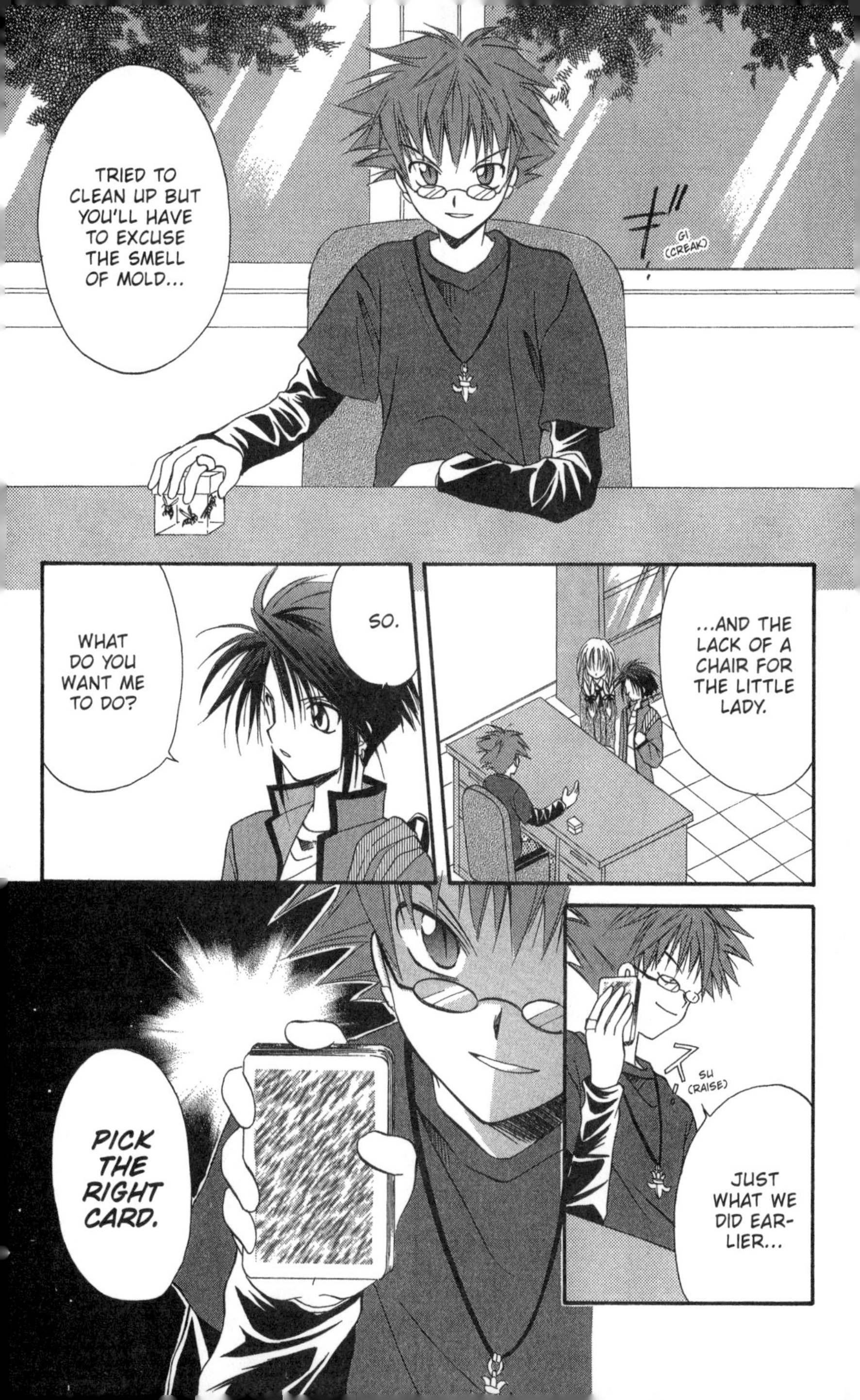
GI (CREAK)
TRIED TO CLEAN UP BUT YOU'LL HAVE TO EXCUSE THE SMELL OF MOLD...
...AND THE LACK OF A CHAIR FOR THE LITTLE LADY.
SO.
WHAT DO YOU WANT ME TO DO?
SU (RAISE)
JUST WHAT WE DID EARLIER...
PICK THE RIGHT CARD.

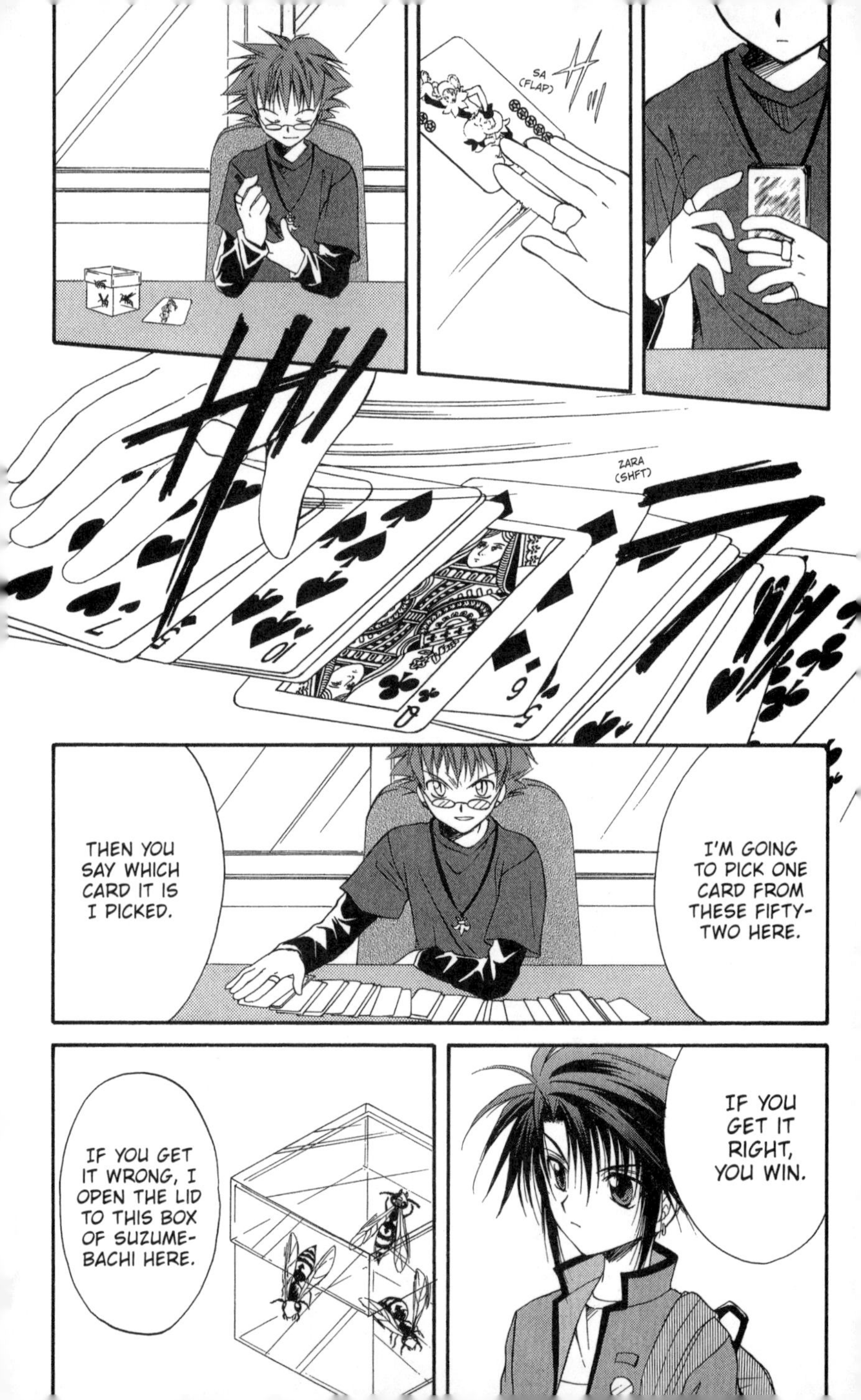
SA (FLAP)
ZARA (SHFT)
I'M GOING TO PICK ONE CARD FROM THESE FIFTY-TWO HERE.
THEN YOU SAY WHICH CARD IT IS I PICKED.
IF YOU GET IT RIGHT, YOU WIN.
IF YOU GET IT WRONG, I OPEN THE LID TO THIS BOX OF SUZUME-BACHI HERE.

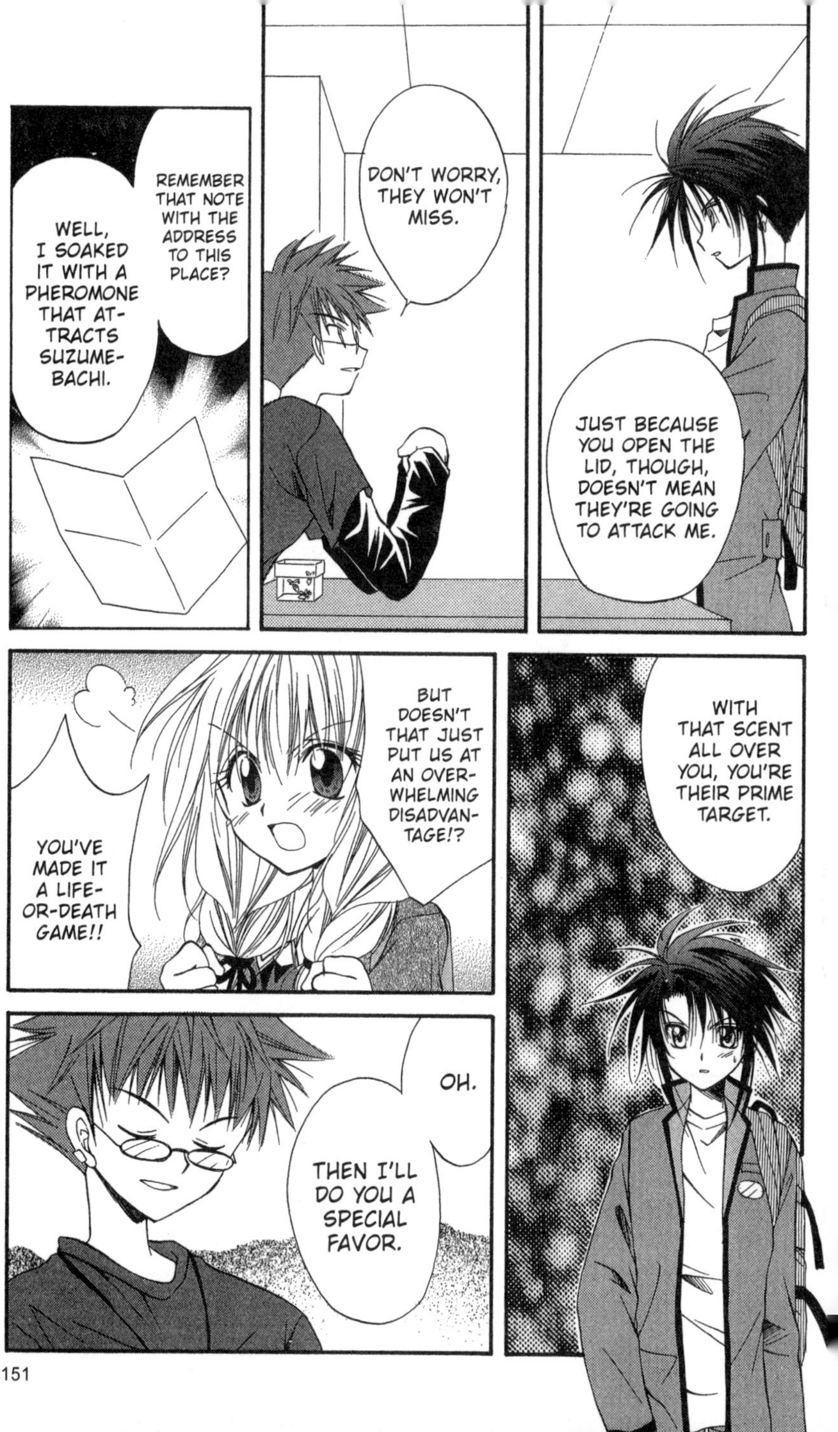
JUST BECAUSE YOU OPEN THE LID, THOUGH, DOESN'T MEAN THEY'RE GOING TO ATTACK ME.
DON'T WORRY, THEY WON'T MISS.
REMEMBER THAT NOTE WITH THE ADDRESS TO THIS PLACE?
WELL, I SOAKED IT WITH A PHEROMONE THAT AT-TRACTS SUZUME-BACHI.
WITH THAT SCENT ALL OVER YOU, YOU'RE THEIR PRIME TARGET.
BUT DOESN'T THAT JUST PUT US AT AN OVER-WHELMING DISADVAN-TAGE!?
YOU'VE MADE IT A LIFE-OR-DEATH GAME!!
OH.
THEN I'LL DO YOU A SPECIAL FAVOR.

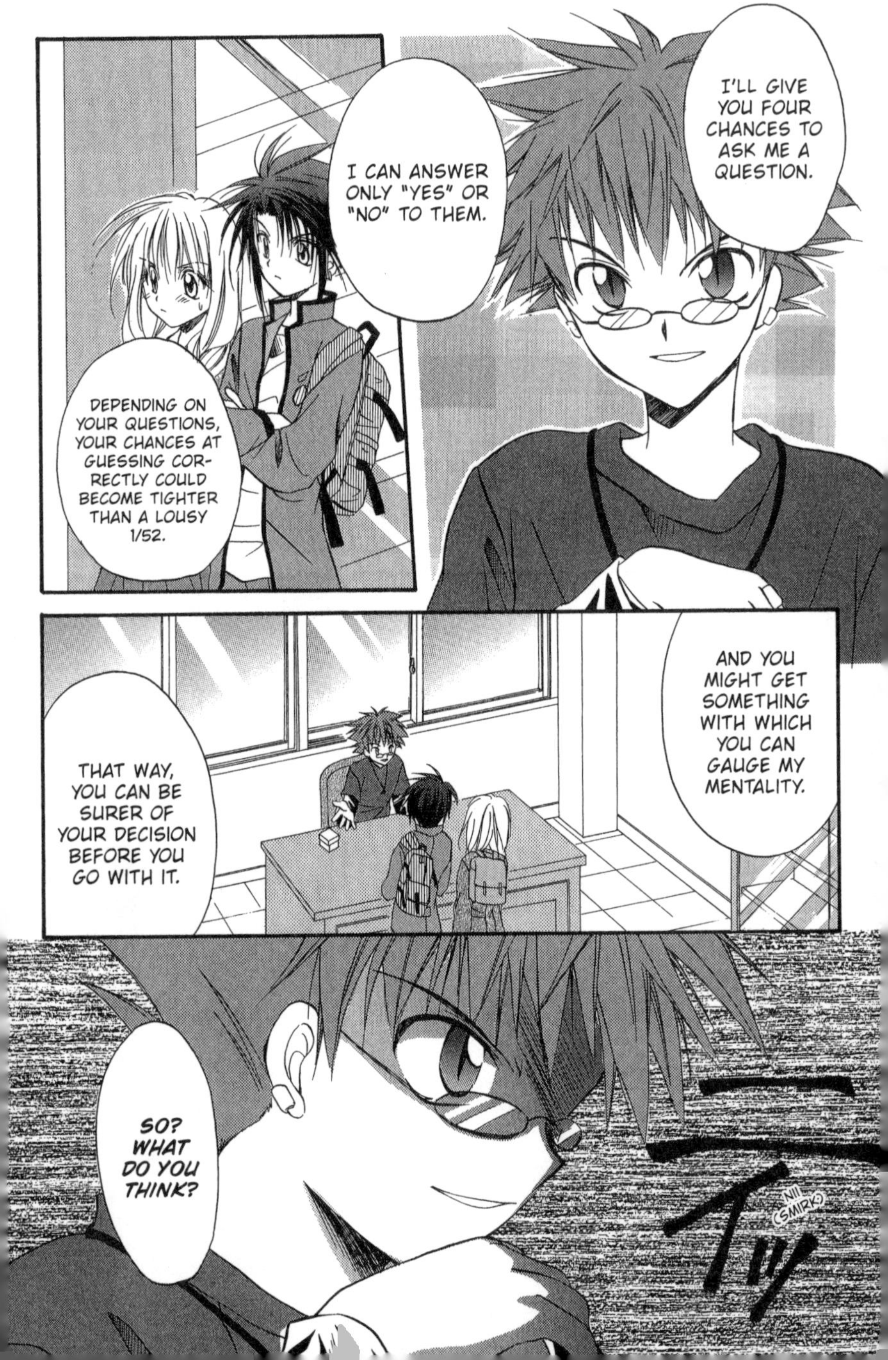
I'LL GIVE YOU FOUR CHANCES TO ASK ME A QUESTION.
I CAN ANSWER ONLY "YES" OR "NO" TO THEM.
DEPENDING ON YOUR QUESTIONS, YOUR CHANCES AT GUESSING COR-RECTLY COULD BECOME TIGHTER THAN A LOUSY 1/52.
AND YOU MIGHT GET SOMETHING WITH WHICH YOU CAN GAUGE MY MENTALITY.
THAT WAY, YOU CAN BE SURER OF YOUR DECISION BEFORE YOU GO WITH IT.
SO? WHAT DO YOU THINK?
NII (SMIRK)

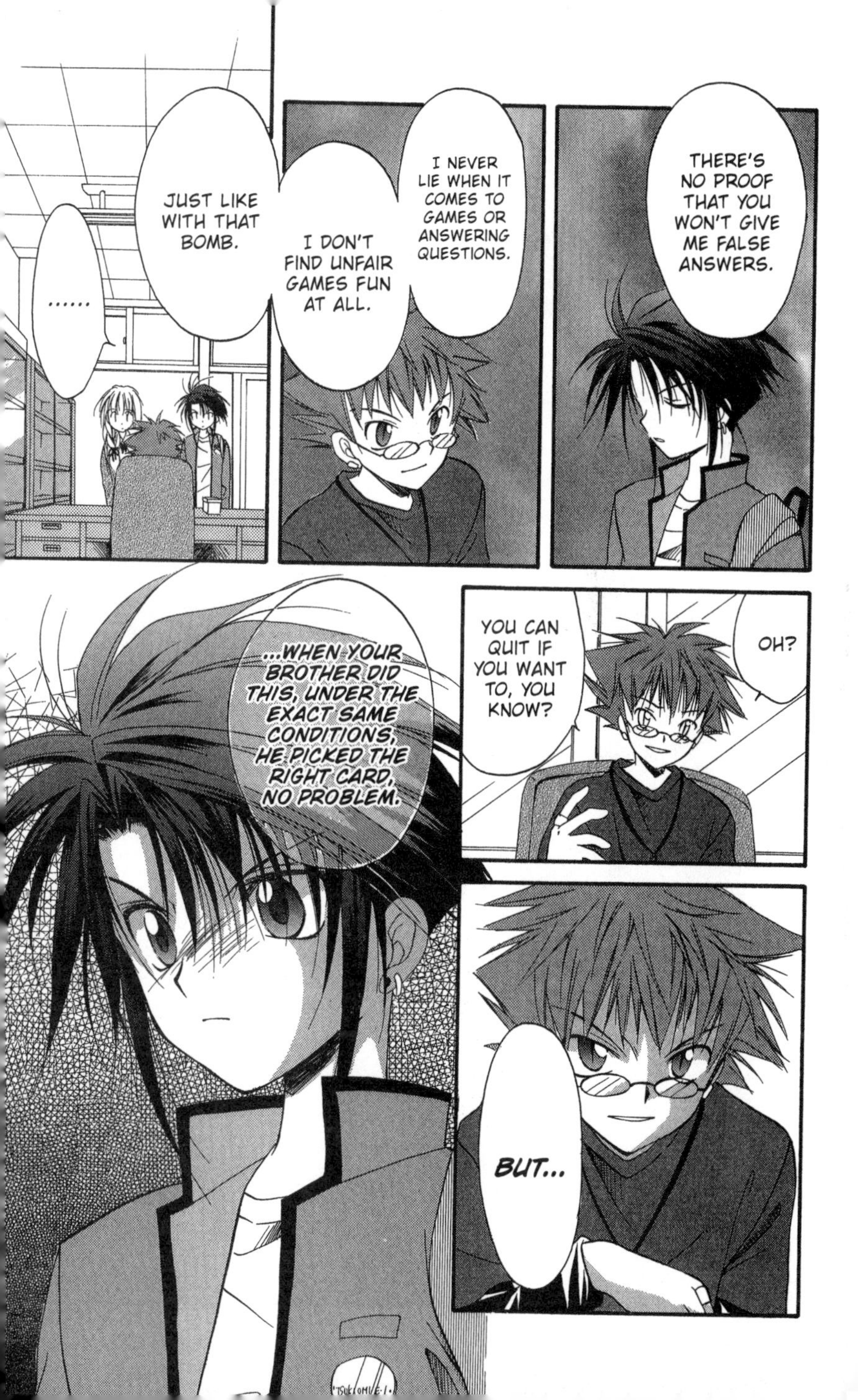
THERE'S NO PROOF THAT YOU WON'T GIVE ME FALSE ANSWERS.
I NEVER LIE WHEN IT COMES TO GAMES OR ANSWERING QUESTIONS.
I DON'T FIND UNFAIR GAMES FUN AT ALL.
JUST LIKE WITH THAT BOMB.
......
OH?
YOU CAN QUIT IF YOU WANT TO, YOU KNOW?
BUT...
...WHEN YOUR BROTHER DID THIS, UNDER THE EXACT SAME CONDITIONS, HE PICKED THE RIGHT CARD, NO PROBLEM.

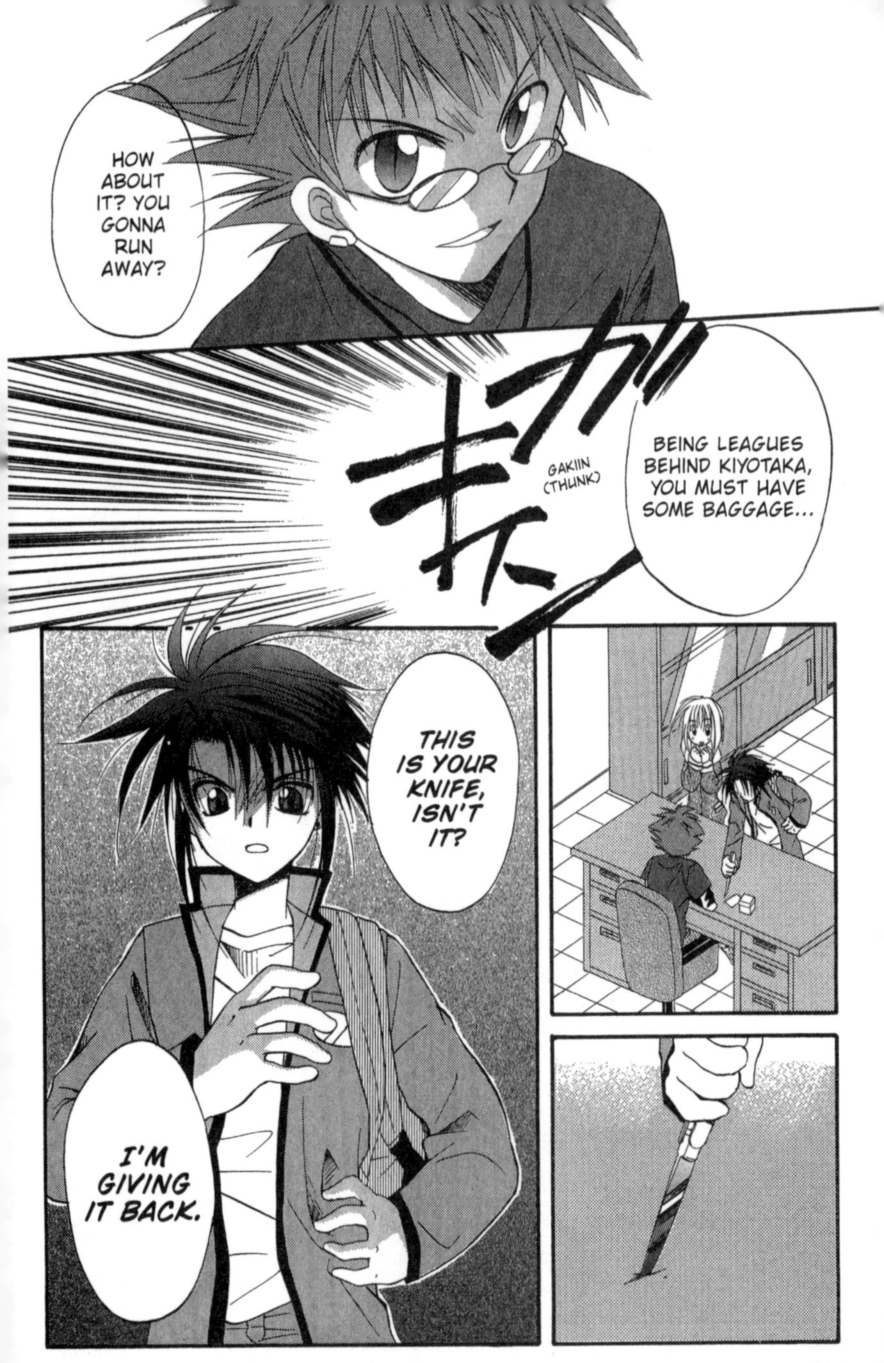
HOW ABOUT IT? YOU GONNA RUN AWAY?
BEING LEAGUES BEHIND KIYOTAKA, YOU MUST HAVE SOME BAGGAGE...
GAKIIN (THUNK)
THIS IS YOUR KNIFE, ISN'T IT?
I'M GIVING IT BACK.

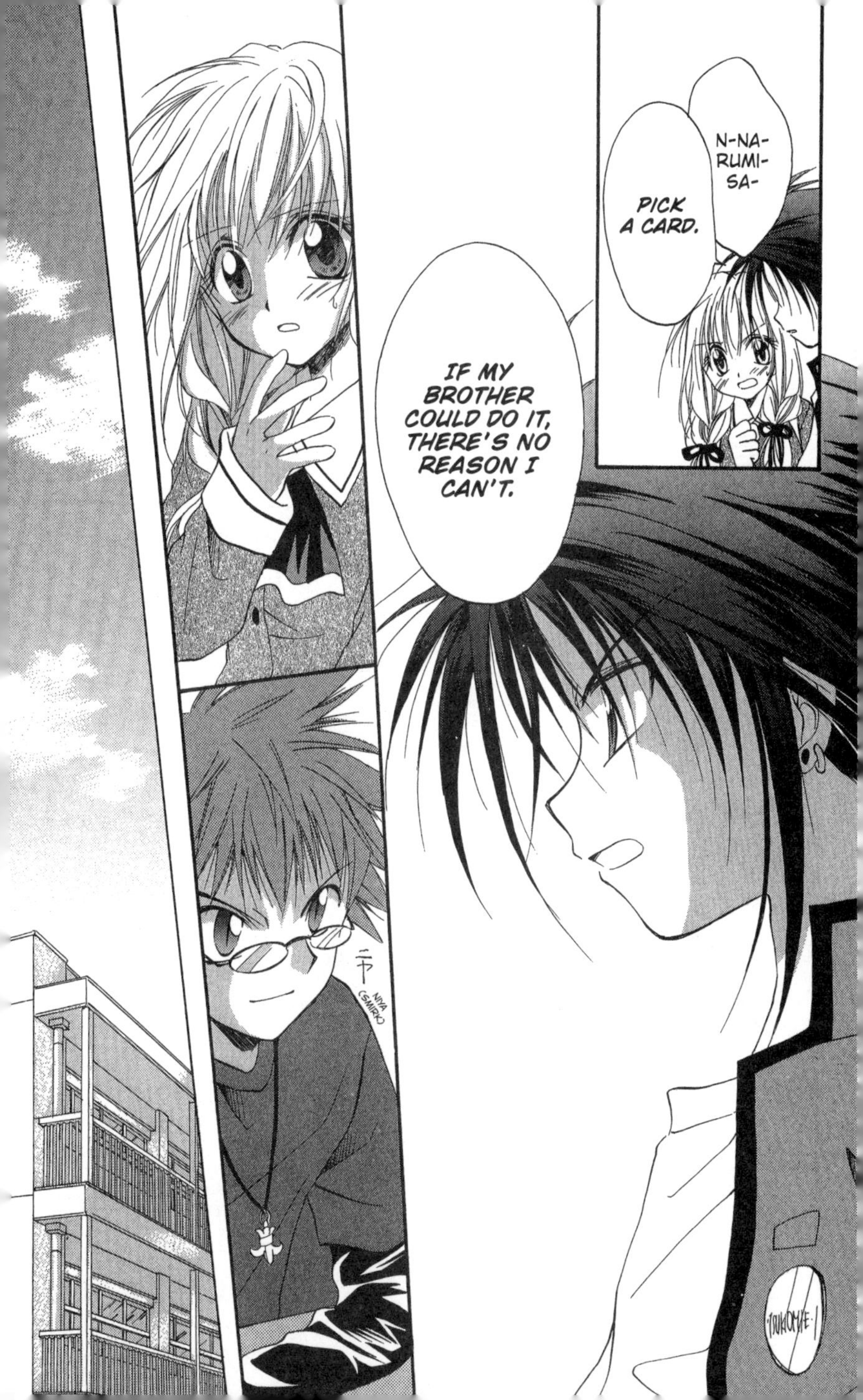
N-NA-RUMI-SA-
PICK A CARD.
IF MY BROTHER COULD DO IT, THERE'S NO REASON I CAN'T.
ニヤ
NIYA (SMIRK)

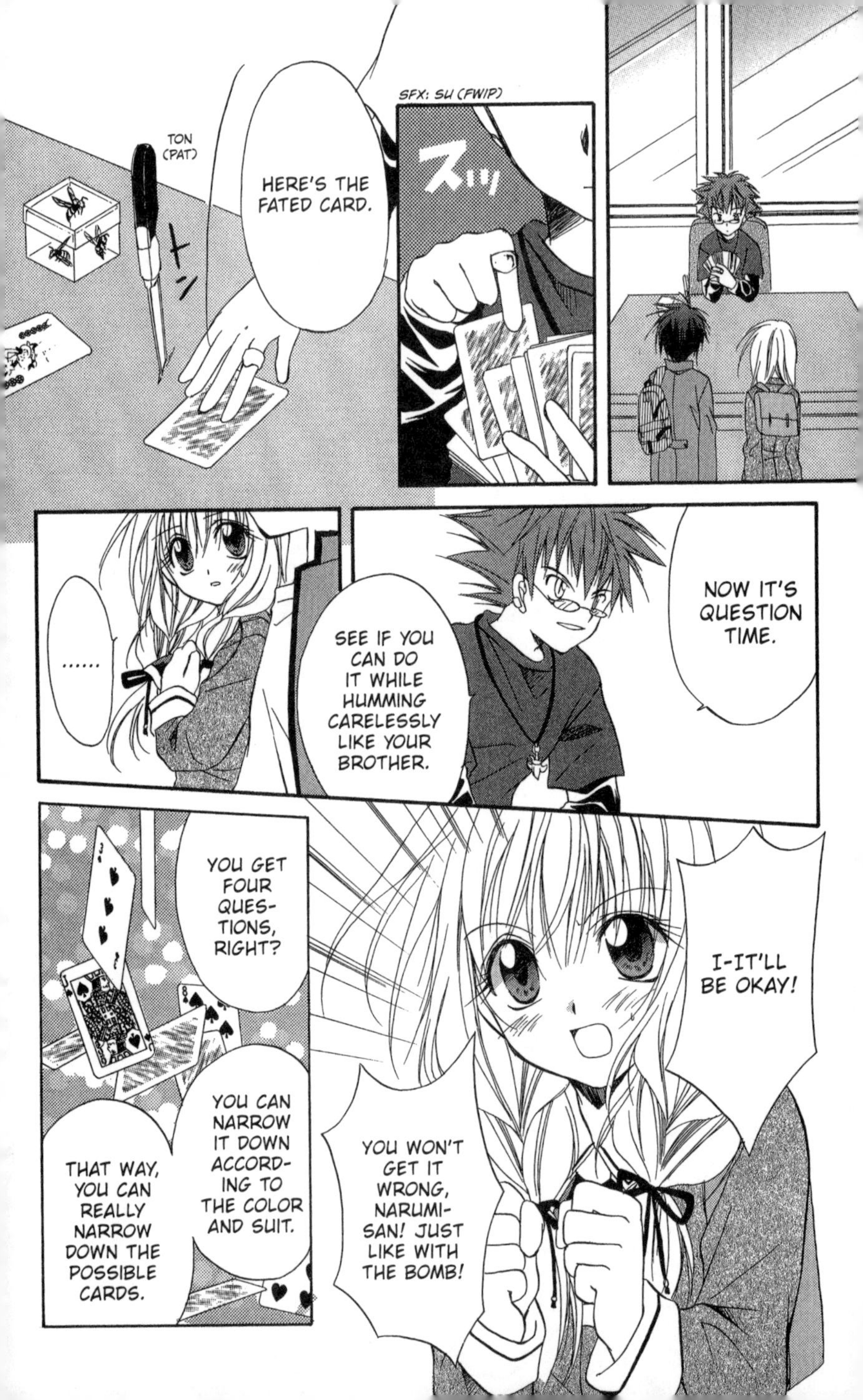
SFX: SU (FWIP)
HERE'S THE FATED CARD.
TON (PAT)
NOW IT'S QUESTION TIME.
SEE IF YOU CAN DO IT WHILE HUMMING CARELESSLY LIKE YOUR BROTHER.
......
I-IT'LL BE OKAY!
YOU WON'T GET IT WRONG, NARUMI-SAN! JUST LIKE WITH THE BOMB!
YOU GET FOUR QUES-TIONS, RIGHT?
YOU CAN NARROW IT DOWN ACCORD-ING TO THE COLOR AND SUIT.
THAT WAY, YOU CAN REALLY NARROW DOWN THE POSSIBLE CARDS.

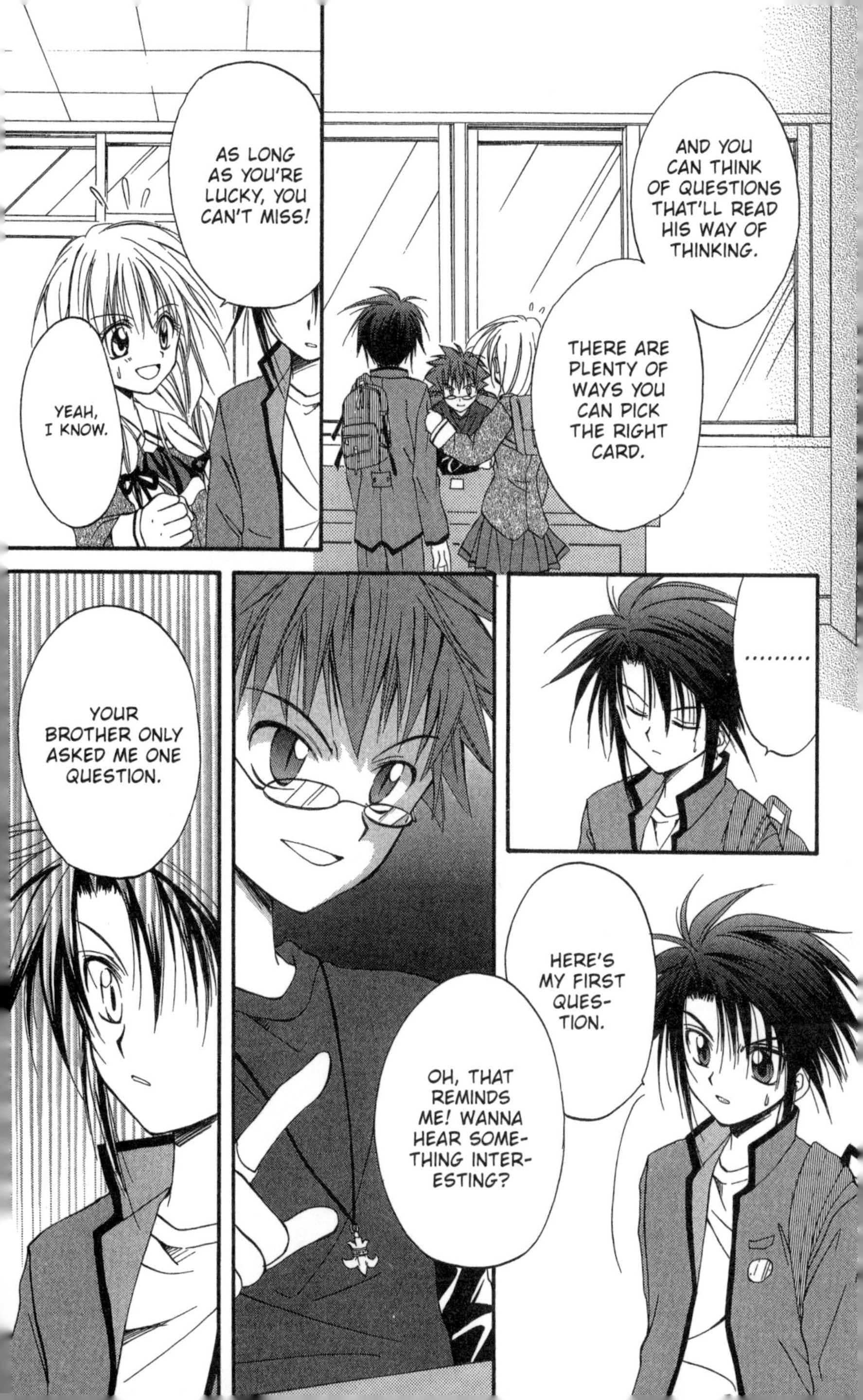
AND YOU CAN THINK OF QUESTIONS THAT'LL READ HIS WAY OF THINKING.
THERE ARE PLENTY OF WAYS YOU CAN PICK THE RIGHT CARD.
AS LONG AS YOU'RE LUCKY, YOU CAN'T MISS!
YEAH, I KNOW.
....
HERE'S MY FIRST QUES-TION.
OH, THAT REMINDS ME! WANNA HEAR SOME-THING INTER-ESTING?
YOUR BROTHER ONLY ASKED ME ONE QUESTION.

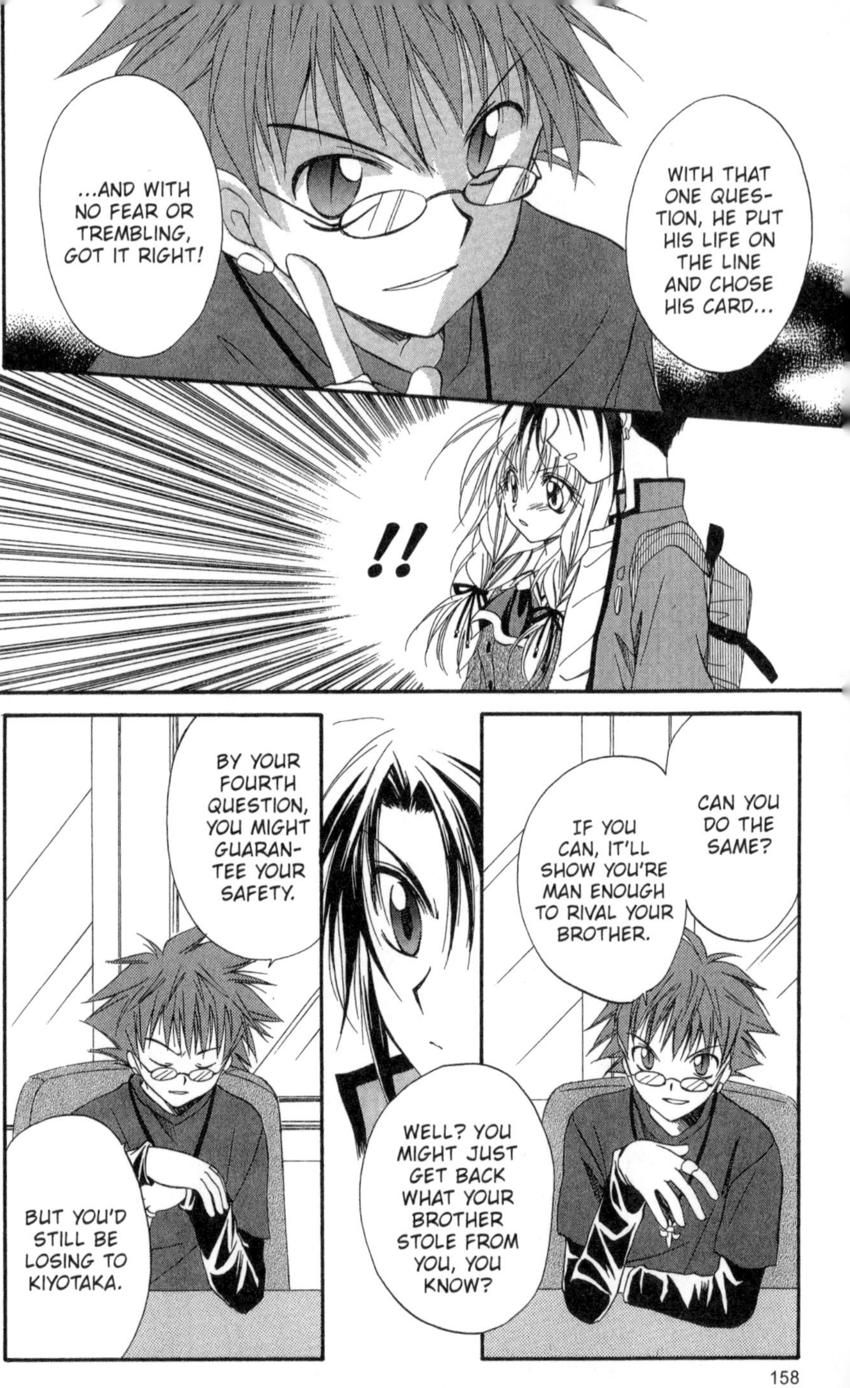
WITH THAT ONE QUES- TION, HE PUT HIS LIFE ON THE LINE AND CHOSE HIS CARD...
...AND WITH NO FEAR OR TREMBLING, GOT IT RIGHT!
!!
CAN YOU DO THE SAME?
IF YOU CAN, IT'LL SHOW YOU'RE MAN ENOUGH TO RIVAL YOUR BROTHER.
WELL? YOU MIGHT JUST GET BACK WHAT YOUR BROTHER STOLE FROM YOU, YOU KNOW?
BY YOUR FOURTH QUESTION, YOU MIGHT GUARAN- TEE YOUR SAFETY.
BUT YOU'D STILL BE LOSING TO KIYOTAKA.

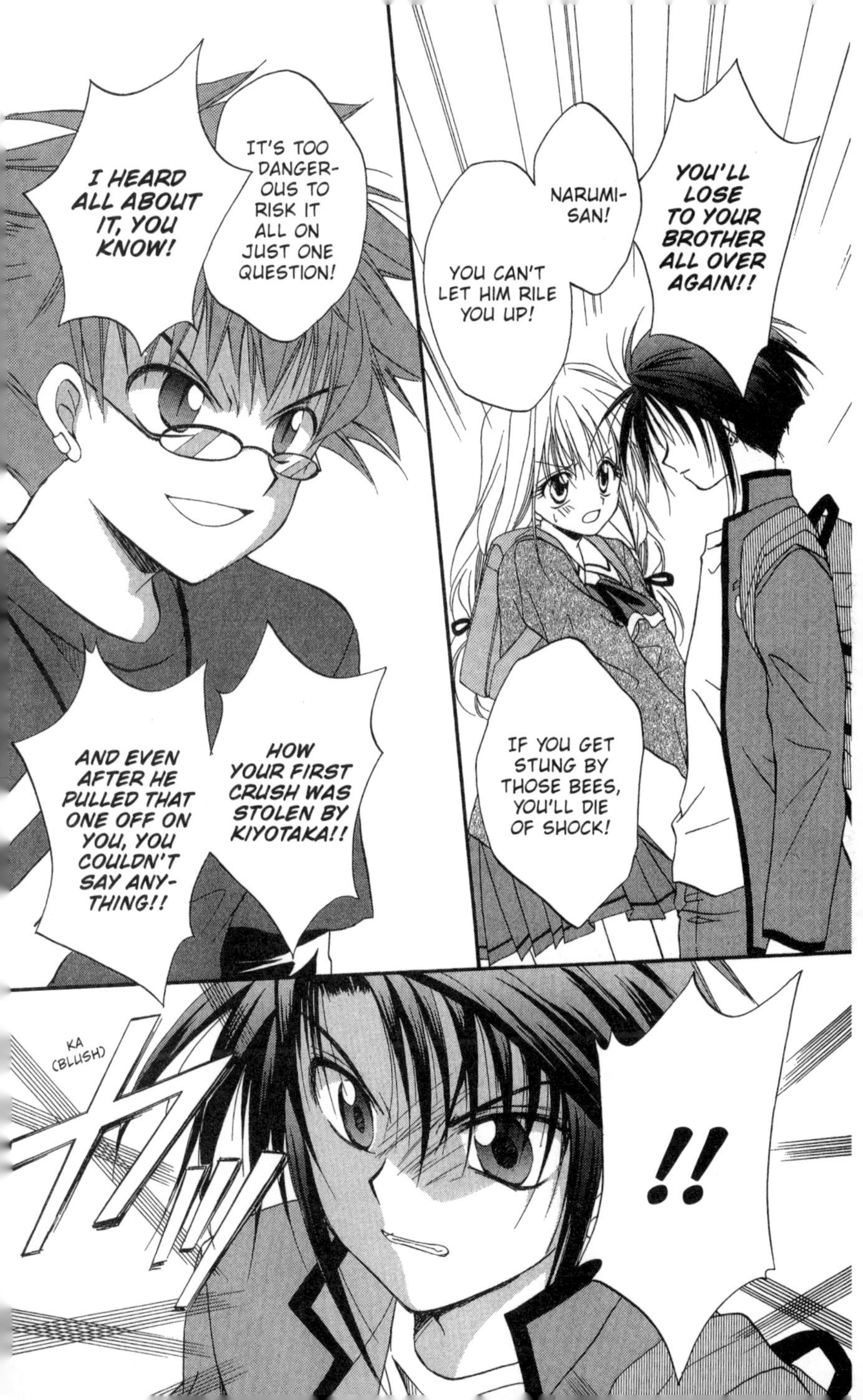
YOU'LL LOSE TO YOUR BROTHER ALL OVER AGAIN!!
NARUMI-SAN!
YOU CAN'T LET HIM RILE YOU UP!
IF YOU GET STUNG BY THOSE BEES, YOU'LL DIE OF SHOCK!
IT'S TOO DANGER-OUS TO RISK IT ALL ON JUST ONE QUESTION!
I HEARD ALL ABOUT IT, YOU KNOW!
HOW YOUR FIRST CRUSH WAS STOLEN BY KIYOTAKA!!
AND EVEN AFTER HE PULLED THAT ONE OFF ON YOU, YOU COULDN'T SAY ANY-THING!!
!!
KA (BLUSH)

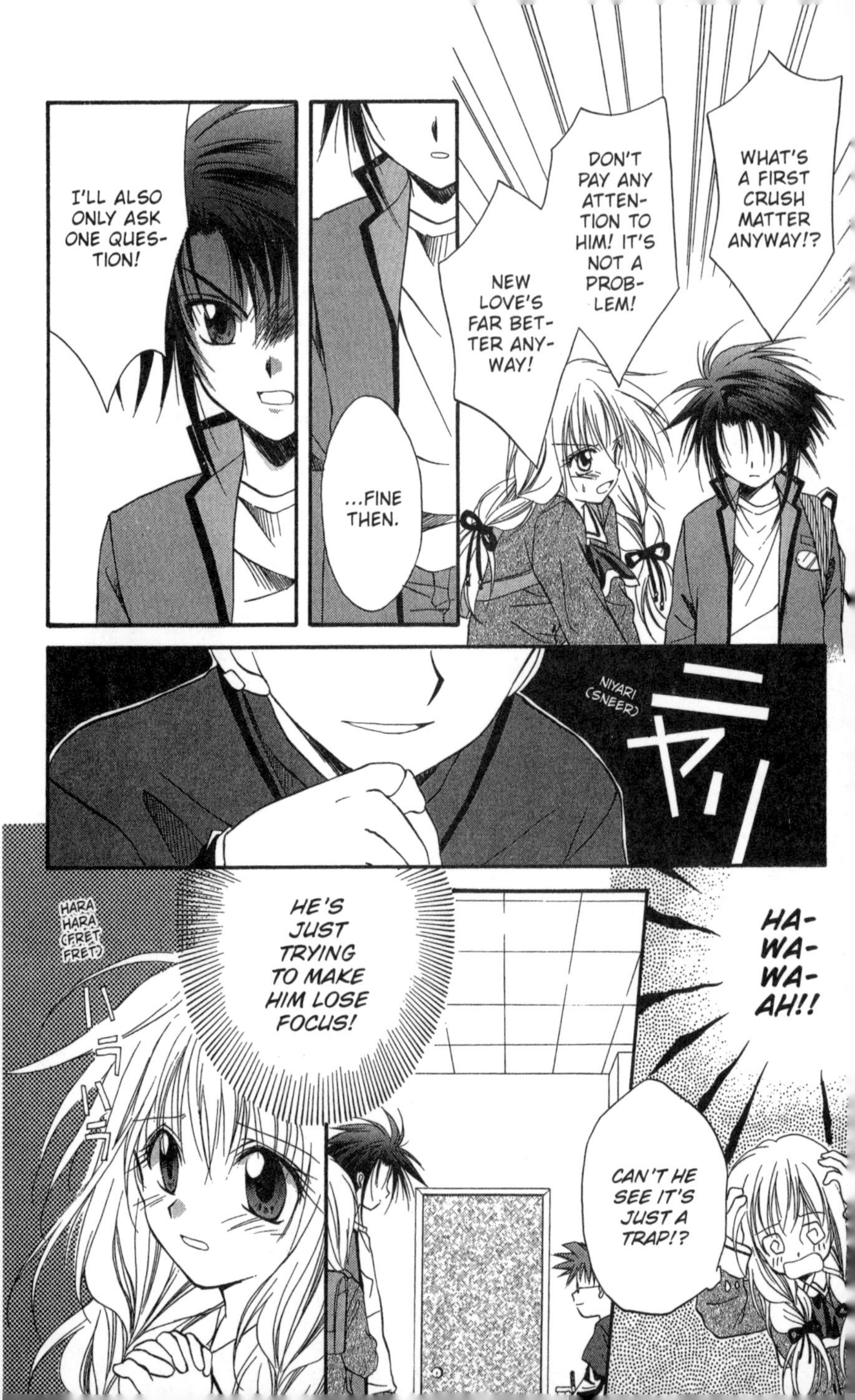
WHAT'S A FIRST CRUSH MATTER ANYWAY!?
DON'T PAY ANY ATTENTION TO HIM! IT'S NOT A PROBLEM!
NEW LOVE'S FAR BETTER ANYWAY!
...FINE THEN.
I'LL ALSO ONLY ASK ONE QUESTION!
NIYARI (SNEER)
HA-WA-WA-AH!!
CAN'T HE SEE IT'S JUST A TRAP!?
HE'S JUST TRYING TO MAKE HIM LOSE FOCUS!
HARA HARA (FRET FRET)

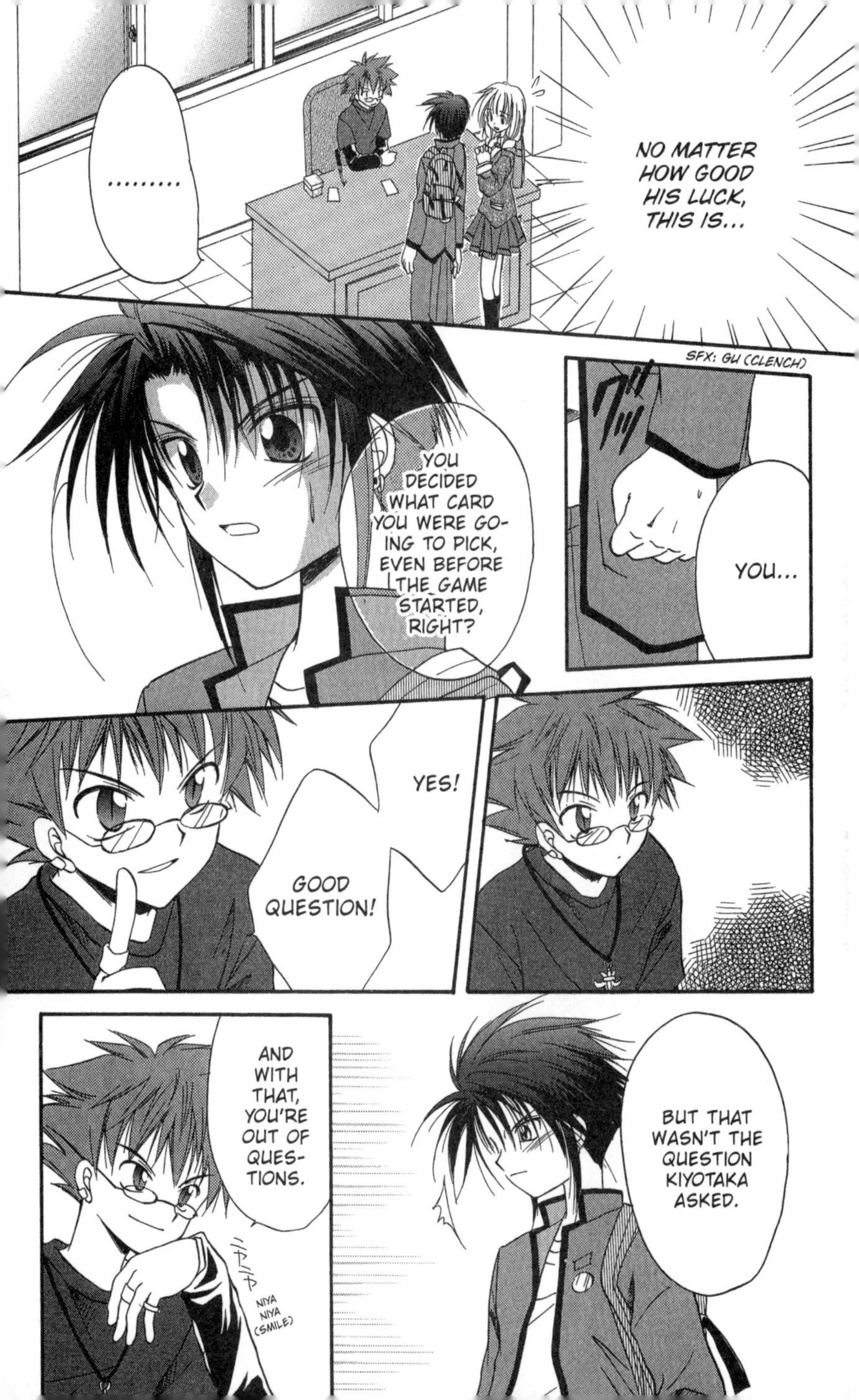
NO MATTER HOW GOOD HIS LUCK, THIS IS...
....
SFX: GU (CLENCH)
YOU...
YOU DECIDED WHAT CARD YOU WERE GO-ING TO PICK, EVEN BEFORE THE GAME STARTED, RIGHT?
YES!
GOOD QUESTION!
BUT THAT WASN'T THE QUESTION KIYOTAKA ASKED.
AND WITH THAT, YOU'RE OUT OF QUES-TIONS.
NIYA NIYA (SMILE)

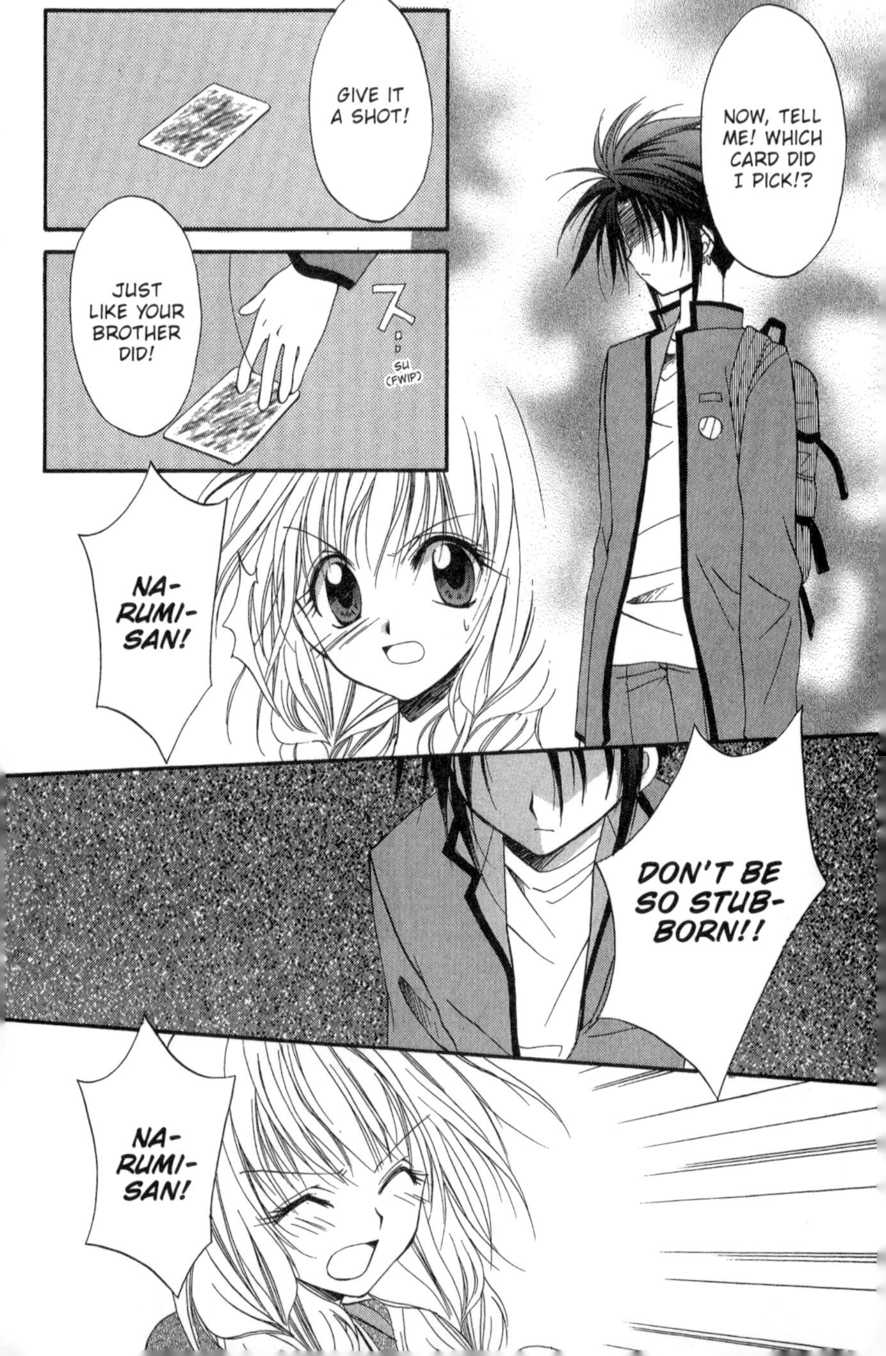
NOW, TELL ME! WHICH CARD DID I PICK!?
GIVE IT A SHOT!
JUST LIKE YOUR BROTHER DID!
ス
SU (FWIP)
NA-RUMI-SAN!
DON'T BE SO STUB-BORN!!
NA-RUMI-SAN!

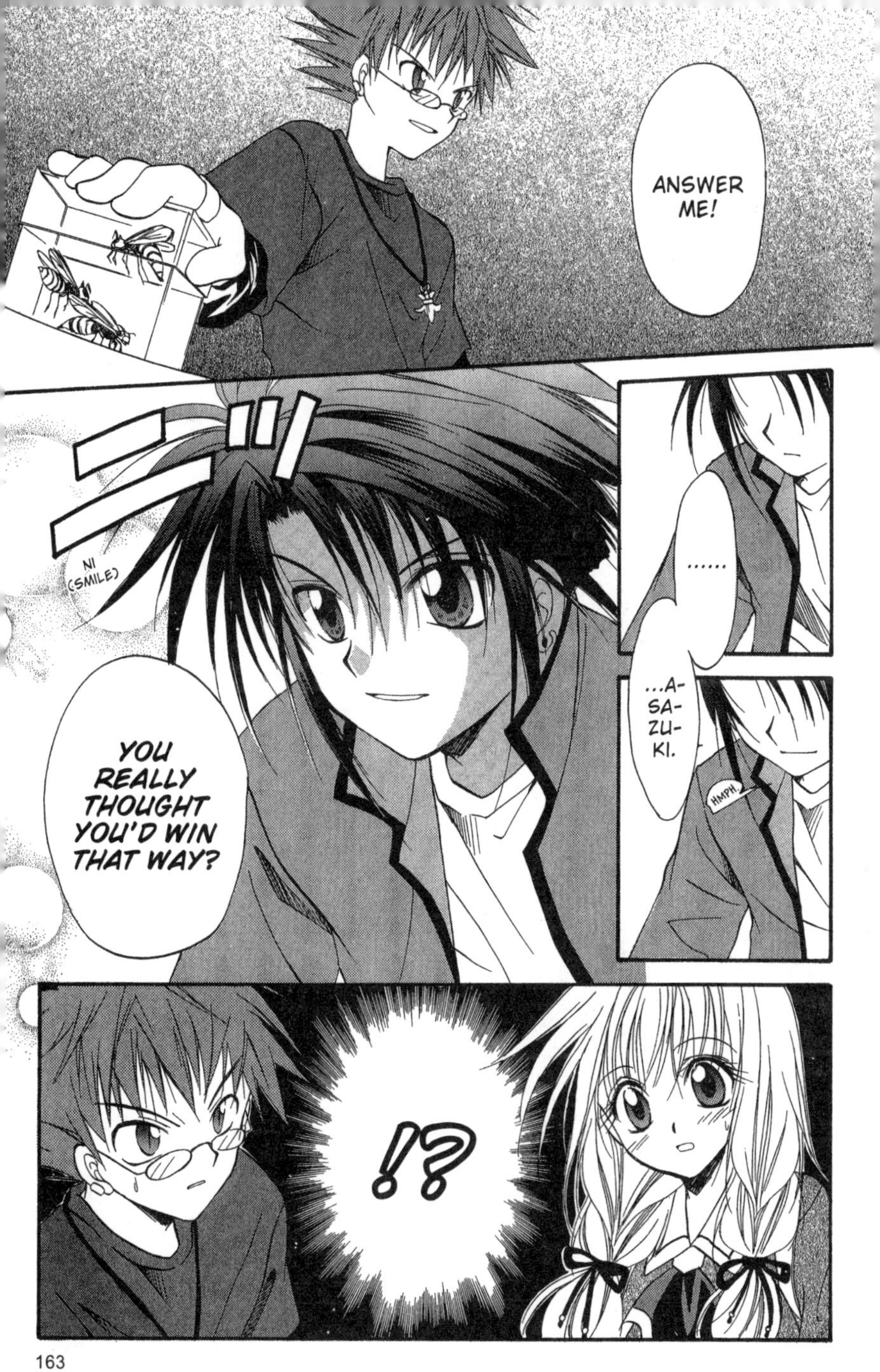
ANSWER ME!
......
...A-SA-ZU-KI.
HMPH.
NI (SMILE)
YOU REALLY THOUGHT YOU'D WIN THAT WAY?
!?

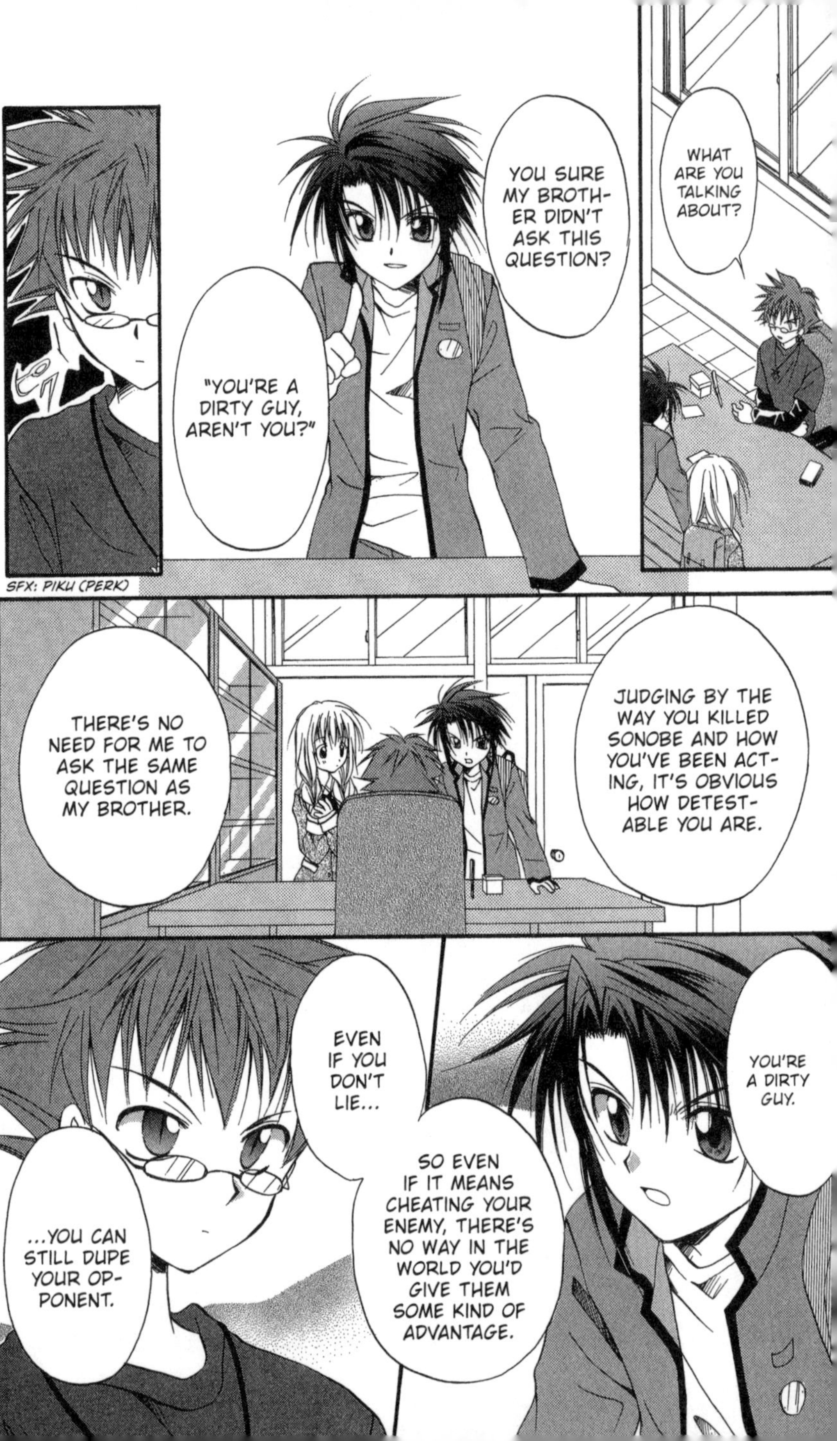
WHAT ARE YOU TALKING ABOUT?
YOU SURE MY BROTHER DIDN'T ASK THIS QUESTION?
"YOU'RE A DIRTY GUY, AREN'T YOU?"
SFX: PIKU (PERK)
THERE'S NO NEED FOR ME TO ASK THE SAME QUESTION AS MY BROTHER.
JUDGING BY THE WAY YOU KILLED SONOBE AND HOW YOU'VE BEEN ACTING, IT'S OBVIOUS HOW DETESTABLE YOU ARE.
YOU'RE A DIRTY GUY.
SO EVEN IF IT MEANS CHEATING YOUR ENEMY, THERE'S NO WAY IN THE WORLD YOU'D GIVE THEM SOME KIND OF ADVANTAGE.
EVEN IF YOU DON'T LIE...
...YOU CAN STILL DUPE YOUR OPPONENT.

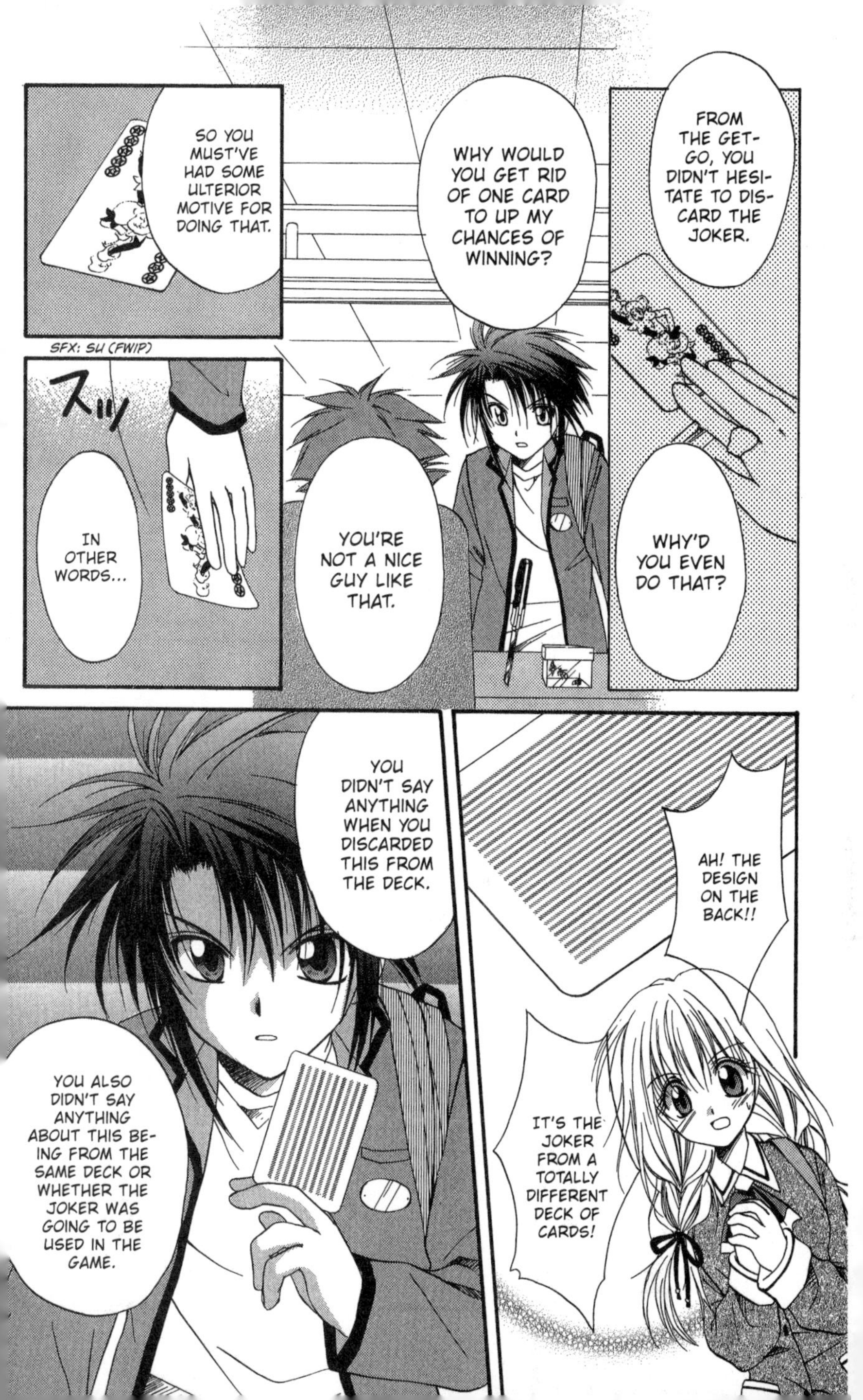
FROM THE GET-GO, YOU DIDN'T HESITATE TO DISCARD THE JOKER.
WHY'D YOU EVEN DO THAT?
WHY WOULD YOU GET RID OF ONE CARD TO UP MY CHANCES OF WINNING?
YOU'RE NOT A NICE GUY LIKE THAT.
SO YOU MUST'VE HAD SOME ULTERIOR MOTIVE FOR DOING THAT.
SFX: SU (FWIP)
スッ
IN OTHER WORDS...
AH! THE DESIGN ON THE BACK!!
IT'S THE JOKER FROM A TOTALLY DIFFERENT DECK OF CARDS!
YOU DIDN'T SAY ANYTHING WHEN YOU DISCARDED THIS FROM THE DECK.
YOU ALSO DIDN'T SAY ANYTHING ABOUT THIS BEING FROM THE SAME DECK OR WHETHER THE JOKER WAS GOING TO BE USED IN THE GAME.

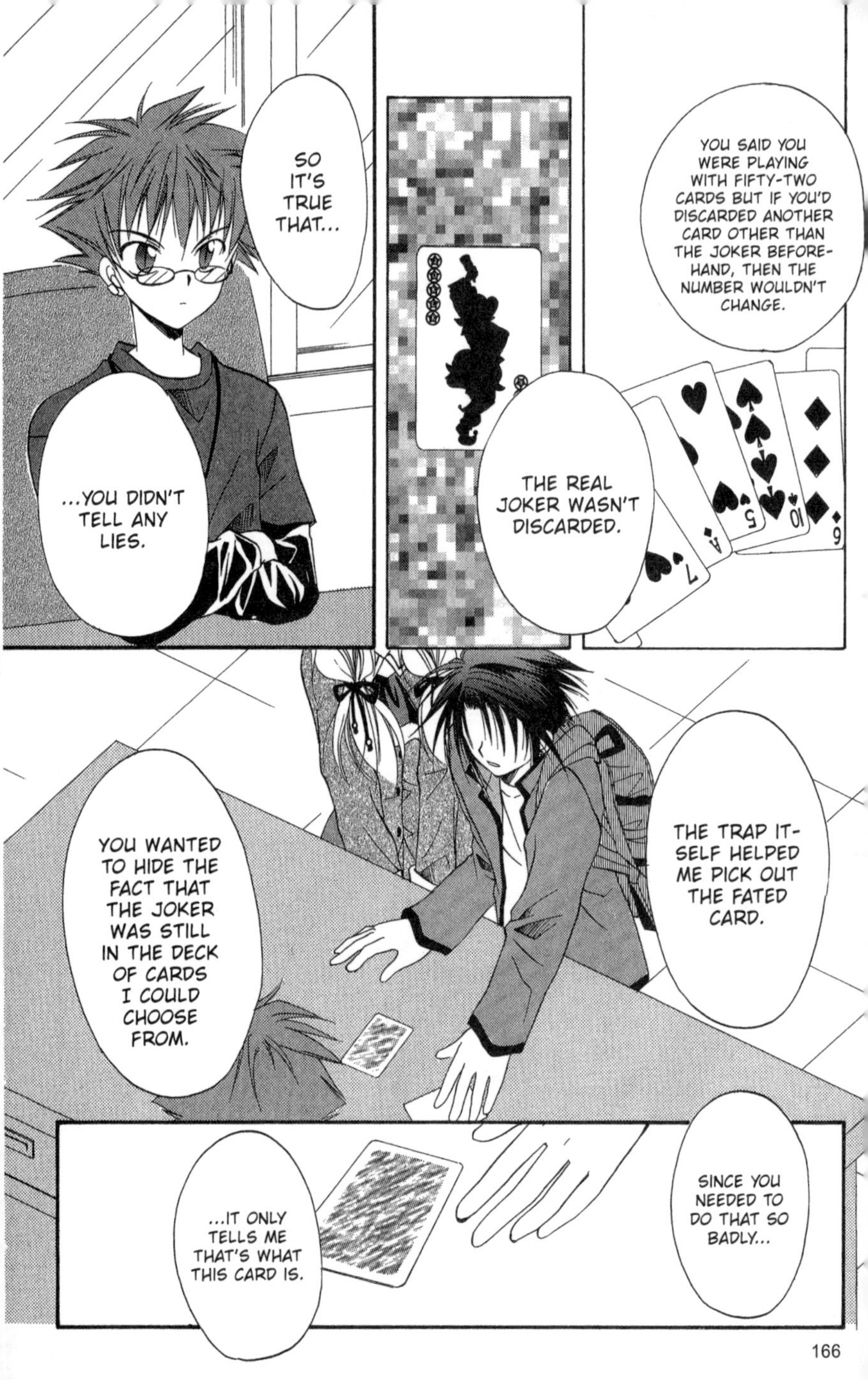
YOU SAID YOU WERE PLAYING WITH FIFTY-TWO CARDS BUT IF YOU'D DISCARDED ANOTHER CARD OTHER THAN THE JOKER BEFORE-HAND, THEN THE NUMBER WOULDN'T CHANGE.
THE REAL JOKER WASN'T DISCARDED.
SO IT'S TRUE THAT...
...YOU DIDN'T TELL ANY LIES.
THE TRAP IT-SELF HELPED ME PICK OUT THE FATED CARD.
YOU WANTED TO HIDE THE FACT THAT THE JOKER WAS STILL IN THE DECK OF CARDS I COULD CHOOSE FROM.
SINCE YOU NEEDED TO DO THAT SO BADLY...
...IT ONLY TELLS ME THAT'S WHAT THIS CARD IS.

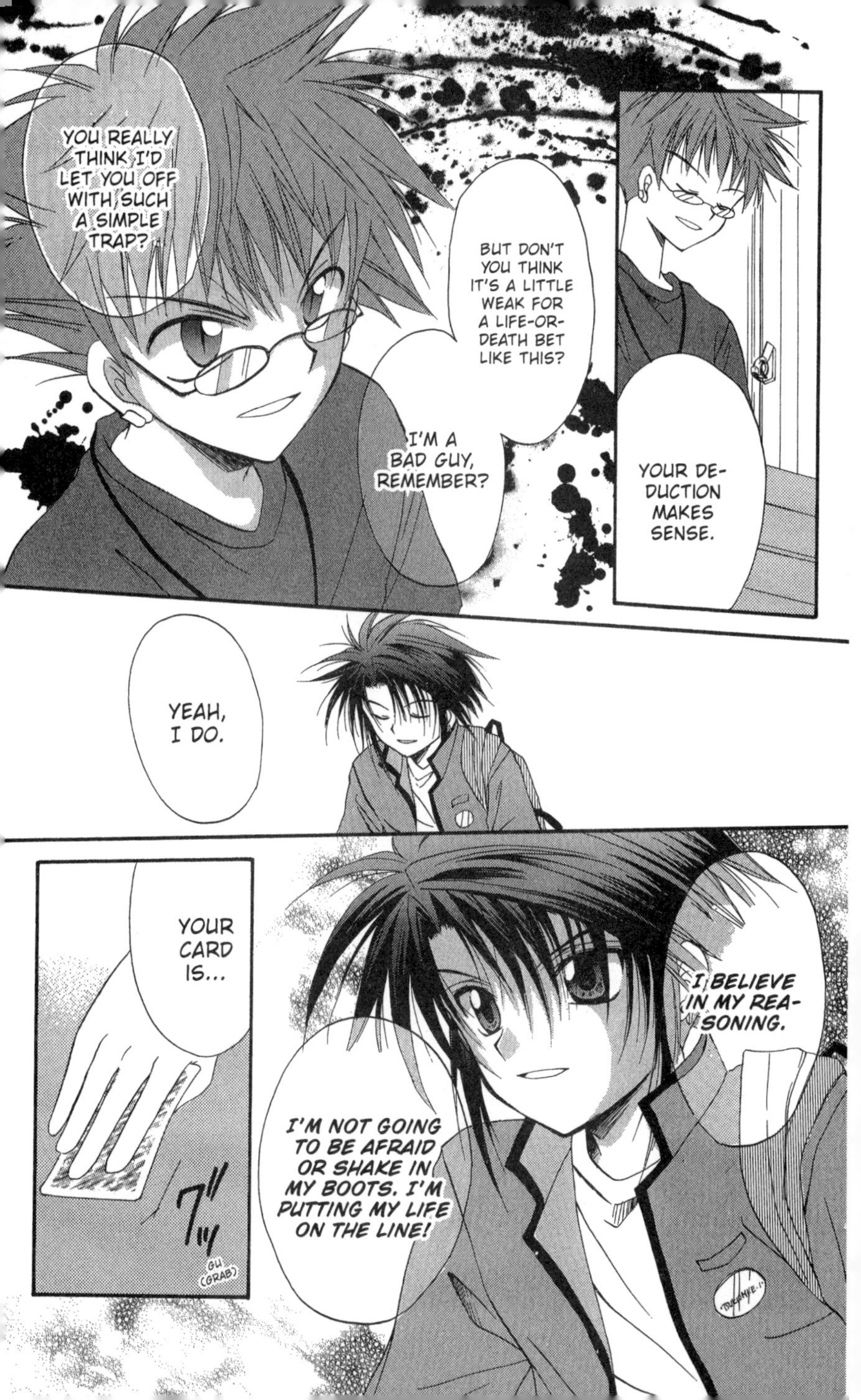
YOUR DE-DUCTION MAKES SENSE.
BUT DON'T YOU THINK IT'S A LITTLE WEAK FOR A LIFE-OR-DEATH BET LIKE THIS?
I'M A BAD GUY, REMEMBER?
YOU REALLY THINK I'D LET YOU OFF WITH SUCH A SIMPLE TRAP?
YEAH, I DO.
I BELIEVE IN MY REA-SONING.
I'M NOT GOING TO BE AFRAID OR SHAKE IN MY BOOTS. I'M PUTTING MY LIFE ON THE LINE!
YOUR CARD IS...
GU (GRAB)

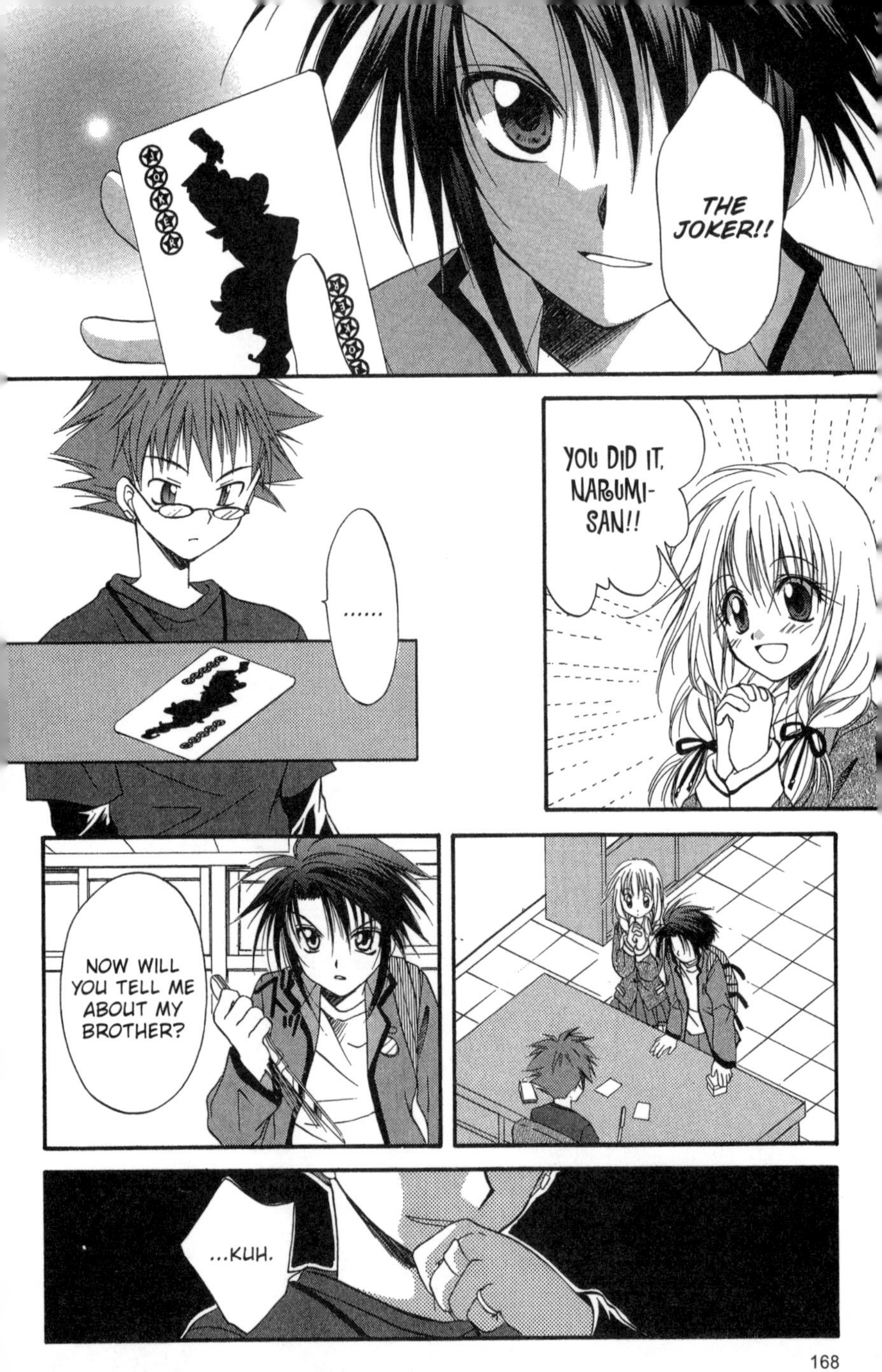
THE JOKER!!
YOU DID IT, NARUMI-SAN!!
......
NOW WILL YOU TELL ME ABOUT MY BROTHER?
...KUH.

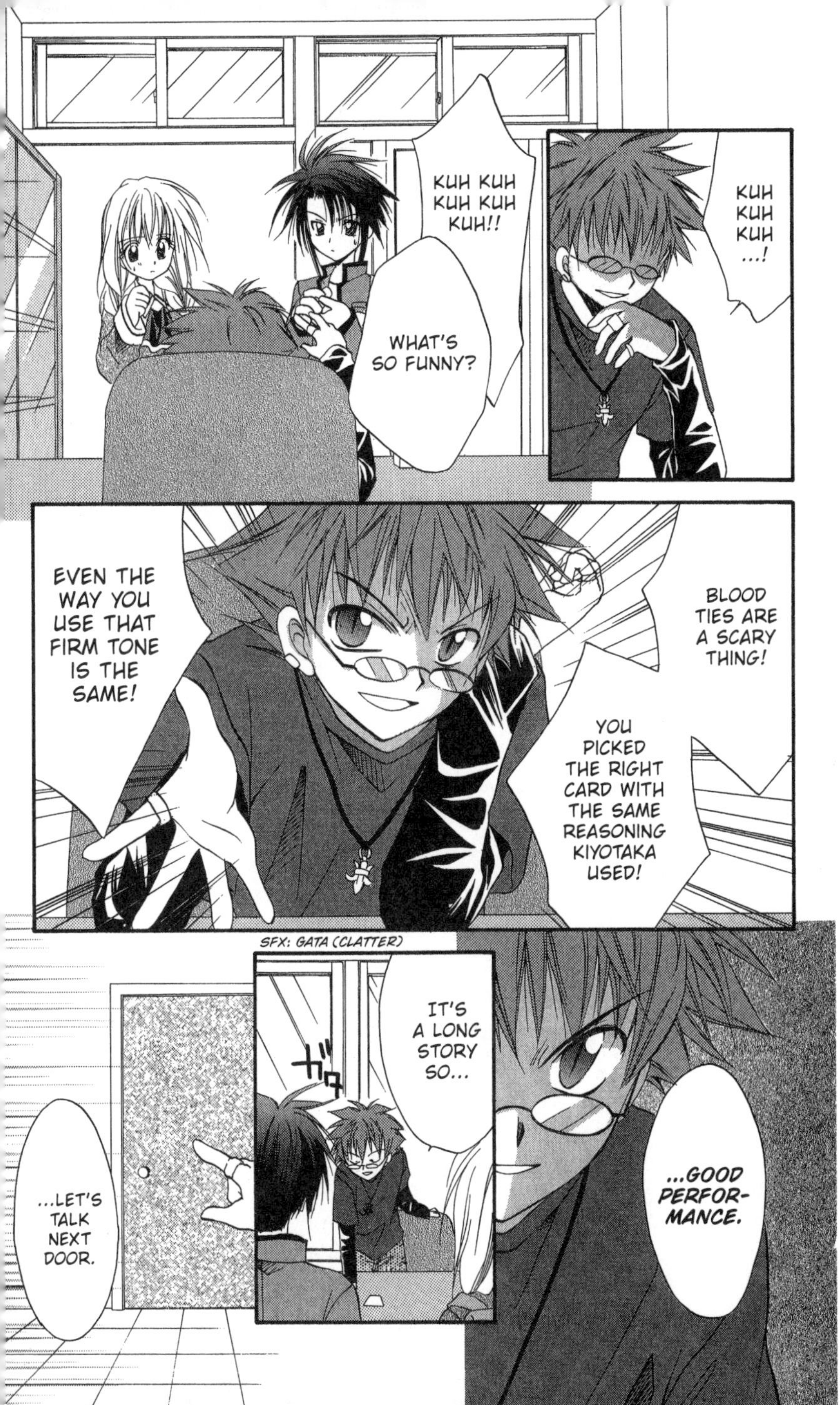
KUH KUH KUH ...!
KUH KUH KUH KUH KUH!!
WHAT'S SO FUNNY?
BLOOD TIES ARE A SCARY THING!
YOU PICKED THE RIGHT CARD WITH THE SAME REASONING KIYOTAKA USED!
EVEN THE WAY YOU USE THAT FIRM TONE IS THE SAME!
SFX: GATA (CLATTER)
...GOOD PERFORMANCE.
IT'S A LONG STORY SO...
ガタ
...LET'S TALK NEXT DOOR.

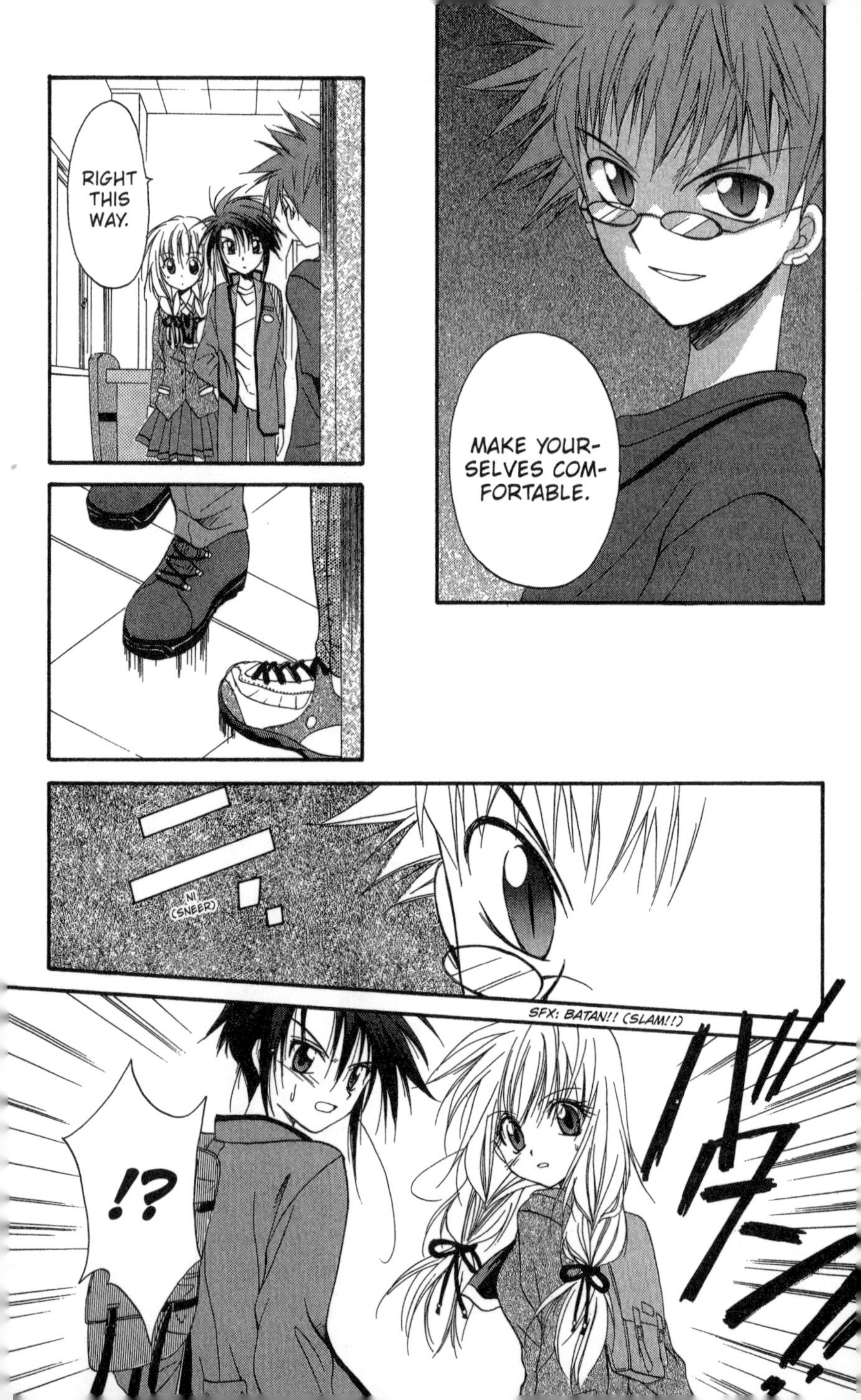
MAKE YOUR-SELVES COM-FORTABLE.
RIGHT THIS WAY.
NI (SNEER)
SFX: BATAN!! (SLAM!!)
!?

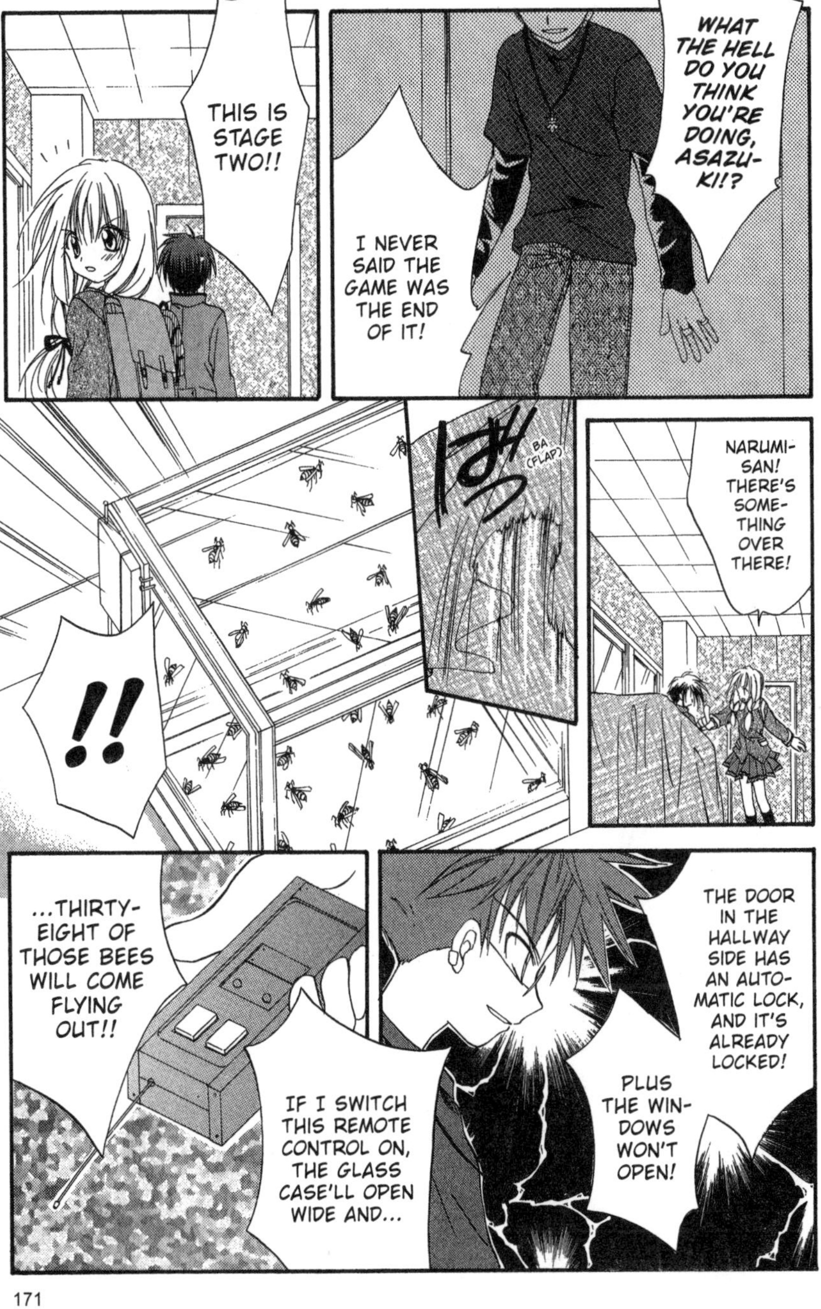
WHAT THE HELL DO YOU THINK YOU'RE DOING, ASAZU-KI!?
I NEVER SAID THE GAME WAS THE END OF IT!
THIS IS STAGE TWO!!
NARUMI-SAN! THERE'S SOME-THING OVER THERE!
BA (FLAP)
!!
THE DOOR IN THE HALLWAY SIDE HAS AN AUTO-MATIC LOCK, AND IT'S ALREADY LOCKED!
PLUS THE WIN-DOWS WON'T OPEN!
IF I SWITCH THIS REMOTE CONTROL ON, THE GLASS CASE'LL OPEN WIDE AND...
...THIRTY-EIGHT OF THOSE BEES WILL COME FLYING OUT!!

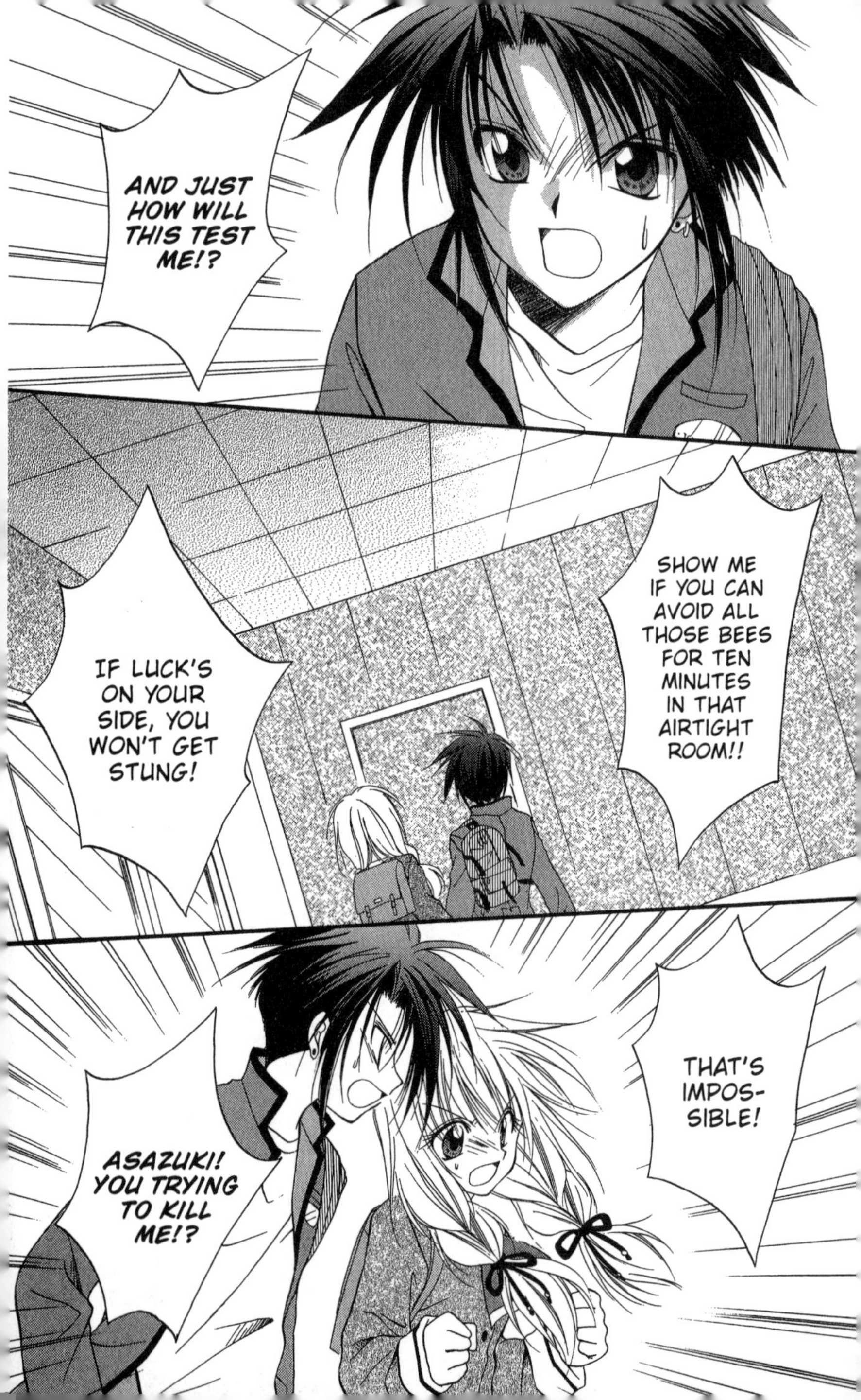
AND JUST HOW WILL THIS TEST ME!?
SHOW ME IF YOU CAN AVOID ALL THOSE BEES FOR TEN MINUTES IN THAT AIRTIGHT ROOM!!
IF LUCK'S ON YOUR SIDE, YOU WON'T GET STUNG!
THAT'S IMPOS-SIBLE!
ASAZUKI! YOU TRYING TO KILL ME!?

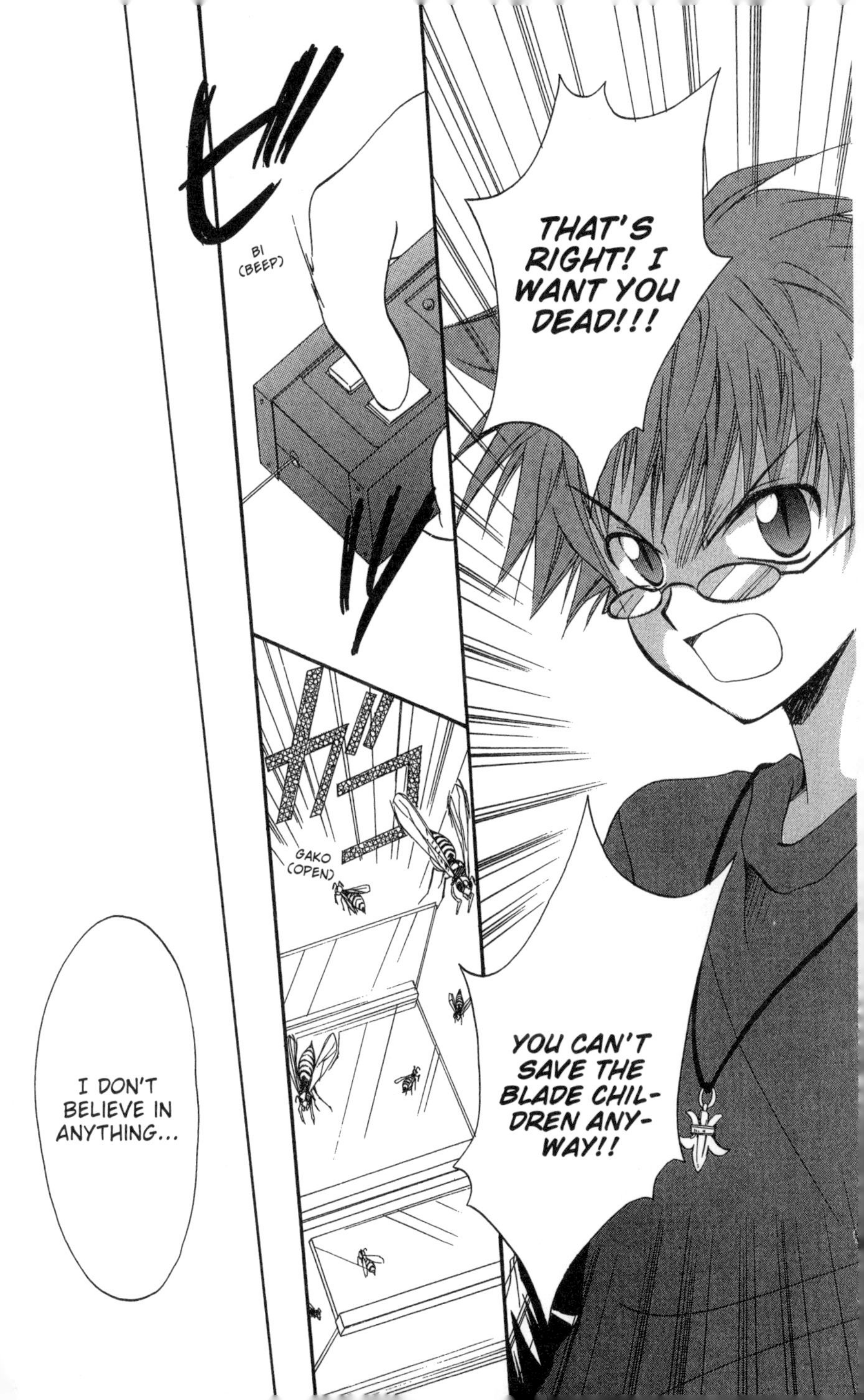
THAT'S RIGHT! I WANT YOU DEAD!!!
YOU CAN'T SAVE THE BLADE CHIL-DREN ANY-WAY!!
BI (BEEP)
GAKO (OPEN)
I DON'T BELIEVE IN ANYTHING...

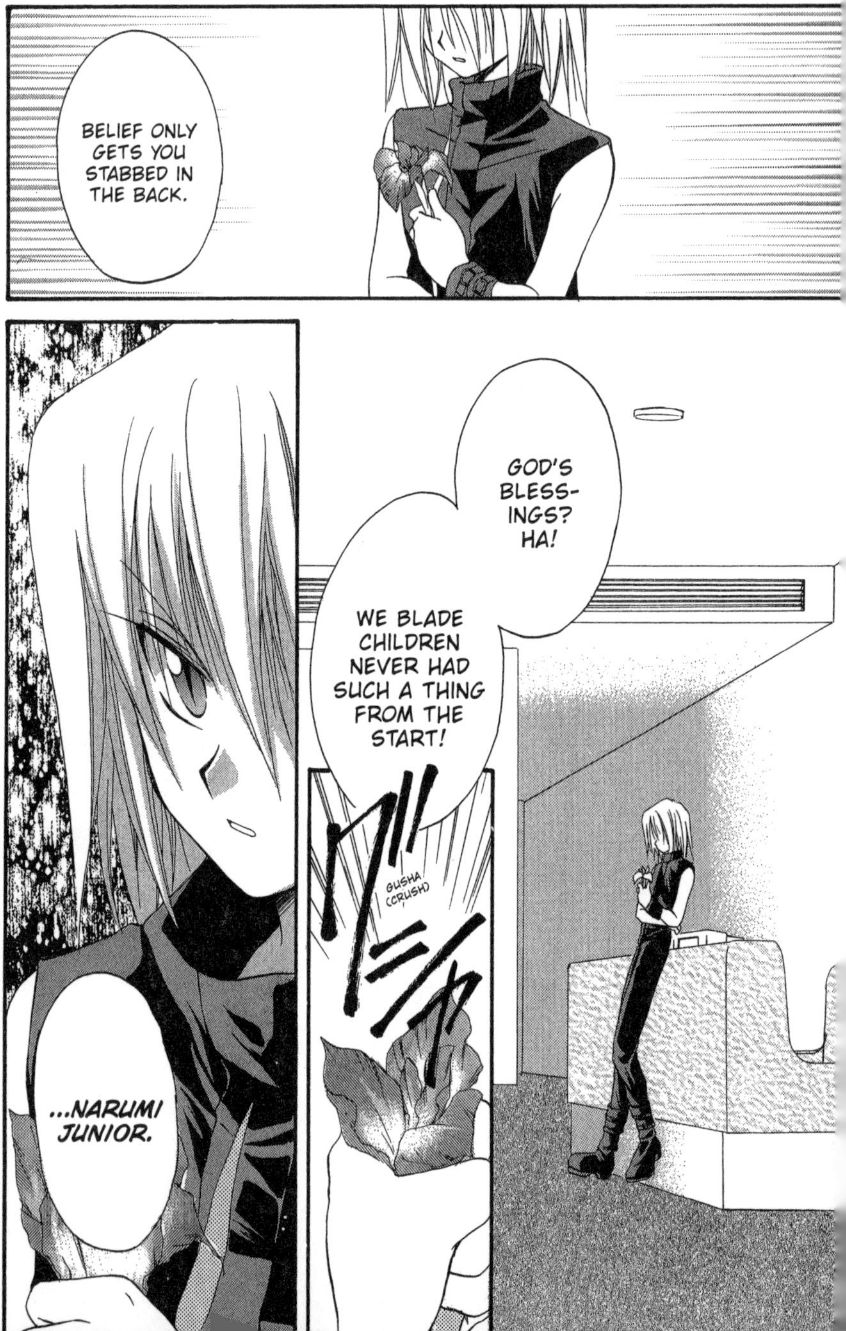
BELIEF ONLY GETS YOU STABBED IN THE BACK.
GOD'S BLESS-INGS? HA!
WE BLADE CHILDREN NEVER HAD SUCH A THING FROM THE START!
GUSHA (CRUSH)
...NARUMI JUNIOR.

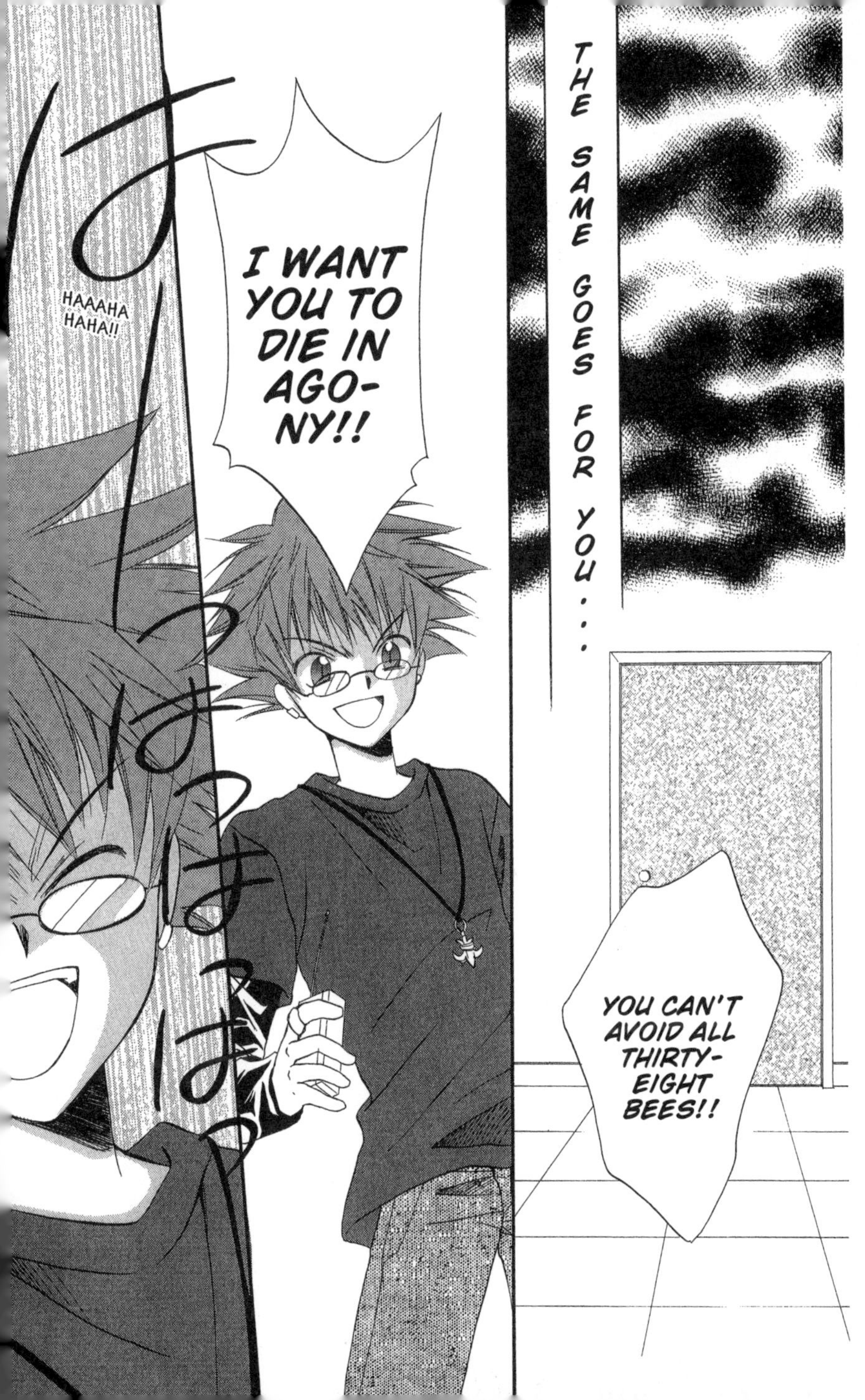
THE SAME GOES FOR YOU...
YOU CAN'T AVOID ALL THIRTY-EIGHT BEES!!
I WANT YOU TO DIE IN AGO-NY!!
HAAAHA HAHA!!

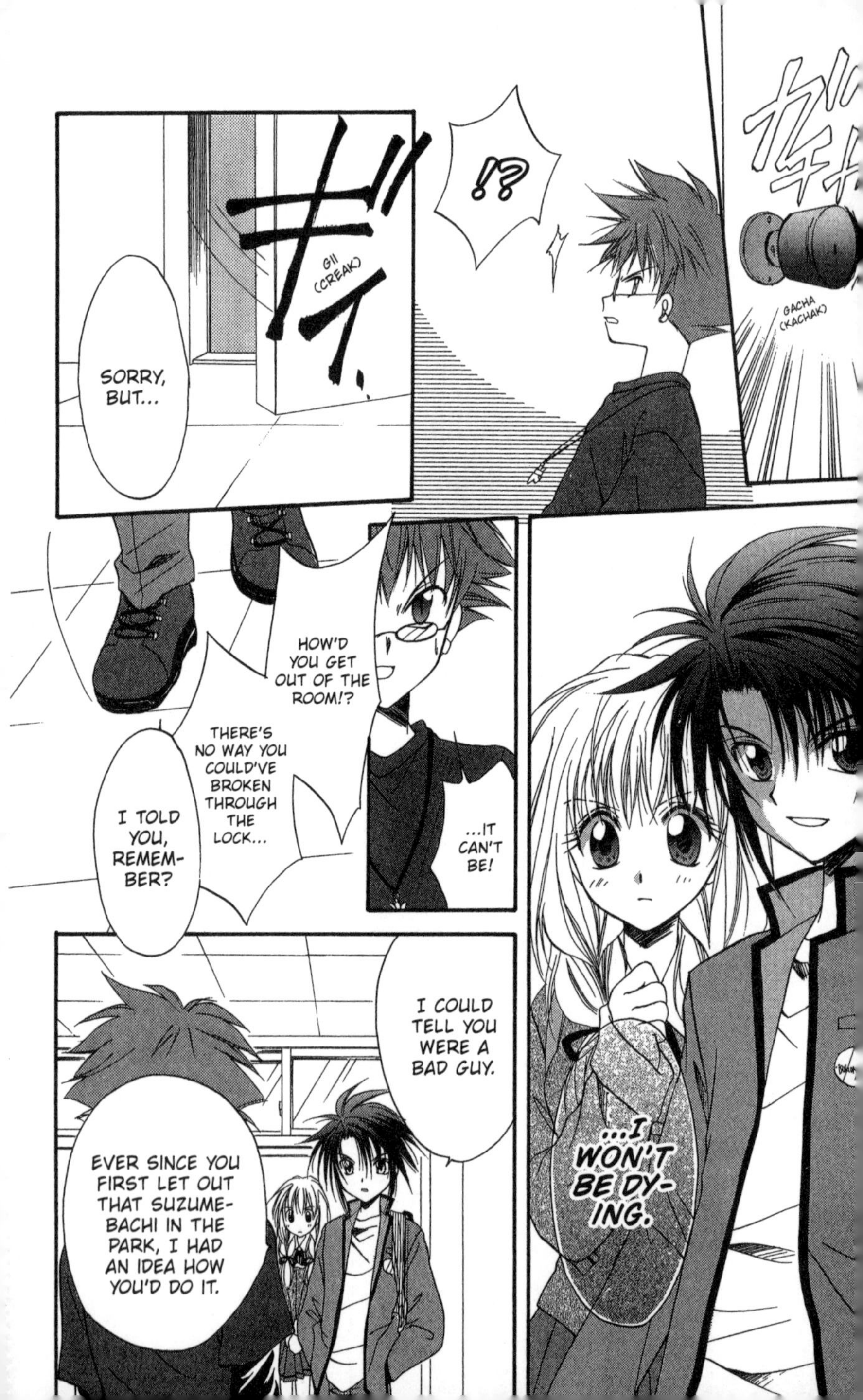
GACHA (KACHAK)
!?
GII (CREAK)
SORRY, BUT...
...I WON'T BE DY-ING.
HOW'D YOU GET OUT OF THE ROOM!?
THERE'S NO WAY YOU COULD'VE BROKEN THROUGH THE LOCK...
...IT CAN'T BE!
I TOLD YOU, REMEM-BER?
I COULD TELL YOU WERE A BAD GUY.
EVER SINCE YOU FIRST LET OUT THAT SUZUME-BACHI IN THE PARK, I HAD AN IDEA HOW YOU'D DO IT.

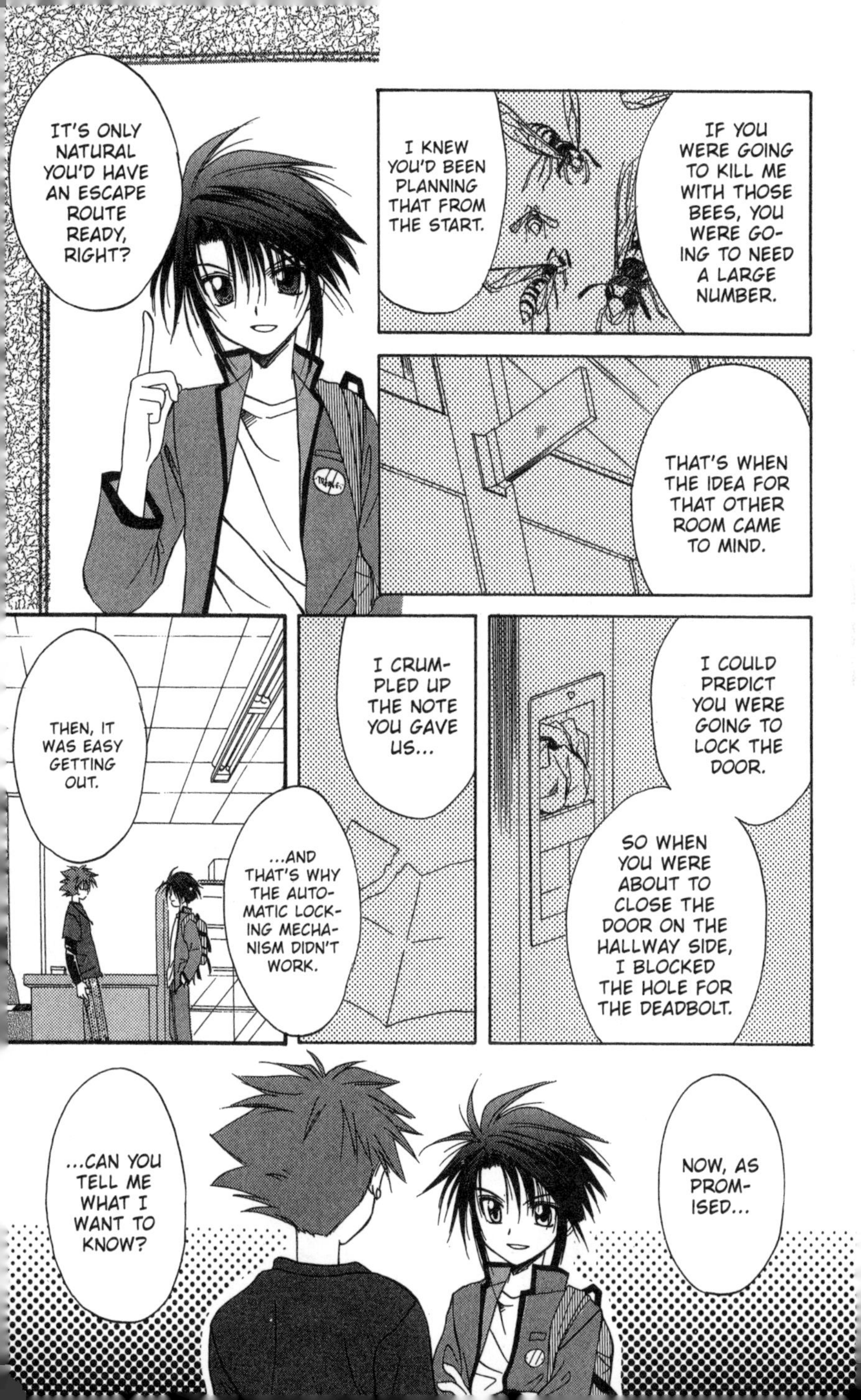
IF YOU WERE GOING TO KILL ME WITH THOSE BEES, YOU WERE GOING TO NEED A LARGE NUMBER.
I KNEW YOU'D BEEN PLANNING THAT FROM THE START.
THAT'S WHEN THE IDEA FOR THAT OTHER ROOM CAME TO MIND.
IT'S ONLY NATURAL YOU'D HAVE AN ESCAPE ROUTE READY, RIGHT?
I COULD PREDICT YOU WERE GOING TO LOCK THE DOOR.
SO WHEN YOU WERE ABOUT TO CLOSE THE DOOR ON THE HALLWAY SIDE, I BLOCKED THE HOLE FOR THE DEADBOLT.
I CRUMPLED UP THE NOTE YOU GAVE US...
...AND THAT'S WHY THE AUTOMATIC LOCKING MECHANISM DIDN'T WORK.
THEN, IT WAS EASY GETTING OUT.
NOW, AS PROMISED...
...CAN YOU TELL ME WHAT I WANT TO KNOW?

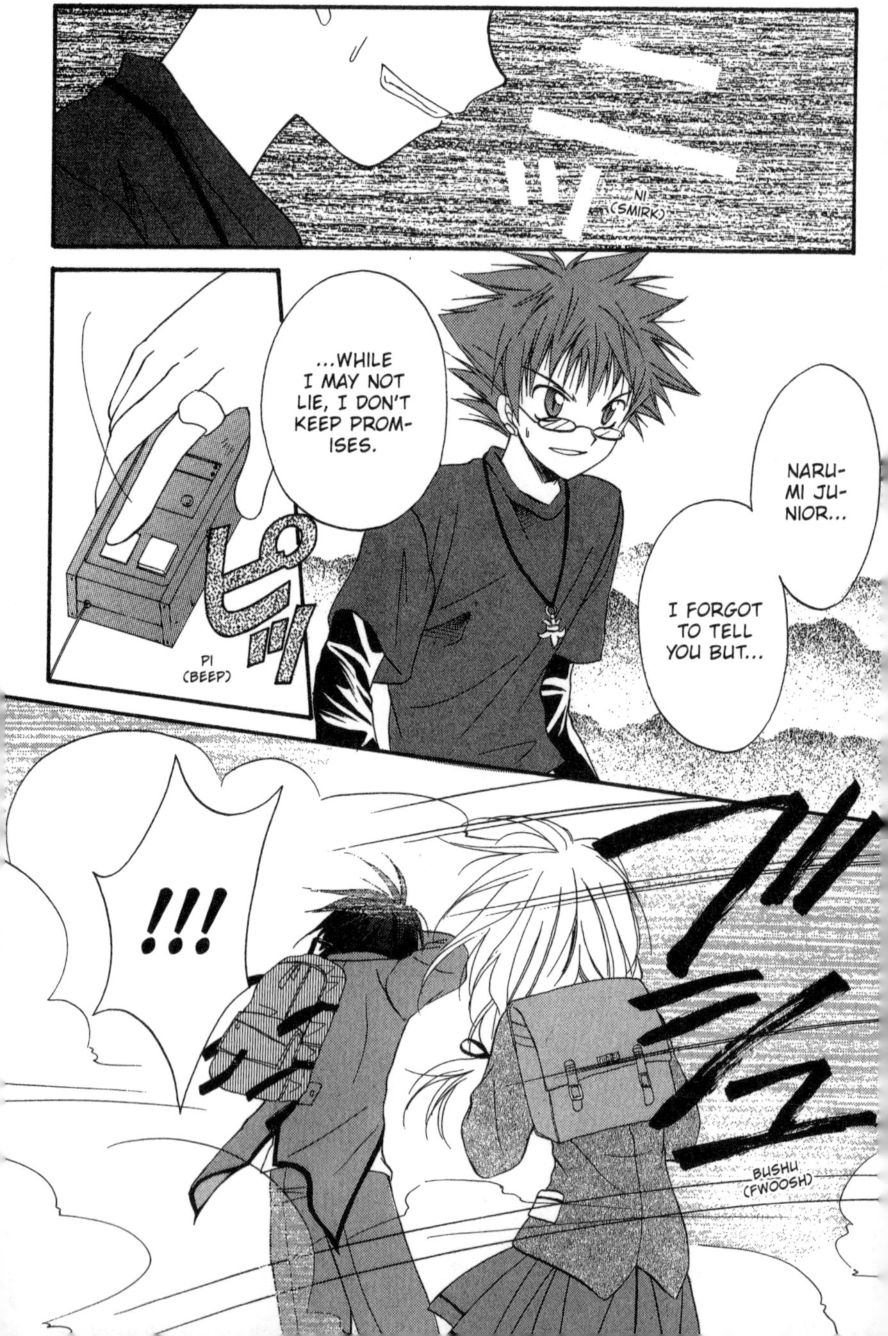
NI
(SMIRK)
NARUMI JUNIOR...
I FORGOT TO TELL YOU BUT...
...WHILE I MAY NOT LIE, I DON'T KEEP PROMISES.
PI
(BEEP)
!!!
BUSHU
(FWOOSH)

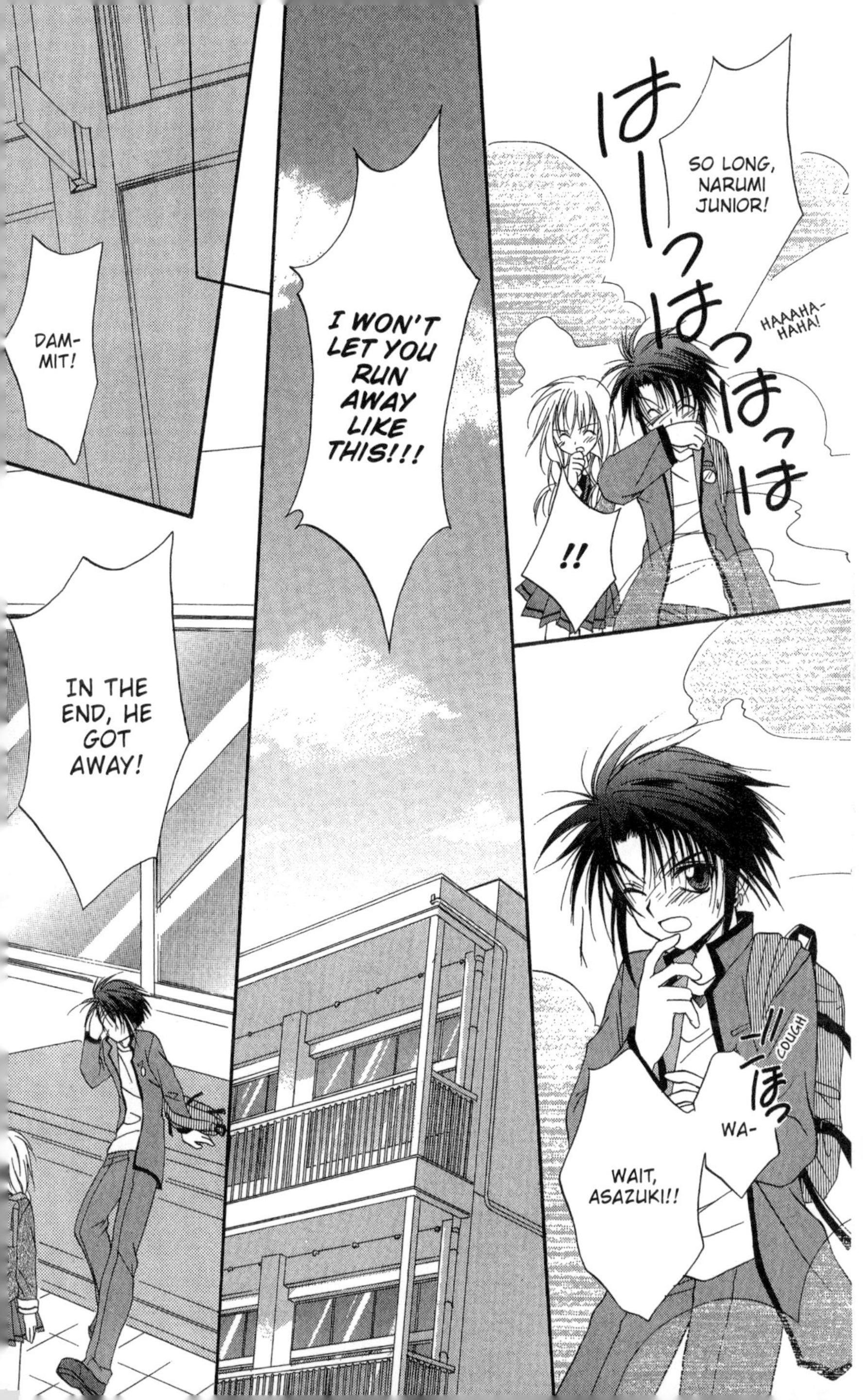
はーっはっはっは
SO LONG, NARUMI JUNIOR!
HAAAHA-HAHA!
!!
COUGH
WA-
WAIT, ASAZUKI!!
I WON'T LET YOU RUN AWAY LIKE THIS!!!
DAM-MIT!
IN THE END, HE GOT AWAY!

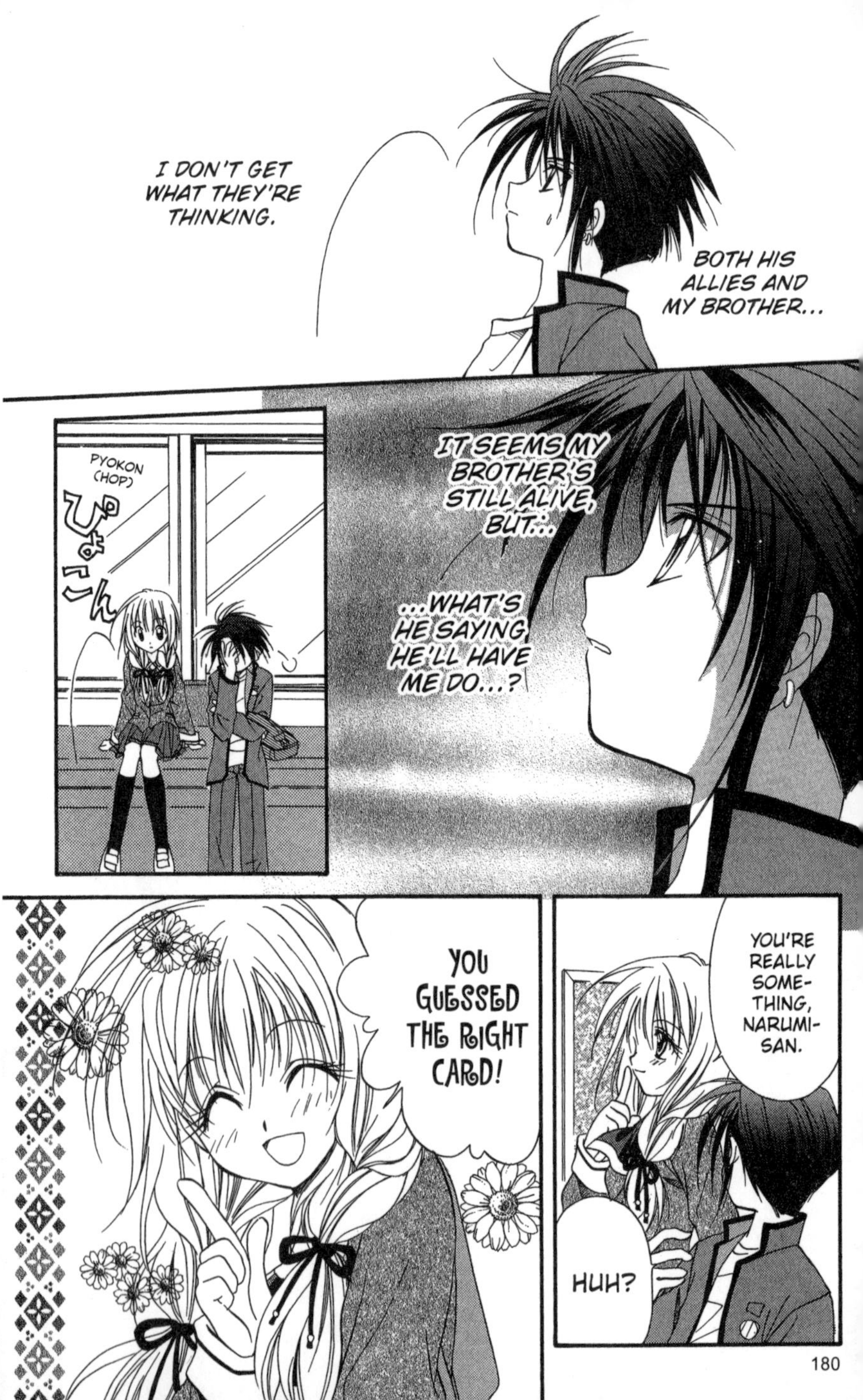
BOTH HIS ALLIES AND MY BROTHER...
I DON'T GET WHAT THEY'RE THINKING.
IT SEEMS MY BROTHER'S STILL ALIVE, BUT...
...WHAT'S HE SAYING HE'LL HAVE ME DO...?
PYOKON (HOP)
ぴょこん
YOU'RE REALLY SOME-THING, NARUMI-SAN.
HUH?
YOU GUESSED THE RIGHT CARD!

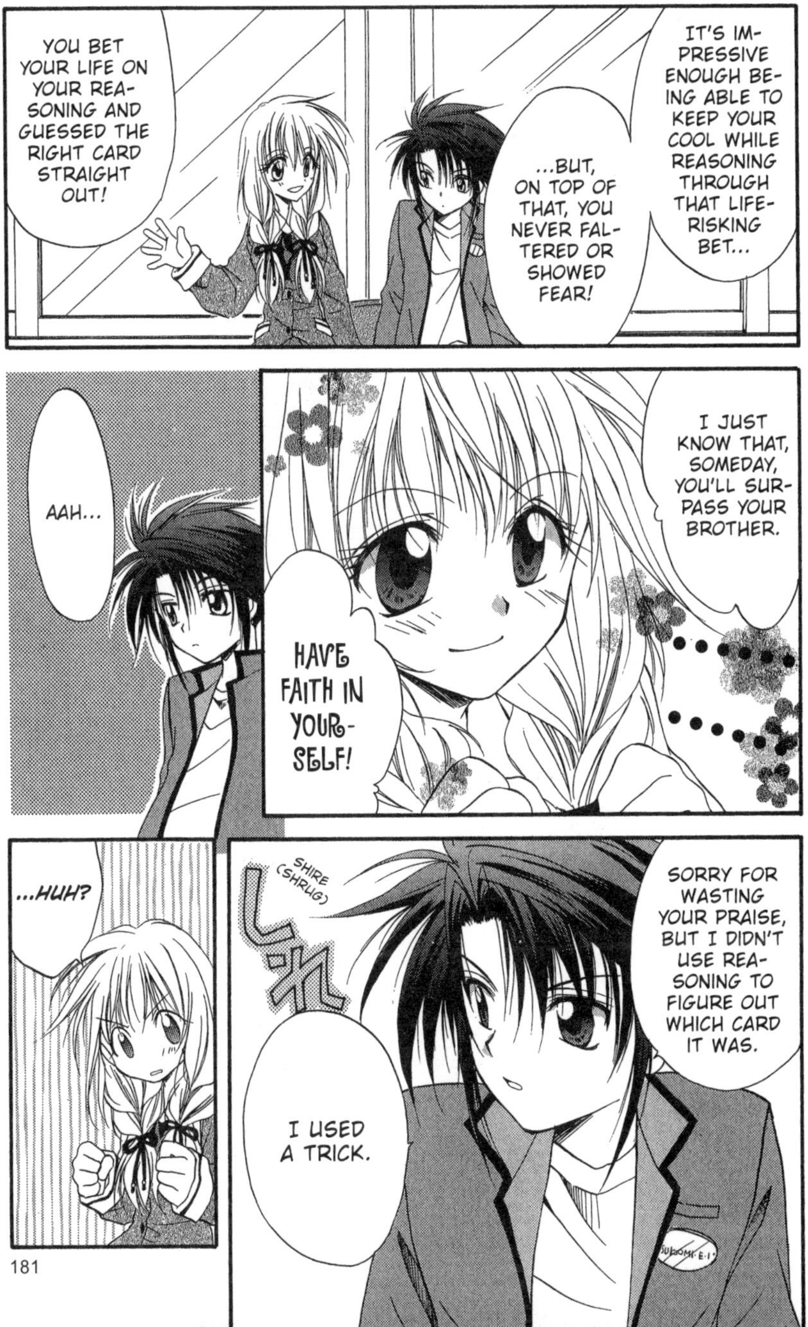

IT'S IMPRESSIVE ENOUGH BEING ABLE TO KEEP YOUR COOL WHILE REASONING THROUGH THAT LIFE-RISKING BET...
...BUT, ON TOP OF THAT, YOU NEVER FALTERED OR SHOWED FEAR!
YOU BET YOUR LIFE ON YOUR REASONING AND GUESSED THE RIGHT CARD STRAIGHT OUT!
I JUST KNOW THAT, SOMEDAY, YOU'LL SURPASS YOUR BROTHER.
HAVE FAITH IN YOURSELF!
AAH...
SHIRE (SHRUG)
SORRY FOR WASTING YOUR PRAISE, BUT I DIDN'T USE REASONING TO FIGURE OUT WHICH CARD IT WAS.
I USED A TRICK.
...HUH?

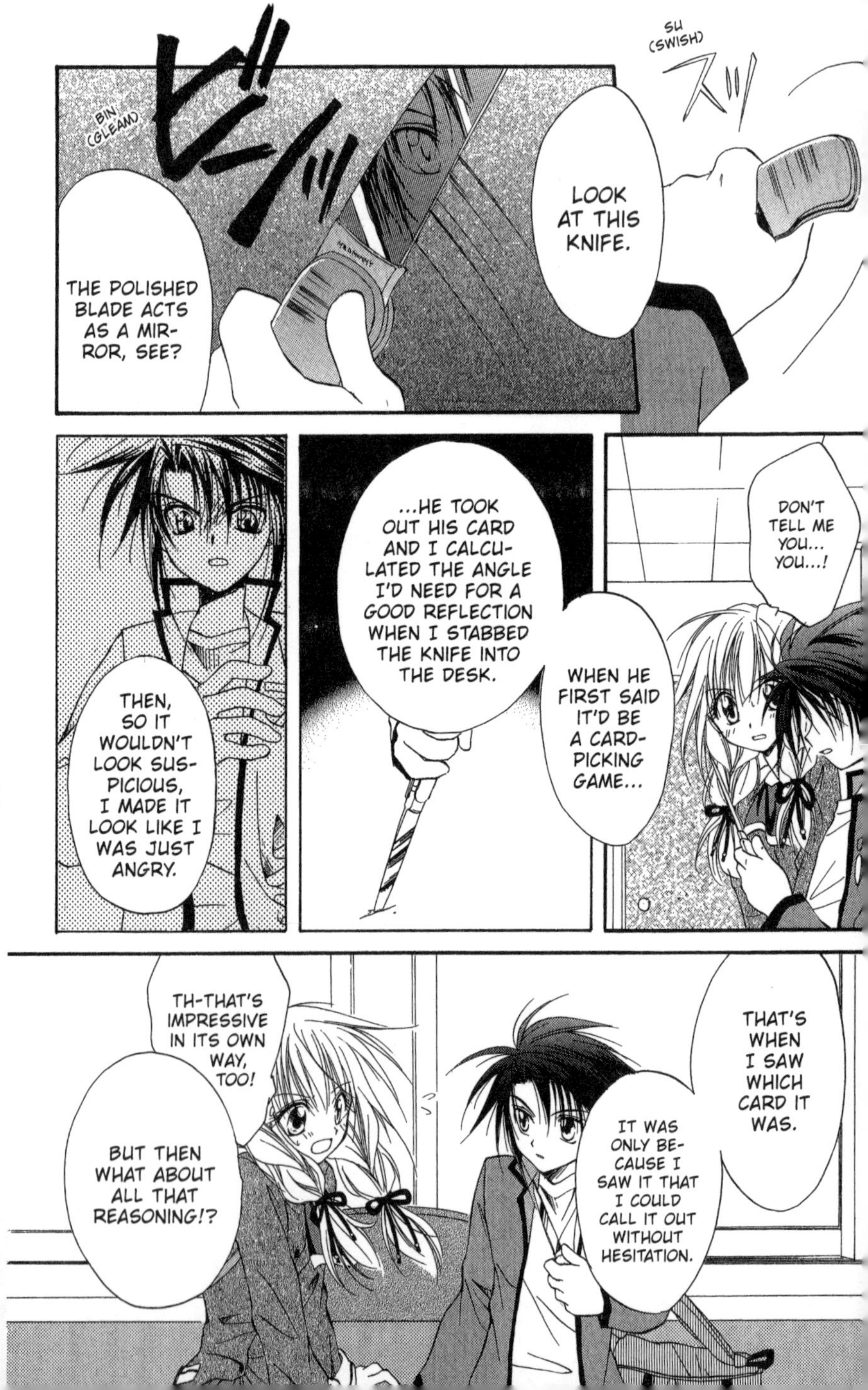
SU (SWISH)
LOOK AT THIS KNIFE.
BIN (GLEAM)
THE POLISHED BLADE ACTS AS A MIRROR, SEE?
DON'T TELL ME YOU... YOU...!
WHEN HE FIRST SAID IT'D BE A CARD-PICKING GAME...
...HE TOOK OUT HIS CARD AND I CALCULATED THE ANGLE I'D NEED FOR A GOOD REFLECTION WHEN I STABBED THE KNIFE INTO THE DESK.
THEN, SO IT WOULDN'T LOOK SUSPICIOUS, I MADE IT LOOK LIKE I WAS JUST ANGRY.
THAT'S WHEN I SAW WHICH CARD IT WAS.
IT WAS ONLY BECAUSE I SAW IT THAT I COULD CALL IT OUT WITHOUT HESITATION.
TH-THAT'S IMPRESSIVE IN ITS OWN WAY, TOO!
BUT THEN WHAT ABOUT ALL THAT REASONING!?

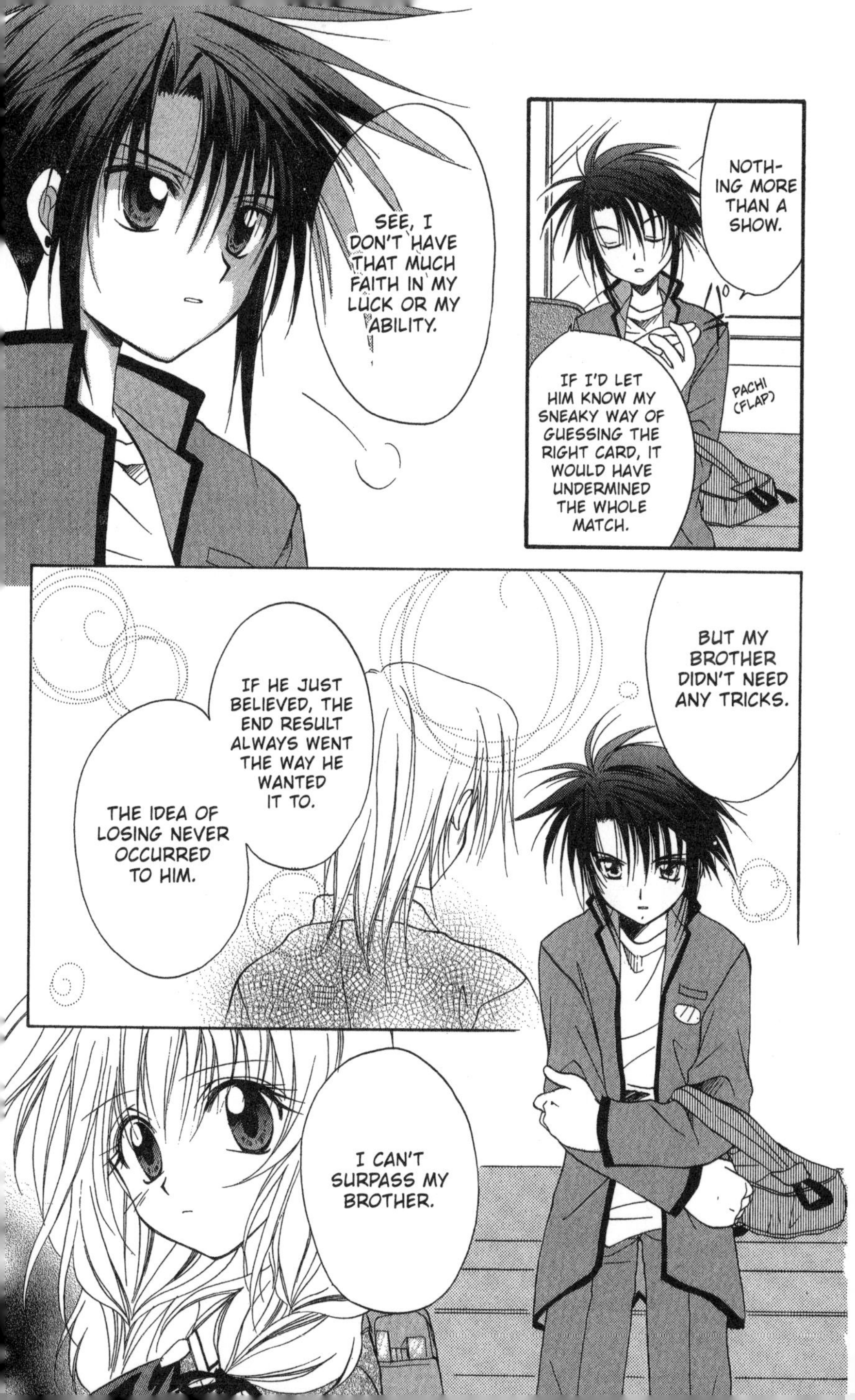
NOTHING MORE THAN A SHOW.
IF I'D LET HIM KNOW MY SNEAKY WAY OF GUESSING THE RIGHT CARD, IT WOULD HAVE UNDERMINED THE WHOLE MATCH.
PACHI (FLAP)
SEE, I DON'T HAVE THAT MUCH FAITH IN MY LUCK OR MY ABILITY.
BUT MY BROTHER DIDN'T NEED ANY TRICKS.
IF HE JUST BELIEVED, THE END RESULT ALWAYS WENT THE WAY HE WANTED IT TO.
THE IDEA OF LOSING NEVER OCCURRED TO HIM.
I CAN'T SURPASS MY BROTHER.

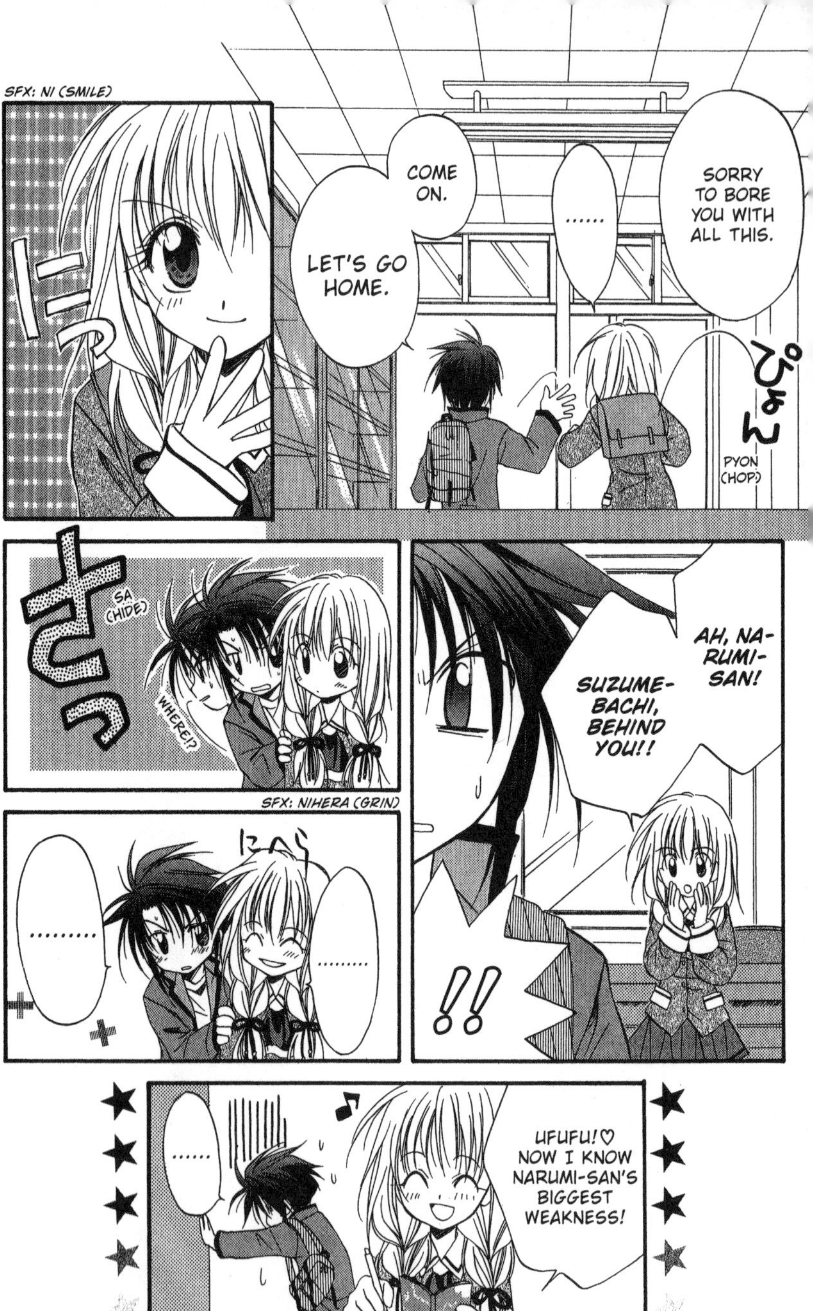
SORRY TO BORE YOU WITH ALL THIS.
......
COME ON.
LET'S GO HOME.
ぴょん
PYON (HOP)
SFX: NI (SMILE)
にっ
AH, NA-RUMI-SAN!
SUZUME-BACHI, BEHIND YOU!!
!!
さっ
SA (HIDE)
WHERE!?
SFX: NIHERA (GRIN)
にへら
....
....
UFUFU!♡ NOW I KNOW NARUMI-SAN'S BIGGEST WEAKNESS!
......

Spiral THE BONDS OF REASONING 2 THE END

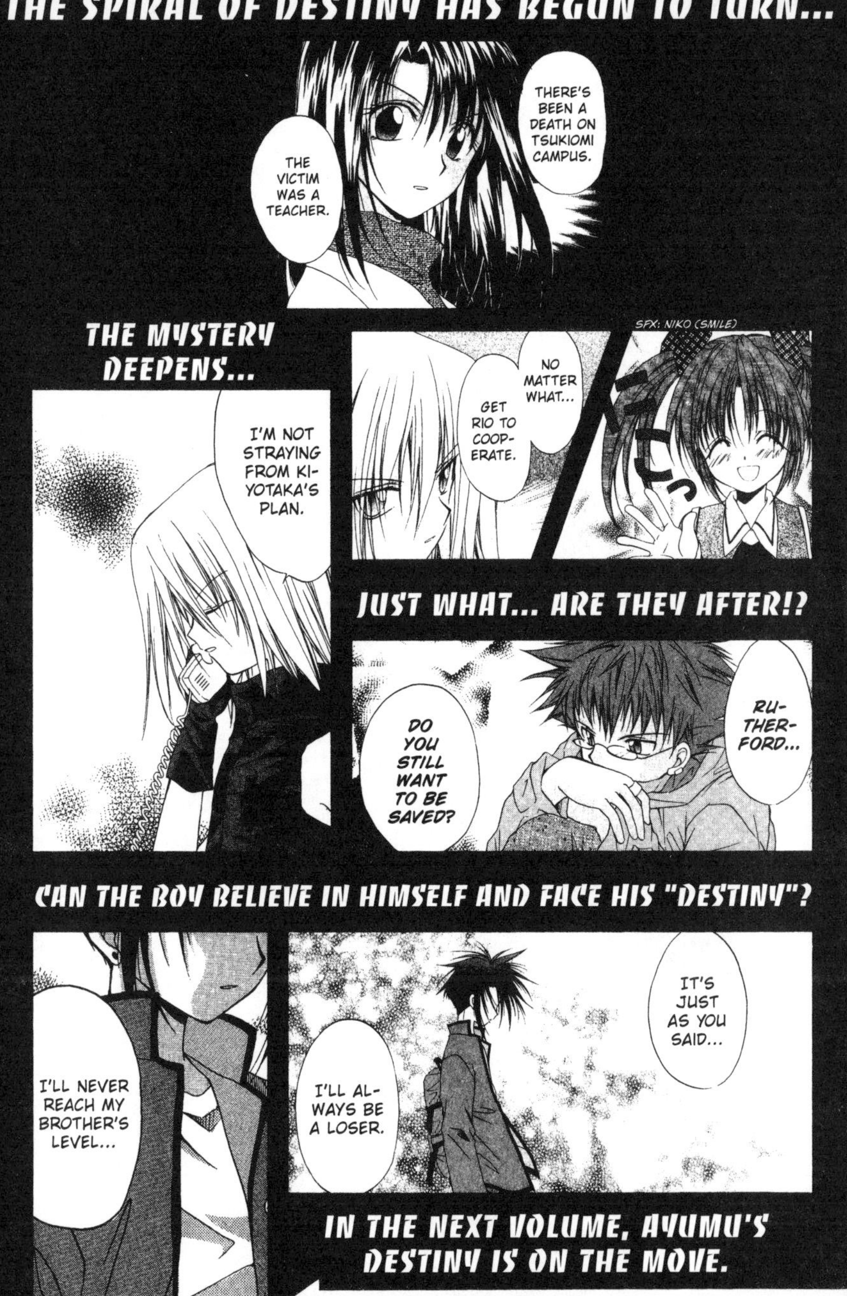
THE SPIRAL OF DESTINY HAS BEGUN TO TURN...
THERE'S BEEN A DEATH ON TSUKIOMI CAMPUS.
THE VICTIM WAS A TEACHER.
THE MYSTERY DEEPENS...
SFX: NIKO (SMILE)
NO MATTER WHAT...
GET RIO TO COOP-ERATE.
JUST WHAT... ARE THEY AFTER!?
RU-THER-FORD...
DO YOU STILL WANT TO BE SAVED?
I'M NOT STRAYING FROM KI-YOTAKA'S PLAN.
CAN THE BOY BELIEVE IN HIMSELF AND FACE HIS "DESTINY"?
IT'S JUST AS YOU SAID...
I'LL AL-WAYS BE A LOSER.
I'LL NEVER REACH MY BROTHER'S LEVEL...
IN THE NEXT VOLUME, AYUMU'S DESTINY IS ON THE MOVE.
To be continued. Please wait!

spiral work diary

~THE GLOSSARY USED BY OUR STAFF~

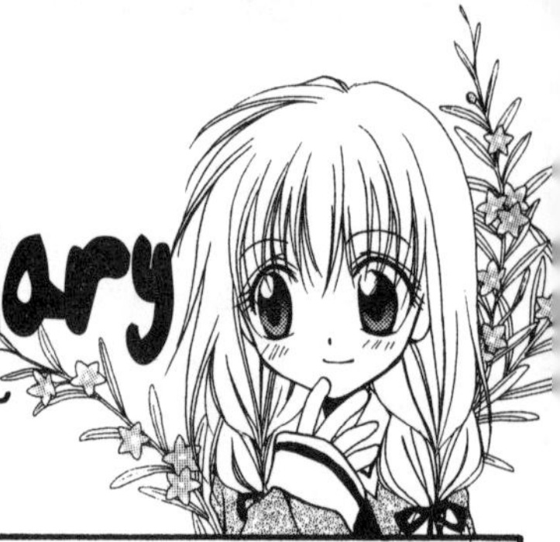

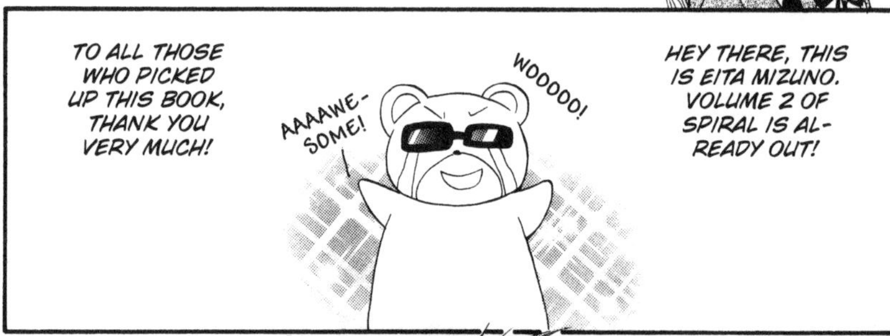

HEY THERE, THIS IS EITA MIZUNO. VOLUME 2 OF SPIRAL IS ALREADY OUT!
WOOOOO!
AAAAWESOME!
TO ALL THOSE WHO PICKED UP THIS BOOK, THANK YOU VERY MUCH!

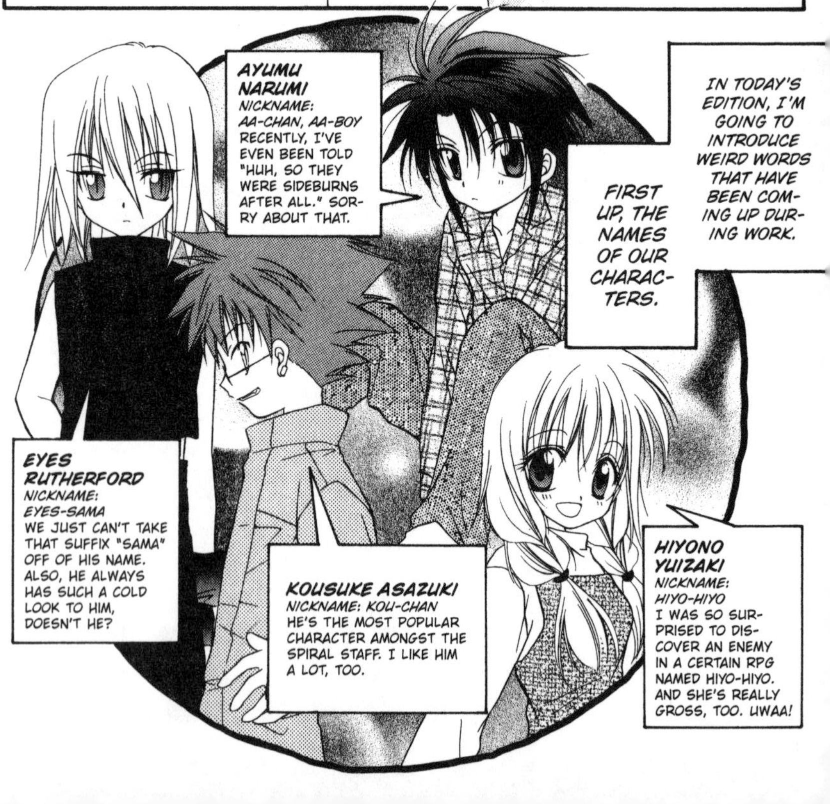

IN TODAY'S EDITION, I'M GOING TO INTRODUCE WEIRD WORDS THAT HAVE BEEN COMING UP DURING WORK.
FIRST UP, THE NAMES OF OUR CHARACTERS.
AYUMU NARUMI NICKNAME: AA-CHAN, AA-BOY RECENTLY, I'VE EVEN BEEN TOLD "HUH, SO THEY WERE SIDEBURNS AFTER ALL." SORRY ABOUT THAT.
HIYONO YUIZAKI NICKNAME: HIYO-HIYO I WAS SO SURPRISED TO DISCOVER AN ENEMY IN A CERTAIN RPG NAMED HIYO-HIYO. AND SHE'S REALLY GROSS, TOO. UWAA!
KOUSUKE ASAZUKI NICKNAME: KOU-CHAN HE'S THE MOST POPULAR CHARACTER AMONGST THE SPIRAL STAFF. I LIKE HIM A LOT, TOO.
EYES RUTHERFORD NICKNAME: EYES-SAMA WE JUST CAN'T TAKE THAT SUFFIX "SAMA" OFF OF HIS NAME. ALSO, HE ALWAYS HAS SUCH A COLD LOOK TO HIM, DOESN'T HE?

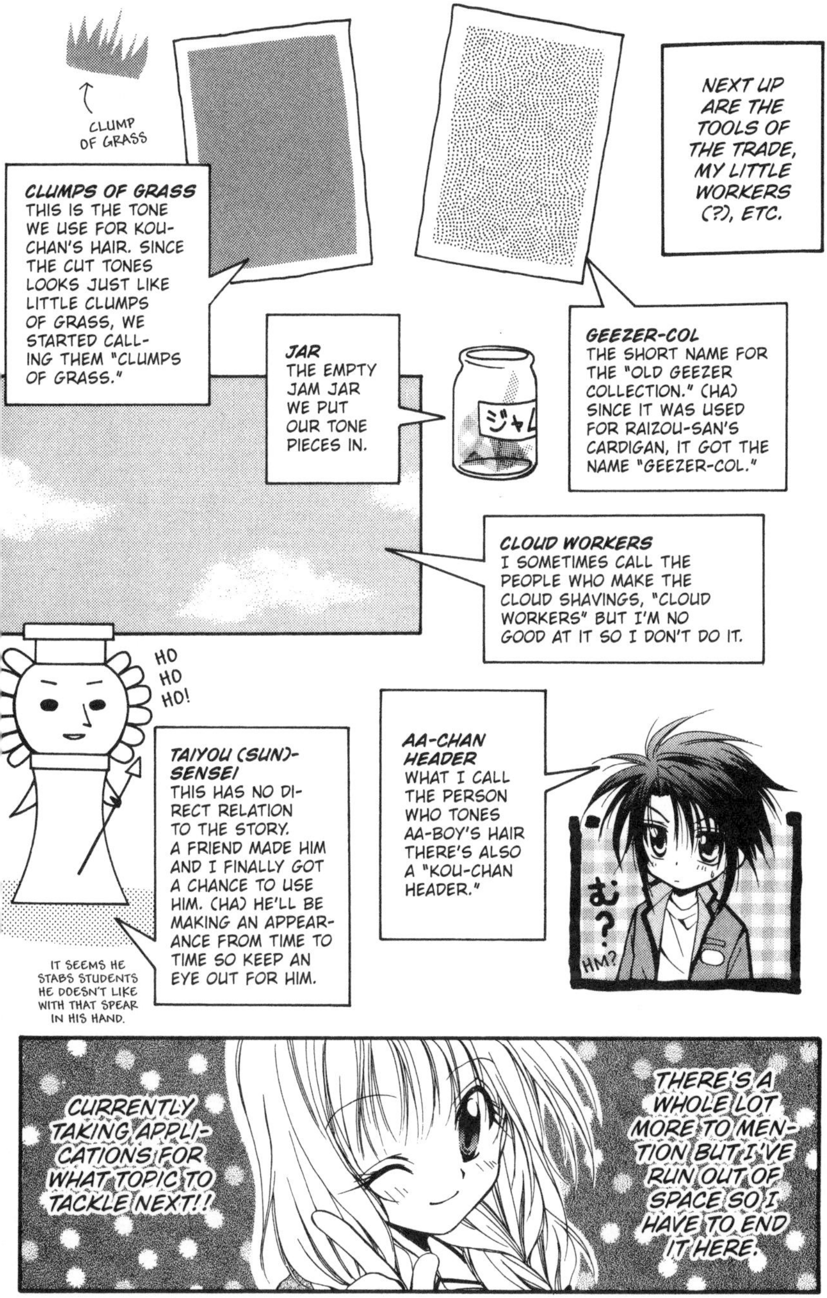

NEXT UP ARE THE TOOLS OF THE TRADE, MY LITTLE WORKERS (?), ETC.
GEEZER-COL
THE SHORT NAME FOR THE "OLD GEEZER COLLECTION." (HA) SINCE IT WAS USED FOR RAIZOU-SAN'S CARDIGAN, IT GOT THE NAME "GEEZER-COL."
CLUMP OF GRASS
CLUMPS OF GRASS
THIS IS THE TONE WE USE FOR KOU-CHAN'S HAIR. SINCE THE CUT TONES LOOKS JUST LIKE LITTLE CLUMPS OF GRASS, WE STARTED CALL-ING THEM "CLUMPS OF GRASS."
JAR
THE EMPTY JAM JAR WE PUT OUR TONE PIECES IN.
CLOUD WORKERS
I SOMETIMES CALL THE PEOPLE WHO MAKE THE CLOUD SHAVINGS, "CLOUD WORKERS" BUT I'M NO GOOD AT IT SO I DON'T DO IT.
AA-CHAN HEADER
WHAT I CALL THE PERSON WHO TONES AA-BOY'S HAIR THERE'S ALSO A "KOU-CHAN HEADER."
む?
HM?
HO HO HO!
TAIYOU (SUN)-SENSEI
THIS HAS NO DI-RECT RELATION TO THE STORY. A FRIEND MADE HIM AND I FINALLY GOT A CHANCE TO USE HIM. (HA) HE'LL BE MAKING AN APPEAR-ANCE FROM TIME TO TIME SO KEEP AN EYE OUT FOR HIM.
IT SEEMS HE STABS STUDENTS HE DOESN'T LIKE WITH THAT SPEAR IN HIS HAND.
THERE'S A WHOLE LOT MORE TO MEN-TION BUT I'VE RUN OUT OF SPACE SO I HAVE TO END IT HERE.
CURRENTLY TAKING APPLI-CATIONS FOR WHAT TOPIC TO TACKLE NEXT!!

Hello, this is Kyo Shirodaira. I'm delighted that Volume Two has been published. Thank you very much to all those who bought it!

Now then, in this volume the chapters strayed a bit from the basic mystery manga premises of "Who-dunnit?" and "What was the trick?" My apologies to those who prefer that kind of plot. However, I hope you don't have trouble thinking of this, too, as just another form of mystery.

With the mystery behind the "Blade Children" deepening, Ayumu being put in danger, and new characters popping up, it's gotten to the point where even I, the creator, am wondering what will happen next.

At any rate, there might still be some chapters that stick to the basic formula but Ayumu and Hiyono's wits and bravery will keep opening up new paths so please look forward to their further adventures in deduction.

By the way, Hiyono-chan is such a cutie, isn't she? I know I'm saying this as the creator but I find her to be a very free-spirited, active, and good-looking girl.

Initially, when I was writing the original Chapters One and Two, I had no hand at character design so I just wrote Hiyono to play a minor role as the info-supplying assistant (at the time, I was actually writing the story with a lot of affection for the sister, Madoka, instead).

However, with Mizuno-san's designs came improvements that couldn't be any better. My manager even said it was good, so that must mean it was *really* good. This is just between us, but in the earliest stages of the story, her name wasn't "Hi-yono," it was actually a very simple name. But we've decided

AFTERWORD

to keep that name *a trade secret*!

Anyway, Hiyono has unexpectedly turned into a great character and has far exceeded my expectations in this intense story by taking up a far more significant role indeed. (The truth is I hadn't planned for that at all. I was planning on having Madoka take the better role.) As this story goes on, I'm sure she'll take on even more surprising roles. Please look forward to them. Also, I feel that Rutherford, who also appeared this time around, will turn out to be more than he seems.

One last announcement...

The GAN-GAN website (http://enix.co.jp/gangan/) is still serializing the *Spiral: The Bonds of Reasoning* side-story novel. It's a basic mystery story focusing on Ayumu's brother, Kiyotaka, and his work as a detective. I'm working really hard on writing it. Madoka also shows up as her pre-marriage self (this is probably redundant, but I just really like Madoka). *[Editor's note: This Web site is no longer active.]*

You can still enjoy and easily understand this story even if you don't read the side-story but for those who have the chance, please check it out.

As time permits, I'm also working on a catch-the-criminal novel that comes with a present (trust me, this is absurdly hard to pull off), so for those of you who are interested in rare presents, please take up this challenge!

Well, I hope we meet again in Volume Three!

KYO SHIRODAIRA

Spiral 2

THE BONDS OF REASONING

Omake!

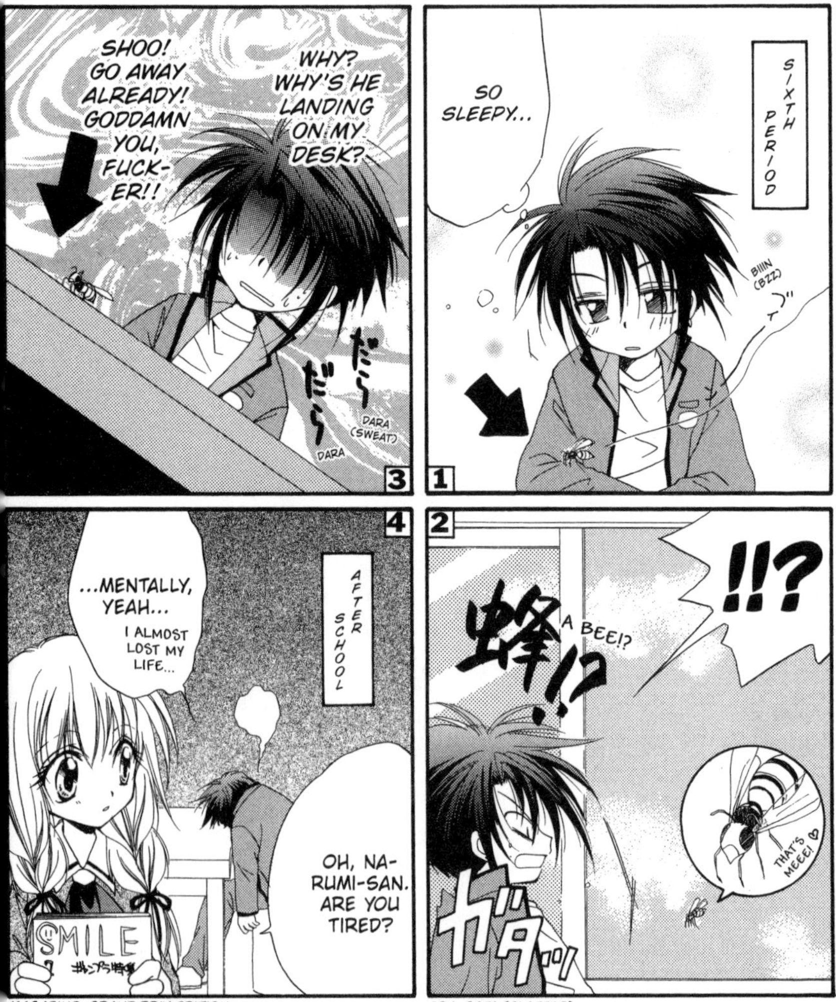
1
SIXTH PERIOD
SO SLEEPY...
BIIN (BZZ)
2
!!?
蜂!?
A BEE!?
THAT'S MEEE! ♡
ガタッ
3
WHY? WHY'S HE LANDING ON MY DESK?
SHOO! GO AWAY ALREADY! GODDAMN YOU, FUCKER!!
だら だら
DARA (SWEAT) DARA
4
AFTER SCHOOL
OH, NA-RUMI-SAN. ARE YOU TIRED?
...MENTALLY, YEAH...
I ALMOST LOST MY LIFE...
SMILE

MAGAZINE: GRAND PRIX EDITION

SFX: GATA (CLATTER)

TRANSLATOR'S NOTES

p11
"Raimon" contains the character for **"rai"** which means "lightning."

p36
Paulownia is a tree native to China and its wood is very light, fine-grained, soft, and warp-resistant. It is often used for chests, boxes, and clogs.

p38
The **Koujien** is a famous Japanese dictionary equivalent to Webster's or the Oxford English Dictionary. It's very thick and is a primary resource for the Japanese language.

p134
Suzumebachi, the insects that Kousuke cultivates and uses when threatening Ayumu, are giant Asian hornets. Their Japanese name means "sparrow bee," presumably because sometimes they are as big as sparrows. They are aggressive and their sting often requires medical attention.

SPIRAL
The Bonds of Reasoning
2

by Kyo Shirodaira and Eita Mizuno

Translation: Christine Schilling
Lettering: Marshall Dillon and Terri Delgado

Yen Press
Hachette Book Group USA
237 Park Avenue, New York, NY 10017

Visit our Web sites at www.HachetteBookGroupUSA.com and www.YenPress.com.

Yen Press is a division of Hachette Book Group USA, Inc. The Yen Press name and logo is a trademark of Hachette Book Group USA, Inc.

First Edition: January 2008

10 9 8 7 6 5 4 3 2 1

WOR

Printed in the United States of America